LUCY MERCER RUTHERFURD
Eleanor's Rival,
FDR's Other Love

LUCY MERCER RUTHERFURD
Eleanor's Rival,
FDR's Other Love

CHRISTINE M. TOTTEN

ELIOT WERNER PUBLICATIONS, INC.
CLINTON CORNERS, NEW YORK

Library of Congress Cataloging-in-Publication Data

Names: Totten, Christine M., author.
Title: Lucy Mercer Rutherfurd : Eleanor's rival, FDR's other love / Christine Totten.
Other titles: Eleanor's rival, FDR's other love
Description: Clinton Corners, New York : Eliot Werner Publications, Inc., 2018. | Includes bibliographical references and index.
Identifiers: LCCN 2015037590 | ISBN 9780989824972
Subjects: LCSH: Rutherfurd, Lucy Mercer. | Roosevelt, Franklin D. (Franklin Delano), 1882–1945 – Friends and associates. | Roosevelt, Franklin D. (Franklin Delano), 1882–1945 – Relations with women. | Roosevelt, Franklin D. (Franklin Delano), 1882–1945 – Marriage. | Social secretaries – United States – Biography. | Presidents – United States – Biography. | Roosevelt, Eleanor, 1884–1962.
Classification: LCC E807 .T68 2016 | DDC 973.917092 [B] – dc23
LC record available at https://lccn.loc.gov/2015037590

ISBN-10: 0-9898249-7-7
ISBN-13: 978-0-9898249-7-2

Copyright © 2018 Eliot Werner Publications, Inc.
PO Box 268, Clinton Corners, New York 12514
http://www.eliotwerner.com

Printed in the United States of America

PREFACE

The bond that tied Franklin Delano Roosevelt to Lucy Mercer was not forged overnight. Neither temperament lent itself to sudden outbursts of passion. Both Franklin and Lucy guarded their emotions and were disinclined to surrender to love at first sight.

On the other hand, once their devotion to each other was established, it proved durable—lasting from 1917 until FDR's death in 1945—and unaffected by their marriages. Lucy served the ailing Winthrop Rutherfurd with every ounce of her energy while she reserved every beat of her heart for Franklin. FDR took care to respect Eleanor's status as his "Missus" while craving Lucy's presence.

The myths about the nature of Franklin and Lucy's relationship cling stubbornly to their posthumous images. They have not changed since their lifetime. Biographers still write that Franklin became acquainted with Lucy through Eleanor's decision to hire the young woman as her part-time social secretary. This legend can be dismissed because Franklin was at work in the Navy Department in the hours Lucy worked with Eleanor at home.

In reality, Franklin came to know Lucy at the social events of the British Embassy in Washington where she was always welcome as one of the most popular guests. The time Lucy spent in Franklin's circle varied considerably. It was concentrated mainly in the war years beginning in July 1917, picking up again in the late summer of 1941.

During the decades in between, Franklin continued to reach out to Lucy. Now Mrs. Winthrop Rutherfurd, Lucy moved out of her former circle of friends and out of Franklin's orbit. But he did not hesitate to approach Lucy again, wholly unexpectedly. Unimpeded by her husband, FDR marked the period from 1926 to 1928 as a time of regular contact, with Lucy as the recipient of a regular flow of his letters. Their mainly one-sided correspondence concerned neither Franklin nor Lucy's spouse. Eleanor had long overcome her shock of September 1918 when she found letters from Lucy in her husband's luggage.

The next unpleasant experience, which found an echo in Eleanor's second autobiography of 1949, was Franklin and Lucy's continued contact behind her back. Her hurt was soon erased when Eleanor rose quickly as a celebrity in her own right.

* * *

Lucy's gentle reactions to events in her surroundings were no match for Eleanor's dynamic temperament in dealing with controversy. Lucy did not offer much cause for wrestling down a rival; she denied Eleanor the satisfaction of a good fight.

As an articulate First Lady, Eleanor was the more passionate and emotionally alert of the two women. She kept posterity electrified with her sequence of love-like affairs, permitting men like her body-guard Earl Miller and women like Lorena Hickok to become intimate friends.

Lucy rarely revealed that FDR resided in secret chambers of her heart. Rather, she offered an elegant solution for possible complications caused by her friendship with the president. She prepared the way for her daughter Barbara to be enthusiastically adopted by Franklin as his goddaughter, a second daughter beside Anna.

Franklin, Eleanor, and Lucy were equally eager to avert the public's eyes from any spectacle of interaction among the three of them. Lucy remains a "mystery woman" to this day—but also a woman of perennial appeal. The close examination of her personality and behavior in times challenging her moral fiber proves, however, that she is worthy to be remembered in one breath with Franklin and Eleanor.

* * *

The material for these revelations was found in Lucy's correspondence, which to date has never been published.

With the exception of the 1919 group picture of the Roosevelt family, all photos are taken from family albums belonging to Lucy's sister Violetta. Vio's descendants authorized the use of these pictures by the author. Permission was granted by Lucy's niece Mrs. Lucy Mercer Blundon and her granddaughters Mrs. Lucy Knowles and Mrs. Alice Knowles, to whom I am most grateful.

CONTENTS

> **PART II.**
> **LUCY AS MRS. WINTHROP RUTHERFURD**

PROLOGUE

WAYS TO DISCOVER LUCY

FDR'S MOST PERSONAL LETTERS

NOT A SINGLE love letter is to be found in the four volumes of Franklin Delano Roosevelt's *Personal Letters*. None of FDR's biographers quote an authentic, verbatim profession of love from a man accustomed to hiding his innermost feelings. Only a few words from the depth of his heart, which were long kept secret, have survived on paper.

The president's unofficial writings were part of his legacy, inherited by his widow at his death in 1945. Eleanor chose her thirty-four-year-old son Elliott as the publisher of FDR's personal letters. She herself took an active interest in the selection of the messages to be published. There was much to choose from. Like his grandfather Warren Delano II, Franklin was virtually addicted to writing letters. He kept every shred of correspondence that reached his desk. His wife frowned upon the urge to collect that Franklin inherited from his mother. For the widowed Eleanor, it left an embarrassment of riches to deal with. To thin out a surplus of personal documents, it made sense to exclude the most private items from publication.

As a boy, Franklin did not have many secrets to keep. There were no special feelings for a lady friend to express in writing until he became a student at Harvard. He was twenty in 1902 when he fell seriously in love for the first time. He tried in vain to win the hand of a beautiful aristocratic Boston girl, Alice Sohier. Thirty years later, in 1932, Alice looked back without regret on the courtship of the young man now elected president. There is no trace of his letters to her.

Franklin was consoled about the loss of Alice by the affection of his distant cousin Eleanor. The correspondence between September 1903 and their wedding in March 1905 was voluminous, even by Victorian standards. Franklin had been the man of Eleanor's dreams since she was thirteen. The handsome young student from Groton had saved her from the lot of a wallflower when he invited her to dance with him at a country club ball in Orange, New Jersey.

As First Lady, after more than three decades of marriage to Franklin, Eleanor saw the personal relationships of her youth in a new light. Describing her getting together with FDR, Eleanor skimmed over the three months that led to her engagement and did not mention that it was Franklin's mother who helped her win his heart. Sara was impressed by Eleanor's closeness to the White House. She was even more captivated by the fine character of the eighteen-year-old girl. Eleanor would make a perfect "helpmeet" for Franklin. Sara introduced the girl in warm terms to her brother Warren III. As head of the Delano clan, he functioned as its arbiter for acceptable marriages. Sara suggested that he invite Eleanor to Steen Valetje, his estate north of Hyde Park, to meet "the nicest, most intelligent and thoughtful girl" she ever knew.

In June 1903 Sara took Eleanor's measure at three house parties in a row, arranged in Franklin's honor at Hyde Park. Sara did not give up when her son did not fall right away for the girl of her choice. It was disappointing that Franklin did not write to Eleanor while on a trip to England the following month. Undeterred, Sara asked the girl once more for a visit in August. Eleanor was to stay with her in her summer home on the Canadian island Campobello. Franklin would join them there on his return from Europe.

As a houseguest on the estate of Sir Hugh and Lady Edith Cholmeley in Lincolnshire, Franklin had hesitated to end a heady flirtation with their daughter Aline. Walking on Campobello's beach with the refreshingly different Eleanor, he felt attracted to her in a new way. He had admired her fine character in Hyde Park in June; he now responded to the sparks of affection that flew from Eleanor's eyes to his.

After the girl left for her grandmother's home at Tivoli on the Hudson, Franklin sent his new friend a note—including "a token from the sea," perhaps a pretty sea shell. These lines started the most significant series of private letters that FDR ever wrote. Eleanor's thanks for Franklin's note, her first written communication with FDR, was dated September 3, 1903. An enthusiastic correspondent herself, Eleanor would soon plead with Franklin to write more often. She told him that she "hated to add another burden to too many" when she urged Franklin to answer her letters late at night, after his work for the Harvard paper, the *Crimson*. Eleanor told him that she felt "absolutely lost" on a day without a word from him.

Keeping up with Eleanor's flood of messages was no mean task. On a given day, she would write six pages on her dainty ladies' stationery in the afternoon, then follow up with another five pages in the evening, and continue writing the next morning. Although Franklin apparently did not reply as often as Eleanor hoped, the mail from him added up. Eventually, Eleanor hoarded a huge cache of Franklin's letters to her. She treasured them and reread them from time to time.

It could be expected that she would have carefully preserved every line, every word of love she received from Franklin. This was not to be. Before Eleanor published the first volume of her memoirs in 1937 under the title *This Is My Story*, she tossed large bundles of old letters into her fireplace at the White House. Among them were all of Franklin's letters from the first phase of their acquaintance.

Eleanor dealt differently with her own answers to those letters from her husband that she later destroyed. She carefully preserved her part of the correspondence before it was deposited in the FDR Presidential Library at Hyde Park.

Eleanor's replies to Franklin's lost first letters provide at least indirect insight into their content. They imply that that her new friend's tone was initially cordial but not amorous. Franklin talked about his life as a student in a light vein. Eleanor thanked him politely for looking up her brother Hall, then a student at Groton. In a touch of flirtatious jealousy, Eleanor asked whether "someone else" might not deserve Franklin's "token from the sea" more than she did herself.

Evelyn Carter, the distinguished young English lady Eleanor had in mind, also had her eye on Franklin.

While Franklin had been flattered by Evelyn's attention, Eleanor soon captivated more and more of his affection. She clearly stayed ahead of Franklin both in the number and in the warmth of the letters the two young people exchanged. On November 25, 1903, Eleanor introduced him to a sonnet by Elizabeth Barrett Browning, the favorite poet of her generation. She chose the line: "Unless you can swear 'For life, for death!' – Oh, fear to call it loving!"

The quote expressed Eleanor's own longing for a firm oral commitment from Franklin's side, for an expression of his love in words. However, this was not Franklin's way of loving. Instead of showering her with vows and passionate letters, he provided the ultimate proof of his devotion by action. Giving their relationship a dramatic turn, Franklin committed himself to his friend for life. He now definitely offered Eleanor the clear-cut profession of love she had been waiting for in vain.

At Thanksgiving, when Franklin's aunt Kassie Delano Collier allowed the young people to walk without the habitual chaperone on the banks of the Nashua River near Groton, he used the precious moment of privacy to propose marriage to Eleanor. His bold move was unexpected and surprised Eleanor as much as it startled his mother. Sara's promotion of Eleanor as Franklin's future wife had overshot its goal. Sara doubted whether her happy-go-lucky son of twenty-one was ready to take on the responsibilities of marriage. She felt that he should first finish his studies and earn a law degree.

The tone of Franklin and Eleanor's correspondence between September and Thanksgiving 1903 did not indicate any plans for a future together. Eleanor had been formal to the point of being stiff in addressing her friend simply as "Dear Franklin" and signing off as "Your affectionate cousin, Eleanor Roosevelt." She reminded her readers later that a lady of her time had to be a tad more reserved in the use of endearments than her admirers. But Franklin apparently set the bar low in the effusiveness of his letters. Before he proposed in November, he had called her just once his "darling" in his secret a-line-a-day diary.

Once she was engaged, Eleanor put more feeling into her letters. She addressed her fiancé as "Franklin, dear" and moved on to "Dearest Boy" or "Dearest." By 1904 she no longer signed off with "Devot-edly, always, Eleanor" but with "Lovingly devoted." In the fashion of her time, Eleanor wrote her endearments ending a message along the side of the first page of a letter, on top of her own previous writ-ing. Victorians liked discretion. It was in good taste to make fond words difficult to read.

Regrettably, there was not much tenderness to be masked in Franklin's letters to Eleanor after their honeymoon in 1905. Franklin's letters to his wife, which unlike the early letters have been preserved, were written in the same vein as the letters to his mother. They usually started out "Dearest Eleanor" and ended "Devotedly." Whenever the couple traveled separately, Franklin used the conven-tional dutiful phrases of missing her in his letters.

Did Eleanor, a romantic at heart, destroy FDR's early letters to her because she was disappointed by the lack of loving fervor in his lines? Eleanor's young friend, protégé, and biographer Joseph Lash did not think so. His explanation for Eleanor's decision to burn FDR's letters reflects his dislike of the president. Lash had reason to resent FDR, whom he suspected of encouraging the FBI to secretly investigate his leftist leanings. In his later writings, Lash pointed to the coldness, fickleness, and lack of gratitude of Franklin as a hus-band. He concluded that Eleanor could not bear to reread Franklin's allegedly exuberant love letters of their youth, once he had betrayed her with his affection for another woman.

*   *   *

As a young mother, Eleanor herself indicated by the matter-of-fact tone of her letters to her husband that they were first of all partners managing a large family. Being lovers was secondary. After a dozen years of an unsentimental marriage, Eleanor was all the more shocked when she discovered in September 1918 that Franklin was carrying on a correspondence with a friend of the family. No outsider knew what level of intimacy Eleanor found in Lucy Mercer's letters to Franklin. Apparently, they were destroyed after Eleanor read them at his sickbed in Manhattan.

For almost two decades, it seemed as if Franklin had overcome his infatuation with Lucy. There is no evidence that Eleanor ever learned that he reached out again to Lucy after eight years of complete separation from each other. She was Mrs. Winthrop Rutherfurd when FDR approached her in a quest for a new correspondence. Four of his very formal letters to her, from the time between 1926 and 1928, are now open to public scrutiny. They have been made accessible only recently by the FDR Library. A much more private and revealing message from Franklin to Lucy survived in the form of a note. Eleanor did not know it existed. She was saved the pain of realizing how enamored Franklin still was with Lucy in 1941.

In the eighth year of his presidency, FDR indicated in a few lines that Lucy was dearest to his heart. He used the word "forever" to define his feelings for her. Nobody but Mrs. Lucy Rutherfurd was to read his confession, scribbled on small lined pages, torn from a pad of ordinary paper.

It looks as if Lucy could not get herself to part with this precious document even after she destroyed all of Franklin's letters in the summer of 1945, shortly after his death. It might just as well have inadvertently escaped Lucy's deliberate erasing of all evidence of his love for her. The note remained untouched as long as she lived. Lucy's heirs kept it in a safe in Manhattan. When it was finally examined after more than four decades of disregard, the crucial two words of the brief document were declared "illegible" by a first commentator. Its importance was never recognized. The note is not dated, does not address Lucy by name, and is simply signed "F."

With the permission of Lucy's granddaughters, I was allowed in 2007 to study FDR's intimate words in a Manhattan law office. I found it difficult to concentrate on Lucy's papers under the watchful eyes of a lawyer, a trustee of the Rutherfurd family foundation. Uncomfortable at taking so much of her time, I felt better when I could provide her with a few clues about the collection of Lucy's childhood memorabilia laid out in front of me. The attorney warmed up to me when I was able to fill in many of the empty spaces in the typewritten transcripts of FDR's letters, guarded by her in the family archive.

One of these gaps, formed by the two mysterious omitted words, demanded more attention than I could afford at that moment. When I studied them at leisure, they proved to be worth deciphering. Unlike FDR's cautious letters to Lucy from the twenties, his note from the fall of 1941 was highly emotional. This was a time of upset for FDR. He was shaken by the death of his mother and by the permanent immobilization of Missy LeHand, his secretary turned caring friend. The president's personal assistant in his last years, William Hassett, touched by rare breaks in FDR's usual disposition of serene detachment, considered his boss "deeply sentimental" underneath a hard shell.

The two puzzling words were written in response to an event that brought FDR much joy in weeks of sorrow. He met Barbara Rutherfurd in person for the first time in his office in October 1941. Long curious about Lucy's only biological child, the youngest in the family after her five Rutherfurd stepchildren, Franklin had been fascinated by reports on the twenty-year-old girl. He too had an only daughter Anna, who was the apple of his eye.

FDR immediately shared his delight in Barbara with Lucy. "This littlest Babs is all that I dreamed," he jotted on the first available piece of paper. Calling Barbara "just the dearest thing in the world," FDR paused. He added, pensively, in brackets, barely readable, "'cept one." In two words he reserved his highest tribute for Lucy herself. Franklin's indirect profession of love was followed in the last sentence by an outcry. It combined nostalgia for the past with a promise for the future. He responded with a passion to Lucy's recent mention of joint memories from the time of their first acquaintance, more than two decades earlier. "I do remember the times—so well— *à toujours et toujours.*"

Slipping into French, their language of love, he lent the words "forever and ever" a special weight. Hints, allusions, and half-hidden recollections were all that Franklin and Lucy permitted themselves to share. In 1941 he was fifty-nine and she was fifty. Both were burdened by worries and responsibilities. Both believed in the inviolability of marriage. They were tied with fond respect to their spouses, determined not to hurt their feelings under any circumstances.

Franklin and Lucy always kept strictly to themselves what they felt for each other. Their reticence encouraged observers around them to talk all the more. Roosevelt watchers eagerly spread their speculations about an alleged scandalous relationship that began in the First World War and was resumed in the Second World War. After Franklin died in 1945, Lucy in 1948, and Eleanor in 1962, speculation about "the other woman" in FDR's life clouded the memory of the president.

FDR'S MISTRESS OR HIS SOUL MATE?
MYTHS AND TESTIMONIES

Nobody will ever know with absolute certainty whether Franklin and Lucy veered from their moral principles and found enough privacy for sleeping together.

Two schools of thought present starkly differing perspectives about Franklin and Lucy's romance. The dominant first group labels Lucy categorically as FDR's kept woman. The second one, convinced that Lucy and FDR's relationship was a platonic attachment of remarkable restraint, is headed by contemporary members of the Roosevelt, Mercer, and Rutherfurd families. Ellie Roosevelt Seagraves, FDR and Eleanor's oldest granddaughter, has expressed her belief in the innocence of Franklin and Lucy's encounters in oral history interviews since the 1970s. Her testimony, and her personal encouragement to devote new effort to an in-depth study of Lucy's role in FDR's life, spurred me to fill in the sparsely known outlines of Lucy's existence with concrete facts.

The granddaughters of Winthrop and Lucy Mercer Rutherfurd, Lucy and Alice Knowles of Aiken, South Carolina, agree with Mrs. Seagraves. They want to see their grandmother's friendship with FDR interpreted on the basis of factual evidence, rather than as the sum of salacious hearsay. On numerous visits the Knowles sisters supplied me with unpublished family papers and pictures in their possession that turned out to be invaluable for my work.

The relative who knew Lucy most intimately expressed the deepest disgust at the distortion of Lucy's image that reduced her to the object of FDR's desires. Mrs. Lucy Mercer Blundon was named after her beloved Aunt Lucy by her mother Violetta Mercer Marbury. Vio and her sister Lucy spent most of their lives close together in a perfect symbiosis. Four visits with Mrs. Blundon at her home in McLean, Virginia, each lasting many hours, opened my eyes to Lucy as her loved ones saw her. In these long conversations, Mrs. Blundon gallantly overcame her hearing problems and her initial reluctance to talk about very personal matters. I am grateful for her confidence, and for her permission to copy unpublished family papers. Entrusted by Mrs. Blundon with the use of her mother's extensive photo albums, I was able to compensate for the lack of diaries explaining Lucy's youth.

I always had a hard time taking my eyes away from Mrs. Lucy Mercer Blundon. She was a *grande dame* of the old school, a virtual reincarnation of her namesake aunt Lucy Mercer. Mrs. Blundon was lovely to look at, a very private person but warm, thoughtful, and charming even in her late eighties. I was crushed when her widower, Montague Blundon, told me that she had suffered a fatal heart attack in February 2010, and that I had lost in her "a great friend and admirer."

"Monty" Blundon lived only two years longer than his wife. He handed on her mission as family historian to their daughter in Vermont, Ludy Blundon Biddle. Monty distanced himself firmly from the views of most men in his circle. They had a gut feeling about an ordinary, full-blown affair of FDR and Lucy based on regular sexual encounters. Instead Monty sided with the female relatives of his wife who were convinced of a chaste love between Franklin and a lady of moral standards that were not negotiable.

Mr. Blundon's successful detective work, debunking myths about Franklin spending a night with Lucy in a motel, proved as compelling as his personal recollections of summers spent with Winthrop and Lucy Rutherfurd on their estate at Allamuchy, New Jersey. The reminiscences of contemporary members of the Rutherfurd family seamlessly complemented the memories of the Mercers' descendants. The collection of observations and papers obtained from both families resembled a treasure trove of countless small chips of information. It was my task to assemble them into a large mosaic, a sequence of pictures illustrating how Lucy Mercer Rutherfurd's fate evolved.

HIDDEN CORNERS IN LUCY'S LIFE

The initial panels of my mosaic, depicting the first twenty years of Lucy's life, surprised even contemporary members of her family. Nothing was known about Lucy's formative years overseas. Roosevelt biographers, accustomed to a wealth of facts about the youth of Franklin and Eleanor, were frustrated searching for an equivalent in the background of FDR's important friend. All accounts of Lucy Mercer began in 1913 when she was twenty-three years old and appeared as Eleanor Roosevelt's social secretary. Lucy's change into a new person as an admired great lady in the 1920s and 1930s was again ignored by writers, even though it was crucial for her last, most intense friendship with FDR in the 1940s.

Since decisive periods of Lucy's life were never explored, her influence on the president could not be properly assessed. The stereotypical formula about Lucy's characteristics is limited to facts of her birth. It labels her simply as a Catholic from an impoverished aristocratic family. Repeated in numerous biographies of FDR, this limitation to Lucy's outer circumstances misses the core of her relationship with the president: the beneficial effect on his frame of mind flowing from a gentle, wise, and motherly person tempered by adversity and reduced circumstances.

Franklin's initial fascination with Lucy as a lovely young lady was easy to grasp for FDR's biographers, but they were at a loss how to explain his puzzling later efforts to keep Lucy in his life. The question why Franklin never ceased to seek Lucy's presence remained unanswered. Calling her simply "a nice person" would not do. A look at Lucy's upbringing by nuns, and at her absolute devotion as a wife, rules out the theory of sexual bonding with FDR.

To solve the riddle of Lucy's lasting appeal for the president, it was essential for me to trace the testimony of others under her spell— primarily her family and friends in Aiken, South Carolina.

TRAVEL IN LUCY'S FOOTSTEPS

Tracing Lucy Mercer Rutherfurd's role in FDR and Eleanor's lives came as the second step in my work on the personal history of the Roosevelts. Yearly journeys to the FDR Library in Hyde Park, between 1989 and 2011, served to explore the influence of Franklin's mother Sara on his leadership.

Travel was as essential as study in archives for getting to know the *dramatis personae*, as the Delanos liked to call the main actors of their family, and historical detective work on site was as helpful for discovering Lucy as it had been for understanding Sara and Eleanor. My husband—before our retirement my colleague as a professor at Clarion University of Pennsylvania—was not only my main support at work in the FDR Library, the Houghton Library at Harvard, and the Wilson Library at the University of North Carolina. He was also my travel marshal when we followed in the Roosevelts' and Delanos' footsteps in America and France, in Switzerland and Germany, and all across the eastern United States.

The highlight of many interviews with witnesses from Lucy's world was our day with Mrs. Pamela LeBoutillier. She resided in a pillared temple of the arts hidden deep in the Long Island woods. A *grande dame*, a contemporary version of a figure from an Edith Wharton novel, she offered unsurpassed views of society life in Aiken. Since her youth Pam had been an intimate friend of Lucy's daughter Barbara. Linked to the next generation after Lucy as godmother to Lucy's granddaughter Lucy Rutherfurd Knowles, Pam's memories covered a long span of time—from the 1920s to the present. A model of gracious hospitality, she helped me visualize Lucy at the top of the social ladder in a world long gone. Her vividly remembered personal experiences on April 12, 1945, added a new facet to the oft-told story of FDR's last day.

I had to rely on our daughter Katherine for on-the-spot research into Lucy's formative years in Austria. She interviewed Austrian historians, scholarly sisters in prominent convents, and a reticent countess related by marriage to Lucy's temporary mother Agnes Carroll Heussenstamm.

I felt closest to Lucy on a bright fall morning in 2008, when I woke up in the bed that had belonged to Lucy's daughter Barbara in Aiken, South Carolina. It was thrilling to find in an inconspicuous wall cabinet a present that FDR had sent to Lucy by way of Barbara.

LUCY'S OBSERVERS

The more I immersed myself in Lucy Mercer Rutherfurd's life, the less she resembled the vixen she has been made out to be by a long line of writers. Her denigration reached a peak in the 1970s, in spite of the publication of a major, well-balanced account that served as the basis for all following chronicles of Lucy. It came out in 1968 under the title *Washington Quadrille: The Dance Beside the Documents*. Its author, Jonathan Daniels, was the son of FDR's former boss Josephus Daniels, secretary of the navy in the Wilson administration. In

1943 President Roosevelt honored Jonathan Daniels with an appointment as his administrative assistant, and in 1945 he made Daniels his press secretary.

Less responsible, more sales-oriented writers about Franklin and Lucy included the president's own sons James and Elliott. Their books—published in 1973—reflected the view of Lucy as FDR's mistress expressed earlier by Joseph Lash in his bestseller *Eleanor and Franklin.* Lash based his conclusions on his own assumptions and accepted without question the gossip of FDR's jealous Oyster Bay relatives. The ladies' speculations were precisely what the public wanted to hear. They revived old, slanderous clichés about Lucy Mercer. Under new, misleading labels, Lucy came to be known as a seductress, as a "secretary" who betrayed her employer Eleanor, and as a "governess" for the children of Winthrop Rutherfurd.

The historian Arthur Schlesinger, Jr., foresaw the growth of this widespread scandal mongering. In 1966 and 1967, he wrote two magazine articles to stem the tide. He called the sensational reports about Franklin's friendship with Lucy "wrested terribly out of proportion." Schlesinger insisted that "Eleanor Roosevelt, Franklin Roosevelt, and Lucy Mercer all emerge from the story with honor." He tried to oppose the tendency of the media to "transform a strong and loving friendship into some kind of scandalous revelation."

FDR and Eleanor's daughter Anna Roosevelt Halsted welcomed Schlesinger's conclusions. She had a special stake in promoting the truth about Lucy, because she had arranged the president's innocuous dinner meetings with Mrs. Rutherfurd in 1944. In the 1960s Mrs. Halsted was univocal with Schlesinger in her concern about the salacious overtone in new interpretations of her father's friendship with Lucy. The fallout in the media from the cultural revolution of 1968 increased Mrs. Halsted's pain. The era's acceptance of casual sex and "open marriage" made Victorian restraint and self-denial more improbable than ever.

Lucy's observers overlooked that her long closeness to FDR was rooted in his appreciation of her beneficial influence on his spirit. She earned his affection as a deeply caring, intelligent, and well-informed friend. Lucy made FDR's interests her own—from his love of nature, of trees and birds, to his love of country, and from there to his concerns for all mankind. While journalists suspected from

Lucy's relationship to Franklin at best a prominent man's pillow talk with a mistress, Lucy actually served as a trusted sounding board for the president's deepest thoughts. Whether they were sitting together at their private dinner table in the White House, or in the open at an outlook under the pine trees near Warm Springs, they talked about heady subjects. FDR revealed his view of present domestic politics and presented to his listener his plans for the future in foreign policy. He relied absolutely on Lucy's discretion, while he was not always sure whether Eleanor the columnist was reliable in keeping his secrets to herself.

Observers of the triangle situation, created by the appearance of another woman in the Roosevelts' marriage, initially limited their focus to the tragic consequences for Eleanor of the shock caused by the revelation of Lucy's letters to Franklin in September 1918. More recently admirers of Eleanor in the new millennium looked at the turmoil caused by Lucy in Eleanor's heart and mind in a positive light. They pointed out that Eleanor's rival played a crucial role as a catalyst for her transformation from a conventional society matron into one of America's great politicians and role models for generations to come.

Joseph Alsop, who complained in 1982 that the story of Franklin and Lucy had "never been properly told before," stressed the benefit to his psyche that his cousin Franklin derived from his closeness to Lucy. Not only did it play "pretty nearly as great a role in Franklin Roosevelt's life and career as his tragic infantile paralysis," but it also "transformed for good [Franklin and Eleanor's relationship] from a normal marriage into a highly successful working partnership." Alsop's mother Corinney, Eleanor's first cousin, considered it as more important that Franklin's "disappointment in a strong and strongly felt love did much to banish the 'feather duster' side in Franklin Roosevelt, and to deepen, toughen, and mature his character and personality even prior to his paralysis."

As Franklin and Lucy's platonic love fades into the past, its innocence loses ever more credibility. Contemporary observers scoff at Victorian standards before the First World War. It is well known that Eleanor called sex "an ordeal." Conventional wisdom concludes that a virile man of thirty-five like Franklin, enjoying openly the company of a beautiful lady, must have had an adulterous affair with her.

Alsop's new interpretation of the triangle relationship formed by FDR, Eleanor, and Lucy was full of praise for all three of them. They "all met this crisis in their lives . . . in the grandest style, to a degree that one can only admire nowadays, although their version of the grand style is likely to bewilder all too many persons in the 1980's." As a member of the Roosevelt's Oyster Bay clan, and a grandson of Theodore and Elliott Roosevelt's sister Corinne Roosevelt Robinson, Joseph Alsop had known all of Eleanor and Franklin's Oyster Bay and Hyde Park relatives since childhood. Alsop's insights were tucked away in his biography of his cousin, titled *FDR: A Centenary Remembrance*—an unwieldy publication in the format of a coffee table book.

After the turn of the twenty-first century, conflicting new voices retold the old story. Ellen Feldman's poetic novel of 2003, titled *Lucy*, adopted the perspective of Franklin and Eleanor's sons, seeing sex as the ultimate fulfillment of FDR and Lucy's relationship. A year later Resa Willis differed with a more nuanced approach in her slim volume *FDR and Lucy: Lovers and Friends*.

Joseph Persico proved himself the most radical proponent of the theory that the attraction of Lucy for FDR was purely sexual. In his 2008 book *Franklin and Lucy*, he revived old beliefs in the continuity of their sexual bonding, even in the years following FDR's paralysis by polio. An experienced author, Persico encouraged biographers and journalists to once again assume as a matter of course that Lucy was FDR's mistress.

The scarce substantive information about Lucy's life and personality was not increased by new research in the first decades after the year 2000. Errors and misrepresentation were handed down from one writer to the next, but the basic formula of Lucy's evaluation as a historical figure remained within the limits set by Jonathan Daniels in 1968. Nevertheless, the awareness of Lucy's impact on FDR and Eleanor's fate has risen to an ever-higher level in the Roosevelt literature. Peter Collier's concept of interweaving the history of Theodore Roosevelt and Franklin Roosevelt's clans in his 1994 book *The Roosevelts: An American Saga*, was expanded in 2014 by Geoffrey C. Ward and the filmmaker Ken Burns in a large volume called *The Roosevelts: An Intimate History*. The book turned into a printed document the images and text of the PBS series of documentary films on the Roosevelts, adding Eleanor Roosevelt—Theodore's niece and Franklin's wife—to the three star-constellation in the firmament of American presidential history.

Lucy's chaste frame of mind is hard to imagine in the twenty-first century. Her relationship with FDR is automatically listed as an earlier chapter in the chronicles of overflowing presidential libido. Lucy seems to belong in a similar niche with a Marilyn Monroe or a Monica Lewinsky. On the other hand, Henry Kissinger's formula of power as "the ultimate aphrodisiac" does not fit Lucy's attraction to Franklin.

While research on Eleanor continues to regard Lucy as her nemesis, it fails to recognize a distinct advantage in her husband's preoccupation with an unselfish friend like Lucy. The impeccable Mrs. Rutherfurd presented a relatively benign challenge to Eleanor's standing in her marriage and with the public. A perfect lady of high moral principles, Lucy always stayed out of the general view. She was ever careful not to mar the appearances of an intact marriage of a man holding high office. In her place another more self-seeking and ruthless woman might have caused serious harm to the president's reputation.

New evidence of Lucy's modesty and lack of vanity is still turning up. A letter from Lucy to FDR's personal secretary Grace Tully, dated April 9, 1945, was found in 2010. It shows her as thoughtful and tactful as ever to the very end of FDR's life. Lucy only agreed to come to Warm Springs after Miss Tully assured her that "the Boss" specifically asked for her visit. Lucy's response to Franklin's longing for her turned out to be a blessing for both of them. Lucy was rewarded for the rest of her life by the knowledge that her coming had benefited a very sick man. The president was comforted by her tenderness in his last days, and by her beloved presence in the hour of his death.

PART ONE

LUCY AS MISS MERCER

Lucy's Mother Minnie Tunis Mercer was a queen of Washington Society.

CHAPTER I

BORN OF THE BLUEST BLOOD

LUCY'S MOTHER, MINNIE TUNIS MERCER: HEIRESS OF MERCHANT PRINCES

LUCY GETS OUT reads a neatly printed line under a photograph from the 1890s. Shiny black colors dominate the picture, from the rumps of two stately horses to the top hat of the coachman holding the reins. The image evokes a golden Cinderella coach, with a tiny princess descending steep steps.

A little girl of about five, Lucy is the brightest spot in the picture from the Mercers' family album. She almost disappears under a wide-brimmed, frilly white hat that matches her white summer dress. Large, dimly outlined residential buildings in the background indicate that Lucy had just arrived home in the family carriage. An even more faded photo shows Lucy and her older sister Violetta hugging soft-bodied dolls. Their dolls were huge even by the standards of Victorian times, when little girls were expected to develop motherly feelings playfully at an early age.

It is not known whether Vio and Lucy's mother expressed special tenderness for her young children. With an array of nurses and governesses at her call, it is unlikely that she cared for them herself. The chronicles of Washington's high society at the time speak only about the brilliant trail left by Mrs. Carroll Mercer on the capital's social scene. Minnie Leigh Tunis Mercer (later often called Minna), was well

5

endowed with assets that made her sparkle in her circle: she combined blue blood, beauty, wealth, ambition, and regal bearing.

Her background was both opulent and aristocratic. Through her mother, whose given name was Henderson, Minna belonged to one of the first families of North Carolina. Caroline Earl Henderson had married "down" socially, but "up" in wealth. Her husband John Tunis could trace his ancestry only to his grandparents. When Violetta and Lucy Mercer reconstructed their family tree for six generations, they had to leave twenty-three slots on the Tunis side blank. But there were plenty of other ancestors to fill in the tree, which blossomed with illustrious names from as far back as colonial days.

When the time came for Lucy Mercer and Franklin Roosevelt—both genealogy buffs—to compare their family histories, Franklin lost out to Lucy by a wide margin. His Roosevelt and Delano ancestors could not remotely compare in historical importance to Lucy's forebears, at least according to the snobbish standards of the Victorian era. In fact, the aristocratic Mrs. Schuyler Van Rensselaer had declared in *History of New York in the Seventeenth Century* (1909) that "at no pre-Revolutionary period was the Roosevelt family conspicuous nor did any member of it attain distinction."

The founding father of the American Roosevelt family, Claes van Rosenvelt, had arrived in New Amsterdam as a humble Dutch farmer around 1650. His grandsons John (Johannes) and James (Jacobus) Roosevelt eventually became successful merchants. In 1858 John's descendants, called the Oyster Bay Roosevelts, produced President Theodore Roosevelt, the uncle of Eleanor. In 1882 James's descendants, called the Hyde Park Roosevelts, yielded President Franklin Roosevelt—the first statesman among five generations of wealthy New York City businessmen since his great-great-grandfather Isaac Roosevelt, born in 1726, who stood out with his political prowess as a member of New York's Constitutional Convention and the State Assembly.

By contrast, Lucy's ancestors—the Mercers and the Carrolls, the Masons, the Pages, and the Spriggs—were counted among Virginia and Maryland's prominent families for many generations. Lucy's ancestors on her father's side had their roots in large, princely estates. Enterprising scions of landed English families, they acquired immense plantations in the colonies in the late 1600s and served as

colonels and generals in the War of Independence. Later, as statesmen and governors of southern states, they helped shape the new
nation.

The family tree of Lucy's mother, Minnie Tunis Mercer, paralleled
that of the two Roosevelt dynasties. Like the Hyde Park and Oyster
Bay Roosevelts, it was dominated by well-to-do businessmen of social distinction. Minna's father was the third John Tunis in as many
generations—all highly regarded as merchant princes in their native
Norfolk, Virginia. When Minna's great-grandfather, the first known
John Tunis, died on December 8, 1830, the community of Norfolk
"mourned his death as a public loss." His epitaph lists a number of
charitable works and praises him as a philanthropist, acting upon
his "troublesome conscience." Norfolk remembered Minna's great-
grandfather for his "usefulness and public spirit as a citizen, for his
intelligence and integrity as a merchant, and for his benevolence and
sterling worth in all relations of social life." A model family man, he
was praised as "a devoted husband and a kind and indulgent parent."
Theodore Roosevelt, Sr., President Theodore Roosevelt's father, can
be regarded as Tunis's equivalent in the Roosevelt family. Born just
one year after the death of Tunis, Roosevelt Sr. (known as Great-
heart) stood out as the benefactor of many charitable institutions,
like New York's Newsboys Lodging-House.

When Minna's grandfather (the next John Tunis) died, the citizens
of Norfolk erected a monument in "loving tribute to one who gave
his life in the service of this stricken community during the prevailing epidemic . . . administering to the wants of the sick, until he himself fell a victim of its ravages." Just fifty years old, this John Tunis left
a noble heritage and a large fortune to his own son John Edward
Tunis. Unfortunately, the son died only eleven years after his father at
the age of thirty-one. John Edward's early death on February 23,
1866, would have tragic consequences for his aristocratic wife Caroline and their three-year old daughter Minna. It eventually also overshadowed the lives of the granddaughters he never knew, Violetta
and Lucy Mercer.

In times of need, and especially when young women were in distress about affairs of the heart, the relatives of Lucy Mercer's maternal grandmother Caroline Henderson Tunis provided moral and
practical support. The Scottish Henderson relatives could trace their

prominence to the Jamestown colony. One of their descendants, Samuel Henderson, moved to North Carolina as justice of the peace and high sheriff. Pleasant, the youngest of his five officer sons, won distinction as a major. In times of peace, he served as superior court clerk of Orange County, North Carolina, and as steward of the University of North Carolina.

Pleasant's son Alexander, a surgeon in the U.S. Navy, was Lucy Mercer's great-grandfather. His marriage to the high-born Elizabeth Earl Johnson enhanced the social standing of their daughter Caroline Earl Henderson. But Caroline, Lucy Mercer's grandmother, did not choose a scion of an old family for a husband. Instead she married John Edward Tunis III, Norfolk's richest merchant. When their only daughter Minna was born on June 18, 1863, the young family's good fortune seemed sealed. As far as anybody in Norfolk could tell, neither Caroline nor Minnie Tunis would ever want for anything. But John's early death spelled disaster for mother and daughter.

*   *   *

John Lowell, Jr., a lawyer of Pemberton Square in Boston, was entrusted with the posthumous management of John Edward Tunis's fortune. Although the terms of Tunis's will are unknown, Mr. Lowell's letters to Minna contain references to many family tragedies that occurred after her father's death. Caroline was only twenty-five when she was widowed. After she remarried and had children with her second husband Andrew Sigourney, she appears to have lost her claim on her inheritance from her first husband. By the time Minna came of age, she was in charge and acting as her father's only beneficiary. But she was unprepared for the responsibilities of an heiress. Her father had not lived to teach her how to use money wisely.

Initially, Minna's mother Caroline held the purse strings at the discretion of Mr. Lowell. But young Minna borrowed substantial sums— as much as $3,800 at a time—from funds held by her mother as her guardian. The money in Minnie Tunis's young hands might have amounted to a quarter of a million in today's dollars. By the summer of 1887, when Minna was twenty-four, she had won the upper hand after many years of disputes over money. Minna's mother and half sister now depended on the young woman's generosity. While Minna received monthly payments of four hundred dollars from Boston, her mother had to do with monthly payments of less than two hundred dollars.

Mr. Lowell, the family lawyer, proved to be a kind and wise man. In a fatherly way, he tried to soften the temperamental Minna's harsh judgment. On July 15, 1887, Minna's mother Caroline—who had become addicted to narcotics—turned to the family lawyer for help. "She is very anxious to go to Europe to live," Mr. Lowell reported to Minna, "and from what she says and what has happened to us this time I am satisfied that the only chance of freedom from annoyance for you is to let her go." Minna would have to foot the bill. Mr. Lowell advised her "to pay for her [mother's] passage, to give her some money to start with (but not much) and to increase her monthly payments to 200 dollars."

By April of the following year, Mr. Lowell's strategy seemed to have worked. He wrote Minna, "Your mother is much better. Dr. Folson tells me she has not touched any morphine or other narcotics for at least 3 weeks; that she is very sorry for what she may have said or done to you. Would it not be well if you and she could be on good terms with each other once more."

Sympathetic to the plight of his clients, Mr. Lowell acted beyond the call of duty as the manager of the Tunis legacy. But advising Minnie Tunis was a thankless job. She regarded her attorney mainly as a spigot that spouted cash, a fixture to be turned on forcefully until it yielded its last drop. Mr. Lowell understood Minna's youthful assertiveness. While the widowed Caroline Tunis was preoccupied with a new husband and a new family, the fatherless Minna suffered from the turbulent relationship with her mother. Nobody had offered the girl a realistic view of the world. Minna did not know the joys of contentment but rather followed the whims of her strong personality. She had received good "school training," as she said, in Raleigh, North Carolina. She was energetic and independent. Ambitious and lured by the glitter of the Gilded Age, she was willing to use gold to pave her way to the pinnacle of high society.

Young men, eager to help Minna spend her money, soon swarmed around the sweet lure. The lively heiress was not just pretty; she was gorgeous. She stunned her suitors with her perfectly proportioned profile resembling a Roman empress, and with the promise of soul in her large dark eyes. Minna had the presence of a young lady of class who was used to getting what she wanted.

A well-born Englishman, Percy T. Norcop, was different enough from her other admirers to catch Minna's fancy first. But after three years of marriage, she had reason to wonder about his motives for courtship. When Percy played around, Minna filed for divorce. On June 19, 1886, it was "appearing to the Court that the charges of adultery contained in the plaintiff's bill, have been sustained by the evidence adduced." The divorce decree stressed that the defendant, Percy T. Norcop, would be "divested of any property and estate of the plaintiff, acquired by virtue of the marriage." Minna acted aggressively to protect her fortune, though she knew full well that divorce would cast a shadow on her standing in society and in church.

Minna found a friendly refuge in North Carolina while she let the waves of scandal calm down. She could not lean on her mother but in her large, close-knit southern clan, there were numerous uncles, aunts, and cousins glad to offer her the comforts of family solidarity. The Hokes, Minna's distinguished relatives in Lincolnton, North Carolina, were happy to make her part of their family. Only two decades earlier, Major General Robert F. Hoke had enjoyed being called Lee's best general. His son William A. Hoke excelled as a jurist. Long after he offered advice to his cousin Minna, the younger Hoke gained prominence as chief justice of North Carolina's Supreme Court.

William's sister Sallie was less brilliant but good naturedly filled the role of Minna's companion in Lincolnton. Cousin Sallie was not forceful enough for mothering—and certainly not for chaperoning— a freshly divorced young woman of great vitality. This was all the more reason for Minna to take Sallie along when she put an end to her self-imposed exile in North Carolina. In Washington, where major social success beckoned, Minna established herself as the hostess of the Hendersons and the Hokes.

In the spring of 1887, Mr. Lowell reluctantly agreed to Minna's purchase of a house on P Street, even though the real estate she inherited in Norfolk was not doing well. Minna asked her lawyer not to tell her mother where the new house was located. At the same time, she rebelled against his suggestion to "be careful and buy furniture that is not expensive." Minna sent to Norfolk for her inherited furniture, but she also extracted two thousand dollars from Mr. Lowell for fine new furnishings. Setting up a house to perfection was her passion. She knew that she was good at it. A generation later she would share her skills with her daughter Lucy, who inherited her exquisite taste.

LUCY'S FATHER, MAJOR CARROLL MERCER: MARYLAND ARISTOCRAT, GRANDMOTHER'S BOY

Shortly after her arrival in the nation's capital, Minna became a Washington hostess to be reckoned with. Congressmen and senators flocked to her home at 1744 P Street, near Dupont Circle. It was described by one of her Hoke relatives as "so rich and beautiful that it strikes everyone who comes in."

Friends of friends introduced her to presidential social circles surrounding the young Mrs. Grover Cleveland. But in her days as Mrs. Norcop, Minna had already discovered two aristocratic Maryland families that attracted her more—the Carrolls and the Mercers. Minna was fascinated by a good-looking marine lieutenant who combined both names. He had an edge over many suitors who sought her hand. Carroll Mercer, six years her senior, was a suave society man who had seen the world as an officer. On June 16, 1880, at the age of twenty-three, he had been commissioned as a second lieutenant in the Marine Corps. In 1885 his longest overseas assignment took him all the way to the Isthmus of Panama.

Carroll was known as a charmer but also as a kindhearted friend of nature. He radiated the mystique of nobility. Together with his brother, he had been raised by his grandmother, one of the *grande dames* of Washington society. From a distance Minna had long admired Mrs. William T. Carroll. In the young woman's eyes, the distinguished matron surpassed all of Washington's prominent ladies. But before Minna gave serious consideration to Lieutenant Carroll Mercer's courtship, she wanted to meet his grandmother and find out whether the Carrolls and Mercers deserved their fame.

Minna knew that Carroll Mercer had lost his mother, Violetta Lansdale Carroll, when he was a child. When Violetta's two little boys were rescued by their grandmother Sarah Carroll, they were brought close to another proud family's heritage. Sarah, also known as Sally,

Lucy's father Major Carroll Mercer is pictured here after
his discharge from the army.

had grown up in style as the daughter of Governor Samuel Sprigg of Maryland. The governor's wife, the distinguished Violetta Lansdale, was the first of three Violettas in the family. Sarah Sprigg's marriage to William T. Carroll, clerk of the U.S. Supreme Court, was a widely celebrated social event. William's father, Charles Carroll of Bellevue, had inherited great wealth from his own father, Charles Carroll of Duddington Manor. He was a first cousin of the most famous Carroll, the last surviving signer of the Declaration of Independence.

William T. Carroll raised no eyebrows when he married his mother's niece. Marriages between first cousins were common in a small, exclusive society with a limited number of eligible partners. A similar scenario led to frequent intermarriages among the first families in the Hudson Valley. A century later Theodore Roosevelt would congratulate his niece Eleanor for "keeping the name in the family" with her marriage to Franklin Roosevelt. But they were cousins only through a common ancestor five generations back.

The numerous cousins in Lucy Mercer's noble family tree were much more closely related than their peers in New York State. There was a Sophia Sprigg in Lucy's ancestry in addition to her great-grandmother Sarah Sprigg. But all that counted was their descent from the founding father Thomas Sprigg, who had won thousands of acres in land grants after he came to Maryland from England in 1658.

Minnie Tunis was impressed by the life stories of Carroll Mercer's ancestors, but she was thoroughly charmed by his grandmother's graciousness and self-confidence. Minna could always count on a warm reception at the great lady's home, the legendary Carroll House. Mrs. Sarah Sprigg Carroll had good reason to welcome one of Washington's most eligible heiresses under her roof. She regarded Minna as an ideal match for her motherless grandson Carroll Mercer. The young man was like a son to Sarah, having been brought up under her care together with his brother John Francis Mercer. But although Carroll had inherited the bluest of blue blood, the riches of his planter forefathers had melted away over the previous two generations.

Carroll received a good education at Columbian College, a forerunner of George Washington University. Seeking a career in the military, he followed family tradition. He could count on excellent connections as he rose through the ranks. Two brothers of Carroll's mother Violetta Lansdale had served as generals. There was, however, no lush plantation in Carroll's background to enable him to retire to the life of a gentleman farmer.

Carroll's physique was imposing. Close to six feet tall, he entered a room with panache and won general respect with his impeccable, gentlemanly manners. A keen interest in naval matters set him apart from his fellow officers.

Carroll's father Thomas Swann Mercer died prematurely, only twenty-two years after he and Violetta were married in 1856. It was Carroll's good fortune that his grandmother could receive Minna, the young lady he courted, in a palatial mansion on beautifully landscaped grounds. Carroll House stood on property left in trust to Sarah by her father, the ex-governor. Many Washington dignitaries, including former President James Monroe, enjoyed her hospitality. Sarah could not guess that in only a few years Carroll's daughters Vio and Lucy, her own great-granddaughters, would romp happily in the lovely garden.

When Minnie Tunis set foot in Mrs. William T. Carroll's place at 18th and F Streets—now listed in the National Register of Historic Places—the grandeur of the Sprigg and Carroll family legacies was tangible. Her hostess was happy to fill her in on the Mercers' fame as well. She could sense that Minnie Tunis was determined to marry up. As a prospective member of the Mercer family, Minna needed to know that the Mercers of Aldie and Meikleour were "oulder than ould Perth," according to an ancient verse often cited by Scottish historians. The Mercers could trace their family in Scotland back to 1200. The renown of the first known John Mercer was established at the time of King Richard II.

* * *

After John Mercer's descendants emigrated from England, they rose rapidly in the ranks of the landed gentry in the American colonies. John Mercer of Marlborough, the legendary founding father of the Mercers' dominion by the Potomac River and Chesapeake Bay, was Carroll Mercer's great-great-grandfather. He died at the age of sixty-four in 1768—a Crown lawyer, the owner of large estates, and the father of nineteen children.

His heir Colonel John Francis Mercer, a student and friend of Thomas Jefferson, served as governor of Maryland from 1801 to 1803. When Marlborough—his inherited mansion in Stafford County, Virginia—burned down, he moved to Cedar Park, the Maryland estate of his wife Sophia Sprigg. The mansion, located by the West River near Annapolis, still belonged to Mr. and Mrs. Mercer when young Carroll was born there in 1857. Colonel Mercer, "generous to a fault," had sacrificed a large portion of his "noble fortune" to the cause of the Revolution. He paid out of his own pocket for the horses, arms, and munitions of his regiment.

The family's finances never recovered from the drain. Carroll's father Thomas Swann Mercer worked as a physician. He had to sell Cedar Park and move to Washington. But his marriage to his cousin Violetta Lansdale, from another dynasty of planters, added to the distinction of the Mercer family.

The prominence of the Mercers was beyond question, but it was the dignity and charm of Carroll's grandmother Sarah that finally won over her guest. Minna had taken one of her trusted Hoke cousins along on the visit that would decide her future. The young man echoed Minna's awe upon making closer acquaintance with the "Carroll Mercer kin." Writing home to Lincolnton, North Carolina, Mr. Hoke praised them lavishly as "elegant people and Mrs. Carroll is an elegant old lady."

Minna's fascination with her prospective in-laws was sealed by the presence of Sarah Carroll's daughter. Carroll Mercer's aunt, an older sister of his late mother Violetta, was married to a Count Esterhazy. Also named Sarah, she spelled her nickname "Sallie" to distinguish herself from her mother's nickname "Sally." Minna's Hoke cousin remarked about the lady, "The Countess could talk one to death in 15 minutes by the watch." But in Minna's eyes the Countess Esterhazy had everything she would have wished for in a mother-in-law, had Carroll's mother Violetta lived to fill the role.

Mrs. Sarah Carroll and her namesake daughter, the cosmopolitan countess, served as Minna's role models. Minna tried to emulate the Carrolls not only in their smart living, but also in the depth of their faith. The spiritual side of the Carrolls impressed her profoundly. Their historic roots in the Roman Catholic Church set the Carrolls apart from the Anglican traditions of most planter families. Minna's conversion to Catholicism, and her decision to raise her daughters Vio and Lucy as Catholics, represented a deliberate break with the Mercers' Episcopalian heritage.

When Minna's idol Sallie Carroll married the Austrian Count Esterhazy, she fit seamlessly into the Catholic tradition of the Austro-Hungarian Empire. Minna would not have been averse to a similar turn of fate for her daughters Violetta and Lucy. Surprisingly, Minna's romantic visions almost came true.

Minna sensed right away a kindred spirit in the Countess Esterhazy. She had been the darling of Washington society in Abraham Lincoln's time. The wedding of Sarah Virginia Carroll to Maximilian Ernst Maria, Count Esterhazy, took place on June 6, 1870, in Washington. Count Esterhazy was serving as secretary to the Imperial and Royal Austro-Hungarian legation at the American capital when he fell in love with one of the most enchanting ladies in President Lincoln's entourage. The lovely Sallie Carroll had been widowed at twenty-seven. Her husband Charles Griffin, a general in the Civil War, had died from yellow fever in Galveston, Texas, three years earlier.

In the six years of her first marriage, Sallie Carroll Griffin rose to the zenith of Washington society. The *New York Herald* called her wedding in the mansion of her father William T. Carroll, clerk of the U.S. Supreme Court, "one of the most brilliant assemblages ever witnessed in Washington." Eventually, Sallie was perhaps even better remembered for triggering Mary Todd Lincoln's perpetual jealousy. It seems that Mrs. Sarah Griffin shone a tad too brightly at White House balls. In his *Illustrated Weekly,* Frank Leslie commented that "Mrs. Griffin was simply but tastefully attired in a corn-colored silk headdress of bright crimson flowers. She was observed of all, as she leaned on the arm of the President."

Sallie Carroll's second marriage, to an Austrian diplomat, added to her glamour. Her new husband, Count Maximilian Esterhazy, belonged to the Forchtenstein branch of the historic clan. The Esterhazy name became famous in 1683, when a member of the family distinguished himself as a military leader in the successful defense of Vienna, which had been besieged by Turkish invaders. A hundred years after this time, names of the music-loving brothers—Prince

Paul II and Prince Nikolaus I Esterhazy—were forever linked to the composer Franz Joseph Haydn as his patrons.

Sallie's husband, the wealthy lord of large estates in Hungary, was just a count rather than a prince. But Sallie filled the role of countess superbly, even after she was widowed a second time in 1883. Mrs. Edith Benham Helm, social secretary to First Ladies Edith Wilson and Eleanor Roosevelt, called Countess Esterhazy "a very charming person with a lovely voice and must have been a great beauty when young." In 1912, when Sallie was seventy-two and living in London, a society observer joked that Washington's Carroll Mercer "in all probability will inherit something from his Aunt Sallie, the Countess Esterhazy, provided she does not lavish everything she possesses on her young admirers."

By 1917 Sallie Carroll Esterhazy had become a legend in England. At her death a requiem mass was celebrated in Westminster Chapel. Against all expectations, it was not her nephew Carroll Mercer but his recently widowed wife Minnie Mercer who was eligible to become the beneficiary of a legacy from the countess.

CARROLL AND MINNIE MERCER'S ROMANCE: IDYLL IN EGYPT

Money was no concern for Minna at the time when Countess Sallie was about to become her relative by marriage. Minna was well aware that her union with Carroll Mercer—just as the marriage of her own mother and father, Caroline Henderson and John Tunis—combined the allure of new money with the appeal of famous old names. Minna and Carroll shared both a preference for a casually elegant lifestyle and the ambition to rule at the top of society. They were congenial, they were in love, and they made a stunning couple.

Minna had the means and determination to stay close to her beloved, even when his military assignments put an ocean between them. Seeking Carroll out overseas added the adventurous touch to her romance that Minna craved. She wanted a life out of the ordinary, setting her apart from her peers.

To realize her grand plans, Minna had been pulling more impatiently than ever at her financial leash. Her father had deliberately kept it short. There was still only one way for Minna to get at her money, and it passed through the narrow channel of Mr. Lowell's consent. In the fall of 1887, the family attorney had declared Minna's repeated request to buy an estate in North Carolina "out of the question." Seven months later, though, Mr. Lowell was amenable to a less expensive proposal. He approved his client's plan to marry Carroll Mercer in London and went along with her intention to live with him overseas after the wedding. On April 10, 1888, Minna received a letter of credit to use abroad, "$3000 for the six months you are to be away."

At first Mr. Lowell balked when Minna asked for steamer tickets to London, but it was not easy to resist the prodding of a persistent young lady with a great zest for life. In spite of his protests that he was no travel agent, Mr. Lowell came around. On June 8 he wrote Minna, "I have engaged two berths, nos. 217 and 218 on the *Germanic* for June 20th. These are all that are left on the *Germanic*."

When Minna sailed to London on the White Star ocean liner *Germanic,* she was properly chaperoned. As her companion, she invited her cousin Sallie Hoke, who had always hoped to go to Europe to study music. The watchful eyes of an Episcopal bishop, Theodore Benedict Lyman of the Diocese of North Carolina, would assure the Henderson relatives that Minna would not fall in with the fast crowd on board that drank "champagne and cocktails from morning to night."

Minna did not at all like the idea that she would soon turn the ripe age of twenty-five. She wished to live on without regard to birthdays, she told the Hokes, adding the exclamation, "Pray for us at church." Her prayer for staying young would be answered for almost sixty years until she died in 1947, vivacious and rebellious to the end.

The rapid ticking of life's clock encouraged Minna's pursuit of an immediate wedding with Carroll. After she joined him in London, a copy of her and Percy's divorce decree arrived from Lincolnton, just in time for the ceremony on July 30, 1888. It took place "according to the Rites and Ceremonies of the Established Church" at Saint Martin-in-the-Fields, an Anglican church in Trafalgar Square. Sallie Badger Hoke served as one of the witnesses. The bride always stressed that the officiating Reverend John F. Kitto was "the Queen's Chaplain."

The newlyweds started their honeymoon in Paris and Italy. Before long Lieutenant Mercer had to report back for duty on his naval vessel, the USS *Quinnebaug*. His new wife followed on a commercial ship. She finally caught up with him in a remote corner of the eastern Mediterranean. The *Quinnebaug* was moored in Alexandria, Egypt, from November 28, 1888, to April 10, 1889—allowing the young couple a delightful time together under a warm winter sun. The young Mrs. Carroll Mercer had her fill of the exotic living she had missed in boring Lincolnton.

At a time when properly timid young matrons from the District of Columbia would consider a trip across the river to Alexandria, Virginia, an adventure, Minnie Mercer was exhilarated at being stranded in Alexandria, Egypt. Here she was, in her fifth month of pregnancy, in an ancient but utterly foreign Arab country. Egypt was poor, in political and economic chaos. Only six years earlier in 1882, Alexandria—the country's major port—had been bombarded from the sea by British warships putting down a revolt.

Minna was separated from home by more than four thousand miles, facing a string of rocky return voyages on steamers through the Mediterranean and the Atlantic. But the venturesome Minna was having the time of her life. She was well cared for by Carroll, the man she wanted. He in turn was entitled to protection by British soldiers, who had been guarding the small British-American colony since the 1850s.

A number of prominent Americans had remained at Egypt's leading port since the time of westernization under Ismail Pasha. One of them, Judge Victor Clay Barringer, happened to belong to the vast circle of Minna's relatives from North Carolina. Minna could not make much of his scholarship in Roman and Muslim law, but she was grateful for the hospitality extended by the Barringers. She raved in letters to Sallie Hoke about their "really charming" little garden and she delighted in breakfasts of local specialties, like tiny eggs and small fruity bananas.

Even in her idyll on the Mediterranean coast, Minna could not sit still. On a trip with Carroll up the Nile to Cairo, inland heat and gusts of dusty wind could not discourage her from exploring the wonders of the desert. The pyramids inspired awe but the Sphinx made her laugh. She joked with Carroll that its flat-nosed expression in stone reminded her of her cousin Sallie Hoke.

Though far away from her duels by correspondence with Mr. Lowell, Minna's perennial discontent with the state of her finances caught up with her. She was six months pregnant. On January 25, 1889, years of uncertainty about the scope of her inheritance came to an end with the final settlement of her father's estate. In a solemn statement, Mr. Lowell informed her that the entire estate was worth somewhat more than three hundred thousand dollars, the equivalent of about three and a half million dollars a century later. Part of the fortune was termed "unproductive real estate in Norfolk, Berkley and Newark." Mr. Lowell warned Minna that her yearly net income would not exceed $6,968.21.

The financial disappointment was soon softened by Minna's joy at the birth of her first child. Her daughter Vio, named after her late grandmother Violetta Lansdale Carroll, was born on March 31, 1889. Judge Barringer called little Violetta Mercer a beauty.

When bad news followed from Boston on April 13, 1889, Mr. Lowell communicated with them delicately by way of Minna's husband, respecting the vulnerability of a new mother. "My dear Sir," he wrote Carroll Mercer, "I take the liberty of writing you not wishing to annoy Mrs. Mercer at this time." A rainstorm had destroyed a portion of her warehouse and wharf property in Norfolk. Consequently, a quantity of slack lime had caught fire, but fortunately the property had been protected by insurance. Earlier Minna's cousin William A. Hoke had written Mr. Lowell to ask him to cancel the insurance, but the letter arrived too late, after the storm had done its damage. In his letter to Carroll Mercer, the attorney took the opportunity to vent his annoyance with the interference from Mrs. Mercer's relative in North Carolina. Until this time Mr. Hoke had been mainly entrusted with safekeeping Minna's inherited jewels. Mr. Lowell noted now that more than two thousand dollars had been paid in premiums for the insurance. It would have been "a foolish waste of money to cancel it," he remarked tartly. In any case, the loss of rental income at Norfolk was going to diminish Mrs. Mercer's cash flow for some time to come.

Minna gallantly dismissed the unpleasantness of getting along on two hundred dollars a month less. She had taken in stride the challenges of giving birth one month early in a remote and undeveloped country. She was young, strong in body and spirit. With an infant at her breast, she remained brave even when she had to say goodbye to her husband. Carroll sailed west on the *Quinnebaug* on June 12; shortly afterward Judge Barringer escorted mother and child to a rocky steamer, on the first leg of their long voyage home.

THE CAVE DWELLERS' DAUGHTERS:
VIO AND LUCY GROWING UP IN SPLENDOR

On April 26, 1891, two years after Minna and Vio left Egypt, a second beautiful daughter was born to Carroll and Minnie Mercer. Baby Lucy looked like an angel. Most records give 1744 P Street in Washington as the address of her birth. Her middle name, Page, alluded to an illustrious line of forebears on her father's side. The Pages were renowned for women of great charm and great virtue. Their men combined the management of large plantations with scholarship in the law and letters.

Lucy Page Mercer grew up as a city girl. Aside from New York City, the nation's capital offered America's upper class the most favorable environment for enjoying the Gay Nineties. Washington flourished with the growth of the federal government and the increase in number of its legislative representatives. High society recruited its members from the Senate and the House, mixing them with descendants of proud old families from colonial times. It also embraced men who had recently amassed great wealth in a nation that was flexing its new industrial muscle. Recognition of the United States as a fledgling world power caused an influx of important foreign embassies into the city. But in spite of the recent upswing, Washington society stayed small. Members of the elite knew each other and competed fiercely, vying for top social recognition.

As a rule, the wives of the great entrepreneurs of the time (*the* Mrs. Astor of New York, née Caroline Schermerhorn) had the leisure and ambition to become trendsetters. But only the super-rich had their own ballrooms. Minnie Mercer rose to prominence on a smaller scale. She mainly used her skills as a discerning hostess. In contrast to William Backhouse Astor, who left the staging of great social events to his wife Caroline, Minna's husband was always at her side, actively promoting their standing in the capital's pecking order.

In June 1890, when Carroll resigned his military commission, he was described simply as a "gentleman" on his daughter Lucy's birth certificate. Unencumbered by a profession, Carroll was free to direct all his energies to the exclusive social clubs of his circle. He ranked high in the Cave Dwellers Club, a society unique to Washington. Although it had a strange-sounding name, the concept was a success that proved to be long lived, lasting through two world wars and great social change. In modified form it has survived to the present day.

Long after the Gilded Age, Marietta Minnigerode Andrews explained the raison d'être of the Cave Dwellers Club of her era in a 1928 book *My Studio-Window: Sketches of the Pageant of Washington Life*. "This term, which is a little too suggestive of a limited horizon, is one highly relished by those to whom it properly belongs, and much coveted by such as aspire to be classed with the blue blooded and considered inheritors of old traditions."

Before the turn of the twentieth century, the Cave Dwellers Club at 1710 Eye Street was the Mercers' special domain. But Carroll also held a superior position in the exclusive Metropolitan Club and was elected to the first board of governors of the Chevy Chase Club. A new type of club, the latter promoted riding and hunting far out in the Maryland countryside. For its main event of the 1892 season, the Pink Coat Ball in December, part of the ballroom had been converted to a hunters' woodland festooned with bowers of greenery. The men— prominent in government, business, and the diplomatic corps—wore colorful hunter's coats. The ladies were resplendent in gowns with touches of glowing scarlet. Everybody had a glorious time until the ball ended at five o'clock in the morning. Minnie Mercer felt that she had truly arrived when she read in the *Washington Star*'s social pages that Mr. and Mrs. Carroll Mercer were regarded first among the participants of the ball.

Looking back at the Mercers' role in Washington's fin de siècle elite, where they cut "quite a swathe," one historian praised Minna as "easily the most beautiful woman in Washington society." He recalled in 1912 that "to be invited to one of her dinners was in itself a social distinction that qualified one for admission to any home."

Maintaining her social position took much of Minna's money, time, and organizational talent. By the mid-1890s the priorities in the

Mercer household were clear. A large staff had to keep their home in showcase condition. Extraordinary cooks had to be hired and supervised for outstanding dinner parties. In a family where the parents were always on the go, the caretakers of the Mercers' little daughters had to be chosen with special circumspection.

Vio and Lucy spent the first stage of their childhoods in the care of nurses. By this time they were being raised by a governess and indulged by their great-grandmother Carroll. Their mother rarely showed up in the nursery or the schoolroom. She was the distant fairy queen, bending over the girls' beds for goodnight kisses before she stepped out, a vision in silk and velvet, filling the air with enchanting fragrances.

There is no indication that Vio and Lucy felt shortchanged by their mother's absences. This was the order of things they knew. They were happily aware of their refined surroundings and preserved its memory in stately picture albums. The girls' mother was at the center of many photos. Standing ramrod straight, with her head held high, Mrs. Carroll Mercer was the model of a great lady in elegant attire. A whole page of pictures was devoted to Minna's superior skill in interior decorating. It showed various views of the Mercers' social rooms, their luxurious furniture, and their interesting curtains and pillows. Lucy's sister printed the words RHODE ISLAND AVENUE in large letters on the first page, marking the site of the family's mansion. It was located prestigiously off Connecticut Avenue, close to the place where the Cathedral of Saint Matthew the Apostle was being erected.

As a decorator, Minnie Mercer took pride in staying at the cutting edge of contemporary furnishing trends. She excelled in the fashionable "ebonization" of Victorian living rooms, adding drama to ornate sideboards and cabinets with dark, tinted, or naturally black woods. In the formal entry hall, huge carved elephant heads at the bottom of the staircase added the exotic touch expected in a sophisticated home. While Minna's own "mother's room" reflected lighter moods, the luxury of the Gilded Age permeated the whole first floor, resplendent with lavishly upholstered armchairs and sparkling mirrors.

Minna, who liked to surprise visitors with abrupt changes in style from one room to another, carried her era's fascination with the Orient to an extreme. Japan, which had been open to the West since 1854, offered unusual models of elegant interiors. Minna wanted Carroll, the master of the house, to be portrayed in a kimono amid the sparse Oriental interior of a room she designed. He played along happily with his wife's favorite decorating theme.

It is difficult to date a rare picture of the whole family seated at the dining room table, although its formality points to a special occasion. The Mercer girls wear their long blond hair unbraided; they turn their backs to the camera and their father sits between them. But their mother, whose name is here spelled "Mina," is seated in the center. She presides at a setting fit for princes, adorned with fine crystal, silver, and a bowl of roses. In the background a uniformed butler waits for her call. The portrait of a noble family dining in their splendid home marked not only the peak of their good fortune. It also heralded the beginning of the end of their time in the sun.

CHAPTER 2

THE SILVER SPOON SLIPS OUT

FATHER GOES TO WAR

The darkening of the picture taken at the Mercers' festive dining table is obviously the result of more than one hundred years of aging, but it is also symbolic. When Vio was nine and Lucy seven, the bright sky over their childhood clouded over.

The change was felt acutely by the children on the day when their father once more put on an officer's uniform, left the house, and went to war. According to Minnie Mercer's petitions for her pension as an officer's widow, the former marine lieutenant enlisted in the army as a volunteer. He was appointed "captain in charge of commissary subsistence" on June 16, 1898. On January 31, 1899, he was promoted to major and "chief commissary of subsistence of volunteers."

The Spanish-American War began in April 1898. The legendary storming of San Juan Hill on July 1 led to the surrender of nearby Santiago, Cuba, on July 17, virtually ending the hostilities. Captain Mercer had prosaic duties in the commissary sector of the army, but he considered himself close enough to action to share the fame of the Rough Riders. His wife thought highly of the value of his services "in command of needs at San Juan Hill—where Col. Theodore Roosevelt received cargoes & the companies of officers and soldiers."

Captain Mercer's service close to the great man lent an aura of distinction to the members of his family. As an adult, his daughter

Lucy shared it proudly. By the time Lucy entered the orbit of Franklin and Eleanor Roosevelt Roosevelt in 1913, her father's wartime service was generally regarded as a patriotic act. But when Carroll Mercer followed Theodore Roosevelt's call to Cuba in 1898, close friends labeled his return to military life a "graceful escape."

Carroll had indeed left his luxurious home under heavy pressure. The Mercers' rise to the top of Washington society had been achieved at a price. Minna had blithely ignored the fact that her inheritance was no match for the fortunes of the super-rich, like the Astors and Vanderbilts. Initially, her legacy had appeared so enormous that she refused to believe it could ever run out. But soon her correspondence with the manager of her trust, John Lowell, Jr., grew irritable on both sides. The word "impossible" cropped up more and more in the attorney's replies to Mr. and Mrs. Mercer's entreaties. Mr. Lowell had a hard time keeping his clients from squeezing the last penny out of their shrinking estate.

Before Minna was married, she had occasionally tried to generate additional income by nagging her father's debtors. In a letter of October 8, 1887, Minna demanded from Richard P. White of Philadelphia, "Your Norfolk debt must be paid by January 1st." Mr. White minced no words in his return letter. He reminded the young lady that he had been her friend and adviser. He scolded her, "It is much easier for you to sit down and say that impossibilities shall be accomplished by a certain day than it is for me to relieve you of the consequences of your former follies."

Minna's lawyer was taken aback by her brusque approach. He finally told her, "I must decline to answer any letter written in the tone of yours of July 17." Minna's husband was just as disrespectful when he interfered in her correspondence with the Boston attorney. Mr. Lowell was incensed by Lieutenant Carroll Mercer's roughly expressed lack of confidence in his professional skill. He reminded him in a letter of February 10, 1890, that "as trustees of Mrs. Mercer's estate" he and his partner would "manage her property on strictly business principles . . . whether your letters to us are courteous or otherwise."

"THEY SPENT IT ALL": SHEER GOSSIP?

There was no end to the frustrations of the young couple. Mr. and Mrs. Carroll Mercer were at the mercy of the trustees standing between them and their money. Their anger grew at the same rate as their income from the trust dwindled. But they were not as cavalier about their finances as Minna's relatives from North Carolina would have it. Her Henderson cousins had no inhibitions about broadcasting around town their disapproval of Cousin Minnie's plush lifestyle. Even Vio and Lucy's descendants believed Elizabeth Henderson's often-quoted explanation for the disappearance of the Tunis fortune: "Pooh, they just spent it!"

But reality was more complex. The indignant Henderson ladies disregarded causes of the Mercers' cash problems that were beyond their control. The stock market crash of 1893 ruined more astute stockholders than the Mercers. The young Carroll and Minnie Mercer knew next to nothing about staying afloat in a depression. Their cousin Elizabeth was equally ignorant when it came to financial matters. She had settled in Washington with her father John Steele Henderson, a member of Congress from Salisbury, North Carolina. Like Minna, she would also marry an officer, the ensign Lyman A. Cotten. Elizabeth and her sister Mary were intimately familiar with the capital's parlor talk and filled with envy of the Mercers' elegant tastes.

Actually, Carroll and Minna's financial eclipse turned out not to be complete in the long run. Mr. Lowell's letters show that he was an honest and well-meaning steward of John Tunis's legacy. While Mr. Lowell looked to the future of his young clients, it became clear at the time of the crash that he was no match for Minna's father as a savvy entrepreneur. The attorney did not know how to roll with the punches of the marketplace. A large part of the Tunis fortune, invested in commercial real estate, was as vulnerable to changes in the shipping industry as it was to the forces of nature. Mr. Lowell cited a typical mishap, a fire that had destroyed a General Baker's house in Suffolk, which once had provided a substantial rental income for Minna.

Mr. Lowell was determined to prevent the complete draining of the Tunis estate by the young Mercers. He did not give in to their demands, but rather used all his legal power to teach them frugality.

Though the value of the Mercers' trust eroded in several episodes of adverse economic conditions, it apparently recovered a little and continued to yield some return for years to come. Pictures from the early 1900s show that Minna did not live in poverty. She had enough money to enjoy her traditional summer vacations and to dress as smartly as ever as a guest in fashionable resorts on the East Coast.

By that time Minna had adjusted to the reduction of her income, but from about 1897 on she was neither willing nor able to support her husband financially. A more modest way of living had wreaked havoc on the Mercers' marriage. Minna became irritable in her new role as a frugal housewife. It had been fun living with a husband equally fond of amusement, equally eager to get ahead in society's race for applause. Now the rug of consensus was pulled out from under them. Disharmonies between the spouses surfaced in all aspects of everyday living.

Carroll's return to life as an officer in distant countries removed him from disputes with his wife over housekeeping bills. It also offered his wife a temporary solution for many of her practical problems. First of all, it helped Minna save face in the eyes of her peers by explaining the drastic changes in her housekeeping. Economy was to be expected when the head of the family was absent, serving his country overseas.

From then on Minnie Mercer surrendered to a character trait that had been suppressed while she found satisfaction as a celebrated homemaker. It now became undeniable: Minna was a restless soul, not willing to stay in one place for any length of time. After her estrangement from her husband, a crucial divide in her life at the turn of the century, Minna's perpetual moving between different residences became a virtual addiction. She lived variously in houses, apartments, hotels, and homes of friends—always transient and ready for an abrupt change.

Minna's daughters Vio and Lucy were profoundly affected by her restiveness. Suddenly and painfully, the little girls were cut off from their roots. It hurt all the more after they had lived as well-protected little princesses throughout their childhoods. When the atmosphere in their once gracious home grew tense, and their parents grew hostile, the two sisters held on to each other. They learned the importance of money the hard way. But only too soon they were to suffer

Vio and Lucy (right) stand on the grounds of the
Holy Child Academy near Philadelphia.

Lucy and her classmates gather in the garden
of the convent in Vienna.

the most painful consequence of the family's dissolution. They had
to leave home and were sent to boarding school.

FROM BROKEN HOME TO CONVENT SCHOOL

As a rule, members of a wealthy family of the Victorian era would
have kept their teenage daughters at home with private teachers or
enrolled them in an exclusive private school attended by the daugh-

ters of their peers. When the girls reached the age of eighteen, all schooling would end with their "coming out in society." Without a doubt Minnie and Carroll Mercer would have liked to choose this traditional pattern for the education of their daughters. But they had lost their fortune, and with it the means for Vio's and Lucy's proper schooling according to the code of their class.

Minna tried to make the best of the girls' misfortune by sending them to a relatively inexpensive convent school in Pennsylvania, west of Philadelphia. The Holy Child Academy on Sharon Hill enjoyed a good academic reputation and was located within easy reach of Washington. But it lacked the snob appeal of the elite boarding schools that were considered appropriate for daughters of prominent families like the Mercers and the Carrolls. The girls' enrollment happened without fanfare. Neither letters nor diaries survive from this time of crisis in their lives. There was not much to brag about to the society pages concerning the Mercer daughters' solid but unfashionable schooling.

Vio and Lucy faced up bravely to their new Spartan life at the convent school. They kept the memories of their first school years alive in photo collections. Lucy added a booklet of written messages from this time to their keepsakes. Together these documents tell a vivid story of Vio and Lucy's first steps into the world outside their crumbling parental home. Another source of information, opened by a contemporary archivist of the Order of the Holy Child in Pennsylvania, added important clues that help illuminate the influences on Lucy's frame of mind between her tenth and fifteenth years.

In many descriptions of Lucy Mercer's relationship with FDR, her chaste behavior and her refusal to press for his divorce is ascribed simply to her Catholicism. Such a statement, superficial to the point of being misleading, does not do justice to the impact of faith on Lucy's personality. Her religious feelings guided her far beyond self-denial in her romantic attachment to Franklin Roosevelt. For Lucy her Catholicism was not just a coincidence of birth into a devout family of a specific faith. It was a defining part of her identity, a mark of distinction—and eventually a moral obligation. Lucy's mother, marked by the religious zeal of the newly converted, emulated the devotion of Lucy's great-grandmother Sallie Carroll. Minna taught her girls from childhood that the distinction of their forefathers was rooted deeply in their leadership in the Roman Catholic Church.

Lucy had reason to be especially proud of Charles Carroll of Carrollton, the most distinguished member of the clan. A U.S. senator and the last surviving signer of the Declaration of Independence, he used his political power as a Catholic leader to help secure the independence of the colonies. In his last words, spoken at the age of ninety-five, Charles had counted among his blessings his "continued health," "great wealth," and "public . . . applause." But he concluded that "the greatest satisfaction to myself is that I have practiced the duties of my religion."

In 1688 the signer's grandfather Charles Carroll, an immigrant to the English colonies from Ireland, chose to settle in Maryland because he expected its royal charter of religious tolerance to protect his Catholicism. Although religious persecution caught up with him in spurts in his new country, Charles was able to acquire huge estates under the patronage of "the . . . Lord Proprietor, Charles, Lord Baltimore," the Roman Catholic founder of the colony. The Carroll estates extended over half a dozen counties of Maryland along the Potomac River down to the Virginia border. The jewel in the crown of their land—comprising almost sixty thousand acres—consisted of the ten thousand acres surrounding Doughoregan Manor, the main residence of the owners. Doughoregan's proximity to Washington would lend it a special importance in Lucy's adult life.

In 1776, when Charles Carroll of Carrollton and Benjamin Franklin were sent by the Continental Congress on a diplomatic mission to Canada, they were accompanied by Charles's cousin John (1735–1815). Also a great religious leader, John Carroll had enjoyed the support of George Washington. In 1786 he initiated the founding of a Catholic academy that became Georgetown University. The first Catholic bishop in the United States and since 1811 the archbishop of Baltimore, John Carroll was regarded as a symbol of American religious liberty.

At a time when little Lucy Mercer was no longer a rich girl, her distinguished family background still commanded the respect of her classmates and teachers in a Catholic school. The Carrolls had traditionally received the best in religious education. When Charles Carroll of Carrollton was asked how he could "rise so early and kneel so long," he replied that he had learned the skill at the age of ten at the Jesuits' College of St. Omar. A century and a half later, Lucy was also ten years old when she was roused early in a convent school.

* * *

The Order of the Sisters of the Holy Child Jesus was centered in Pennsylvania, not too far from the Maryland border. The Holy Child Academy on Sharon Hill was small but was considered "one of the most prestigious girls' private schools in the Philadelphia area." It was run by the sisters of the Society of the Holy Child Jesus, founded by Mother Cornelia Connelly and six of her fellow sisters in 1864. The new school was distinguished by small classes of eight to ten pupils each. The total enrollment in grades one to twelve amounted to around sixty girls at the time of the Mercer sisters' enrollment. The nationalities of the teaching staff reflected the order's ties to the British Isles and Italy.

Violetta Mercer preceded her sister Lucy at Sharon Hill. Vio's name was listed in the school's *Alumnae Address Book* on January 6, 1898, almost three months before her tenth birthday. This was the only time when the girls' father, Major Carroll Mercer of 1730 H Street, Washington, appeared in the role of a parent. In the subsequent entry, he was replaced by the girls' mother. Minna had taken control of the children when her husband rejoined the armed forces. Vio was sent off to school while Lucy remained a little longer under her mother's care.

Beginning on October 1, 1899, Mrs. Carroll Mercer was listed by the Holy Child Academy as the parent in charge. The order's sisters were not always sure where Mrs. Mercer lived. In their yearly entries, Minnie's various addresses appear vague; sometimes the field is left blank. "Araby" and "Frederick County" come up as place names; during one year Mrs. Mercer resided with a well-to-do friend and her address was listed as "c/o Mrs. J. Ferguson in Hempstead, L.I." In 1900, when Lucy was nine, her name appeared in the school records all by itself, without a parental address. On September 23, 1901, Vio and Lucy were registered together, again without any parental address. In the fall of 1902 and 1903, their mother turned up once more, but with two addresses: 1761 N Street and the Hotel Richmond in Washington. No parental address was given in 1904. In 1905 Mrs. Mercer was listed as living at "M + House, Montclair, N.J." In 1906 she was not listed at all.

Despite their mother's migrations, Vio and Lucy's parents did not altogether disappear from their lives. At least they paid their tuition at the boarding school. But the girls could not return to a parental home. They had no father to lean on and their mother was peripatetic and given to unpredictable wanderings. In the absence of a permanent residence, the door to a new shelter opened for Vio and Lucy. It was the Church, acting as a surrogate mother, taking them under her mantle, kindly and firmly.

A page in Vio's photo album dated 1904 opens a window onto the girls' new surroundings. Simply labeled "At the Convent," the pictures were taken outside the order's main buildings. The two sisters were tall for their ages, fourteen and twelve. Lucy had not yet reached her full height. She still wore her lush blond hair down while Vio looked more adult with an upswept hairdo. Dressed alike, in simple dark smocks over white blouses, they were surrounded by a wide-open space.

The order's chapel and its impressive four-story red brick school building had been erected in 1890, a decade before Lucy studied there. The adjacent convent flourished as the novitiate for the Holy Child sisters. In 1940 it was moved to nearby Rosemont, Pennsylvania. The school's enrollment peaked in the 1960s, until a shortage of teaching sisters gradually forced the order to give up its educational mission at Sharon Hill. Although the attractive school grounds still exist as a public park, popular to this day for walking and bicycling, the chapel and school were demolished in 1978, to the regret of the institution's neighbors. Decades after her years at Sharon Hill, Lucy might have remembered the stately red brick building for its uncanny architectural resemblance to the Rutherfurd mansion at Allamuchy, New Jersey—where, as the owner of a palatial residence, the widowed Lucy would host her old friend President Franklin Roosevelt in August 1944. His visit would inaugurate his most determined push for Lucy's company in the last year of their acquaintance.

*   *   *

When Lucy was ten, at the beginning of her life as a schoolgirl, she started collecting handwritten entries in a small booklet bound in brown leather. The binding is now crumbling but the booklet is still preserved by Lucy's descendants as one of their grandmother's most prized possessions. Lucy's album of autographs, her "signature book" as it was called by granddaughters Lucy and Alice Knowles, was identical in format to the "poetry album" kept by many young ladies of her time. An exceptionally beautiful poetry album, created by Sara Delano, was given by FDR to his presidential library as a memento of his mother's teenage years. Like Sara's collection of endearments, Lucy Mercer's autograph album presents an intimate picture of its owner's youth. With contributions from family, teachers, and friends, Lucy's album offers insights into the years between 1901 and 1913, a little-known period in her life.

The album was apparently given to Lucy by Vio in June 1901 to commemorate Archbishop Ryan's visit to the academy on Sharon Hill. The archbishop had come from Philadelphia to preside at the confirmation of a group of pupils, including Lucy Mercer. The first entry in the album, written by Vio in a youthful hand, was addressed "To dear Lucy" and reflected the sadness of children abandoned by their parents. It said, "Full many a shaft at random sent / Finds mark the archer little meant / Full many a word at random spoken / May soothe or wound a heart that's broken."

At this time children received First Communion at a relatively late date. Lucy had been eleven at the big event on May 29, 1902. There is no mention in the academy's journal of the presence of either of Lucy's parents. But Lucy had already made many friends. A little later, at a children's retreat on March 16, 1902, Lucy collected the first large cluster of contributions to her album. In rhyme and prose, the signers offered lofty ideals and practical advice aimed at preparing the little girl for a difficult outside world.

Two initial pages, starting out the album in a distinctive hand, were obviously written by a high-ranking sister, possibly the Mother Superior. They center on formidable ethical demands, appropriate for much older students. With a voice of authority, "M.A." expressed her wish that Lucy exercise self-knowledge and self-control "in acting the law we live by without fear." Her mentor expressed a maxim that would echo in Lucy's ethics at crucial junctions of her life. It insisted, since "Right *is* Right," Right had to be followed, with "wisdom in the scorn of consequence." A second page just contained the words "God bless you."

In a lighter vein, teachers and classmates added their own advice. Lucy's instructor of French, addressing her fondly as "Chère Lucette," expected her to breeze through a French text. It told Lucy that the hard nut of duty is easily cracked by a determined will. Just as FDR nurtured a long-lasting affection for his French-Swiss governess Mademoiselle Sandoz, Lucy enjoyed a special bond with her French instructor at Sharon Hill. The teacher's name is not known. She signed off as "ta Mamidelle." This term, which may have been Lucy's invention, appears to combine "Mama" with "Mademoiselle."

Lucy had learned elementary French from a governess before she became quite fluent in French at Sharon Hill. Her most advanced schooling, at her next convent school overseas, again improved her command of the language.

In her adult life as Mrs. Rutherfurd, Lucy conversed daily in French with Marie, her personal maid from France. Only in her last decade, when Lucy was in her fifties, did her mastery of French take on high emotional importance. Her friend FDR chose to communicate with her in French as an easy way to keep their telephone conversations as private as possible. Franklin had more confidence in his French linguistic skills than they merited. He was teased about the imperfections of "Roosevelt French" in his public life. In his personal life, his French was good enough to be elevated to the language of the heart in his exchanges with Lucy.

There is no parallel in FDR's communications with his wife that points to an equal role of a foreign language in talking and writing to each other. Eleanor's multilingual skills, acquired at Allenswood, were formidable. Yet Lucy matched Eleanor's fluency in French and surpassed Eleanor in her familiarity with German. Both learned some Italian in their schools. An entry in Lucy's album from Sharon Hill—written by her teacher of Italian—explains her familiarity with this language, which Lucy put to good use in her married life. As a young mother in South Carolina, Mrs. Winthrop Rutherfurd liked to converse in German or Italian with her multilingual husband whenever they did not want to be understood by the children.

* * *

Vio and Lucy had reason to be grateful for the wide range of their instruction at Sharon Hill. They found their social circle, and even their own family, well represented among the girls at the Holy Child Academy. Someone with the initials E. H. B. signed Lucy's album as "your cousin." Three girls could proudly write the abbreviation "E de M" underneath their signatures. The *Enfants de Marie*, French for the Children of Mary, were chosen for their academic excellence. But all friends of Lucy were highly erudite, well versed in world literature. They knew Longfellow and Bates and quoted Victor Hugo in French.

Entries of July 20, 1902, show the girls on a summer vacation of the Mercer family at Cape May, New Jersey. Around the same time, two undated whimsical messages—allegedly left by Lucy's parents in her album—were not actually written by Minnie and Carroll Mercer. They might have been based on typical utterances of Lucy's father and mother. But they were turned into a joke, presented as authentic sayings of the girls' parents.

The first message, appearing in Vio's hand, was later labeled by Lucy herself on the bottom margin as a contribution from "Violetta Mercer." It was addressed "To bad little Johny [sic] Appleseed" and was signed "Lovingly[,] Papa." It said, "God gives our features / We make our faces. If thou would'st be beautiful / Do beautiful things." According to Lucy, the second entry was penned by one Teresa Reggio. It began, "To dear little Johny [sic] Appleseed" and it ended "Lovingly[,] Mama." It said, "Love many, trust few, but always paddle your own canoe." Minnie was quoted in character, proud and independent.

A June 21, 1903, entry was genuine, written by Lucy's father himself and signed "Dad." It looked distinguished with his elegant handwriting. Carroll's advice for his twelve-year-old daughter is engaging. "Be gentle to the clam," he told Lucy, "Never mention mint in the presence of the lamb / Give the stranded jelly fish a shove into the sea / Always be kind to animals / Where ever they may be."

By this time the girls' father had taken second place in their lives as a guardian, but they loved him no less. He would forever be their hero, the warrior in foreign lands, the bold world traveler. Vio and Lucy's memory of their father was firmly linked to his adventures in the tropics. In loving tribute Vio had re-created her father's time overseas in a beautifully arranged special photo album. It showed that Carroll Mercer's service in the Spanish-American War took place under General Nelson Appleton Miles's command in areas of little danger. His assignments moved him from Cuba to Puerto Rico to Manila in the Philippines. The photographs depicting his sightseeing were taken with a good camera. They included street scenes and images of dilapidated mansions. One picture shows Carroll in a white suit, looking like any other tourist in Manila, paying the driver of a donkey-drawn cab.

Carroll's daughters liked to dwell on these parts of family history, even though their father's return to military life had increased his physical and emotional distance from his family in Washington. He acted responsibly, supporting his wife and daughters as long as he could. To her great chagrin, Minna had failed in her efforts to have her husband retained in the peacetime army.

Even into his forties, Carroll cut an impressive figure—portly and sporting a fashionable mustache. By the time he arrived on the West Coast at the end of his service overseas, his physical condition had deteriorated alarmingly. In her 1919 petition for a widow's pension, Minna painted a pathetic picture of his yellow complexion and swollen legs. On April 11, 1901, a medical board at the U.S. Army General Hospital in San Francisco had indeed found him "suffering from chronic diabetes, complicated by chronic interstitial nephritis [Bright's disease]." It was "mild in form" and slow in progress. Nevertheless, Captain Mercer "was mustered out and honorably discharged" on June 30, 1901. He could no longer act as a provider for his family. Carroll was on his own, described simply as a "gentleman," a man without an earned income.

It is not clear how long Minna and Carroll stayed together under one roof after his discharge from the service. But though they went their separate ways, they were never divorced. The Pension Act of July 16, 1918, would lend unexpected importance to the fact that Minnie L. Mercer was the widow of a veteran who never remarried.

According to gossip in Washington's *Town Topics*, Carroll Mercer lived "any old way." He never overcame the misfortune of a fire that destroyed all his belongings, including his correspondence and papers. A few written traces suggest that he took up residence in apartments, clubs, and boardinghouses. During Vio and Lucy's last years at Sharon Hill, he clearly played only a marginal role in their lives. In spite of his new passive role as a parent, Lucy's poetry album reflects the girls' unshakable affection for their charming and easygoing "Dad." They tried to stay in touch with him even after their mother made all decisions for them. Photos show that it was "Mother" who now cared for the girls during school vacations.

LITTLE SISTER LUCY: NOWHERE TO GO

By 1903 Lucy saw her father only occasionally. There was no sign of reconciliation between her parents. An undated photo in the Mercer family album depicts the couple in an obviously arranged theatrical pose. A balding, remorseful Carroll has fallen to his knees and begs his wife to forgive him. But an imperious Minna turns her head away from the supplicant, indicating that she has had enough of him. The fact that Carroll and Minna acted out this scene, and had it photographed for the family's records, shows that they at least preserved a sense of humor amid tragedy.

As their financial situation grew ever more precarious, Carroll and Minna were further estranged. Toward the end of 1904, between November and December, there was a sudden drop in Lucy's grades, a classic symptom of depression in children upset by the separation of their parents. The entries in Lucy's album grew sparse, although they would not end completely until 1913.

There is no reason given for the disappearance of the Mercer sisters from the records of the Holy Child Academy after 1906. Their parents might not have been able to continue tuition payments at the school, but they made no effort to enroll the girls elsewhere.

Lucy, the younger and more vulnerable of the sisters, found herself in an especially delicate situation. Vio was by now seventeen. But fifteen-year-old Lucy could not be considered a graduate from school by any stretch of imagination. Deprived of shelter in the convent, with no money for a proper conclusion of their education, the girls had no place to go. Their parents had separated and had a hard time making ends meet. The future looked bleak indeed. Vio's daughter

Lucy Mercer Blundon later summed up their predicament with the words "They only had each other."

*   *   *

If two sisters grow up as closely together as Vio and Lucy, one of them tends to become the leader. It was a great blessing for Lucy during the misery of her mid-teens that she had a strong, bright older sister. Vio took after her mother as a born fighter. She was well suited to take the lead in their loving camaraderie, always willing to stand up for her gentle little sister. Vio wrote most of their letters, took most of their snapshots, and never ceased to teach Lucy about the glory of their ancestors. The sisters' historic first, middle, and last names—reminding them of their prominent birth—were the only outward sign of their standing above the crowd they had left.

Except for a brief interlude during World War I, the Mercer sisters remained within easy reach of each other all their lives. From Lucy's birth to her mid-twenties, they always lived under one roof. They were pulled apart temporarily by Vio's assignments as a nurse and more permanently by her marriage in 1919, but Vio and Lucy always kept a manageable distance between their homes. Their children were of a similar age. Vio gave her only daughter, the later Mrs. Montgomery Blundon, the first name Lucy Mercer. When the sisters were concerned about their mother, living in an old age home, they worked out a sensible plan for sharing the care for her. Lucy died in 1948, only eight months after Vio took her own life. Both Lucy and Vio enjoyed each other's full confidence and exchanged their hearts' deepest secrets. FDR felt indebted to Vio when she helped him in his search for Lucy's company.

Both Vio and Lucy were attractive, though in different ways. Lucy took after her father, with light eyes and soft features. As the girls grew up, the family noticed that Lucy was the more beautiful of the two. Complementing each other in temperament—one was determined and strong willed, the other more gentle—the Mercer sisters made an enchanting team. They were bound more tightly than ever when they embarked together on the greatest adventure of their lives. At the age of eighteen and sixteen, respectively, they were whisked away from homelessness and despair into a world of carefree enjoyment. It was provided by a loving surrogate mother and father in a fairy-tale land across the sea.

*　*　*

When Agnes—a cousin of the sisters' father Carroll Mercer—was alerted to the sad end of the girls' stay at their convent school, she decided to come to their aid. She extended an invitation to her stranded young cousins that proved to be a godsend: they were offered an open-ended, all-expenses-paid residence in their relative's palatial villa. Agnes Carroll, married to Count Anton Heussenstamm, lived in a charming corner of Austria, in the romantic countryside known as Wachau.

Such generosity was not unusual in close-knit Victorian families. Eleanor Roosevelt referred gratefully in her memoirs to her substitute mother, her father's sister Anna Roosevelt Cowles, beloved as her Auntie Bye. Auntie Bye, together with Eleanor's great-aunt Anna Bulloch Gracie—sister to Eleanor's southern grandmother Mittie Bulloch Roosevelt—and great-uncle James King Gracie, became surrogate parents for the orphaned Eleanor and her little brother Hall.

An entry in Lucy's signature book points to Cousin Agnes's sister Ellinor as the benefactor who arranged her rescue. Mary Ellinor Carroll of Carrollton and Doughoregan was born in Baltimore on December 7, 1860, three years before Agnes. The Carroll sisters had been brought to Vienna in their twenties by their stepfather James Fenner Lee, a prominent American diplomat at the Austrian imperial court. Agnes would stay on in Austria as the bride of a dashing count, while Ellinor returned home and remained single. But Ellinor continued to act on her strong sense of family and kept a watchful eye on the precarious situation of her cousin Carroll Mercer's young daughters. She must have been a character. When Lucy asked her to write in her album in the summer of 1902, Cousin Ellinor suggested, tongue in cheek, "The best occupation is recreation—I ain't going to work no more."

Ellinor, of course, was well aware of the precedent her cousin Sallie Carroll had set when she married the Austrian Count Esterhazy in 1870. Her own sister Agnes had married Count Heussenstamm in 1887. Now two lovely girls in the next generation of Carroll descendants were headed for Austria. Vio and Lucy Mercer, both highly attractive and approaching marriageable age, lacked the means for coming out in society at home. Perhaps, family aunts like Ellinor imagined, Vio and Lucy would follow in the footsteps of Sallie and Agnes Carroll, marrying well in Austria.

Ellinor was entitled to a matchmaker's dreams. But even today Elisabeth, the contemporary Countess Heussenstamm and Agnes's successor as owner of the title, thinks along similar lines. Asked about Agnes's possible motives for inviting Vio and Lucy into her home, Countess Elisabeth was quite sure that Agnes had matrimony for the girls in the back of her mind.

It is uncertain to what extent the sisters' mother, Minnie Mercer, approved of these plans. Photos from the winter of 1906 show that Lucy and Vio still visited or even stayed with her. All three ladies appear in heavy coats and muffs in a picture taken in Montclair, New Jersey. Later in the same year, the names of new friends appear in the album. Someone by the name of Mel Knight assures Lucy Page Mercer that "way down in my heart I've got a feelin' for you." The following summer, in July 1907, the sisters posed with their mother and her circle of friends near the Maclara Inn in Bellport, Long Island.

A fragmented message from Lucy to a friend on a postcard glued into the album goes back to the same time. With a well-taken snapshot of an unidentified mansion, Lucy proved herself an accomplished photographer. "Don't you think this is a good picture?" her inscription asks. Lucy shares her dismay about her hostess getting the mumps. She wants the recipient of her card to "Tell Lottie she is a p. of a r. [?] for not writing." She closes with "Lots of love from L.P.M." The sisters liked to use their initials. In casual conversation Vio would refer to Lucy, the baby in the family, as Babs. This widely popular endearment, derived from the Italian *bambino*, was used frequently by FDR when he wrote to Eleanor.

* * *

By 1907, at sixteen, Lucy was challenged by big changes in her surroundings. She found herself in the heart of Europe, inundated by the sounds of German and under the care of a motherly relative she had never met before.

This formative phase in Lucy's life, lasting about five years, cannot be traced in letters or diaries. If they existed, Lucy saw fit to destroy

This photograph of Lucy was taken around the time
of her arrival in Austria.

Lucy poses on the steamer en route to Europe.

Vio sent her mother a postcard from Melk, site of a
well-known monastery on the Danube.

Carroll Mercer appeals to his wife Minna on bended knee.

Surrogate parents overseas:
Agnes Carroll as bride of
Count Anton Heussenstamm

Lucy's cousin Agnes Carroll—seen here on her wedding day—and
her husband Count Anton Heussenstamm served as Lucy and Vio's
surrogate parents during their stay in Austria.

Cousin Agnes and Uncle Toni had been married for many years when they took Lucy and Vio under their wing.

them. Fortunately, Lucy's niece Mrs. Lucy Mercer Blundon preserved a treasure trove of information from this time that makes up for these losses. Her mother Vio (Lucy's sister) documented the years in Austria by taking hundreds of pictures, titling them, and pasting them in chronological order into photo albums. After the girls' return to Washington, their mother must have added to the albums some of the postcards she received from her daughters in Austria. These cards contain at least a few lines here and there in Vio or Lucy's hand, revealing what the girls considered important.

Contact with contemporary sources of information in the places of Vio and Lucy's stay overseas helped fill in the contours of their sojourn. Austrian historians, teachers, nuns, and ordinary knowledgeable people were eager to explore for the historical record the conditions in their country that would have affected the young Lucy Mercer, a close friend of President Franklin Roosevelt.

CHAPTER 3

RESCUE FROM OVERSEAS

SUBSTITUTE PARENTS:
THE KIND COUNTESS AND COUNT

Both Lucy and Vio were in their teens, and highly impressionable, when Cousin Agnes took them in tow. She was actually a cousin of the girls' father, but the motherly great lady acted more like a kind aunt than a cousin. In the Mercers' as well as the Roosevelts' usage, the title Cousin, with a capital C and often abbreviated as "Coz," was applied—in the Shakespearean sense—to any relative outside the immediate family.

In August 1907 the Mercer sisters snapped pictures of each other aboard the steamer that carried them across the Atlantic. They were as well escorted on the journey as their mother Minna had been a generation earlier, when she was about to join her future husband in London. Vio, who carefully recorded the names of their companions in her album, mentioned three dignitaries—a colonel and two American priests—on a page entitled "Steamer."

A group of well-connected society people provided entertainment during the crossing. The suave-looking Mr. and Mrs. Richardson Gibson had been photographed standing close to Lucy and her mother in a row of souvenir snapshots taken the previous month on Long Island. Some traveling companions went with the sisters all the way to Austria. They reappeared in group pictures of laughing young people in the garden of Cousin Agnes's villa.

Like any eighteen-year-old, Vio liked to tease. One of her favorite targets was her younger sister. Vio wrote on a postcard to a friend back home, "Don't teach mother too much bad language in our absence, & don't kick too hard as shoes are rather expensive. Lucy was quite excited about Bullard[;] her head actually went to one side . . . you may notice it in the picture!" In fact, all the young women in the picture tilted their head one way or another, but not necessarily at the three young men in the back row. As always, Lucy's smile was distinctly shy. It took sisterly leg pulling to interpret it as partiality for Mr. Bullard. A W. Bullard had been listed among Mrs. Minnie Mercer's friends on Long Island, but the young man's name never showed up again in any record. Young ladies outnumbered the few young men on the scene of their new home overseas.

In an undated postcard to Mrs. Carroll Mercer, addressed to her at the Algonquin Hotel in New York, Vio expressed the sisters' delight with their Austrian surroundings. Referring to the picture on the card, she wrote, "Dear Mother— This is the monastery of Melk. Everything is very beautiful & the people charming—Have you gotten our letters—I wonder where you are. Mr. Pennington left to-day for the U.S.A. but left his daughter here—Lots of love—Vio."

After Vio and Lucy had departed for Europe, it became more uncertain than ever where Minnie Mercer lived. Although the girls worried about a roof over their mother's head, Minna could be assured that her daughters had landed in a safe haven. So far the Mercer sisters had only known city life in Washington, then the grounds of a convent school near Philadelphia. Suddenly, they found themselves in a historic countryside that attracted and still attracts tourists from all over the world. Their hosts' residence was located on the scenic shores of a small river, at its confluence with one of Europe's great waterways—the Danube.

At this point the experiences of Lucy and Franklin Roosevelt's youth have much in common. The Danube's hilly landscape resembled the Hudson Valley. Just as Franklin Roosevelt came to know the lifestyle of England's landed gentry as a student, in her late teens Lucy gained an intimate view of country nobles' ways in the Continent's great houses.

*   *   *

The Mercer sisters' Cousin Agnes, the Countess Heussenstamm, was the mistress of a relatively small estate. It did not compare with the Cholmeleys' or Foljambes' magnificent properties in England that enchanted the young FDR. But unlike Franklin, who just visited, Lucy lived in her cousin's baronial residence like a daughter of the house. She moved freely among the neighboring palaces and castles, many centuries older than the Cholmeleys' noble Easton Hall in Lincolnshire.

Countess Heussenstamm's villa definitely looked more grandiose than Springwood, the Roosevelts' relatively modest home in Hyde Park. In its architectural ambition, the building matched Algonac, the Delano family seat near Newburgh, New York. The villa's location in Lower Austria was superb. Situated near the village of Matzleinsdorf, it was distinguished by its proximity to ancient Melk. The picturesque little town, just five miles away, was dominated by a world-famous Benedictine monastery. The abbey, towering majestically above the Danube River in baroque splendor, had been founded in the year 1089. Rebuilt many times, it has remained a favorite of discerning travelers to this day. Visitors are still awed by the monastery's medieval library, housing more than one hundred thousand exquisitely hand-lettered manuscripts.

The background of the Heussenstamm family was as illustrious as the site near the Danube where its scion Anton settled. Many male members of the family held the rank of chamberlain at the imperial court in Vienna, at the time ruled by the popular old emperor Franz Josef. Here the handsome young Toni Heussenstamm caught the eye of Agnes Carroll of Doughoregan Manor. She always used the full name of her ancestral seat near Baltimore. Twenty-four years old, Agnes had moved from Washington to Vienna with her sister Ellinor. The girls' mother Mary Cornelia was a distinguished aristocrat in her own right. Born into the prominent Read family of Maryland, she married Albert Henry Carroll of the equally distinguished Carroll clan. Widowed early, with two daughters, Mary found a second husband in James Fenner Lee, a promising young diplomat. He took his wife and his two Carroll stepdaughters along when he was sent overseas from the American capital to the court of the Hapsburgs in Vienna.

At the same time, the young Franklin Roosevelt happened to have a parallel family connection with the court of Vienna. In 1887, when

FDR was five years old, his father James had used his personal friendship with President Grover Cleveland to ask for a favor. The president gave Franklin's older stepbrother Rosy—James Roosevelt Roosevelt—a chance to prove himself as a fledgling diplomat. The position of first secretary at the American embassy in Vienna seemed superbly suited for FDR's half brother. Rosy was fluent in German after intensive study at Ernst Boehme's Institute for Boys and Youth, a private school in Dresden. Rosy's wife Helen was just as comfortable in Vienna's local language. She had pleased her grandfather, William Backhouse Astor, with her eagerness studying German.

William was even richer than his father John Jacob Astor. He provided Helen with a fortune that made it easy for the James Roosevelt Roosevelts to stand out regally among the diplomats representing the United States in the Austrian capital. But Rosy preferred the mild maritime winters on Heathfield, his estate near Ascot in England. The extremes of Vienna's continental climate appalled him. When his diplomatic standing became precarious after the election of Benjamin Harrison, the new Republican president, Rosy left Vienna without regret. He had seen the city mainly from the driver's seat of the fancy four-in-hands that were his passion.

Rosy's stepmother Sara Roosevelt tried to instill different values in her son Franklin. She encouraged him to share her love for Boston's art and music when she spent winters in the city after her husband's death. As a schoolgirl in Hanover, Germany, Sallie Delano had spent her last *groschen* for a cheap seat at the opera. As Mrs. James Roosevelt, she missed no major cultural event in New York City.

Lucy Mercer's relatives had similar preferences. The members of prominent southern families like the Reads, Carrolls, and Lees appreciated the rich cultural life in the sophisticated Austrian capital. It offered all the theater, opera, concerts, and art galleries that gentlemen and gentlewomen of refined taste could desire. Vienna's high-class American guests knew how to enjoy the metropolis as a Mecca for the arts at the end of the nineteenth century.

*   *   *

When the young Agnes Carroll arrived in the multiethnic city on the divide between Eastern and Western Europe, Vienna was moving toward the apex of its creativity. Years after his forced exile following

Hitler's annexation of Austria in 1938, Stefan Zweig—the novelist friend of Sigmund Freud—looked back with nostalgia on his native city. He called the decades before World War I the Golden Age of Security. The art nouveau style of the Viennese secessionist painter Gustav Klimt appealed to society's upper echelons. The irresistible tunes of Johann Strauss the Younger (the Waltz King) enraptured dancers everywhere, from palace ballrooms to rural wine gardens.

It was a fascinating world, opened by Agnes's stepfather James Fenner Lee to the adventurous young girl. As the U.S. chargé d'affaires at the Hapsburgs' seat of power, representing a nation rapidly growing in importance after the Civil War, Mr. Lee commanded respect. Receptions, dinners, and glorious balls vied for the presence of the American diplomat's engaging wife and her charming daughters.

Two years after their arrival, Mr. and Mrs. Lee awed Austria's court with an American-style grand wedding. They were as anxious as Count Heussenstamm's family to demonstrate that the American bride, Miss Agnes Carroll of Carrollton and Doughoregan Manor, was of equal rank with her Austrian groom, Anton Alexander Otto, Graf von Heussenstamm zu Heissenstein und Graefenhausen.

The count's family tree was impressive. It reached back to 1075; one of the family's castles, dating back to at least 1211, was situated in the same Hessian landscape near Frankfurt that FDR knew so well from his boyhood summers at Nauheim. A Sebastian von Heussenstamm had been one of the Holy Roman Empire's prince-electors as archbishop of Mainz (known in French as Mayence) from 1545 to 1555, almost three hundred years before John Carroll became America's first archbishop.

The last descendant of Sebastian Heussenstamm's family, carrying the inherited title of marshal of the archbishopric, died in 1965 at the Villa Heussenstamm. Countess Maria was the niece and adopted daughter of the same Countess Agnes (née Carroll) who had been the surrogate mother of Lucy Mercer.

On April 13, 1887, it was fitting that a former governor of Maryland—Agnes's uncle John Lee Carroll—stood in place of the father of the bride when Miss Carroll became Countess Heussenstamm. Court photographers from Vienna's prestigious streets, the Opernring, took magnificent pictures of the shapely American bride. Agnes won all hearts with her sweet expression. The Austrian groom appeared in the uniform of a major in a famous cavalry regiment. The distinguished couple was united in a special ceremony with privileges ordinarily reserved for members of the imperial family. Cardinal Serafino Vannutelli himself, the pope's nuncio, officiated at the wedding in Vienna's papal chapel.

The count and his new countess were a happy match. Agnes's husband Toni was a kindhearted, gentle man, devoted to his energetic American bride. But his glamour was superficial. The Heussenstamms, whose name sounded to Agnes like "Hoissenstom," had difficulties maintaining the appearance of their high social status. Toni had inherited only a fraction of a once imposing old fortune. But as the heiress of an outstanding American family, Agnes commanded a dowry fit to polish the fading luster of old-world nobility. This was a geographic aberration from the usual course of American dowries in Europe. In this time American riches seldom landed in Austrian palaces. Rather, it was England that attracted a great many wealthy daughters of America's Gilded Age to the countryseats of its titled families. The most celebrated case of an American–English union, the marriage of Consuelo Vanderbilt to the ninth duke of Marlborough, was forced upon the girl by her mother and destroyed a budding romance between Consuelo and the young Winthrop Rutherfurd. After losing Consuelo, Winthrop married Edith Morton. As a widower, Winthrop asked Lucy Mercer to be his second wife.

As a young married couple, Anton and Agnes Heussenstamm together acquired a large tract of land outside a settlement called Matzleinsdorf. The groom's mother Caroline, a Countess Harrach, had grown up in the village, the seat of the Harrachs' Zelking–Matzleinsdorf family line. For a time she moved in with her son and his American wife. Family relations were complicated by the strict rules of inheritance. Nephews and nieces were freely adopted whenever an aristocratic couple ran out of heirs. Nonetheless, either Anton or his younger brother Heinrich, Count Heussenstamm, could be expected to inherit Matzleinsdorf's *Schloss*—the old baronial mansion in the village—together with the adjoining estate.

Matzleinsdorf, backed by the foothills of the Alps, sits on the fertile banks of the Melk River, a tributary of the Danube. The village enjoyed excellent train connections to Vienna, fifty miles to the west. It took Anton and Agnes three years to build their dream house on the outskirts of Matzleinsdorf. By 1894 they had finished erecting a large palatial building above the river's floodplain. Vast, well-landscaped gardens were planted immediately. When the couple bought additional acreage in 1912, it was the well-to-do Countess Agnes who signed the purchasing contract as the *Gutsbesitzerin*, the owner of the estate.

While the Villa Heussenstamm lacked the historic patina of neighboring castles, it was brand new and complete with all the modern conveniences a high-class American lady could expect. Appropriately, it was adorned with coats of arms of the Heussenstamms and the Carrolls, side by side above the entrance. But the Heussenstamms had no children. The grand dwelling, set up for happiness of a large family, felt increasingly empty. Rather than accept their fate, the count and countess decided to fill their home with the commotion of young relatives from America. The Heussenstamms' misfortune became Vio and Lucy's good fortune. Beginning in 1907 the Villa Heussenstamm would serve as Vio and Lucy's home away from home.

The precise date of the girls' residence in Austria is difficult to determine. Journalist Jonathan Daniels—who first wrote about Lucy Mercer and Franklin Roosevelt—gives no exact year for their return to America, but he quotes a statement from Lucy's cousin Mrs. Lyman Cotten and an entry in the New York Social Register of 1908 about the girls' schooling overseas "in care of Countess Carroll Heussenstamm." Violetta and Lucy Mercer reappear in the pages of *The Clubfellow and Washington Mirror* on May 22, 1912.

* * *

Agnes's invitation was extended to a third young cousin of the Carroll clan. Marguerite Pennington was accompanied by her physician father when she also arrived at the villa in 1907. Marguerite had seen more of the world than Vio and Lucy. As a child, she had lived long enough in Paris with her mother to change her name from Margaret Mary to Marguerite. She would eventually stay on in Austria and marry a local baron. Her return to the States after the Second World War would take place under dramatic circumstances, with disastrous consequences for Vio and Lucy.

Marguerite's father, the bearded, dignified Dr. Clapham Pennington, is introduced in only one picture from the family photo albums—depicting one of the picnics that Count and Countess Heussenstamm liked to arrange for their guests. But Marguerite Pennington appears constantly in images of carefree social scenes outside the villa. Blond, not quite as tall as Vio and Lucy but very pretty, Marguerite obviously played an important role in Cousin Agnes's plan to surround herself with attractive young relatives from her home country.

A photo of the lithe Lucy, standing erect next to the bent-over Marguerite, expresses a stark symbolism. The girls were obviously amusing themselves with target practice in the park of the villa. Marguerite is aiming a light rifle at a nearby bull's-eye, ready to pull the trigger. The relaxed atmosphere of the scene has nothing ominous about it. Nobody could guess that the same Marguerite would one day pull a more deadly, invisible trigger, hitting the center of Vio and Lucy's heart.

In Vio's pictorial chronicle of life with the Heussenstamms, Marguerite Pennington is gradually shown less frequently. Instead portraits of her brother Charles turned up more often. Countess Agnes's family connection to the Penningtons was not as close as her ties to Vio and Lucy. After all, the girls' father Carroll Mercer, raised by his grandmother Mrs. William T. Carroll, was Agnes's first cousin. Marguerite and Charles Pennington, on the other hand, belonged to a more remote branch of the Carroll family—the Harpers.

The Harpers were remarkable people. The rise of Robert Goodloe Harper from humble beginnings to seats of power had been legendary. A great Carroll heiress had chosen him as a most unconventional husband more than a century earlier. To the initial chagrin of her father, the immensely rich Charles Carroll of Carrollton and Doughoregan Manor, Charles and Marguerite Pennington's great-great-grandmother Catherine "Kitty" Carroll married outside her circle. In May 1801 Bishop John Carroll officiated in Annapolis at the wedding of his Cousin Charles's daughter to Mr. Harper.

For the groom, heavily in debt at the time, the union with Maryland's most coveted heiress had been the ultimate triumph. Robert's supreme self-confidence had propelled him from his father's cabinet-making shop on the North Carolina frontier to study at Princeton.

Supporting himself as a tutor, he relied on his eloquence and good looks to succeed in elective office. A radical southern Federalist, he moved with ease from his seat as congressman from South Carolina to the position of U.S. senator from Maryland—he simply changed his residence to Baltimore. He won military fame in the War of 1812, attaining the rank of general. But Robert Harper failed to make his wife happy. The former Kitty Carroll turned into the epitome of a nagging wife, plagued by many real and imagined ailments. Colorful family lore, propounded by the self-made senator and general, was kept alive by Kitty's descendants. When Countess Agnes Carroll Heussenstamm hosted Charles and Marguerite of the Harper–Pennington branch of the family, together with Vio and Lucy from the Carroll side of the family, she added new piquancy to old feuds.

Robert Goodloe Harper the Federalist and Colonel John Francis Mercer the Maryland Republican leader narrowly escaped a potentially fatal duel. Harper had insulted John Mercer, calling him a "pseudo-Marylander." Just in time he prudently called off the confrontation neither of them wanted, saving Colonel Mercer from having to defend his honor with a pistol.

* * *

As Cousin Agnes's guests, the descendants of the Harpers and the Mercers got along famously. Only a few close relatives noticed that Charles and Lucy took a special interest in each other. Charles Pennington appears first in Vio's photo albums as a tall, somewhat lanky, good-looking young man in casual clothes, romping with the young crowd in the Heussenstamm gardens. His subsequent appearance in the uniform of a lieutenant in the Austrian army comes as a shock. A generation earlier, American public opinion had shifted decidedly in favor of France, turning against the German-speaking countries after the Franco-Prussian War of 1870–1871. These sentiments, coming to a head in World War I, were bound to cause Charles Pennington extreme embarrassment. As an expatriate artist, he eventually had to pay a high price for surrendering to his youthful enthusiasm for the good old Austria he had discovered in Cousin Agnes's world.

Charles Pennington and Fred Tinti, the son of neighbors, were the two young men caught most frequently by Vio and Lucy's camera. The girls' albums were filled with pictures of female friends, and above all with portraits of their surrogate parents. The photos reflect the growing affection between the older couple and their young guests. Vio and Lucy could well have been the Countess Heussenstamm's daughters. Agnes, born in 1863, was exactly the age of the girls' mother Minnie Mercer. Now forty-one, Agnes was beyond hope for children of her own. Her husband the count was born in 1856, two years before the girls' father. Like Carroll Mercer, Anton Heussenstamm had left the military with the rank of major. But Toni had been a career officer longer, serving in the prestigious Cavalry Regiment Number Seven—which proudly counted Franz Ferdinand, the heir to the throne, as its patron.

Ironically, Anton's marriage to Agnes—a lady without a title of nobility and therefore considered beneath his exalted position as a chamberlain of the emperor—disqualified her from presentation at the imperial court. As the daughter of the American chargé d'affaires, Agnes had been welcome at all court events. But as the wife of an Austrian count, she was "excluded on ancestral grounds." On July 18, 1909, *The New York Times* ran an article entitled "Where Americans Lose Caste: Women of This Country Who Marry Titled Austrians and Hungarians Are Barred from the Court of Vienna Where Before They Could Be Presented." In indignant disbelief, the reporter, identified only as "a veteran diplomat," cites an example from a previous generation: "Miss Sarah Carroll, married to Count Maximilian Esterhazy." He focuses on "Countess Anthony von Heussenstamm," who "is a member of the historic Maryland House of Carroll of Doughoregan Manor: that is to say, she has in her veins the bluest of American blood."

There is no evidence that anyone at the villa in Matzleinsdorf held a grudge at the petty snub by the court in Vienna. If the kindly Uncle Toni was upset, he did not express his anger. He showed little of the rigor of a former military man. He preferred the easygoing lifestyle of a country gentleman, frequenting a hunting lodge in the nearby mountains. It was worlds apart from Vio and Lucy's memories of their own father, tied to smoke-filled city clubs that were Papa Mercer's domain.

Whereas Cousin Agnes—like her husband Toni—was firmly rooted in the country, Minnie and Carroll Mercer were at home in the city. Toni and Agnes made Vio and Lucy comfortable in surroundings dominated by horses and dogs. They would teach the girls the joys of gardening, a pastime that Lucy cultivated throughout her life as Mrs. Winthrop Rutherfurd. Lucy's equestrian expertise went barely beyond managing a dogcart, as her granddaughters recalled. But as a young girl she learned to appreciate fine horses, under the tutelage of Cousin Agnes, who entered the stars of her stable in local horse shows.

In Lucy's twenty-eight years as Mrs. Winthrop Rutherfurd, a more important skill—taken home from the Austria of her youth—would pay ample dividends. As the mistress of a large, elegant household, Lucy Rutherfurd knew how to direct a staff of servants. In the great house kept by Countess Heussenstamm at Matzleinsdorf, Lucy had observed Agnes manage a rural estate—an art that she could not learn from her mother in a Washington apartment.

CASTLES ON THE BEAUTIFUL BLUE DANUBE

Although Vio and Lucy do not seem to have attended the grand balls at the court of Vienna, they were sharing happily in the rich social life of the landed gentry. They loved to accompany Cousin Agnes and Uncle Toni on their frequent visits to nearby mansions and castles. Lucy's fond memories of these outings strikingly parallel FDR's remembrances of the homes of English nobles much admired by him in 1903. In letters to his mother, Franklin raved about the fun he had joining his English hosts (the Cholmeleys) on visits to titled neighbors, like the Duke of Rutland in Lincolnshire.

Lucy and Vio experienced a continental version of similar pleasures. Postcards sent home to America showed pictures of the proud old mansions and historic castles where they stayed. The baronesses and countesses of their acquaintance served fine meals, prepared by carefully chosen cooks. Countess Agnes Heussenstamm paid the price for indulging in the famous regional cuisine. She added more and more girth to her middle, once so well shaped at the time of her wedding. Vio and Lucy, on the other hand, stayed as svelte as they were upon their arrival in Austria. They did not gain weight in spite of indulging in famous local specialties, like hearty beef stews with horseradish sauce or decadent desserts combining apricots and chocolate, hazelnuts and whipped cream.

Pictured here are castles of Lucy's relatives and friends.

As a guest at the country gentry's tables, Lucy gained valuable experience for her later duties as hostess of elegant dinners. Putting together a tempting buffet for fox-hunting parties was a highly valued skill for ladies of her class in many countries—whether they resided in Lower Austria, England's Lincolnshire, Aiken, South Carolina, or New York's Hudson Valley. FDR's mother prided herself on creating memorable hunters' buffets at Hyde Park.

The Mercer girls' parents had shined at balls in Washington that imitated hunting parties. Vio and Lucy themselves participated in similar society events in Austria and took snapshots of the hunters and their hounds. The photos reflected the differences between the hunting traditions in America and continental Europe. Uncle Toni and his peers hunted on foot rather than on horseback. The Austrian aristocrats did not wear the red coats of their English and American counterparts; neither did they ride with a pack of hounds chasing their prey. Instead a few specially trained hounds led their masters to the deer on hunting grounds they owned or rented. The hunters, clad in dark forest green with hunting rifles slung over their shoulders and an obligatory "brush" of mountain goat bristles on their felt hats, were picturesque objects of the Mercer girls' cameras.

The names and titles of Uncle Toni's hunting friends, listed carefully by Vio in her album, pointed to varied European backgrounds. There was a Count Cassis and a Baron José Hammerstein, a Count Ségur and a Baron Eichelburg. A hunting party at Matzleinsdorf was hosted by Count Heinrich Kaspar Heussenstamm, known as Riki— Uncle Toni's brother. Riki's daughter Maria was ten years younger than Lucy Mercer. Lucy, who adored all children, could not take enough pictures of the little countess. Maria's brother Alexander, heir to the Matzleinsdorf estate, would have two daughters. The older one, Elisabeth, is the present-day Countess Heussenstamm. She resides in a former administration building on the old estate and is well aware of Lucy Mercer's historic importance.

The Baron and Baroness Tinti, who lived in an ancient castle at Poechlarn on the Danube not far from Melk, treated the Mercer sisters like members of their family. The Tintis' daughters, Dita and Ella, became Vio and Lucy's best friends. Lucy would never stay as a guest in a more extraordinary building than the Tintis' castle. The building rested on the relics of antique fortifications, erected on the northern border of the Roman Empire. Around the year 800, the strategic spot on the Danube had become a stronghold of Charlemagne's empire. It was said to have been the seat of Ruediger of Bechlarn, the famous troubadour of the Nibelungen saga. This was the powerful historical legend that had fascinated the thirteen-year-old Teddy Roosevelt when he stayed with the Minkwitz family in Dresden, Saxony, and was tutored by their daughter Anna. Theodore was now president of the United States. At the time when Vio and Lucy Mercer absorbed European history from living with their friends Ella and Dita Tinti, they could not guess how significant their links to the Roosevelts would become in but a few years.

The Mercer girls and the Tinti daughters had a lot of down-to-earth fun together. On vacation in Liesingau, a small resort village in the Styrian Alps, they went hiking in the mountains and swimming and rowing on a lake. In a photo taken during that holiday, Ella and Dita Tinti sport knee-length swimsuits that peek out from under tightly wrapped bathrobes. The picture is titled "After the Bath." On a postcard from Liesingau to her mother, Vio wrote that she and Lucy were "to stay with the Tintis until Sunday. Cousin Agnes will join us there Thursday on her way home. The place is in Styria & 3 hours from here—it is their hunting place—we expect to have a big time."

Cousin Agnes made sure that the girls grew to know Europe beyond Austria. In one of many pictures taken during their travel in France, Lucy sits gracefully on the ground at the entry to an elegant residence at 40 Boulevard des Invalides, a private home in the heart of Paris. After their visit to the capital, pleasant summer weather permitted the ladies to roam the French countryside. The picture of their vehicle is hilarious. An open automobile, driven by a hired chauffeur, is overflowing with a surplus of young and not-so-young ladies. They are packed frighteningly tight, crammed together into a car resembling a horse-drawn carriage more than a modern automobile. A major destination of the travelers was one of the renowned Loire castles, disappointingly wrapped in scaffolding.

At the end of their travels, Lucy looks happy in the pictures taken at home, in the house and gardens of Cousin Agnes and Uncle Toni. Frolicking in the gardens of the villa, the sisters and their friends were all dressed in identical clothes, obviously sewn by the Heussen-stamms' seamstress. The girls, wearing a variation of local folk costumes, described themselves as "Peasants" in a tongue-in-cheek caption under their group portrait. Their dresses consisted of gathered skirts—cut from a flowery cotton—combined with tight-fitting bodices, aprons, and wide-sleeved white blouses. It was obvious that Cousin Agnes had the local traditional *dirndl* dresses in mind when she had a flattering adaptation custom tailored for her guests. Agnes was taken with the charm of her adopted country and had enough sense of humor to go along with her young guests' horseplay. One of their pictures, taken in the estate's orchard, presents three of the girls' visitors grazing piglets on a leash. Another one shows Vio and Lucy perched high up in two niches in the villa's wall, spaces that were usually reserved for statues of saints and cherubs.

THE EDUCATION OF LUCY PAGE MERCER

In spite of the abundant *joie de vivre* in the Villa Heussenstamm, life in Austria was not all fun and games for the Mercer sisters. Cousin Agnes took her obligations as a surrogate mother seriously. Without making much ado about it, she provided her young American relatives with a sterling education. The years of learning during the girls' sojourn in Austria have never been appropriately described. Even the present-day members of Lucy's immediate family know next to nothing about her life as a student.

Jonathan Daniels tried hard to incorporate this part of the Mercer family history in his book *Washington Quadrille*. In the end he had to admit that his research had led nowhere. He frankly declared himself unable to describe Lucy's formative years. He could not find any account of Lucy's schooling comparable to Eleanor Roosevelt's description of her years of learning as they were recorded in her autobiography. The frustrated chronicler of Lucy and Violetta's youth stated with a sigh, "No record exists of their education abroad such as Eleanor wrote of her troubles and triumphs during her schooling in England. The Mercers were not given to self-documentation." Daniels speculated, "The Austrian nuns provided the kind of education deemed required by a young lady of the time with emphasis on prayer as well as pedagogy."

Daniels underestimated the dimensions of a reality unknown to him. Vio's photo albums, together with records kept by Austrian arch-

The Benedictine abbey at
Melk had been rebuilt
several times since the late
Middle Ages.

Vio and Lucy spent many happy
hours at the Villa Heussenstamm,
home of their cousin Countess
Agnes and her husband Toni.
The villa's orchard was especially
popular as their playground.

ivists and school historians, offer rich documentation of the Mercer girls' advanced studies. Their instruction was far more intensive than the teaching offered in the relatively modest academic program at Eleanor's boarding school, Allenswood near London. In fact, Lucy Mercer enjoyed the very kind of steady and challenging systematic schooling that Eleanor regretted later having missed.

In the fall of 1899, when Eleanor had just turned fifteen, she was sent to England to attend a highly regarded boarding school, considered a cut above the traditional Swiss finishing schools. The curriculum at Allenswood included the usual subjects considered suitable for upper-class young ladies. It guaranteed fluency in French, German, and Italian, as well as familiarity with major poetry and literature. But the school's founder, the charismatic Mademoiselle Marie Souvestre, went beyond her calling. She dutifully nurtured the acquaintance with the fine arts expected from a refined young lady, but she also dared to lead her charges to intellectual questioning. Eleanor was grateful to be invited by her teacher to express her own opinions.

Nevertheless, Mademoiselle Marie Souvestre's bold spirit could not change the fact that a large part of Allenswood's school day was devoted to games and sports, apart from the teaching of non-academic subjects. Eleanor missed out on the study of the natural and social sciences, economics, and political history. Interrupted by a return to the States, her boarding school experience lasted barely two years. Still, Eleanor's exceptional intelligence, thirst for learning, and copious reading balanced the shortcomings of her education. First of all, Eleanor had to make up for a late start in the schoolroom. Only in 1891, when an aunt discovered that the seven-year-old Eleanor could not read, was she finally taught the "three R's."

Lucy and Vio were distinguished from Eleanor by the excellent basic instruction they received as little girls. In the first decade of their lives, their parents could still afford to engage superior governesses as their teachers. When their home broke up, the girls were taken over by nuns at a convent school in Pennsylvania with an extraordinary academic reputation. When they moved on to Austria, the quality of the Mercer sisters' education rose from a high level at home to the finest schooling for young women anywhere. From age ten until her early twenties, Lucy enjoyed enviable schooling.

There was a fine small convent school for girls right in Melk, within easy reach of Countess Agnes's young American guests. It had been set up in 1902 by nuns, the Daughters of the Divine Redeemer. But it was not good enough for the ambitions of the countess to teach her substitute daughters. Agnes aimed for the order's largest and most renowned boarding school, located in the capital. It did not matter that it was an hour by train away from Melk. Mother Alphonse Maria, the founder of the order and its first schools, had been born Elisabeth Eppinger, a simple country girl from Alsace. She impressed on her followers—eventually numbering in the thousands—that they were tools of God, privileged to serve their fellow men. It was their mission to care for the sick as nurses and to tend to poor children as teachers.

Mrs. Carroll Mercer had to give her consent for her daughters' enrollment in the best school Cousin Agnes could find. The trans-Atlantic mail was exasperatingly slow. At the end of August 1907, Vio wrote her mother in New York, "We are anxious to hear about your decision for the convent but by the time you get this we will have heard. We are having a lovely time and cousin Agnes is dear."

Minna's consent arrived in time to permit Vio and Lucy to become boarders in the school at the center of the order's motherhouse in Vienna. It provided instruction at the highest possible level. Among its staff of nuns were the first women to hold advanced academic degrees from the University of Vienna. They were qualified to prepare teachers for service in public and private schools. Starting in the 1850s, the Daughters of the Divine Redeemer had begun to create a sizable compound of schools at a choice inner city location in Vienna. It ranged from kindergarten to middle school to high school and beyond, including a teachers' training college. The buildings occupied a whole city block between the convent's main house on Kaiserstrasse and a parallel thoroughfare, Kenyongasse. The order owed the extraordinary dimensions of its campus to a wealthy childless couple who had given the nuns a whole estate, complete with several buildings, gardens, and meadows.

As in Eleanor's school, instruction in French was entrusted to native speakers. Fluency in German was acquired as a matter of course by attendance of classes taught in German, the nuns' native tongue.

In addition, students from distant parts of the Austrian Empire brought to school in Vienna their Slavic tongues, spoken in the east of the realm, or their Italian spoken on the Dalmatian coast. In contrast to a finishing school's focus on the fine arts, the convent school stressed the sciences, geography, and history. Religious instruction combined philosophy and basic theology. On the girls' report cards, the academic subjects came first. Music and art, gymnastics, and ladies' needlework followed. The importance of character building was reflected in grades for "conduct" and "diligence."

The Mercer girls lived in an enclave of quiet amid the bustle of a vibrant metropolis. There was little distraction from the outside world. Even in the twenty-first century, time seems to stand still for a visitor passing through the gate of the sisters' motherhouse on Kaiserstrasse. Integrated into its urban neighborhood, the building still is a part of a long row of ordinary houses on a busy city street. To this day streetcars roll by.

Little has changed inside the convent walls since Lucy's days in Vienna. High dormitory and classroom buildings look down upon remnants of gardens. A special corner, formed by two high walls and filled with greenery, serves to this day as the traditional spot for taking student pictures. Amazingly, the same corner appears on one of the most informative photos Vio and Lucy took back to America. In the course of the century that has elapsed since that time, the tall statue of Christ in the background has disappeared—a victim of erosion caused by big city pollution. The trees filling the corner don't seem to have grown much since the Mercer sisters walked in their shadow.

But this is unmistakably the very place where an important group picture with Vio and Lucy Mercer was taken in November 1907. Vio wrote "At the Convent in Vienna" in big letters on the picture's bottom border. In the right-hand margin, she identified by name herself, Lucy, and fourteen of the seventeen students in the picture. They all look gracious, solemn, and self-assured, dressed alike in formal attire. They wear crosses over wide dark robes, held together by tasseled cords at the waist.

The numerous Slavic first and last names on the picture, interspersed with a few Anglo-American names, point to the cosmopolitan makeup of the student body. In the center of the group portrait, flanked by the Mercer girls, is a dark-skinned "Helène" [sic], likely from French Africa.

The part of the Continent that became Lucy's home in Vienna lay far to the east of the European countries familiar to the Roosevelts. The imperial Austrian government had failed to grant the Slavic countries under its jurisdiction equal standing with the ruling Germanic and Hungarian elite. But the Roman Catholic Church drew wider circles. Characteristically, the Daughters of the Divine Redeemer—called the Sisters of the Divine Savior after 1985—attracted young women from the eastern and southern parts of the empire. They were proud to count among their alumnae Czech, Slovak, Croatian, and Serbian girls, including the daughter of the mayor of Belgrade.

Vio was eighteen, Lucy sixteen when the group picture was taken in 1907. Most of their classmates look a little older, mature enough to be sent out as teachers in parochial schools all over the empire. By contrast, Eleanor Roosevelt's classmates—shown in a carefully staged group picture outside the Allenswood School—belonged to a different class. They also came from many different countries but they belonged to the moneyed social elite. They all expected to marry well, as Mademoiselle Souvestre hoped so fervently for Eleanor. Lucy's classmates, on the other hand, came from more modest backgrounds. They expected to find jobs as schoolmistresses.

Neither Eleanor nor Lucy brought home many pictures from their schoolrooms or playgrounds overseas. But the sisters at Lucy's school in Vienna preserved an album of photos commemorating the founding of their teachers' training academy in 1904. It shows only a few male professors; most of them were teachers of geometry, science, and music. The labs are remarkably well equipped. In a zoology classroom, large glass cabinets containing stuffed birds and drawings of wild ducks point to special stress on ornithology. Fierce-looking hawks are balanced on slender girls' hands. It is astounding to think that Lucy Mercer would have been able to converse knowledgeably about birds with FDR, himself a child prodigy in ornithological know-how.

The young teachers in training shared the ascetic living conditions of all students. Their neatly made beds in the dorm stood so close together that it was hard to move between them. The walls were bare, except for a picture of the Madonna and a glass candleholder. In the dining hall, lit by gas lamps dangling from high ceilings, the long benches in front of rows of tables had no backrests.

The austerity of the girls' quarters did not prevent the Daughters of the Divine Redeemer from keeping their charges happy. Memoirs of an alumna, Stephanie Haas, center on the sunny side of the sisters' rule. Mrs. Haas, the mother of a famous contemporary Viennese actress, stressed "old Austria's" joy of living as a balance for the girls' simple everyday routine. Called to a first prayer at 6:15 in the morning, the students underwent at least five hours of instruction, followed by quiet study. At some grade levels practical work—such as gardening or assistance with the sisters' charitable activities—complemented the students' work at school desks.

Weeks of concentrated study were highlighted by excursions to scenic spots. In the hilly countryside leading to the mountains of the Alps, the girls hiked and picked wild blueberries and strawberries. Holy days were celebrated exuberantly. Although the daily fare was sparse, the sisters proved worthy of a long tradition of Viennese culinary excellence at the high points of the church year. Festive apple strudels and chocolate tortes were produced by master bakers. In December all students took part in cutting out a huge assortment of Christmas cookies.

At the end of the school year, artistic girls with nimble fingers were honored in an exhibition of choice needlework. Lucy Mercer, naturally gifted in sewing and stitching, had a chance to acquire state-of-the-art skills. Her granddaughters have preserved her muchused knitting needles to this day. In the spring of 1945, Lucy could hold her own among FDR's female companions, excelling with fancy crocheting on the sofa of the Little White House in Georgia.

Lucy's inborn good taste in clothes had no opportunity to unfold at the convent school. The students wore their formal school uniforms only on holidays. Throughout the year simple smocks would do. The "interns" (the boarding school students) wore straw hats in summer and felt hats in winter, but Vio and Lucy's substitute mother Agnes made up for the lack of fashionable clothing at the convent. The countess splurged on expensive finery for the girls' time away from school. Portraits of Lucy around the age of twenty show her in a

fancy white cotton dress accentuating her slim waist. She takes obvious pleasure in a wide-brimmed hat covered with roses.

Lucy Mercer's niece Lucy Mercer Blundon—the daughter of
Lucy's sister Violetta Mercer Marbury—and her son, nicknamed Tad,
characterized Lucy's time in Austra with an oft-repeated anecdote. It
was based on Cousin Agnes's weakness for fine lingerie and her generosity in decking out her young relatives with an elegant wardrobe.
Vio and Lucy never forgot how shocked the order's sisters were
when they discovered the frilly nightgowns the girls had brought
along to the dorm. The nuns declared these garments fit for prosti-
tutes. Deeply embarrassed, they realized too late that their new
charges had never heard of such women.

On the other hand, Vio and Lucy were taken aback when the sisters expected them to bathe with their undershirts on. Over the
years, they grew accustomed to such extremes of modesty and took
the nuns' lofty ideals of chastity with them back to America. They
never rebelled against the restrictions of their upbringing with later
undisciplined behavior. When Lucy entered FDR's orbit as Eleanor's
part-time secretary, she was as innocent and unworldly as Eleanor
later described herself in her autobiography.

*   *   *

While Mademoiselle Souvestre alerted Eleanor Roosevelt to the social problems of her time, the Mercer sisters learned about the weak-
est members of society in school. The nuns at their convent
regarded social service as their way of loving God. Around the turn of
the century, the fast-growing backstreet ghettos of Washington could
have supplied Vio and Lucy with ample evidence of the struggle for
survival among the poorest of the poor. But neither their father's associates in exclusive clubs nor their mother's friends in luxurious
parlors stressed empathy with the lower classes.

Vio and Lucy were aroused to the suffering of the poor by the
hands-on engagement of nuns who served as their mentors and
role models. At a time when infectious diseases ran rampant, when
smallpox and cholera terrorized large sectors of the city, the nuns
earned widespread respect for their heroic service as nurses. Un-
afraid of deadly contagion, they carried on their work in the middle
of devastating epidemics. They made the treatment of lung dis-

eases their specialty. Tuberculosis, the bane of the poor, was widespread in Vienna.

The dark side of the glamorous city, concentrated in a belt of misery on its outskirts, was the main target of the sisters' charitable crusades. Recent industrialization had attracted an army of indigent workers from undeveloped corners of the realm. The labor of these men and women ("guest workers" in the parlance of the following century) was gladly accepted in the thriving capital. But the newcomers were not covered by the most rudimentary social services that were taken for granted by residents in the older parts of the city. The Daughters of the Divine Redeemer established an outpost of charity at the Croatendoerfl, a small village of Croat immigrants where no German was spoken. There was no school, no hospital, and no church in the slum-like quarter. Undeterred by the village's record of crime, the nuns tried to fill in for all three missing institutions. Word spread like wildfire among the sisters when one of them, on a mission of mercy, had been attacked from behind in the dark. She had been thrown to the ground on her lonely way back to the convent. Her cries for help were lost in the night.

The Daughters of the Divine Redeemer were not intimidated. Danger prompted them to expand rather than end a special service that distinguished them from other charitable orders. Whenever the sisters heard of a family whose mother was incapacitated or missing, one of the sisters would visit the afflicted home as an angel of mercy. She would keep house for the family's widowed father and extend loving care to the half-orphaned children.

Approximately a decade later, at the point that marked the major divide in her life, Lucy would follow the example of these role models from her youth. Moved by the misery of a widower left to raise six children as a single father, she would come to the rescue in 1920. Lucy's compassionate response to the needs of the Rutherfurd family would turn into the calling of a lifetime.

MALE ATTENTION

It is not clear why or when Vio and Lucy left Austria and returned to their mother in Washington. Minnie Mercer welcomed them back as gracious, well-educated young ladies. Quite possibly, Minna was disappointed to find her daughters still single in their early twenties. Cousin Agnes was definitely saddened by Vio and Lucy's failure to follow in her footsteps and win a good husband in Austria. In every other respect, the countess had much reason to be proud of her two surrogate daughters' progress overseas. Vio had been motivated to train as a nurse; Lucy had gained a professional introduction to the education of young children. Both had received a superior general education in Vienna.

Only one of the three American girls invited by Agnes, Marguerite Pennington, fulfilled her hostess's matrimonial expectations. Marguerite married a baron and remained in Austria. Agnes did all she could to promote the interest of eligible suitors in the other two girls, Vio and Lucy. Yet there is no hint, in word or picture left for posterity, to indicate romantic ties between Vio and a young man in the countess' circle. There are, however, faint traces of documentation showing how Lucy's gentle appeal boosted Agnes's hopes that she would follow Marguerite Pennington's example.

In an age of great reticence about affairs of the heart, the evidence of male admiration for an eligible young lady remained well veiled. A picture of one of the Heussenstamms' evenings out in Vienna offers a rare clue to their efforts to build bridges to Lucy's heart for a highly desirable suitor. The formal portrait shows the family in fancy attire, fit for attendance of a theatrical performance or a festive meal at a restaurant in the capital. In the foreground Vio tenderly grasps Cousin Agnes's left hand with both of hers. The countess gazes fondly at the girl she loved as much as a daughter. Lucy stands in the back, in all her demure beauty, with an absent smile on her face. She is framed by two gentlemen. Uncle Toni, on her left, looks much older than he did at the time of the girls' arrival in Austria in 1907. On Lucy's right stands a tall, young officer in dress uniform. Count Ernst Meraviglia-Crivelli was obviously favored by Count and Countess Heussenstamm in their plans for Lucy's future. They had invited him to come along as Lucy's escort and included him in their family portrait. The handsome count is visibly enraptured by Lucy and turns his head toward her with a smitten smile. But Lucy looks straight ahead, giving no sign of special feeling for her admirer.

Ernst was highly desirable as a husband. The count was a distant relative of the Heussenstamms—attractive, well to do, from a respected family, and madly in love with Lucy. Vio acknowledged the importance of her sister's suitor by giving his Italian-sounding family name, Meraviglia-Crivelli, a place in her album. She included a special picture of Count Meraviglia on another page of her pictorial chronicle. It shows him sitting in a smart landau behind his coachman, stopping in front of a local "Hôtel."

Nothing came of the count's courtship of Lucy. It is idle to speculate whether Lucy, turning a cold shoulder to her surrogate parents' choice for her, brought about a falling out in her relationship with the count and countess that led to the sisters' departure from Austria. The assumption that such an emotional crisis was triggered by a delicate attachment of Lucy to another young man, right under Cousin Agnes's nose, stands on even more uncertain ground.

A close look at Lucy's male companions in Austria does suggest, however, that there was a competitor for the attention given to her by Count Meraviglia. In Vio's pictorial record of life in Austria, there was no young man more conspicuous in the young crowd at the Villa Heussenstamm than Charles Pennington. Marguerite's brother was even shown in one of Vio's photos in direct juxtaposition with Lucy. In the discreet way of her age, Vio pointed delicately to a special relationship between Charles and her sister. She took a picture with Charles on the left and Lucy on the right. They were engaged in the same game, letting a yo-yo dance up and down on a string connected to two short sticks. Vio's dash, put between Charles's and Lucy's was symbolic. To those familiar with the circumstances, it linked the two young people as friends.

The double portrait would be less meaningful if Lucy had not permitted Charles years later to leave a cryptic message in her autograph book. The last pages of Lucy's album are marked by a mysterious double entry in a man's hand. It appears without a signature or date and follows another entry written in 1913—a nostalgic poem composed by one of Lucy's former classmates at Sharon Hill. Sometime around 1913 Lucy had asked a friend to add a message to her album of endearments. His two-page contribution, in English and German, represents the last entry in Lucy's collection of affectionate links to her life.

The limited number of young men, photographed in Austria by Lucy's sister Vio, leaves little doubt about the author's identity. Another possible admirer of Lucy, the Tinti sisters' brother Freddy, appears only marginally in Vio's album. The frequent photographs of the Mercer girls' distant cousin Charles Pennington make him all the more conspicuous as their companion. Freddy only knew German; Charles was fluent in English and German. Charles had been raised in America but was deeply immersed in Austrian culture. He was uniquely qualified to leave a double message on facing pages in Lucy's album—one in English, the other in German. Written in the same bold hand, the first message was gruff and not very funny. The second, more melancholy message hinted at an unhappy love. Both entries gave off an air of resignation.

The English message read, "If you save your money, you're a Grouch. / If you spend it you're a Loafer / If you get it you're a Grafter, / If you don't get it you're a Bum—So whats [sic] the use—." Expressing a general disenchantment with life, these sentiments were straightforward. While the ten words in German on the facing page could not be more puzzling to an outsider, Lucy would understand their secret significance. She could read between the lines of an apparently impersonal text that said, *Es waren zwei Königs Kinder / Ich glaube sie hatten sich lieb!* Lucy had no difficulty translating the two sentences into English. They said, "There were two children of Kings; I think they were in love!"

These lines paraphrased a widely known old folk ballad about the tragic fate of two lovers, the Romeo and Juliet of another time. Lucy's friends, the Tinti sisters, might have taught their guests the sentimental tune on balmy summer evenings at a sing-along. Everybody knew the words: "There were once two children of Kings, so much in love with each other. But they could not get together—the water between them was much too deep."

The gulf dividing Charles Pennington and Lucy Mercer indeed proved too deep to be bridged. Being cousins presented no problem—their common ancestors on the Carroll side went far back into the seventeenth century—but Charles had little to offer as a provider. Worse, he had embarrassed the family by going overboard in his infatuation with the land on the Danube. After seeing much of Lucy at the Heussenstamms, Charles apparently remained devoted to her in the following years, when they went separate ways.

It remains an open question whether Lucy ever had a lasting affection for Charles, but she cared enough to invite him to write in her album, reserved for those who counted in her life. If anything in Lucy's early twenties should have resembled a love doomed to end in heartbreak, it would have been a foretaste of Lucy's sorrow over Franklin Roosevelt at the age of twenty-seven.

*   *   *

When Vio and Lucy returned to the States around 1912, they were long past eighteen, the age of introduction to society. Their parents had never been able to fund the expensive rites of "coming out." Their mother still cared for them; she moved back to Washington from New York to receive her daughters. But Minna did not settle again in a joint household with her husband Carroll. The spouses continued to live apart, Carroll in more strained circumstances than Minna.

Even if the girls' wealthy cousin in Austria had tried to help out again, Agnes would have been cut off from the girls by the outbreak of World War I in 1914. Like most of their aristocratic peers, the Heussenstamms had to cope with disastrous losses in fortune and prestige. By 1921 Countess Agnes was using the numerous extra rooms of her villa for bed-and-breakfast guests, many from the United States. Several of them would stay for months and even years. Among her longtime guests was Agnes's sister Ellinor Carroll, who had befriended Vio and Lucy in 1902. Ellinor died in Matzleinsdorf in 1924 in her sister's care.

Agnes had also stayed in touch with Sophie Walker Lee, from her stepfather's side of the family. It was Sophie who spoke for her mourning American family in the announcement of Agnes's death in 1942. Count Toni had passed away before her in 1929.

For Violetta and Lucy, their education in Austria soon became more of a liability than an asset. In the passionately anti-German mood of the war years, it was not opportune to mention ties with enemy countries. But Lucy was always good at holding her tongue. Though the sisters were more comfortable in the lilting Viennese dialect they had spoken during their years in Austria, they now conversed in the French they had acquired in classrooms. Violetta would soon come as close to military duty as a woman could, serving as an army nurse with the Allied forces overseas. There is no trace of renewed contact of the Mercer sisters with Cousin Agnes after the war. Nobody knows whether Lucy had fond or frustrated feelings looking back on her years in Austria.

Whatever public opinion decreed about Lucy's life overseas, her education in a distinguished convent school commanded respect. But the job market for young ladies without specific qualifications was limited. We know from Minna's pension file that Lucy needed a regular job to complement her sporadic work as an interior decorator.

CHAPTER 4

RETURN TO REALITY

BACK HOME, RICH IN HERITAGE

Once more Lucy and Vio had only each other when they arrived home. They were poor, except for a wealth of famous forefathers. Vio was the sisters' leader in the study of their illustrious ancestry, but Lucy was equally well versed in genealogy. The girls' aristocratic background would be an asset in the pursuit of their most urgent goal: finding husbands before they were too old to compete on the marriage market. Their mother, disappointed to welcome back her daughters as singles, now waited for her Cinderellas to charm two princes in Washington's ballrooms. Matrimony was preferable to a career. It was not easy to parlay noble descent into bread and butter.

Minna and her estranged husband set miserable examples. Papa Mercer had tried his luck as a manager of elite social clubs, but had been devastated by a fire that destroyed his possessions and valuable papers and was now seeking solace in alcohol. Too proud to take advantage of his friends from the good old days, Carroll Mercer never stayed long with any of them. The girls' mother also tired of being a houseguest. By 1912 she had settled in a respectable Washington apartment complex, the Decatur, at 2131 Florida Avenue. According to a May 22, 1912, article in *The Clubfellow and Washington Mirror,* her daughters Vio and Lucy had returned to their mother's care. The girls had last been seen vacationing with her in 1907. The society paper noted that Mrs. Mercer worked in an art establishment in the northwest part of Washington. She had "placed both her daughters in self-supporting positions; one a trained nurse; and the other an inside decorator."

Minna could still draw on her old reputation as the creator of Washington's most spectacular interiors, including her own. It was to be expected that her daughter Lucy would serve as her mother's apprentice. Lucy had an eye for elegance in clothes and furnishings. Art instruction overseas, as well as classes in sewing and needlework, had sharpened her senses of shape and color.

Minnie Mercer was a savvier businesswoman than her daughter. Yet whether she was rich or poor, Lucy's mother never had as much money as she needed. It was only too easy for her to let her good credit in Washington lead her down the slippery slope of debt.

This photograph of Lucy was taken around the time
she met Eleanor Roosevelt in 1923.

Even in their impoverished state, the adorable Mercer sisters and their stately mother were welcome in Washington's high society. Local old families liked to add the luster of the Mercer girls' nobility and charm to their dinners. Foreign embassies, staffed largely by men, needed eligible young ladies for their elaborate parties. The energetic and efficient Violetta Mercer, commanding popular respect as a nurse, had little time for social events. But the lovely Lucy, as bright and well organized as her sister, had time to spare. She was still searching for a profession into which she could fit.

LUCY IN THE ROOSEVELTS' ORBIT

After the election of 1912, Lucy saw many new faces at Washington's grand parties. Among the recently arrived officials and their wives, Mr. and Mrs. Franklin Roosevelt—both of them tall and strikingly distinguished—stood out.

Franklin Delano Roosevelt's move to the capital from staid Albany, New York, had encouraged his ambitions. With his appointment as assistant secretary of the navy he had landed his dream job, taking him a decisive step up the ladder to high office. His cousin and role model, Theodore Roosevelt, had shown the way as assistant secretary of the navy under President William McKinley. Franklin's family background predestined him even more than Theodore for the position: like all Delanos, he loved the sea with a passion.

Franklin's enthusiastic promotion of Woodrow Wilson's presidency at the Democratic National Convention in Baltimore in 1912 had earned him the perfect job offer after Wilson's inauguration on March 4, 1913. On the seventeenth of the month, his eighth wedding anniversary, Franklin raved to his wife, "The delightful significance of it all is only beginning to dawn on me." In his note of the same date to his mother, he told Sara that he had been thinking of her when he took his oath of office. FDR gave his triumphant letter special flourish by signing it with his full name. He vowed that he would master this job, even if it took all summer to get on top of its intricacies. In high spirits he declared, "I am baptized, confirmed, sworn in, vaccinated—and somewhat at sea! For over an hour I have been signing papers which had to be accepted on faith—but I hope luck will keep me out of jail."

The first two sentences of Sara's joyful reply to her son filled a whole page of her dainty ladies' stationery. She began, "You can imagine the happiness you gave me by writing to me yesterday. I just *knew* it was a *very* big job, & everything so new that it will take time to get *into* it."

Franklin was too excited over the promise of his position to give much thought to the consequences of his move to Washington, the city where the South began. While he did not mind living under a hotter sun, his wife and mother were all the more anxious. When summer began to get humid on the Potomac, Eleanor was glad that her mother-in-law took the children north to the cool Hudson River breezes at Hyde Park. On June 26 Sara commiserated with Franklin and Eleanor, "You are having it rough." She expected that "you stand it well at night" but "the day will be horrid for my poor Eleanor." On the other hand, Sara mused, Washington "seems a good climate for children" in winter, "good for our lambs as it is not severe."

After Eleanor escaped north to the family's summer retreat on Campobello Island in New Brunswick, Sara expressed concern for Franklin, working at his new job in great heat. She advised him to "get Milly to give you nice home food when possible and take daily exercise and drink water and you will keep perfectly well I am sure."

As soon as Sara joined her daughter-in-law on Campobello, she could reassure Franklin that "Eleanor seems very happy and looks so well, and loves having Maude." Eleanor's maternal Aunt Maude, a welcome guest, distracted her from missing Franklin too much. Campobello again offered a cool refuge for Eleanor the following summer at the end of her fifth pregnancy. "It was pure luck that I decided to come Sunday," FDR wrote to his mother, congratulating himself for being at his wife's side when Franklin Delano Roosevelt, Jr., was born on August 17, 1914.

Eleanor stayed on the island until October 1. With a new baby on her hands, the avalanche of social duties approaching with the winter season appeared more crushing than ever. She explained later that she needed a social secretary "to arrange my calling list, and answer and send invitations." Eleanor gave no name when she wrote, "I finally engaged one for three mornings a week."

Much evidence supports the widely held assumption that it was Eleanor's aunt Anna Roosevelt Cowles who suggested that she hire

Lucy Mercer for the part-time job. Anna, Mrs. William Sheffield Cowles—Theodore Roosevelt's sister—had a splendid record in judging and matching people of her acquaintance. The Mercers had once lived down the street from Admiral Cowles's residence. Anna heard enough of Miss Lucy Mercer's fine qualities to think of her when her favorite niece needed help. Since the fall of 1913, Eleanor and Franklin had rented the Cowles' old-fashioned but cozy residence on 1733 N Street. Eleanor felt at home in the house where her Aunt Bye (Anna) had lived before she moved to her husband's homestead in Farmington, Connecticut.

Anna Roosevelt Cowles had two nicknames. Her Oyster Bay Roosevelt relatives called her Bye; to her Hyde Park Roosevelt cousins she was Bamie. Anna had been uncannily successful in directing the personal affairs of both branches of the Roosevelt family from behind the scenes. She had encouraged her widowed brother Theodore to propose to Edith Kermit Carow, the estranged sweetheart of his youth. A few years earlier, James Roosevelt of Hyde Park had been deeply grateful to Bamie for helping him win the hand of Sara Delano. Anna's nephew Theodore Robinson felt equally indebted to her. Auntie Bye had promoted his unlikely union with the Astor heiress Helen Rebecca Roosevelt, the daughter of FDR's half brother Rosy.

Less than a year later, Anna happily celebrated another family wedding she had also helped bring about. On March 17, 1905, her "doe-eyed" niece Eleanor married the man of her heart, Franklin Roosevelt. Anna remembered well that the handsome Franklin Roosevelt had been Eleanor's dream husband even before she was sent to boarding school in London. Prior to Eleanor's return in 1902, following her grandmother's directive to appear as a debutante in society, Franklin had only taken notice of the girl as the niece of the president.

But Anna wasn't the only one who envisioned Eleanor as a perfect match for Franklin. His mother idolized cousin Theodore Roosevelt and his family. Sara held up the great man as an example for FDR since he had been a schoolboy at Groton. At the same time, she fondly remembered Theodore's brother Elliott and his orphaned daughter Eleanor. Encouraged by her friend Anna Cowles, Sara had been able to open Franklin's eyes to the allure of the "Angel" in Eleanor's pure heart in the summer of 1903.

As FDR's wife, Eleanor lived up to her mother-in-law's expectations. She served diligently as her husband's dutiful helpmate and excelled as a model mother of many children. But the marriage favored by Auntie Bye and Cousin Sallie may not have been as carefree as they had expected. Overwhelmed by obligations, hurt by a lack of sensitivity on her husband's part, Eleanor began to nurture resentments.

Eleanor would turn thirty in the fall of 1914. Her first child, Anna, had been born in 1906, her son James in 1907. Her third child, the first Franklin, Jr., had only lived from March to November 1909. But he was followed fast by her fourth child, Elliott, in 1910. Eleanor was pregnant with her fifth child, the second Franklin, Jr., when she followed the suggestion of Anna Cowles to hire Lucy Mercer as her secretary. FDR first mentioned Lucy as a member of the Roosevelts' household, assisting the family chauffeur in domestic chores, in an undated letter to his wife that can be placed between May and June 1914. Eleanor's wise aunt understood better than any outsider the challenges faced by the young woman.

Hoping to give her niece a lift by hiring efficient help for her, Anna Cowles thought of Miss Mercer as the ideal candidate. She had placed promising young ladies as social secretaries before. An earlier protégée, Edith Benham Helm, had nothing going for her but solid charm and her background from an old naval family when Mrs. Cowles arranged her employment by the wife of the British ambassador James Bryce. Mrs. Helm ended up marrying an admiral. Later, when Eleanor was First Lady, she would hold the position of her social secretary in the White House.

Lucy Mercer had the right qualifications to embark on a similar course. Mrs. Helm vouched for Lucy, whose "family were old friends of mine." From the beginning of her employment by the Roosevelts, Lucy was more than just secretary to the lady of the house.

Not only did Miss Mercer bring valuable social connections to her work; she would also be an asset to Franklin and Eleanor Roosevelt in her capacity to act as a bridge to the South. Mrs. Cowles and her brother Teddy had observed a resurgence of interest in Lucy's ancestral heritage in a new wave of literature, swelled by the "reconciliationist" movement gaining ground after the Civil War. Thomas Nelson

Page, one of the popular authors who extolled the glamour of the Old South, was Lucy's cousin.

"I didn't know that there was anybody in Virginia who cared whether I went to hell or not," President Theodore Roosevelt had exclaimed when he read in the introduction to a reconciliationist book that "there was a woman in Virginia who prayed for him every day." When he found out that she was Page's mother, he sent her a photograph of himself, dedicated "To Mrs. John Page, with [the] regard and esteem of Theodore Roosevelt."

Initially, Eleanor saw her new secretary mainly through the eyes of Auntie Bye and Uncle Theodore. It was her husband Franklin who came to know Miss Mercer from a different angle, as a member of Washington's vibrant social scene. While he was adjusting to life in the capital, two of Franklin's best friends discovered Lucy as a distinguished southern blue blood.

DOUGHOREGAN MANOR.
MARYLAND.

Doughoregan Manor in Maryland was the seat of the Carrolls of Carrollton. A wing of the mansion served as the country refuge of FDR's friend Lathrop Brown.

FRIENDS: FDR, LATHROP BROWN,
NIGEL LAW, AND LUCY MERCER

Theodore Roosevelt was more apt to listen to echoes of the old regime of aristocratic slaveholders than his young cousin and admirer FDR. Teddy had adored his "darling motherling," as he addressed her tenderly as a teenager. Mittie Bulloch Roosevelt had taken her attachment to her home in the South to the residence of her husband Theodore Roosevelt, Sr., right in New York City. Even in the middle of the Civil War, she had dared to hang a Confederate flag from her city window. Raised on Roswell estate near Atlanta, Mittie regarded the cluster of small wooden slave cabins close to the mansion as inseparable from the memory of her home. Massive white pillars in front of a heavy entrance door guarded the world of her childhood from intruders, from strange people and strange ideas.

The mind of Franklin's mother had been cast in a different mold. As a young woman, she called herself as Yankee as Plymouth Rock. She never forgot her elation in Northampton when all the church bells tolled in celebration of Lee's surrender. Franklin proudly shared with his mother the high moral ground of the abolitionists. However, in his mother's view there was also an endearing aspect of the South to be found in the refinement of its society.

Sara instilled in her son a profound admiration for true nobility, wherever it was found. Wealth alone did not make anyone superior. Money had to be combined with an elegant, cultured lifestyle, a wide, cosmopolitan horizon, and stress on education rather than material gain. For Sara and Franklin Roosevelt, these principles knew no borders between North and South. When Lucy Mercer's stories of the world of her ancestors in Virginia and Maryland confirmed for FDR that they were more similar than different from his own role models in the Hudson Valley, he accepted a new view of the southern aristocracy. He regarded it as congenial and worthy of closer scrutiny.

Regarding himself as a farmer, FDR could understand George Washington's pride as a landowner. Thomas Jefferson's love of books and learning was as tangible a characteristic of the lord of the manor as Franklin's own ambitions for Springwood's library at Hyde Park. The Roosevelts and Delanos belonged to the upper echelons of an all-American society, including the land south of the Mason–Dixon Line. Two of FDR's close friends, Lathrop Brown and Nigel Law, were equally eager to become connoisseurs of southern society. All three men became acquainted at almost the same time with a young lady who appeared as an incarnation of gracious ancestors. Miss Lucy Page Mercer was a contemporary messenger from the world of Mount Vernon and Monticello.

On weekday mornings, when Miss Mercer sorted out Eleanor's invitations on her employer's living room floor, FDR was at his desk in the Navy Department. He came to know Lucy in his hours of leisure, at social events in the company of his peers. His old Harvard roommate Lathrop Brown, the closest companion of his student years, had also moved south in 1913. FDR's mother and Lathrop were fond of each other; the boy was as at home in Hyde Park as another son. His election as a Democratic congressman from New York City brought Lathrop and Franklin together again in Washington. The name Brown appeared consistently in records of get-togethers of Franklin's friends.

To escape Washington's oppressive summer heat in the age before air conditioning, Lathrop acquired a country refuge in nearby Maryland. Renting a wing of the sprawling Doughoregan Manor, he entered the world of southern nobility.

Doughoregan Manor, the original homestead of Charles Carroll (known as the "Signer"), had been enlarged with additions on all sides by subsequent generations. Each new wing was a mansion by itself. The manor's absolute rural seclusion was protected by the Carrolls' fierce sense of privacy that is upheld by their descendants to this day. This was a perfect place for Lathrop and his wife Helen, from a Boston Brahmin family, to receive discriminating houseguests like Franklin and Eleanor Roosevelt. Lathrop's landlord Charles Carroll, a descendant of the Signer and the contemporary head of the leading branch of the clan, took pride in his international connections. Together with his wife Marie-Louise Suzanne, a granddaughter of the scholar and ambassador George Bancroft, Charles had just returned from years of living in Paris. Very likely he included a visit with a close relation during his frequent travels in Europe. His first cousin Agnes Carroll was married to the Austrian Count Anton Heussenstamm and lived in a fairy tale villa near the Danube.

*   *   *

While FDR's old buddy Lathrop Brown drew wealth from his family's real estate empire in New York City and prestige from his wife's high-society Boston origins, Nigel Law—FDR's new aristocratic friend in Washington—was a distinguished English diplomat. Befriending Nigel, the third secretary of the British embassy, Franklin was once again following in the footsteps of his most famous relative. At the beginning of his career, his cousin Theodore Roosevelt had also chosen as a confidant a man in the same position at the British embassy: the English nobleman Cecil Spring-Rice. As a friend of England, FDR's great "kinsman" (as his mother called Theodore) was predestined to show his young cousin how to rise in rank, possibly all the way to the White House.

Franklin emulated Teddy's everyday habits, like wearing pince-nez glasses and spicing his speech with many a "bully." Yet he was not able to create a perfect equivalent of Theodore's attachment to Spring-Rice in his friendship with Nigel Law. On his first round of duty at the British embassy, long before Sir Cecil returned to Washington as the British ambassador in 1913, he had been a power both in Theodore Roosevelt's political thinking and in his personal life. Cecil had served as best man at the Roosevelt–Carow wedding and was anchored firmly in the affection of Teddy's wife Edith.

In contrast to Cecil, Nigel Law had not endeared himself to Franklin's wife Eleanor. In her eyes Nigel dominated the assistant secretary's life away from home. Eleanor excelled as the hostess of intimate dinners for close friends, but she despised big, noisy parties like the crowded receptions and dances at the British embassy. This, however, was the place where Nigel Law reigned supreme among the fun-seeking young people. Here Franklin found not only congenial company but also familiar faces. His aunt Katharine Delano Collier (also known as "Kassie") belonged to the group of Washington's Anglophiles who were regular guests at the embassy. Together with her son Warren Robbins and her daughter Sara Collier, Kassie served as both witness and watchdog of Franklin's behavior in his favorite social circle.

Whereas FDR's Collier relatives had arrived recently in Washington from England, Nigel Law had lived in Austria before his assignment to the United States. He quickly learned that his recent impressions of life in Vienna paralleled the experiences of the popular Miss Lucy Mercer. He admired Lucy as a cosmopolitan among Washington's provincials, a true blue blood whose family history touched the past of his own forebears. Nigel's friendship with Mr. Roosevelt and Miss Mercer grew in tandem, beginning at the same time and ending almost simultaneously.

FDR had been attracted to Nigel Law since the young diplomat's arrival on the *Lusitania* in November 1914. On June 28 of that year, Archduke Franz Ferdinand—heir to the crown of the Austro-Hungarian dual monarchy—had been assassinated in the wake of a Serbian conspiracy at Sarajevo in Bosnia. By August 4 Europe was engulfed in an explosive conflagration. In four years of war, the alliance formed by Russia, France, and Britain was joined in 1917 by the United States.

Right at the outbreak of hostilities, Nigel Law had to leave Vienna, now a major enemy capital along with Berlin. In Washington he enjoyed the enthusiastic support of Franklin Roosevelt, the assistant secretary of the navy, for his diplomatic mission: boosting Britain's purchase of war supplies. Eight years Franklin's junior, Nigel was "close akin to the loftiest of British nobility," according to *Town Topics,* Washington's society paper. This was an exaggeration but it fit with FDR's expectations. The young aristocrat warmly returned FDR's spontaneous affection. Law was equally impressed with the Roosevelts. He described Franklin as "the most attractive man whom it was my good fortune to meet during my four years in America."

At the time when Nigel became acquainted with FDR, he remarked that Franklin appealed to his friends above all with his "gaiety and kindliness." Nigel stressed that FDR "always seemed to be considering the feelings of others and doing all he could to make those in his company happy and cheerful. He was intensely interested in other people, not I think as a mere study in diverse humanity, but because he liked all people. He was intensely patriotic, but next to his own compatriots I think he preferred the English to other nationalities and during the period of American 'neutrality' he never disguised his strong pro-Ally sympathies." In June 1916 Franklin took Nigel to a du Pont wedding, then introduced him to his mother at Hyde Park. Sara was delighted with her son's new best friend.

Looking back fondly on FDR, and recalling the way the young crowd at the British embassy saw him, Nigel described him as "a fine physical specimen in the days I knew him, delighting in all sorts of outdoor activity. But he was not just a gay athlete, for he had a deep understanding of politics and a sound knowledge of history and foreign affairs, strong convictions and ideals and a deep desire to serve his country with all his powers. In my own mind I gave him the highest praise an Englishman can give a man, that he was a perfect example of an English Country Gentleman."

Nigel Law was accepted enthusiastically by Washington society. His recently acquired first-hand knowledge in European affairs put him much in demand as a conversationalist on the capital's dinner party circuit. His comments were seen as an interesting sequel to the reports of Miss Lucy Mercer, who had preceded his stay in Austria. It soon became clear that the British nobleman and the beautiful American blue blood had more in common than their recent familiarity with Austrian society.

More than a century earlier, Nigel and Lucy's forefathers had been competitors. Nigel's great-granduncle Thomas Law had arrived in Washington in 1796 as one of its earliest financiers. He married but could not hold Elisabeth Custis, the adventurous daughter of George Washington's stepson. Mr. Law's losses in land dealings were linked to the superior business prowess of Lucy's clever ancestor Daniel Carroll of Duddington Manor.

Lucy knew the circumstances well. She preserved a *Washington Post* clipping—included in Violetta's collection of family memorabilia—that showed to what extent Daniel Carroll had controlled the land in the heart of the city. The present-day Capitol grounds formed the jewel in his crown of invaluable real estate. According to the article, Daniel Carroll, "the richest and most important" owner of the property, brilliantly entertained several presidents and "the leading men of the day." His mansion, surrounded by six acres of parklands and flowerbeds, was protected by a high brick wall. In 1885 two unmarried daughters of the Carrolls were still living there, before it had to "make way for rows of small houses . . . a severe blow to the city which thus lost one of its most beautiful and historic relics."

In Nigel's eyes it added to Miss Mercer's distinction that she had lived in Austria as the surrogate daughter of Countess Agnes Carroll, the wife of a chamberlain of the emperor. At the British embassy in Vienna, on his first overseas assignment after graduating from Cambridge, Nigel became well acquainted with Austrian nobility. He knew all about the popularity and personal tragedies of the old Austrian emperor Franz Josef. Like Lucy, Nigel had experienced the rigidity of the Hapsburgs' court.

* * *

Franklin, Nigel, and Lucy were children of their time, worshipping crowns and adoring the landed gentry. Eleanor alone dared to be different. As she grew in stature, she associated with members of all social classes.

Among American presidents Franklin Delano Roosevelt stands out as the champion of the common man. But he demonstrated persistently in his personal life that he was not a common man himself. His parents convinced him that he was a blue blood and that he had to act like one. His mother impressed him specifically with the illustrious origins of the Delano family. Only in 1995 did the banker Frederick Baldwin Adams, Jr., a great-grandson of FDR's uncle Warren Delano III, prove beyond a doubt that the family's founding father— Philippe de la Noye—was not the offspring of princes of the Holy Roman Empire. Rather, he actually belonged to a family of refugee wool carders from Flanders. The enterprising eighteen-year-old Philippe had sailed as the only Delano in his group of immigrants from Leiden in Holland to the Puritans' colony in New England, arriving in Plymouth on November 11, 1621.

FDR was not aware of these facts. He did not look at the Delanos' rise as a triumph of commoners but thought of his ancestors as high-ranking aristocrats. Consequently, he regarded all European nobles as his relatives. In a letter written four months before his death, Franklin addressed Charlotte, Grand Duchess of Luxembourg, as "Dear Lottie." He mourned the destruction of one of her palaces, Clervaux Castle, in the war, but rejoiced, "I seem to be lucky in that the DeLannoy Chateau seems to be still intact."

Like the president himself, U.S. Army historians were taken in by the name de Lannoy. They did not realize that the name was common to princes and burghers alike. Neither FDR's forefather Philippe de Lannoy nor his ancestors were the owners of Clervaux Castle, which rather belonged to a Belgian prince of the same name. The army historians who eagerly tried to satisfy the president's interest in the history of his alleged ancestral castle provided many details about the castle's real owners since the twelfth century. In reality, they were irrelevant for FDR's true-to-the-facts genealogical research. Nevertheless, the history of Clervaux assumed a special luster for FDR when Lucy shared details about her past associations in Europe with Franklin. Lucy's surrogate father Anton Count Heussenstamm was proud of the numerous archbishops who once possessed the famous castle. Among them appeared an archbishop of Mainz, who enriched his family tree.

When FDR arrived in Washington in 1913 as a high government official, he cultivated his image as a part of nobility from two continents. Nigel Law the high-born Englishman, and Lucy Mercer the southern aristocrat, were company from similar backgrounds. In addition, they were fellow genealogy buffs. Franklin was immediately comfortable with Nigel Law, a son of Sir Algernon Law of the House of Ellenborough. The two friends, Nigel and Franklin, were equally eager to find blue blood in their ancestry. Both were awed by the historic importance of Lucy Page Mercer's forefathers.

LUCY PAGE MERCER:
A DAUGHTER OF THE OLD SOUTH

Lucy Page Mercer could entertain a history enthusiast like FDR just by making past bearers of her first, middle, and last names come alive. When her parents called their younger daughter Lucy Page, they had been inspired by the recently published *Genealogy of the Page Family in Virginia*. Its author, Dr. Richard Channing Moore Page, was a physician in New York and Lucy's distant cousin. He followed his Page ancestors from their emigration as English cavaliers in the 1600s to their status as affluent landowners in the colonies. Over the course of two centuries, the Pages had produced prominent statesmen, professors, and many beautiful women.

As Mrs. Rutherfurd, Lucy Mercer handed down to her daughter what she knew about her ancestors. In 1940 Lucy encouraged eighteen-year-old Barbara to closely study a small manuscript, describing the history of her maternal forebears. Barbara Rutherfurd corrected small errors in the typewritten text by hand. The story of an earlier Lucy Page, raised in the orbit of George Washington, was a gem in the Mercers' chronicles.

Colonel John Page, born in England in 1627, had left three flourishing plantations in York County, Virginia, to his heirs. His estate included three ships, water mills, and a treasure trove of money and gold rings. Like many fellow planters, he increased his wealth by marrying a well-to-do young widow. His second wife Mary Mann, the widow of the Honorable Matthew Page, brought the famous Rosewell mansion into his possession. The legendary homestead of the Pages was tied to high points of early American history. According to family lore, Matthew Page settled on the spot where the great Indian chief Powhatan had ruled and where Powhatan's daughter Pocahontas had saved the life of Captain John Smith. It was said that the Pages' close friend Thomas Jefferson drafted his version of the Declaration of Independence, right before he went to Philadelphia, in the brick-and-marble Rosewell mansion.

A Page family historian, the venerable Bishop Meade, pointed to a grandson of the original Colonel John Page—the John Page of North End, Gloucester County, Virginia—as the link tying the Pages to the Carters, one of Virginia's most illustrious families. John's mother Judith Carter was the daughter of the famous Robert "King" Carter. The King's descendant George Carter turned his Oatlands plantation into a showplace. For generations to come, the hospitable place attracted many prominent visitors, among them Franklin and Eleanor Roosevelt.

According to Bishop Meade and Dr. Richard Page, John Page of North End first won renown as a patriot soldier who served with George Washington "in one of his western expeditions against the French and Indians." Next John became "a Representative in the House of Burgesses" and was appointed "visitor" of the College of William and Mary. During the Revolution he "contributed freely from his private fortune to the public cause." By 1802 he reached his highest rank as governor of Virginia. Bishop Meade praised him as "a well-read theologian and zealous churchman" and "the most affectionate domestic character."

Governor John Page named his youngest child Lucy after a beloved half sister Lucy, the charming Mrs. George W. Baylor. As a widow, Lucy Page Baylor had not been able to forget her late "dear George" and refused to listen to a distinguished colonel's "addresses" to marry him. In the way of her time, Lucy's brother cajoled her into a second marriage anyway. Her suitor "put it all to rights by saying, 'Lucy, you don't know what is good for you. Your brother John and I arranged it all!" Twisting Lucy's arm worked. Lucy and her second husband lived happily together ever after.

Lucy Page Baylor fit an established pattern where harmonious second marriages were common. In an era when infectious diseases swiftly took the lives not only of infants but also of their mothers, many young planters were widowed early. With half-orphaned children on their hands, they rushed to find a new wife, preferably a widowed relative. Love often flourished more freely after a second or third wedding than in a first union. A marriage of convenience was fine as long as it linked old names and brought in large dowries; on the other hand, a union based on infatuation was suspect. Any violation of "the habit of marrying well" was sharply censored.

Daniel Carroll of Duddington Manor was incensed and minced no words when his son Charles presented him with Mary Hill as his second wife. Mary was the daughter of a wine merchant who did not belong in the planters' circle. Daniel's brother, the "Signer" Charles Carroll, was equally indignant about the intrusion of the Hills into his exclusive clan. He exploded, "My nephew who is not capable of doing a wise thing, has lately done the foolishest thing he ever did, for he has taken to himself a wife, the daughter of Mr. Henry Hill."

Mary and her father Henry Hill did indeed leave a conspicuous gap in the genealogical fan chart of their descendant Lucy Mercer. The Hills' forefathers were unknown. Where Lucy's other ancestors could deliver illustrious names for her family tree since colonial times, Henry Hill provided only blank spaces on her chart.

The famous Charles Carroll of Doughoregan Manor might well have encouraged his nephew to choose a second wife to enhance his social standing. Charles admitted that his new bride, Mary Darnall, was "a little too young" to get married. He was right: at fifteen, Mary was less than half his age. She was also a little too closely related, even by the planters' liberal standards. Her mother, also named Mary Darnall, was Charles' first cousin. Charles did not care. The political power of his future father-in-law, Colonel Henry Darnall, more than compensated for this flaw of the union. The colonel, overseer of Lord Baltimore's interests in Maryland, held innumerable high offices and marriage to his daughter promised invaluable future favors. The opportunities that this alliance brought Carroll "can scarcely be exaggerated," his chronicler appraised the groom's shrewdness. Charles was lucky. Mary Darnall gave birth to seven children in a marriage that grew in mutual affection.

*   *   *

It fit this sober emotional atmosphere that another Virginian planter, George Washington, did equally well in 1759 when he married Martha Dandridge, the rich widow of Daniel Parke Custis. Romantic feelings and ardent courtship were considered secondary. The material gains of the match were as obvious as its immaterial advantages. George not only added eight thousand acres to his land; he also found great personal satisfaction in the stepchildren and step-grandchildren brought into his life by Martha.

George and Martha Washington, the peers and friends of Lucy Mercer's ancestors, set an example for a happy second marriage in their social group. Lucy might have had this familiar pattern of matrimony in Old Virginia and Maryland in the back of her mind in 1919, when she was in doubt whether to accept the hand of Winthrop Rutherfurd, an aristocratic widower twice her age.

Lucy's last name was as rich in historic connotations as her middle name. A well-renowned ancestor John Mercer, married to Catherine Mason, was a Crown lawyer and active opponent of the notorious British Stamp Act. He became the surrogate father of his nephew George Mason. When John's brother-in-law George Mason III drowned in 1735 during a crossing of the Potomac, the three fatherless Mason children were taken into John and Catherine Mercer's custody. Their distinguished mansion Marlboro was situated at the far end of Potomac Neck. The Mercers received one thousand pounds of tobacco annually from the widowed Ann Mason to help them raise her children. John Mercer's devotion as a foster father proved priceless for the gifted little George Mason.

John Mercer of Marlboro directed the boy's education and had him "read law" in his office. George Mason never forgot what he owed his uncle when he became a great jurist himself. He authored the Virginia Constitution in 1776 and used the term "inalienable rights" before Thomas Jefferson did.

In April 1769 George Washington tried to form an alliance with George Mason, who by now had outgrown the Mercers' Marlboro. It was their common goal to resist "our lordly masters" in England. It was remarkable that the Virginia planters remained true to their English cultural heritage in spite of their revolt against British domination. The Washingtons, Pages, Mercers, and Carrolls were of one mind in seeking for their offspring a traditional English education in the classics and in law. If they could afford it, they emulated Augustine Washington—the father of George—who sent his two older sons to the mother country for schooling at Eton.

At this point the world of Lucy Mercer's ancestors touched the preferences of the Roosevelts. FDR's prep school, Groton, was modeled on Rugby in England. As a young Harvard man, Franklin adopted his father's ambition to live like an English lord. His roots were important enough for the young man to choose the history of the Roosevelt family at the time of the American Revolution as the theme for his sophomore essay at Harvard.

There were both similarities and divergences in the standing and attitudes of Franklin and Lucy's forebears. The Roosevelts and their peers had risen to high social rank as the result of solid merchants' toil. Lucy Mercer's forefathers, on the other hand, had built their riches on the sweat and tears of men and women in shackles. FDR was not made aware of the difference by his mother or his favorite teacher. His French-Swiss governess, Mademoiselle Sandoz, stressed in her history instruction for Franklin her employers' idolization of George Washington and Thomas Jefferson. She avoided describing the founding fathers as slaveholders in her classes for Franklin.

Franklin was in his thirties when Lucy Mercer's stories about her family's history taught him to see the many-faceted mentality of Virginia and Maryland planters in colonial times from a new perspective. Their patriotic sacrifices in the struggle for independence had not only defined the personal fate of Lucy's prominent ancestors, but had determined the future course of the nation.

Not all Mercers had a blind spot in their conscience when they considered slavery, the source of their wealth. Margaret Mercer was one of the rare rebels against the spirit of her class who refused to accept slavery without question as part of the nature of things. She was born in 1791 as the fourth child of John Francis Mercer, briefly the governor of Maryland. Margaret set a selfless example by freeing her inherited slaves and sending them to a refuge, a missionary colony she founded for them in Liberia. She then invested all her energy and money in establishing a girls' school at Cedar Park, her parental plantation near Annapolis where Lucy Mercer's father was born in 1859. By the time Margaret died in 1846, she had exhausted all her resources and faced poverty. Her noble experiment remained but a footnote in the history of slavery.

For her chroniclers Margaret Mercer not only stood out as a social revolutionary and a model of an enlightened educator; she also exemplified the love of books that distinguished her circle. FDR could

FDR poses with his friend Frank Lane on an excursion to the Virginia countryside. This is the only picture of FDR found in Lucy Mercer's papers, which were inherited by her niece after his death. It escaped Lucy's systematic destruction of Franklin's letters and pictures in the summer of 1945.

readily relate to this distinctive trait of the southern planters. As a passionate book collector, Franklin followed in the footsteps of his grandfather Warren Delano II, who inspired him to build his own superior library at Hyde Park.

Among the southern planters who came alive for Franklin in Lucy Mercer's accounts, George Mason and his guardian John Mercer were notable as members of the fraternity of book lovers that knew no state boundaries. On the Carroll side of Lucy's family, founding father Charles Carroll of Carrollton had made reading and the creation of a large private library a special mark of distinction. At the age of ninety, Charles was devastated by the weakness of his eyes because he had "always taken great delight in reading."

FITTING IN WITH THE ROOSEVELTS

For Lucy Page Mercer, the grounds of Mount Vernon—George Washington's family seat close to the mansions of both their ancestors in Virginia—were the essence of home. But Franklin Roosevelt was thrilled to live now in the orbit of Washington, his childhood hero.

FDR was equally aroused by the vicinity of the White House to his new home. He had seen it inside as a nine-year-old. Dressed in a new Scottish kilt, he had accompanied his father on a courtesy visit to an old family friend, President Grover Cleveland. The heavy man was "utterly worn out by the weight of work and weariness." The president's "strange wish" for the little boy ("that you may never be president of the United States") did not seem so far-fetched in 1913, when a vigorous Franklin returned to Washington at the age of thirty-one, on his way up the ranks in public service.

To succeed in Washington, Franklin had to be comfortable living there. The capital formed a cosmopolitan island in the predominantly rural sea of two southern states, Virginia and Maryland. He had a tie to Baltimore, the native city of his beloved aunt Jennie Walters Delano, but most of the land around Washington was terra incognita for Franklin. He knew Europe better than he knew the American South. Overseas travel had reinforced his identity as a thoroughbred Yankee.

When FDR put down permanent roots in Washington, he realized that he had grown up in a different social, historical, and cultural climate. His wife felt the change even more acutely. Eleanor did not get to know her southern paternal grandmother Mittie Bulloch. Firmly anchored in her family's past in New York, Eleanor never learned to be completely comfortable with the ambience and values of the South. Lucy Mercer was the first southern lady of her class and generation who made a lasting impression on Eleanor.

Franklin's adjustment to the South was a requirement of his new job. It was his good fortune that the secretary of the navy, a newspaper owner from North Carolina and a proud southerner, took a spontaneous liking to his Yankee assistant. When his boss Josephus Daniels irked him with his pacifist views, Franklin kept his irritation in check. Their relationship grew more personal after 1914, when Mr. and Mrs. Daniels accepted the first of many invitations from his mother Sara to visit Hyde Park. They returned Sara's affection warmly and developed respect for her sound judgment.

Josephus Daniels and his wife held Franklin's wife in equally high regard; they also approved of Eleanor's assistant Miss Mercer. Lucy was recognized by them first as a charming young socialite from an illustrious family, second as Mrs. Franklin Roosevelt's secretarial aide. Like other Washington matrons, Mrs. Daniels knew that the Roosevelts' house on N Street was a poor hunting ground for a not-so-very-young lady who needed a husband. Lucy's part-time job did not pay much and filled at most fifteen hours per week. It helped that Lucy liked her work and was impressed with her employer. She certainly tried her best to please Eleanor.

Miss Mercer succeeded in winning over the Roosevelt children, although their written testimony about her was influenced by later events. In contrast to her brothers, Franklin and Eleanor's daughter Anna always stuck to her first appraisal of Lucy, observing that all "liked her warm and friendly manner and smile." In retrospect Anna's brother Elliott mistakenly described Lucy as his father's mistress. He did not mention that he was only between four and eight years old when he knew Miss Mercer in person. He would have hardly noticed at the time that her deep, "smoky" voice compared favorably with Eleanor's shrill, high tones.

Miss Mercer's assessment by FDR's mother was more to the point. When Sara visited her son's family in Washington in the spring of 1915, she had high praise for Lucy. Mrs. James Roosevelt was a lady and could recognize another lady when she saw one. Sara took Lucy's measure in a letter of March 24. "Miss Mercer is here, she is *so* sweet and attractive." Always trying to stem Eleanor's feelings of feminine inferiority, Sara added, "and she adores you, Eleanor." Indeed, Lucy admired Eleanor—seven years her senior—from the first day of their acquaintance to the end of her life.

*   *   *

Eleanor's feelings for Lucy would change in the long run, but at first they were warmly welcoming. Eleanor's compassionate heart was touched when she found many parallels with Lucy's past in her own background. As slender young girls, both were tall and regal, surrounded by an aura of "extreme innocence and unworldliness." Both had noble ancestors and strong-willed mothers, women to be reckoned with. In the first sentence of her autobiography of 1937, Eleanor called her mother—the blond, ethereal Anna Hall—the most beautiful woman she knew. Along the same lines, the spirited, dark-haired Minnie Tunis Mercer had been declared "the most beautiful woman in Washington" and the darling of the capital's beau monde, mainly because of her charming way of living as a *grande dame*. Anna Hall had been a reigning society belle in New York City.

Like Eleanor, Lucy suffered from the severe stress in her parents' marriage after a luxurious early childhood. Although the fathers of both women fared poorly in their later years as the result of excessive drinking, neither of them ever lost the love of their daughters.

When Eleanor returned to Washington after her summer vacation on Campobello Island in 1915, she paid Lucy her ultimate compliment by inviting her twice in a row to her monthly Thursday evening dinner parties. Eleanor was as exacting as her mother-in-law Sara about the intellectual level of conversation at her table. She did not suffer fools lightly and expected all guests to carry their weight in intelligent exchange. Miss Mercer could be trusted. She had seen the world, had received a splendid education, and always knew when to remain quiet.

The first entry in Eleanor's *Dinner Book* that listed Lucy as her guest is dated November 11, 1915. The relatively small party had brought together the highest-ranking members of FDR's innermost circle, which included Secretary of the Interior Franklin Lane and his wife Anne and French Ambassador Jules Jusserand and his wife Eliza. Eleanor also listed "Assist. Sec. of State and Mrs. Phillips." Caroline Astor Drayton Phillips, the wife of Assistant Secretary of State William Phillips, was a first cousin of Helen Astor Robinson, the daughter of FDR's half brother Rosy. Miss Mercer was escorted to the table by a relative of Mrs. Phillips, Mr. Coleman Drayton.

At Eleanor's next big party, on December 2, Miss Mercer was seated beside a rear admiral. All other guests were couples, with the exception of "Miss Delano," the dinner partner of John Barrett. Louise Delano was the daughter of FDR's uncle Frederic Adrian Delano. He had moved to Washington for a new career in public service after becoming independently wealthy in the railroad business. The guest of honor at the dinner for fourteen was FDR's boss himself, the secretary of the navy, accompanied by Mrs. Josephus Daniels.

CHAPTER 5

1917-1918: LUCY AND ELEANOR

PRECARIOUS FAMILY VALUES

Sara never retracted her initial enthusiastic appraisal of Miss Mercer. Still, she was the first to ring alarm bells when her informants in Washington informed her that Lucy appeared to admire her son Franklin even more than she respected her employer Eleanor. Franklin may have returned Lucy's sentiments, but of course it was not permissible for him to show his special feelings for the young lady so openly.

Sara only came to Washington for emergencies. On July 2, 1915, the day after her son had his appendix removed at Washington's Naval Hospital, she was at his bedside before Eleanor could make the long, hot trip from Campobello to Washington.

It made no difference whether Sara was in the capital or Hyde Park; she could always monitor closely what her son was doing. Among the Delanos in Washington, Sara's younger sister Kassie was especially good at keeping track of family members. Kassie was fond of Eleanor and had been instrumental in encouraging her nephew Franklin to propose to Eleanor in November 1903, on the banks of the Nashua River at Groton. Ten years later Kassie and her children agreed with other members of society who raised eyebrows when Franklin publicly favored Lucy Mercer at Washington's grand parties. In the previous decade, Franklin had behaved reasonably well as a family man. He had derived keen pleasure from the arrival of each of his "chicks," though he invested too little time in their upbringing. His youngest child, John Aspinwall Roosevelt, was born on March 13, 1916. Sadly, FDR was fast approaching the unromantic stage of a marriage when a man's children occupy a larger part of his heart than his wife can claim.

On January 29, 1916, Sara wrote her "darling Son," "I am thinking of you on this, the eve of your thirty-fourth birthday, with love and pride and my prayer is constant that you will always have the strength to stand by the right in all things. I know you will, and have continued happiness with your perfectly lovely Eleanor and children." But from 1916 on Sara's letters to Franklin reflected a growing concern about his lack of commitment as a husband and father. It appeared that getting married at barely twenty-three had its risks. FDR had not lived out the urges of bachelor life. He had not had his fill of the turbulent parties that Eleanor detested, and he had not been ready to settle down to the home life that had made his parents contented and happy.

At first Sara did not criticize her son directly. But she obviously had Franklin in mind when she held up as a bad example his Oyster Bay cousin Theodore Robinson, married to Helen Roosevelt Robinson. Sara shuddered at the fashionable pre-World War I trend toward what was later called in the rebellious 1960s "an open marriage." In an indignant letter to Franklin from Hyde Park, she wrote, "Teddy has gone to Hillbrook this afternoon to see 'his best girl' Louise Blagden, all very silly and not a dignified joke for married people and heads of young families. Do you think I am too old-fashioned? I think people go too far now with that sort of joke, and also that very deep love does not permit of it. This tirade is for you alone dear and to be destroyed."

In the opening volleys of Sara's protest against Franklin's unconventional behavior, the term "old-fashioned" played a central role. Sara felt she had to deal with trends of the time rather than with shortcomings in her son's character. She never wavered in supporting the strict ethical values of FDR's father James and his grandfather Warren Delano. Sara was firm in her belief in "the true, the good, and the beautiful." She never ceased to remind Franklin of his father's moral legacy: "Be a good man."

In the summer of 1916, Lucy Mercer appeared for the first time as the catalyst of marital unpleasantness between Franklin and his wife. Eleanor had just settled again on Campobello with the children when she received a letter from Lucy. Apart from trivia about house-keeping problems that cropped up after the departure of the lady of the house, Lucy told Eleanor that she had been invited by FDR to be one of the guests aboard his official yacht, the *Sylph*.

Eleanor was less disturbed by the invitation than by the vision of Franklin and Lucy handling chores together at home. She wrote Franklin on July 23, 1916, full of anger at herself and at FDR for the ineffective handling of business left behind. "Your letter of Thursday is here and one from Miss Mercer. Why did you make her waste all that time [on my] fool notes. I tore them and [L.M.'s] up and please tear any other results of my idiocy up at once. She tells me that you are going off for Tuesday and I hope you all had a pleasant trip but I'm so glad I've been here and not on the Potomac!"

The small, handsome naval vessel at FDR's disposal was the most appreciated perk of his position in the Navy Department. Much earlier the *Sylph* had played an important role during his cousin Theodore Roosevelt's tenure as assistant secretary of the navy. Frequently combining social obligations with recreation for family and friends, FDR spent many happy days on the ship. Most of his guests were his peers, high government officials accompanied by their wives. A single young lady like Lucy Mercer was an exception aboard. Eleanor and the children also showed up infrequently. Though they were treated as the skipper's guests of honor, Eleanor was not too keen on excursions by ship. She was mainly held back by her fear of the sea combined with seasickness and did not want to "fail as a good sailor," as the Delanos described the unpleasant condition. Since the trauma of a near-fatal shipwreck when she was about three years old, she had had an aversion to open water. Eleanor spent the latter part of summer routinely on Campobello and was not around during the main yachting season. She could not get too excited about the *Sylph* and its passengers.

A year later Eleanor's attitude toward Franklin's junkets on the *Sylph* had changed. Her new frame of mind was only a minor part of more profound transformations in the Roosevelts' relationship.

WARTIME REBELLION: A SUMMER'S DREAM

By the summer of 1917, it became apparent that Sara's plea to uphold tradition had been spoken into the wind. The First World War brought an end to lingering Victorian conventions. In succeeding generations of the Roosevelt family, their tolerance of formerly unthinkable libertine attitudes reflected general trends in American society. Franklin abandoned some of the strict moral principles of his parents, but his own children moved even more radically away from his and Eleanor's puritan standards of behavior. The generation gap was especially pronounced in situations where the sanctity of marriage was disregarded and a new, more casual view of divorce and remarriage became acceptable.

War had come in two stages to America—first in diplomatic reaction to Europe's conflicts in 1914, then when the United States joined the hostilities on the side of the Allies in 1917. From the very beginning, FDR had been as impatient as his British friends to move right on to Berlin. His family reacted more slowly. In the summer of 1913, FDR's mother stated with conviction, "I think war would be not only wicked but unnecessary." Two years later Sara called the war "the greatest calamity of our age or of many ages, and it seems too dreadful to be true."

Sara changed her mind when President Wilson asked Congress for a declaration of war on April 16, 1917. She now wholeheartedly joined her son's enthusiasm for the Allied cause. In her personal life, however, she was not as ready to change her perspective as in matters of foreign policy. Sara was upset by the prospect that half a century of stability in moral values, enjoyed since the Civil War, should now come to an end.

Sara observed the effect of new tendencies in family relations in her own immediate family. All the issues that separated Franklin and Eleanor were brought into sharper focus by the outbreak of war. People were less gentle with each other at a time when individual concerns became secondary. Uncertainty about the future called former agreements into question. Franklin no longer hesitated to put more distance between Eleanor and himself. He gave in to his urge to see as much of Lucy as he could, while paying lip service to what was expected of him as a husband and father.

Powerful obstacles prevented Franklin from going overboard with the liberties he took. He was committed to strengthening the navy's role in winning the war. His patriotic passion surpassed all passions of the heart. Burdened with a heavier workload than ever before, Franklin had less time for pursuits of leisure. When balls and parties faded away as a result of wartime austerity, the number of places where he could see Lucy diminished considerably.

Before long Franklin found other ways to enjoy Lucy's company. In early summer he asked both Eleanor and Lucy to be his guests on the *Sylph*. According to the records of Jonathan Daniels, Eleanor accepted only part of the invitation. On June 16, 1917, she joined the party on the yacht briefly on its way from the Washington Navy Yard to Stafford Cliffs, Maryland. It is not known why she left early to return home. The small group of guests who stayed aboard consisted of two marine officers, a married couple well known to Eleanor, and two equally familiar single people—Nigel Law and Lucy Mercer.

Unforeseen events had created a new situation by the middle of the following month, when FDR invited Lucy on a second cruise. By the time the *Sylph* sailed on July 20, Lucy had been released from her employment as Eleanor's social secretary. Her services were no longer needed after the war had brought social life in the capital to a standstill. Yet even now Miss Mercer's services had been too valuable for Eleanor to let her go altogether. Relieved from the routine of paying formal calls, of extending and receiving invitations, Eleanor stepped up her efforts to aid soldiers in her capacity as a member of the Navy League's Comforts Committee. The same ladies who had excelled as hostesses on the merry-go-round of dinner parties now put their energies into producing sweaters and other "woolies," as the wool garments for the men in uniform were called. Miss Mercer was not only recruited to be a member of the growing army of knitting women; she was especially in demand for her managerial skills as an efficient collector and distributor of the donated woolens. Most important, Eleanor could rely on Lucy as her deputy in charge whenever she had to be away.

Lucy, however, wanted to be involved more directly in the war effort. Possibly it was FDR himself who suggested a step that would be both patriotic and pleasant for him personally. In any case, on June

24—just a few days after her trip on the *Sylph*—Lucy enlisted in the navy as a female yeoman. Assigned to secretarial work in the Navy Department, she changed from having Mrs. Franklin Roosevelt as her boss to having Mr. Franklin Roosevelt as her superior.

No other move could have better served FDR's craving for Lucy's presence. He and Lucy now worked together under the same roof. With one swoop of a magic wand, two major walls of separation between them had been torn down: the lack of time and lack of a place to meet. Of course there were still formidable obstacles to their closeness. Franklin and Lucy obviously worked in different rooms. They knew only too well that office walls have more eyes and ears than ordinary walls. But they were better protected from gossip in a place where seeing each other was part of an ordinary working day, than they were in a ballroom where the lorgnettes of critical dowagers would focus on every one of their moves.

*   *   *

By the time Franklin invited Lucy to the cruise on the *Sylph* leaving on July 20, he had come to know her more closely than ever before. He had seen more of her in the three preceding weeks than in the almost four years of her past employment by his wife. He seems to have liked Lucy even better in uniform than in ball gowns. Possibly feeling guilty about his infatuation, Franklin sent an especially detailed report of the trip on the yacht to Eleanor. She had left for Campobello just a few days before the *Sylph*'s departure, exhausted by one of her admirably executed logistical operations—maneuvering five children and a large staff through a complicated network of transportation on the way to her summer home.

Reporting promptly to Eleanor on July 25, FDR called his extended weekend on the water "a joy and a real rest, though I got in a most satisfactory visit to the fleet. Such a funny party, but it worked out wonderfully." Eleanor needed no introduction to the two couples that accompanied Franklin aboard the yacht, the Munns and the Graysons. Eleanor's wartime work as a volunteer had brought her close to Mary Munn (née Mary Astor Paul), the wife of a naval reserve officer and Harvard man, Charles A. Munn. The other prominent lady on the *Sylph*, Altrude Gordon Grayson, had only recently become the wife of surgeon Cary T. Grayson. He would rise fast to the rank of medical director of the navy and serve as personal physician to President Woodrow Wilson, and would eventually be appointed head of the Red Cross by President Franklin Roosevelt.

Nobody could foresee in 1917 that the assistant secretary's familiarity with a leader of the Red Cross would have a sequel in 1941, affecting again a hidden corner of his personal life. Dr. Cary Grayson, FDR and Lucy Mercer's friend on the *Sylph*'s travels, died in 1938. By 1941 it was easy for Franklin as the president to invite Dr. Grayson's successor for a get-together with Lucy's daughter Barbara Rutherfurd. At this time FDR's self-appointed "Goddaughter" Barbara was soldiering on as a humble worker in the lowest ranks of the Red Cross. The twenty-year-old girl would be thrilled to meet the top executive of the organization she served.

At the height of summer in 1917, the Graysons and Munns would appear regularly as supporting members of the cast, defining the brief drama of FDR's greatest closeness to Lucy. Together with Nigel Law, the second single member of the cruising party, Lucy "got on splendidly" with the two married couples aboard. FDR was delighted with his choice of guests. Nigel Law was equally pleased with the composition of the party. In a long handwritten report for his own records, he mentioned Lucy without further comment as an integral part of the *Sylph*'s adventures in July 1917.

The assumption of Roosevelt biographers that Nigel Law was invited on the *Sylph* as a cover-up for FDR's pursuit of Lucy is hard to substantiate. A close look at the circumstances conveys a different picture. The narrow confines of the yacht did not lend themselves to romantic scenes, displays of affection, or clandestine rendezvous. There were too many people around at all times, with the crew and guests in every corner. The Graysons and Munns knew just as well as Eleanor that Franklin could not approach Lucy aboard ship in any inappropriate way; neither did they assume that Nigel and Lucy were invited as a couple. Both young people were interesting personalities in their own right. Widely appreciated as entertaining conversationalists, they added spice to any social get-together. Only in hindsight did it became clear how much it meant to Franklin just to see Lucy nearby every day, watch her smile, and learn about her ties to the historical figures and places on his itinerary.

As the *Sylph*'s skipper, Franklin fulfilled quickly the official obligations of the trip—an encounter with the USS *Arkansas* and Admiral Tommy Rodgers. From then on the yacht followed an unusual route. FDR's choice of stopovers on the James River reflected his fascination with Lucy's family history.

Franklin justified his out-of-the way sightseeing with his predilection for historic homes. He explained to Eleanor, "Those old houses are really wonderful, but *not* comfy!" Very soon, however, the main reason of their attraction for FDR would become obvious. After the yacht briefly visited Upper Brandon and Lower Brandon plantations, Westover emerged as the most important destination of the trip. The estate near the residence of George Washington had played a prominent role in the past of Lucy's family. Lucy Page Mercer's first name was linked to other remarkable ladies named Lucy in a historic family, whose famous seat was located in the part of the James River that the *Sylph* was swiftly approaching.

Lucy Parke had been the first wife of William Byrd II of Westover (1674–1744), the best-known planter among his peers and prestigious owner of Westover plantation. The brick mansion he built at Westover housed his library of four thousand volumes and is considered one of the finest surviving examples of Georgian architecture. He was a member of the Governor's Council, elected to the House of Burgesses, and served as its representative in London. Byrd helped survey the boundary between Virginia and North Carolina and established the town of Richmond. A prolific writer, he is remembered for his diaries and narratives of his surveying trips. Evelyn Byrd, one of Lucy Parke and William Byrd's two daughters, became a legend as a celebrated beauty, shining in Lucy Mercer's family lore. When Evelyn was introduced in London to William Pitt, at the time Lord Chatham, Pitt exclaimed that he no longer wondered "why young gentlemen were so fond of going to Virginia to study ornithology, since such beautiful *Byrds* were there."

For a bird lover like FDR, such a historical pun had a special charm. But his guest aboard the *Sylph,* Lucy Page Mercer, could treat him to yet another story that linked her to Westover—in the part of the James River they were fast approaching. William Byrd II had a second wife, Maria Taylor. They had a daughter Jane, who married

John Page in 1746. Their eleventh child was also named Lucy. This first Lucy Page, born in 1775, would marry Francis Nelson, the fourth son of Governor Thomas Nelson. A descendant of the famous Virginia planter clan, he had attracted the Roosevelts' attention as an outspoken admirer of FDR's cousin Theodore at the time of his presidency.

FDR relished the challenge of telling the lore of the Byrds, Pages, and Nelsons as he was exploring their former territory on stopovers of the *Sylph*. With Lucy Page Mercer at his side, a perfect interpreter of times long past, Franklin became deeply involved in the history of his surroundings. As a deliberate choice, he decided to make the discovery of the famous Westover mansion a highlight of the trip.

Franklin's visit to the renowned place is mentioned in many history books—not because of its links to Lucy Mercer, but because of the amusing rebuke of a high-ranking Yankee government official by a representative of the Old South. Nigel Law himself gave the details of FDR's often-recorded difficult approach to Westover.

> *Franklin and I & some of his party landed at the bottom of the garden & rang the bell. A darkie servant came out & he was told to say that the Under Secretary of the U.S. Navy would be glad to be allowed to visit the house & garden. The servant looked doubtful & soon came back with a curt "no." For a moment we were nonplussed for we particularly wanted to visit this famous old place. Then Franklin had an idea. He said to me, "Maybe they don't like Yankees in these parts. You send in your card." So as a joke I told the man to take my card in which I was described as 3rd Secretary of His Britannic Majesty's Embassy.*

Nigel crossed out the word *our* in the next sentence in favor of *my*.

> *To my surprise he came running back to say "the Master wants you all to come right in." Franklin was much tickled by this Southern rebuff of Federal authority & kept laughing over it all afternoon.*

The incident showed that some of Lucy's peers, descendants of the pre-Civil War elite, had kept their Southern pride intact against their old Yankee foes, in spite of defeat and humiliation.

The memorable journey to Westover cast a glow over the following weeks and Lucy moved into center stage with Franklin. After a brief visit with her husband, Eleanor had left Washington to return to Campobello. Four days later, on August 19, Franklin invited Lucy again. The excursion would take them to the vicinity of historic Harpers Ferry, a scenic place of Civil War fame. This time Nigel Law was not included in the trip. FDR traveled by land instead of water. For a change Lucy appeared as a sole single lady, in addition to just one married couple (the Graysons) serving as chaperones. As usual, Franklin sent an exact account to Eleanor, informing her, "I had a very occupied Sunday, starting off for golf at 9 with McIlhenny, Legare and McCauley, quick lunch at Chevy Chase and off in a car at 2:30 to the Horsey's place near Harper's Ferry. Lucy Mercer went and the Graysons." After walking over the rich farmland and staying for supper with his acquaintances, FDR's party "got home at midnight! The day was magnificent."

*   *   *

These lines—singling out one glorious, refreshing summer Sunday in 1917—were FDR's last written report to his wife about weekends with friends. It is not known how often Lucy Mercer was included in outings when he and Nigel Law simply lunched, dined, or picnicked together, walking in the Virginia woods and swimming or canoeing on the Potomac. Law stressed that "neither of us could take much time off from our duties."

FDR was indeed never distracted from his mission to get the navy ready for war. His longing for Lucy's company took second place on his agenda. Torn between conflicting notions of right and wrong, Franklin sent mixed signals to Eleanor. He knew in his heart that he slighted his wife when he allowed Lucy Mercer a major role in his thoughts and leisure activities. At the same time, he rationalized Lucy's presence on his cruises as perfectly acceptable as long as other guests were around. He was less honest when he routinely professed to be lonely, missing Eleanor terribly.

Soon enough, in an apparently transparent effort to dampen his feelings of guilt, Franklin found fault with the person he wronged. When his dutiful wife left reluctantly for Campobello in July, FDR wrote her on the sixteenth of the month that he had passed "a vile day" by himself. Allegedly, he was not even able to play his customary game of solitaire to relax "as usual" after a hard day at the office. He lunched with Commander Bernard Aubin de Blanpré of the French embassy, then dined with his cousin Warren Delano Robbins. Both Warren (a budding diplomat) and his wife, the former Irène de Bruyn, were fond friends of Eleanor.

In the confusion of his feelings about his wife, Franklin was prompted to change from defense of his emotional betrayal of Eleanor to offense, finding fault with a wife whose behavior was beyond reproach. He started out his new mode of attack from a meek position, writing:

> *I really can't stand that house all alone without you,*
> *and you were a goosy girl to think or even pretend to*
> *think that I don't want you here all the summer, because*
> *you know I do! But honestly you ought to have six weeks*
> *straight at Campo, just as I ought to, only you can and I*
> *can't! I know what a whole summer here does to*
> *people's nerves and at the end of this summer I will be*
> *like a bear with a sore head until I get a change or some*
> *cold weather—in fact you know I am unreasonable and*
> *touchy now—but I shall try to improve.*

If Eleanor had reason to miss the tenderness she craved in her husband's letters, she certainly could not complain about receiving too few of them. Even when tension between the spouses mounted, Franklin wrote Eleanor practically every day. But Eleanor did not excuse the poor quality of FDR's letters because they appeared in large numbers. "I don't think you read my letters for you never answer a question and nothing I ask for appears," Eleanor complained. But Franklin certainly failed to be consistent in his efforts to improve his ways. On July 17 he told Eleanor what she wanted to hear. "It seems years since you left and I miss you horribly and hate the thought of the empty house." Yet on the following day, July 18, Eleanor got a taste of Franklin turning against her in his innermost thoughts.

In February 1917 Eleanor had signed a pledge, written by the Patriotic Economy League, to dress simply and cut expenses on food. Mrs. Edith Morton Eustis, the founder of the league, had been an old friend of Franklin since his childhood days on the Hudson River. She would eventually become a good friend of Eleanor too, and act as Lucy's saving angel in 1919. Eleanor had made every possible effort to show Edith Eustis how seriously she took the league's demands. To serve as a model of patriotic conduct, Eleanor had agreed to be interviewed for the *New York Times* before she left for Campobello. She would explain how to run a household frugally in times of austerity.

Franklin was understandably upset when he read the reporter's article, published under the title "How to Save in Big Homes." The *Times* had given the story a tongue-in-cheek twist, sure to arouse wide attention in Washington society. "Making the ten servants help me do my saving has not only been possible, but highly profitable," Mrs. Franklin D. Roosevelt was quoted as saying. Cornbread was served regularly, meat only once a day; bacon never appeared on the table. The laundress used soap sparingly and everybody was encouraged to eat leftovers.

The Roosevelts' son Elliott, many years later and much indebted to his widowed mother for appointing him the editor of his father's personal letters, tried to repair the damage done by the *Times* article. He interpreted FDR's reaction to the story as "jesting." Actually, FDR vented cold fury when he wrote Eleanor on July 18 without benefit of a greeting or his usual salutation, "Dearest Babs." He fumed:

> *All I can say is that your latest newspaper campaign is a corker and I am proud to be the husband of the Originator, Discoverer and Inventor of the New Household Economy for Millionaires! Please have a photo taken showing the family, the ten cooperating servants, the scraps saved from the table and the handbook. I will have it published in the* Sunday Times. *Honestly you have leaped into public fame, all Washington is talking of the Roosevelt Plan, and I begin to get telegrams of con-*

*gratulations and requests for further details from Pitts-
burgh, New Orleans, San Francisco and other neighboring cities.*

Franklin's sharp reaction was not called for. Instead of comforting his wife, he was apparently prompted by his compromised conscience to chastise her with a sarcasm that hurt. The thin-skinned Eleanor took the criticism hard. She replied, "I feel dreadfully about it because so much is not true and yet some of it I did say. I will never be caught again that's sure and I'd like to crawl away for shame."

Making good on her vow, Eleanor would become a master in the art of watching over her image in the public eye. Twenty years later, under the tutelage of the experienced journalist Lorena Hickok, Eleanor learned to shape the public's view of the First Lady with great skill. By 1935 Eleanor looked back with more misgivings than pity on her deplorable situation in 1917. Nobody was harder on the young Eleanor than the mature Eleanor. She was certainly neither a little "fool" nor an "idiot," as she did not hesitate to call herself in her self-disparaging way. Only thirty-three years old in 1917, tied down by five young children, Eleanor was drifting in currents of gossip she could not control. Washington was indeed talking, but less about her housekeeping than about her marriage.

*   *   *

Franklin's uncle Frederic Adrian Delano understood her plight but even he was nonplussed. Uncle Fred had expressed his admiration for Eleanor many times. His opinion counted. He had authority, enjoying high respect as the newly appointed vice governor of the Federal Reserve Board. Fred even did his best to calm the waves of family criticism about Eleanor's ill-fated *New York Times* interview. Franklin quoted him as saying, "It's fine, but Gee how mad Eleanor will be!" Franklin's mother was just as angry. Sara had learned every detail of Eleanor's public relations flop from her brother Fred. Together with his wife Tilly and their daughter Louise, Fred kept Sara up to date about the unsteady course of her son's personal affairs.

Sara knew that Washington's oppressive summer weather routinely took its toll on her son's health. She had rushed to Franklin's side when he was sick in 1916, but in August 1917 Eleanor was not to be upstaged by her mother-in-law again. She did not shy away from the stiflingly hot journey from Campobello to Washington. It was important to her to tend to her husband herself, after he had been in the hospital for four days with a new throat infection.

Sara, meanwhile, slept in Eleanor's bed on Campobello so that she could watch over the children. Writing Franklin, she emphasized Eleanor's qualities as a model wife. "You certainly were unlucky to get that horrid illness, but I think most fortunate to have the most lovely person to rush to you as she did and stay." Franklin, however, had somebody other than Eleanor in mind to connect with the words "most lovely."

Three days earlier, on August 13, 1917, Sara wrote Franklin, "I know you will be feeling pretty lonely, as Eleanor will have left, and I feel very selfish in my impatience to see her." Eleanor's sudden appearance in Washington was bound to bring the turmoil in Franklin's conscience to a boiling point. When FDR did not express pleasure at her presence, Eleanor responded in kind to his lack of graciousness. She decided that it was high time to remind Franklin of his duties as a husband and father. She had to return to the children; it was Franklin's turn to travel to her, and soon.

Disappointed and angry, Eleanor issued an ultimatum to her husband, demanding his speedy arrival at Campobello. She meant it, she stressed in a sharp note to FDR after her departure on August 15. Her opening sentence, "I hated to leave you yesterday," had more than one meaning. As usual, Eleanor did not take her husband's ailments as seriously as he would have liked. "Please go to the doctor twice a week," she prescribed. "Eat well and sleep well, and remember I *count* on seeing you on the 26th. My threat was not an idle one."

After twelve years of marriage, Eleanor should have known better than to issue ultimatums to her husband. Franklin Delano Roosevelt was never going to be threatened by anybody—not by his wife, his mother, or later European dictators. Sara had learned this lesson when her son was a teenager at Groton. His father James had warned him that he would withhold the money for travel if Franklin insisted on spending a holiday with his Oyster Bay relatives rather than his parents. Franklin had only thirty-five cents to his name but coolly informed his parents that he would borrow the needed money from his Aunt Annie.

Sara knew ways superior to threats in order to get Franklin to Campobello. She pulled at his heartstrings where it hurt. Reprimanding Franklin for failing to give his oldest son enough of his time, she demanded that he spend "some time with dear little James. . . . He will never forget what you do for him now."

Besides, Sara stressed that FDR could not disappoint his children because they were rehearsing a play for him to celebrate his return to the family. Sara described the scene at Campobello. "James just came in and says 'Father knows nothing about the play, it is a surprise for him,' so please forget what I have written! I am counting the days until you get here and I hope you are to be here on the 24th and stay till a week from Saturday Sept. 2nd." Sara ended her message with another well-aimed arrow at Franklin's soft spot for his "chicks." "The three send love, and Anna says, 'It is dreadful not to see one's father for so long, isn't it!' "

Sara's strategy worked: Anna's father did show up promptly on the island. But when FDR left after less than a week, he was more inclined than ever to keep his distance from his wife. A summer of delight at being near Lucy Mercer had brought about a profound change in Franklin's heart.

SOBERING AUTUMN: PART I

Ordinarily, the Roosevelt family moved in predictable patterns by September, once Eleanor was back in town with the children. In the fall of 1917, the routine was broken and the family members' lives were turned upside down. After more than half a year away from home, the children didn't go back to Washington until November. Sara wrote in an undated letter from Fairhaven, "In one way I am rather glad I can't have the family at H.P. for now, as I think the children are very restless and never feel quite settled anywhere." Since May they had spent more time under their grandmother's roof at Hyde Park than under their mother's care in Washington and at Campobello; now they had to adjust to completely new surroundings.

Eleanor had shouldered most of the burden of the family's move from Auntie Bye's comfortable but small home on N Street to a more spacious residence at 2131 R Street.

Eleanor would spend less and less time in her new home. She knew her children were happy at Hyde Park. She still had to visit them regularly, even though switching to a new form of wartime volunteer work in Red Cross canteens proved to be extremely time consuming. By comparison, her past efforts for the Navy League's Comforts Committee appeared downright leisurely.

Initially against her own inclinations, Eleanor loyally sided with her husband in a conflict between two of Washington's political powers. Franklin had wisely kept a low profile in a row between his boss—the secretary of the navy—and the arrogant but influential Colonel Robert M. Thompson, the head of the Navy League. Both men were uncompromising and suggested that the other resign. The straitlaced Daniels, always suspicious of wartime profiteering, was wary of the steel magnates' and shipbuilders' influence on the colonel's powerful organization. Thompson could point to the league's spectacular success, especially in the collection of woolen garments for sailors through its popular Comforts Committee.

When Secretary Daniels undercut the Navy League by barring it from all ships and naval stations, both Eleanor Roosevelt and Lucy Mercer felt the consequences. Lucy and Franklin, at work in the capital, could appraise the situation realistically. It was more difficult for Eleanor, cut off from the Washington scene, to recognize that her husband had to demonstrate solidarity with Secretary Daniels. FDR had all the more reason to detach himself from the Navy League after Colonel Thompson tried to make him dependent on him as a personal friend. But eventually Eleanor was able to have it both ways. While she was devoting all her energies to her work in a Red Cross canteen, her efficient co-worker Miss Mercer upheld her cherished ties to the Comforts Committee.

Lucy might have been too trusting when she assumed that she could remain unfazed by the rivalries of the bigwigs, Daniels and Thompson. She rarely thought of herself, and would have been glad to do her former employer a favor by operating as Mrs. Roosevelt's delegate in the Comforts Committee's endangered "woolies" business. She did not want any remuneration for her sporadic work. In hindsight, Lucy's willingness to take Eleanor's side could be construed as an act of contrition—an attempt to atone for seeing too much of Franklin the past summer. It could also be explained simply by Lucy's fondness for Eleanor and her gratitude for her employer's goodness. In any case, irritations appearing in the correspondence between Franklin, Eleanor, and Lucy in the late summer of 1917 are not as personal as has been alleged. The travels of a check, twice bouncing back and forth between Eleanor and Lucy, are not at all surprising; they were dictated by adherence to the maxim *noblesse oblige* on both sides. The episode is revealing, however, in the tone of the notes accompanying the check as it meandered through the mail. It shows clearly how Eleanor and Lucy felt for each other.

Lucy first returned the check from Eleanor with words that combined high respect and fond camaraderie. "My dear Mrs. Roosevelt," Lucy began, very formally. Then she frankly acknowledged her subservient status. "Of course you are the mistress of the situation and I must abide by your wishes!" The tenor of the letter gets more personal as Lucy goes on. At the end Lucy's sign-off, "Affectionately," seems perfectly natural, expressing a lighthearted complicity with the lady she admired.

"I must return the cheque for subtraction," Lucy declared with regret, "and give you more trouble as the two last wolley [sic] parties were not held—according to the Assistant Secretary's instructions—and on the 21st of July I was not there! . . . I went for a little while last Saturday to answer questions and list what came in—and to tell the dear ladies the distribution would in all probability be resumed. Poor dears, they are so distressed!"

Lucy was in full accord with Eleanor's initial rejection of her husband's instruction to abandon the League's Comforts Committee. She agreed with Eleanor that "Mr. D[aniels] has made a mistake to refuse all garments" from the Comforts Committee, because "people will be discouraged and the volume of work will take forever to pick up if it does at all." Eleanor appreciated Miss Mercer's upholding of the Comforts Committee's merits. On September 8 she explained that Miss Mercer "had done far more work than I could pay for. She is evidently quite cross with me." Eleanor worried about having hurt the feelings of Lucy, her indispensable aide.

Actually, it was Franklin who was really cross. "*You* are entirely dis-connected," he shot back, chiding Eleanor for her lack of sensitivity in making Lucy feel inferior. He countered that Lucy Mercer and Mrs. Charles A. Munn—good friends from trips on the *Sylph*—were doing a constructive job by "closing up the loose ends," instead of fretting about the fallout of the controversy.

Finally, on September 11 Franklin drew a line under the contro-versy. He told Eleanor that "Daniels has chucked the Comforts Com-mittee entirely and is trying to organize a rival set under the Red Cross." In the end Franklin was highly gratified when Eleanor be-came the model of a committed, selfless worker in Mr. and Mrs. Daniels's Red Cross canteens. It was all for the better that Eleanor could also hold on to her ties with the old knitters' circle, because Lucy Mercer stood in for her.

*   *   *

Early fall brought a long delay in the Roosevelts' return to their yearly routine. It significantly postponed the reunion of the family in Wash-ington. The change suited Franklin perfectly. Eleanor's lengthy ab-sence from home allowed him to seek Lucy's presence in his time off, as well as in the office. Ladies of his circle aimed to please him by including Lucy in their dinner parties. Franklin's cousin Joseph Alsop mentioned not only invitations by Alice Roosevelt Longworth to her home, but Edith Eustis welcoming Franklin and Lucy on visits at her Oaklands estate. Besides, the last warm days of the year offered an opportunity for Franklin and Lucy to take brief drives in the country together. On such drives Franklin and Lucy could enjoy the highest degree of privacy ever afforded to them—both now in the First World War, and again in the last stage of their friendship during the Second World War.

James Roosevelt, the oldest son of Franklin and Eleanor, had the fall of 1917 in mind when he first mentioned a supposedly adulter-ous excursion of his father with Lucy. This episode, created in James's imagination, would be promoted by later writers looking for tangible proof of sexual intimacy between Franklin and Lucy. In his book *My Parents: A Differing View*, James himself called the incident the only hard evidence for his theory that his father and Lucy were lovers also in a physical way. He told about a "rather well-kept secret" that "there came to light during this time a register from a motel in Virginia Beach showing that father and Lucy had checked in as man and wife and spent the night."

The story seemed authentic enough, presented by FDR's and Eleanor's oldest boy in a serious biography. Few readers realized that the credibility of books about the Roosevelts by FDR's sons James and Elliott was impaired by the way they were conceived. Neither of the brothers was an experienced author. Both left the major part of their writing to their co-authors (Bill Libby and James Brough, respectively), savvy writers who knew how to construct a book that would be well received by publishers and readers. Moreover, they were not overly concerned about the reliability of their sources. A careful reading of their texts shows that they used information from previously written books about their subject, yet were not familiar enough with the facts to recognize errors of previous authors. Libby and Brough did not worry about such details. They were satisfied with the commercial success of the Roosevelt books. The allure of James and Elliott Roosevelt's personal memories and impressions, of their anecdotes and pieces of family lore, were not affected by the manuscripts' flaws. James and Elliot needed the royalties from the sales of the books and did not mind the liberties their co-authors took. For both of them, financial stress had reached a peak in the 1970s when multiple ex-wives demanded alimony payments.

Whether it was James Roosevelt or his co-author Bill Libby who boosted interest in their jointly written book with the legend of FDR's one-night stand with Lucy in a motel, it did not remain unchallenged for long. Montague Blundon, the husband of Lucy's niece Lucy Mercer Marbury, was greatly annoyed when he read the rumors about FDR and his relative spread under the name of James Roosevelt. Mr. Blundon went to great trouble to prove in a thorough investigation that the tryst could not have happened. The result of his detective work was convincing. His study of old road maps from World War I showed that long winding roads and a lack of gas stations made a trip from Washington to Virginia Beach in the given time impossible.

By 1930, when Jimmy Roosevelt entered the three turbulent decades that were marked by his four marriages, checking into a motel had become routine in illicit affairs. In his experience a motel was the most likely place where his father could have taken Lucy for intimate hours. He could not visualize how much had changed since 1917, when he was ten years old. The practical and ethical obstacles that prevented intimate get-togethers of friends like Lucy and Franklin were no longer insurmountable in the next generation.

Franklin and Lucy had virtually nowhere to go if they wanted to be alone. Their own homes, or friends' homes, were obviously out of the question. Lucy's mother watched over her daughter's virginity with eagle eyes. Besides, fear of pregnancy was a powerful motive in the time before easily accessible birth control. FDR's tight schedule left no time for dallying on the side. Except for frequent trips on military duty, he did not travel. If any leisure time was left, it was routinely spent in clubs.

Above all, however, Franklin and Lucy's high moral principles stood in the way of adulterous behavior. Lucy's standards had been shaped in two convent schools. She admired Eleanor too much to hurt her. She was bound to hold Franklin back rather than encourage any advances. Polly Delano, quoted by James Roosevelt, also vouched for Franklin's integrity. She told her cousin James, "I'm sure your father would never have wanted to make your mother suffer."

As the fall of 1917 came to an end, even occasions when Franklin and Lucy could meet with others present were severely curtailed. The relative ease of living in July and August was swept away by the brisk winds of October. The doubling and tripling of work caused by stepped-up war activities absorbed all of Franklin's free time. "I am inexpressibly busy," FDR summed up the burdens of that period. Eleanor stressed that during the war "the men in the government worked from morning until night & late into the night." FDR had to curtail his golfing hours and his luncheons at the Chevy Chase and other men's clubs. His company at golf, at lunches and dinners, had changed from Nigel Law to "Livvy." Livingston Davis, an old friend from Harvard and his new special assistant in the Navy Department, was now his buddy who kept him away from regular family meals at home.

*   *   *

During the same months, Lucy's placid life was upset by a series of hard blows. The death of her father Carroll Mercer on September 13 brought back more painful memories than pleasant recollections. In the previous few years, since her return from Austria, Lucy's loyalties had been monopolized by her mother. Minnie Mercer's hostility to her disappointing husband surfaced when she decided not to attend his funeral; her hard stance prevented Lucy too from appearing at his graveside. Her sister Vio, an army nurse who might have stood up more forcefully against their strong-willed mother, was far away on the front. The sisters had been more forgiving than their mother of their father's weakness and had maintained a loose contact with Carroll in the gradual unraveling of his last years. Lucy and Vio had tried to be good daughters to both their mother and father, but fate had cast Lucy on her mother's side.

Even though Minna had taken the initiative of separating from her husband, she still expected to profit from being Mrs. Carroll Mercer. She had retained much of her old attractiveness and had a large circle of acquaintances, but she never divorced Carroll and did not remarry. Minna was determined to be cautious, mindful of the disastrous financial consequences suffered by her own mother after Caroline decided to marry a second time.

When Carroll Mercer's last will and testament was read, it turned out—to his widow's chagrin—that it was his second will. Minna had been the sole beneficiary of the first one, signed on June 6, 1893. At this time she was still rich and happy, the mother of four-year-old Vio and two-year-old Lucy. Thirteen years later Carroll's bitterness toward his wife was reflected in his new will, in which he left "all to my children . . . [p]articularly [the] legacy in remainder bequeathed to me by my lamented Grandmother Sally S. Carroll."

Minna was not even mentioned in her husband's second will, dated June 20, 1906. The date coincided with the de facto breakup of the Mercers' marriage. Evidently, Carroll had nothing to hand down from the Mercers on his father's side. He mentioned only what he received from his mother's mother, the Sally Sprigg Carroll who had raised him. As a boy, Carroll had been awed by his rich grandmother. She could afford a double set of servants, one for the day and one for the night. Following the pattern of her time, the old Mrs. Carroll may have tried to safeguard the future of her two little grandsons by establishing a trust for them. They were, after all, the sons she never had—being the mother of four daughters. Apparently, his grand-mother's legacy provided Carroll with the bare necessities after his wife cut him off. Minna, always in hot pursuit of every penny that could be hers, was incensed in 1917 to find herself disinherited by her husband. Even though she could not have lost much money to her daughters, she was annoyed on principle.

Surprisingly, just one month after Carroll died, it was Minna rather than her husband's heirs who received a small fortune. She inherited one thousand pounds sterling, the equivalent of forty-one thousand British pounds today. Minna had fought for the money from her deceased husband's estate in an aggressive legal action. She knew that Carroll Mercer had received it from Sallie, Countess Esterhazy, one of her grandmother's four daughters. Sallie Carroll Esterhazy lived to the age of seventy-two in London. Until the end of her life, she was fondly attached to her nephew Carroll Mercer. He had once been like a little brother to her at Carroll House on 18th and F Streets in Washington. It is hard to believe that the countess's glad initial acceptance of Carroll's bride Minnie Tunis withstood the couple's later estrangement.

Vio and Lucy Mercer, the rightful heirs of their grandaunt Sallie Esterhazy's legacy, were not cut out to engage a lawyer to secure an inheritance from England. Vio served as a nurse overseas; Lucy had neither the assertive temperament nor the experience with lawyers needed for a legal fight. Her mother, on the other hand, had a surplus of both. After Henry E. Davis, a lawyer friend and fellow Washington "cave dweller," succeeded in fetching the Esterhazy bounty for her, Minna tried to hire lawyers in London to squeeze even more money out of Aunt Sallie's estate. Hardened by her youthful skirmishes with the legal guardians of her Tunis inheritance, Minna took it in stride when the English lawyers indignantly dismissed her.

Always veiling her true financial circumstances, Minna never revealed what she did with the newly won money. She had to pay off debts, of course, but their nature and precise amounts remained vague. Her finances were entangled with those of her daughter Lucy, with whom she shared an apartment and a small interior decorating business. Minna liked to play her cards close to her vest, whether she supported Lucy or whether Lucy supported her.

Carroll Mercer's second will was decidedly an embarrassment for his widow. Cut out of his will in favor of her daughters, Minna felt more than ever that Vio and Lucy owed her something. Lucy was right at hand as the target of her mother's displeasure. Why was she still single past her mid-twenties, when she had everything going for her? With her beauty, her chaste charm, her fine education, and her practical skills, Lucy should have presented her long ago with a son-in-law fitting their social station. Minna was still listed in the Social Register and was as popular in society as her daughter. She had derived maternal pride from Lucy's career in the Navy Department. Her daughter had been quickly promoted from yeoman third class to yeoman second class, with a top rating in conduct and a qualification for reenlistment.

Minna was bound to have mixed feelings about the assistant secretary's invitations of her daughter to cruises on his official yacht. To keep a foot in the door of the marriage market, Lucy could not afford the slightest blemish on her good name. She needed all-around acknowledgment of her inborn reserve and dignity. Though Minna herself enjoyed being seen as a rebel against convention by smoking in public, she never underestimated the power of society's rules. She was too realistic to accept willingly the attention paid to her virtuous daughter by a married man.

*   *   *

In the fall of 1917, the disapproval of two strong mothers—Minnie Mercer and Sara Roosevelt—was exacerbated by yet another blow. On October 5, barely three weeks after her father's death, Lucy was unexpectedly discharged from the Navy Department "by Special Order of the Secretary of the Navy." She had served less than four months when she was discharged. In Lucy's search for a reason, two possibilities come to mind. The first was her loyal support of Mrs. Franklin Roosevelt in her skirmish with the secretary of the navy, her husband's boss. Only very recently Lucy had served as Eleanor's liaison to the Navy League's Comforts Committee, Josephus Daniels's nemesis. The second reason, an increasing awareness of Miss Mercer's attraction for Franklin, seems just as likely. The puritanical secretary was acutely allergic to what he had heard about the budding of an unwelcome romance right under his nose.

Warnings could have come not only from Miss Mercer's co-workers, but also from the mother of the assistant secretary. Mrs. James Roosevelt was used to taking troubling matters into her own hands. She was on easy speaking terms with Mr. and Mrs. Daniels, favored guests at her Hyde Park home. They shared her old-fashioned values. At the end of a summer that taxed her patience with her errant son, Sara did all she could to discourage Franklin's infatuation with a lovely young woman.

It is striking that the timing of Secretary Daniels's radical step coincided with Sara's preaching about her son's moral obligations. Returning to Hyde Park from Campobello by way of the Delano homestead in Fairhaven, Massachusetts, Sara had fired a first shot. She advised Franklin bluntly to settle down after his selfish, entertaining summer spent with friends. He was to begin autumn as a devoted family man. She told him to "have less 'junketing' and some real home life."

To make clear what she meant by "junketing," Sara mentioned Franklin's presence at Hyde Park on one of his rare weekend visits from Washington. Once again his wife and children had been waiting for Father. As the advocate of her daughter-in-law and the "chicks," Sara talked straight. Franklin hit back, telling his mother that she did not understand how times had changed. He had done no wrong by today's new moral code. Clinging to her most sacred beliefs, Sara continued the heated controversy in a letter to Franklin dated simply Sunday night. It had not been easy to hold her own when confronting her articulate son, an expert debater.

The important letter, covering twelve small pages, was addressed to "Dearest Franklin [and] Dearest Eleanor." It was actually directed only at her son. Sara's grandson Elliott Roosevelt, in editing *FDR: His Personal Letters* at Eleanor's direction, commented that "the particular issue which guided Sara Roosevelt's pen is unknown." To further veil the letter's obvious intent, Elliott took it out of chronological order and placed it in 1915, two years earlier than it was actually written and well before Lucy's acquaintance with Franklin assumed romantic overtones. Elliott's move fit with Eleanor's strategy of taking the sting out of her husband's pursuit of another woman by not talking about it. Since Franklin and Lucy also believed in burying private matters through silence, the tactic would work for decades.

Seen in its proper context, Sara's letter focused precisely on the core of Franklin's bad habits—the straying from his mother's ideal of marriage. Sara built a golden bridge for her son, inviting him to mend his ways, pointing to a generation gap that could be overcome. Sara condemned any form of friendship between a married man and a single lady, while Franklin condoned it as long as it stayed within proper limits. Sara made allowances for her still youthful son. She recognized the influence of a new age and labeled it "democratic," trying to find a formula for easygoing, folksy indulgence with a "trend to shirtsleeves." Yet in her eyes abandoning the rigidity of starched collars did not cancel the Roosevelts and Delanos' high moral obligations.

Sara distanced herself from the self-righteous snobs of her class. She explicitly wanted to see the "foolish old saying 'noblesse oblige' replaced by the maxim 'honneur oblige.' " This meant scrupulous observance of decency—not as the automatic stamp of noble birth, but as a call to combine a strict secular code of honor with the ethical commandments of her Christian creed. She demanded, "If we love our own, & if we love our neighbor, we owe a great example." Then she added humbly, "My constant feeling is that through neglect and laziness I am not doing my part to those around me."

Even if Sara fell short of living up to her own ideals, she could still uphold them for others. She was not willing "to give up the old fashioned traditions of family life, simple home pleasures & refinements." Her credo was clear. She wanted to hold on to "the traditions some of us love best . . . to *keep up* things, to hold on to dignity & all I stood up for this evening." At the core of the distressed mother's message was her wish. "Well, I hope that while I live I may keep my 'old-fashioned' theories & that *at least* in my own family I may continue to feel that home is the best & happiest place & that *my* son and daughter & their children will live in peace & happiness & keep from the tarnish which seems to affect so many."

Sara's basic trust in the goodness of her son was not shaken. Her unconditional love for her boy outdid passionate criticism, as it had done before 1917 and as it would do many times thereafter. It took only a little time to smooth ruffled feathers all around. On October 30 Sara told Franklin in a conciliatory tone, "It was a great comfort to see you looking so seeming well, much better than two weeks ago."

His family was fine, Sara told him, waiting for him. The three older children were happily at supper in Hyde Park, "the babies in the library with Eleanor."

Sara had done all she could to straighten out Franklin in a direct confrontation. It will never be known whether she also approached Secretary Daniels, the man who had the power to act. Sara constantly tried to strengthen her son's marriage in subtle ways. Her letters are filled with passages building up Eleanor in Franklin's eyes. Her most faithful allies in her campaign to please and flatter her daughter-in-law, the families of her brother Fred Delano and her sister Kassie Collier, now stepped up their moral support for Eleanor. Sara told Franklin that Irène de Bruyn, his cousin Warren Delano Robbins's Argentinian wife, "spoke to Aunt Kassie of Eleanor with such admiration and affection, she is clever enough to see how different E. is from some of her friends!"

COUSIN ALICE

Sara, however, could do little to stop a more distant relative who moved in the opposite direction. Alice Roosevelt Longworth derived a perverse pleasure from driving small wedges between Franklin and Eleanor. Sara had been patient with Alice out of deference for Theodore, Alice's father. Cousin Theodore was still Sara's idol, the role model she had held up to Franklin since his student days.

Sara's grandson Elliott Roosevelt had referred to Alice in 1913 as an important gatekeeper. "F.D.R.'s dinner with Alice and Nicholas Longworth might almost be considered part of his official introduction to his job," Elliott commented. "Theodore Roosevelt's celebrated daughter was a leading figure in Washington society from the time of her father's residence in the White House through her husband's thirteen terms in the House of Representatives."

In the long run, Alice was as destructive to FDR's advancement as she was initially helpful. She admitted later that her deliberate slighting of Franklin was rooted in clan rivalry and personal envy. She did not mention that her deeply flawed relationship with her cousin Eleanor was also shaped by simple one-upmanship. Alice was actually at the zenith of her celebrity when she tried to hurt Eleanor by hurting Franklin. She was still basking in the glow of her days as the White House princess who had kept the country intrigued with her escapades.

As the wife of Nicholas Longworth, the popular Speaker of the House, she had more influence than the wife of the assistant secretary of the navy. She was prettier than Eleanor, more sophisticated and more elegant. Alice's intelligence was not as disciplined as her cousin Eleanor's, but Alice was much wittier and flattered herself to be more fun. As first cousins, Alice and Eleanor Roosevelt were forever destined to be compared with each other. The basic difference between them was that Alice was one of those people who think the world owes them something. By contrast, Eleanor always asked herself what she could do for the world.

Alice begrudged Eleanor her few advantages over her. She used her own difficult beginnings as an excuse for attacks on her cousin. Alice regarded growing up as a half-orphan as a license for contrary behavior. The death of her sunny-tempered mother Alice Lee, two days after Alice's birth, had traumatized her father. Theodore and the child's stepmother, Edith Carow, never dared apply to Alice the strict discipline that dominated the upbringing of the five children they had together. Alice did as she pleased, whether she offended or not. Unlike Eleanor, she was not reined in by a straight-laced grandmother. Even though Eleanor resented the old Mrs. Hall's strict regime, it is clear that her grandmother saved the girl from being as spoiled as her Cousin Alice.

Being the same age as her cousin, Eleanor's virtues gave a sharp edge to Alice's competitive instincts. As a girl, she had irked her father to the point where the president declared that he could manage the country or Alice, but not both. Alice was tired of hearing Eleanor praised for her high principles and good behavior and did not like to see her singled out as her father's favorite niece. As a sharp observer of Lucy's relationship with Franklin, it was to be expected that Alice would jump at the opportunity to belittle Eleanor.

Eleanor was only nineteen when she won a charming husband. Franklin had been the man of her dreams throughout her teens. By contrast, Alice had difficulty finding a husband. She settled finally on Nicholas Longworth, a man fifteen years her senior, distinguished by his important position as Speaker of the House. Of course she could not foresee that Nick would humiliate her with his numerous affairs. Eleanor could be proud of a perfect family with five children; Alice was forty when she gave birth to her one daughter. Paulina was rumored to be the offspring of Alice's extramarital liaison with Senator William E. Borah. Alice was "just giggling" when a cousin asked her about it. Only on the eve of her daughter Paulina's wedding did Alice finally reveal that Senator Borah was her father. Both Eleanor and Alice had lost their mothers too early. But Eleanor was a perennially welcome guest at her mother-in-law's beautiful Hyde Park estate, while Alice felt unwelcome on her rare visits with Nick's antagonistic mother in Cincinnati. Susan Walker Longworth, born in 1845 into a family of Mayflower descendants, was as "formidable" as Franklin's mother. Alice transferred much of her dislike of Susan Longworth to her view of Sara Roosevelt.

Alice had been as well chaperoned as Eleanor before she was married. She had been shocked at the discovery that her husband was not willing to give up his promiscuous bachelor habits. In hurt pride Alice took advantage of her less supervised status as a married woman as an opportunity to play around. Trying to match Nick's risqué brand of humor was part of the game. He was famous for off-color jokes that moved quickly from Washington's salons to New York's parlors.

William "Fishbait" Miller, longtime doorkeeper of the House of Representatives, collected stories about Nick as "one of the freshest womanizers . . . on Capitol Hill." His favorite anecdote described a brash congressman who tried to insult the Speaker. Stroking Nick's bald pate, he marveled, "Your pretty bald pate reminds me of my wife's behind." Instead of exploding, Longworth ran his hand across his own head. Thoughtfully, he retorted, "I'll be damned if it doesn't."

Exemplifying the capital's new spirit of permissiveness, Alice aimed to be just as clever. A famous inscription on her velvet sofa cushion invited her visitors to indulge in malicious gossip; it read, "If you can't say something good about anyone, come and sit by me." Alice always needed ammunition for her main weapon, her sharp tongue. She was gratified when rumors reached her that her cousin Franklin favored a beautiful subaltern in his office. Here was an opening for attack. Alice knew Miss Mercer well as a member of Washington's high society. Lucy would allow her to get at both Eleanor and Franklin. By exposing Franklin's impropriety, she could put his righteous wife in her place. Eleanor, a thorn in her side as the antithesis of her own character traits, held up a mirror to Alice that reflected a vain, irresponsible, insatiably ambitious leader of society. She did not measure up to the dutiful Eleanor—the devoted mother of a flock of children, her husband's intelligent helpmate, a highbrow society matron, and the very model of patriotic service in wartime. Mrs. Franklin Roosevelt was about to outshine Mrs. Nicholas Longworth.

* * *

It was a comfort to Alice to hear through Washington's grapevine in 1917 that her rival was not able to keep her husband's undivided attention. From her perspective Eleanor had proved herself a humorless bore without any *savoir vivre*. Summing up her distaste, Alice spread the *bon mot* that Franklin deserved a good time because he was married to Eleanor. Nobody could tell as vividly as Alice the most widespread story that illustrated Franklin's marital frustrations. FDR's mother knew about it all along but kept quiet. Sara's informants, her nephew Warren Delano and his wife Irène, had witnessed Eleanor and Franklin's startling behavior at a party at the Chevy Chase Club.

Eleanor had demonstrated her disgust at the party's exuberance by leaving at ten. Franklin stayed on for another six hours, dancing and flirting. All Washington heard about Franklin coming home at four in the morning to find his wife stretched out on the doormat. In Alice's colorful description, Eleanor was "looking like a string bean that had been raised in a cellar." Franklin reacted with anger to his wife's explanation that she found herself without a house key but did not want to disturb the servants. He was even more upset by Eleanor's stance as a martyr who did not want to go back to the club because "I knew you were all having such a *glorious time*, and I didn't want to *spoil the fun*."

In Alice's view Franklin's quest for more sweetly tempered company was justified, but she would have preferred a racier friend for him. The coy Miss Mercer was too gentle for the Longworths' bold social circle. Lucy promised little in the way of a truly juicy story and provided no evidence of an extramarital fling. Alice explained later what she thought of Franklin and Lucy, stating, "I think their relationship was very much a lovely boy-meets-girl thing. The rose behind the ear, the whipped-off lock of hair, that kind of thing. It mattered only little." Alice had nothing but praise for Eleanor's rival. "Lucy . . . was beautiful," she raved, "charming, and an absolutely delightful creature. She was always beautifully dressed."

Alice's lack of understanding for Eleanor's sorrow was later put in sharp perspective by Franklin and Eleanor's daughter. Anna stressed in one of her many interviews with Joseph Lash how seriously her mother took the betrayal by her husband. "The Lucy Mercer thing really hurt her," Anna regretted.

Unlike Anna, Alice was intrigued by "the Lucy Mercer thing" and determined to make the most of it. First, she tried to make FDR uncomfortable by teasing him. She confronted him with the fact that he was not alone when he was seen twenty miles out in the country in his open car. "Your hands were on the wheel, but your eyes were on that perfectly lovely lady," Alice provoked the offender. But Franklin was not to be bested by his cousin Alice, who had caught her husband in much more compromising situations. Unruffled, he replied simply, "Yes, she is lovely, isn't she?" And that was it.

Franklin did not let on that Alice had hit a raw nerve. She had evoked memories of a strikingly similar situation from his youth. In 1904, before his engagement to Eleanor was announced to the public, Franklin's godmother Nelly Blodgett had told him that his love was no longer a secret. She had spotted him riding in an open carriage with a lovely girl, unable to take his eyes away from Eleanor. Thirteen years later Franklin was obligated to recall that there had been a time when Eleanor's company filled him with great tenderness. It was painful to realize how far he had drifted away from his initial love for his wife.

Franklin calmly faced more provocations from Alice. While Eleanor was in Hyde Park, Alice invited FDR and Miss Mercer to a dinner party where nothing worth reporting on her gossip sofa happened. Alice also did not get any satisfaction from her efforts to embarrass Eleanor, who was quite proud of herself when she told Franklin how she had shown their nosy cousin the cold shoulder. She had met Alice by chance in the Capitol, Eleanor wrote, when "on the way out I parted with Alice at the door not having allowed her to tell me any secrets. She inquired if you had told me, and I said no and that I did not believe in knowing things which your husband did not wish you to know."

SOBERING AUTUMN: PART II

In the fall of 1917, Franklin was in no mood to discuss his frame of mind with Eleanor. He had been sobered twice in his delight in Lucy. He was first taken aback by the drastic action of his boss when he fired Lucy, then by Sara's admonitions about his behavior. In spite of these reproaches, Franklin was not able to ban Lucy from his thoughts. She was in his heart, whether she kept him company or not.

The time while Lucy stayed directly in contact with Franklin was short. Under ever more unfavorable circumstances, Franklin could not see Lucy as often as he wished. There is no evidence that he spent any length of time with her in the winter and spring of 1918. FDR's daily activities were monitored closely by old and new friends. Livingston Davis, Nigel Law's successor as a favorite companion, was not as overworked as Nigel had been. Livy kept a running diary more full of trivia than essentials. His daily notes provide a framework for the reconstruction of Franklin's leisure hours at this time. Davis, a married man, had his eyes wide open for the "peaches" in his circle, always alert to any erotic emanations from the women around him. Among the breathtaking number of names of Washington beauties who crossed his path as his own companions, and his friends' associates, Lucy Mercer does not appear once.

If FDR saw anything at all of Lucy in a busy fall and winter, it could have been only fleetingly and in a secrecy difficult to maintain. An exchange of notes might have been the only bond that remained from the months when they saw each other regularly.

Lucy suffered more than Franklin from the changes brought about in October. She missed the attention of Franklin, no longer her superior at work and the man she adored against all reason and practical common sense. She now had more time on her hands to mourn the loss of a job she loved and the loss of a boss who was the light of her life. Lucy's mother was not sympathetic at all; she welcomed her daughter's enforced return to a spinster's quiet existence. When

Lucy visited her down-to-earth Henderson relatives in North Carolina, she found solace at the same source where her mother had once sought relief from distress. Elizabeth Henderson Cotten remembered long afterward how Lucy had cried on her shoulder about the misery of a love that never had a chance for fulfillment.

To make Lucy's sadness complete, the jolly crowd at the places where she had shared fun times with Franklin was breaking apart. In a war that turned into a struggle for life and death, the officials of the British embassy were no longer looking for charming high-class ladies to grace their parties. They were seeking military support from America. Both FDR and Lucy Mercer faced a personal loss when the third secretary, Nigel Law, was transferred from the Washington embassy to Paris. Franklin soon found a British substitute for Nigel in Sir Arthur Willert, distinguished as chief U.S. correspondent for the *London Times* and an employee of the British Foreign Office.

Lucy was hit hard by Nigel Law's departure but in a different way than Washington's gossips suspected. Writing in hindsight, many biographers assigned Nigel the role of a cover for FDR and Miss Mercer's involvement with each other. Actually, there was little to cover. Franklin and Lucy were always watching appearances when they could be observed together, and occasions when they could meet alone had practically disappeared.

After the third secretary of the British embassy departed across the Atlantic on a darkened ship, *Town Topics* published a lengthy article linking Nigel and Lucy romantically. In his *Washington Quadrille*, Jonathan Daniels expressed skepticism right away about what he saw as sheer conjecture. On December 13, 1917, the paper had been extremely cautious, reporting rumors that "may or may not be true." Washington's gossip had concerned itself with "a charming young girl highly placed in the official world, and an equally delightful young man, close akin to the loftiest of British nobility." Cupid had scored again, the paper alleged, predicting that "another international alliance will be an event of the near future."

Ignorance of the facts caused sloppy reporting. Lucy had not retired, as the paper claimed, but had been fired. Of course the paper did not know that once before Lucy had had a chance to marry a European nobleman. When she was going on twenty, Cousin Agnes had presented her with the opportunity to become the Countess Meraviglia.

As it was, Lucy sincerely regretted losing a like-minded friend in Nigel, an enthusiastic admirer of FDR. Permitting herself the dangerous luxury of falling in love with a married man, Lucy had no eyes for anybody else. Moreover, Nigel was as far away as Lucy was from being hit by Cupid's arrow. The gentle Miss Mercer was not his type. He soon discovered all the passion and excitement he sought in an exotic lady on the Continent. In Nigel Law's elegant circles, where the mores of the late King Edward VII's licentious court were still in play, the pursuit of a married lady was nothing extraordinary. It was puritan America that continued to frown on moral laxity.

When Nigel met the fiery Anastasia Mouravieff on his next diplomatic assignment in Paris, the aristocratic Russian was the wife of his boss. Sir Joshua Milne Cheetham served as the British minister plenipotentiary. During the next eight years, Anastasia went through the ordeals of a bitter divorce. Nigel, her new suitor, was officially punished for the ardor of his courtship. Unfazed, Nigel persisted and married the woman he called "my Nastia" in London.

After Nigel left Washington, FDR still had a close personal link to the British embassy in the person of his cousin and goddaughter, Sara Price Collier. Franklin would give her away at her wedding to a Scottish nobleman, Lieutenant Charles Fellowes-Gordon, in 1918. The groom was distinguished as the aide to vice admiral Sir William Lowther Grant, commander of the British fleet in American waters.

Sallie Collier was just as fond of Eleanor as she was of Franklin. She kept the older Delano ladies—her mother Kassie and her aunt and namesake Sara—up to date on events in the Roosevelt home. Eleanor had warded off the intrusion of her cousin Alice into her personal affairs but was not in a happy mood. A drab fall and winter did not make up for the marital irritations of summer. Franklin was often away from home, frequently on trips to naval bases.

Once more Eleanor was not getting enough of Franklin's company. She poured all her longing for tenderness into closeness with his mother. Unfortunately, Sara, too, did not have as much time for her as Eleanor wished. This year even Sara's traditional Christmas visit with her grandchildren was put into question. On December 7,

1917, Eleanor pleaded with Sara at the end of eight long pages, "Do come the 22d. I'll get a room for Louise [Sara's maid]. I can hardly wait to see you." Sara did come. She admired Eleanor's stamina in giving a big New Year's party for "Fred & Tilly & Louise [Delano], Kassie & daughter Sallie [Collier]," even though Miss Connochie—the children's governess and Eleanor's second-in-command—was sick in bed.

THE CALM BEFORE THE STORM

Sara always tried to make up for her son's shortcomings as a husband with her own presents and letters to Eleanor. On March 17, 1918, her thirteenth wedding anniversary, Eleanor had to go to church by herself. "Franklin got home for lunch but in the p.m. had to work as Mr. Daniels was away," she explained. But Eleanor gallantly stressed the positive side of her marriage. On March 18 she told her "dearest Mummy":

> *Your letter & telegram came Saturday & your Special delivery yesterday. Thirteen years seems to sound a long time & yet it does not seem long. I often think what an interesting, happy life Franklin has given me & how very much you have done to make our life what it is. As I grow older I have realized better all you do for us & all you mean to me & the children especially & you will never know how grateful I am nor how much I love you dear.*

Though Sara shared many meals with her daughter-in-law, they wrote each other constantly in 1918 and talked by phone on January 7. Eventually, Eleanor's correspondence with Sara swelled to gigantic proportions. "Eleanor's letter very long and interesting," Sara noted in her diary on January 30. On May 16 she still noted, "Very interesting letters continue almost daily from Eleanor." Sara became her daughter-in-law's sounding board. She shared not only reports of Eleanor's wartime volunteer work in a Red Cross canteen, but also learned about her views on the latest political developments.

She lent a sympathetic ear to accounts of the ups and downs of her grandchildren's health. Writing to Sara, Eleanor could be utterly candid in her critical appraisal of the parties she attended, the guests she entertained, their Delano relatives in Washington, and her ever-troublesome servants.

Sara, always adapting quickly to technical innovations, could now add an intimate touch to communication with her daughter-in-law by speaking with her on the telephone. "It is always so nice to hear your voice on Sundays," Eleanor told Sara in March. In early 1918 the loss of written information for posterity as a result of increased telephone communication was still minimal. The Roosevelts and Delanos remained as addicted as ever to routinely writing more than one letter a day.

At the same time, there are unexplained and disturbing gaps in the sequence of the Roosevelt family letters. Many biographers have tried to fill these gaps with speculation. Hundreds of pages of Sara's letters in reply to Eleanor's messages of 1918 and 1919 disappeared as the result of Eleanor's decision to keep this period opaque. This was the second batch of personal letters destroyed by Eleanor when she tossed large bundles of old letters into her White House fireplace before the publication of her first autobiography, *This Is My Story*, in 1937. Their contents might have interfered with the messages she sent about herself. Her first choice for the elimination of possibly controversial family documents had been Franklin's letters to her in the three months leading up to their engagement in 1903. Eleanor had no qualms to destroy letters from 1903 and 1918 because they were her personal property, to be dealt with at her own discretion.

On the other hand, Eleanor's conscience would not permit her to destroy letters that did not belong to her alone. In contrast to Eleanor's selective preservation of old letters, Franklin and his mother made a fetish of saving every scrap of family correspondence. "Please return to me all letters as I keep them," Sara had reminded her son once more in the fall of 1917.

In the following year, Eleanor was approaching one of her most prolific periods as a correspondent. She apologized on February 14, 1918, when an especially heavy workload at the canteen had allowed Sara to get ahead of her by three letters. Sara's diary, kept for virtually every day of 1918, makes up to some extent for the loss of her letters to Eleanor. It sheds light on a turning point in Franklin, Eleanor, and Sara's lives that has been deliberately obscured.

Throughout 1918 Franklin saw little of his mother, even though she continued supporting him in his financial distress. He visited her for two days in February on his way to a naval base in New London, Connecticut, and again on March 2 when she was in bed with the flu. Gratefully, Franklin checked off his mother's gifts in a long letter of March 28. Simple presents, such as "very extra nice shirts and ties," were surpassed by Sara's payment of Anna and James's medical expenses. FDR thanked her profusely, confessing, "You have saved my life, or rather the various Doctors' lives, by making it possible for me to pay them promptly!" He included a form indicating the amount of taxes due for his yacht the *Half Moon* and a bill for life insurance premiums paid regularly by Sara. He also requested that she negotiate a better deal with the Lamonts, the renters of his townhouse at 47–49 East 65th Street in Manhattan.

Sara was glad to do anything that benefited Franklin and Eleanor. Two days later, on March 30, Alice Longworth annoyed Sara again with her divisive influence on Franklin and Eleanor's marriage. Eleanor had reported to Sara, "Franklin and I went to Mr. [Henry] Adams funeral at 2 & I felt very sad for he was a very interesting man & the house had so many associations & now it all ended. . . . Alice invited us to lunch next Sunday almost before the service was over & it offended me & made me angry, it seemed so lacking in feeling." In even greater anger, Eleanor reported that "F. said he'd go."

FDR's contrariness did not make Eleanor's heart grow any fonder. She brushed off Sara's concerns about his health, writing, "I don't think F. looks ill . . . he may be a little tired looking, but I think all he needs is 2 or 3 days off in the country. He only plays 18 holes of golf on Sunday morning which I don't think is very strenuous & he walks to his office always & sometimes home." Eleanor then countered one of Sara's suggestions, saying, "He would never get up earlier for exercises."

Franklin was actually gripped by a general malaise, worrying about bills and children. Anna's deteriorating grades in her private school were especially upsetting. Furthermore, he was frustrated in his career, struggling in vain to become actively involved in the naval battles he tried to influence from his desk. Time was working against him in his drive to get overseas in uniform.

It is not known whether FDR's resentment at being cut off from daily contact with Lucy Mercer led him to seek solace in secret rendezvous, as some relatives later speculated. It is highly unlikely that such meetings took place since FDR was much too caught up in urgent business. Apparently, he did keep Lucy up to date by messages about his career moves at home and overseas until July 1918.

* * *

A close look at Eleanor's correspondence with Sara shows that Lucy stayed in touch with the Roosevelts during this time in a way that none of Eleanor's biographers suspected. They all assumed that Eleanor had become wary of Lucy's closeness to her husband in the contentious summer of 1917, and believed that Eleanor had been suspicious of Lucy's alienation of Franklin's affection long before 1918. Surprisingly, the opposite was true. Eleanor did not see a rival in Lucy until she had proof of it. No prescient instinct warned Eleanor to keep her distance from Lucy because she might became a threat to her marriage. On the contrary, Eleanor had grown ever closer to Lucy by early 1918 and was happy to have Lucy's support for her projects. Her association with Lucy remained as strong as ever until September 1918.

Eleanor herself proved her goodwill toward Lucy in a few words, tucked away at the end of a ten-page letter to Sara that ended with "much, much love always." On February 14, 1918, Eleanor gave evidence that she still appreciated Lucy as an assistant and a friend. If she harbored ill feelings for her former social secretary, she would not have asked Lucy to her house again to sort out woolen garments for sailors, just as she had done in 1917. "Lucy Mercer stayed to lunch," Eleanor mentioned casually to her mother-in-law, "and we had wool all afternoon, then tea." Eleanor worked with Lucy all morning. Using Lucy's first name instead of the more formal "Miss Mercer," as she did in the previous summer, Eleanor indicated that she had moved on to a more personal relationship with her assistant. Their cooperation appears to have lasted through July 1918, when

Eleanor stayed by herself at R Street, busy at the Red Cross canteen in the daytime, then "counting woollen garments and tying them up" during lonely evenings.

The children had been parked again in Hyde Park with Sara, though Eleanor felt guilty about the imposition. In March she jokingly predicted a walkout by Sara's servants. "I do hope they won't all leave when they hear the children are to be with you all summer!" Going on sixty-four, Sara was beginning to show her age. "I am so sorry about your knee," Eleanor exclaimed on April 12. "You simply must not get gout or anything else[;] we need you too much as an active Grandma!"

When Eleanor finally joined the children and Sara for a vacation at Hyde Park, "all had a nice time." Eleanor's sister-in-law Margaret Hall and many friends from Washington visited. Franklin suddenly broke into this tranquil summer idyll of women and children like a whirlwind. He devoted an entire weekend at Hyde Park to saying goodbye. About to cross the Atlantic on an important secret mission for the Navy Department, his presence brought to mind not only the dangers and uncertainties of war but also its glorious excitement. Family and neighbors gave him a hero's send-off.

Sara's brothers Warren and Fred hosted the final leave taking in the city. Sara's entry in her diary for July 9 read, "At 11.30 Captain Mc-Caul[e]y [FDR's aide] came & he & Franklin [left] 'for parts unknown'—Eleanor went [back] to Washington & I came home & *all* the children met me—"

Eagerly awaited news from Franklin was sent immediately from Washington to Hyde Park. Sara badgered her daughter-in-law for more details than she could provide. On July 30 Eleanor finally reported that FDR had enjoyed his first triumph as a negotiator. "My dearest Mama . . . I often think that you must wish his Father could be here to be proud with you of Franklin."

This letter marked the end of Eleanor's known correspondence with Sara for two and a half months. The next preserved communication from R Street to Hyde Park was written on October 11, Eleanor's birthday. Much would happen in between, but little was said about it.

DRAMATIC MYTHS, DRAB REALITY

Sara and Eleanor made a good team, working together for the Hyde Park Red Cross. They took care of the children when Miss Connochie left for a two-week vacation on September 2. James's bout with poison ivy and Elliott's upset stomach were minor flaws in the string of one "glorious day" after another, until Sara and Eleanor were suddenly aroused on September 10 by ominous news from Paris. Dora Delano Forbes had seen her nephew and warned that "Franklin was not well."

Nine days later one of the longest entries ever in Sara's diary described the shocking details of Franklin's return to her townhouse at 47–49 East 65th Street.

> *Sent car to Hoboken to meet Franklin & any of his staff he cares to bring—An hour after Butler left, a telephone from Elliott Brown says that Franklin has a light case of pneumonia. A doctor must meet him & he must be moved in an ambulance. Eleanor went in Ad. Ucher's car for Dr. Draper & then to the "Leviathan"—Thro' Dr. Tomkins we got day & night nurses. My dear Franklin arrived in the Navy ambulance with Dr. Draper & 4 Navy orderlies carried him up to his bed, and Miss Clark was ready for him—*
> *Temp. 103—a little lower than yesterday—Later Dr. Ely came from Southampton.*
> *Dr. W. Gilman Thompson is to see him tomorrow—*
> *Patches on both lungs, double pneumonia, following grippe.*
> *E. & I dined with Warren at Delmonicos.*

The next evening Sara continued more calmly, "Miss Dumoulin had charge all night—fairly comfortable—Temp. this morning 102½. . . . Dr. W. Gilman Thompson tells Drs. Ely & Draper he thinks with great care he may not have a *very* bad case. Must stay in bed 8 days after the temperature is normal, & then *very* quiet for weeks." On September 1, 1918, Sara had to go to Hyde Park to get ready for Margaret Hall, the wife of Eleanor's brother. By September 2 Sara reported that Franklin still had to be "very quiet" and added that "Dr. Draper comes two or three times a day. There are lots of flowers."

Sara's old patent medicine, keeping a precious patient "very quiet," again worked its magic. It meant making sure that her son was completely relaxed, protected from any physical or emotional exertion. On September 26 Sara wrote contentedly, "Franklin enjoys having Eleanor read to him, & is very comfortable still just as quiet & not sitting up." After another week Sara's diary sounded cautiously optimistic. "All of us excited as Franklin & Eleanor get back [to Hyde Park] this P.M." At Hyde Park the patient "must be quiet & not get tired."

When Sara could no longer postpone an urgent errand in the city, Eleanor wanted her to look for a new nurse "to take Flora's place." The family of Sara's brother Warren Delano III was crying out for help. There was "serious illness at Steen Valetje [Warren's estate near Barrytown, north of Hyde Park], Warren and Lyman have pneumonia, one maid is very ill with it—ten cases in the house." Sara helped out at Steen Valetje until she had to rush south from her brother's place to Hyde Park to prepare for her son's transfer to Washington. By now he was well enough to get restless in Hyde Park's "quiet." On October 17 Sara took Franklin and Eleanor in her car for a stay overnight "at 47," her townhouse in Manhattan. The next day she had them chauffeured to the 1:50 train for the capital.

On November 2 Sara's grandchildren were finally picked up by their parents for their return to Washington. Anna, James, and Elliott had lived under Sara's roof for more than six months; Johnnie and Franklin, Jr., almost as long. For Thanksgiving the family gathered again in Sara's townhouse in New York. To meet Franklin and Eleanor, "a lot of people came to tea, Blanpré, Morgenthau etc." Jennie and Warren Delano were well enough by then to take the Thanksgiving feast off Sara and Eleanor's hands. They invited the whole clan to a "delightful dinner at 39," the Delanos' New York City residence.

*   *   *

Eleanor enjoyed being wrapped up in comforting Delano family warmth, but the tribulations of the year 1918 would not subside. A string of meetings with Sara for Christmas shopping was interrupted by a new severe blow: all five Roosevelt children came down with the flu at the same time. Elliott was hit especially hard. "I feel anxious & telephone daily as Elliott has pneumonia," Sara fretted before she sent a hard-to-find qualified nurse to R Street.

Eleanor called ever more urgently for Sara herself on December 17, because "I always feel safer when you are by." Sara obliged. Together with Franklin and Eleanor, she attended a party at the British embassy in the capital. Sara was also on hand, as Eleanor wished, for James's eleventh birthday on December 23. On the twenty-fourth she spent "most of the day at Franklin & Eleanor's. They had a Christmas tree & supper for 12 soldiers from Mrs. Lane's Convalescent Home & 12 sailors from the Naval hospital."

Sara's strenuous shuttle between Washington and New York would not abate. When she returned to the capital on December 28, she stayed "at Franklin's" to ease the children's feeling of being left behind. Their fears had suddenly become reality: both their parents were to go to France for almost two months. Long into the night, Sara was kept busy "in Eleanor's upstairs sitting room, she & Franklin writing & packing." On the morning of December 30, Franklin gave away his goddaughter Sally in a wedding to Charles Fellowes Gordon. In the afternoon Franklin, Eleanor, Sara, and James went to New York. But their ship, the *Levinthe*, broke down and was not yet ready for them.

It was a blessing that Eleanor was kept frantically busy in the three months between Franklin's arrival on a stretcher on September 20 and her departure with him on his second overseas tour of duty at the end of December. Every single week had been hectic. There was not a minute when Eleanor was not preoccupied, struggling with one big practical problem after another. This stress was beneficial; it protected her from the necessity to come to confront one of the worst emotional experiences of her life that descended upon her in the tumultuous days of her ill husband's return from Europe. Only gradually did Eleanor muster the strength to cope with a blow that hit her on—or shortly after—September 20, 1918. The sudden revelation that her husband had carried on a loving friendship with Lucy Mercer behind her back shook the foundation of her existence and left her dumbfounded. She could not get herself to relieve her anguish by sharing it with well-meaning others. She would not have talked to outsiders about her marital troubles for anything in the world. Victorian taboos against discussing openly intimate matters kept her silent.

CHAPTER 6

HIDDEN ROMANCE, OPEN FALLOUT

DAMAGE AND REPAIR

While Eleanor did not make her hurt an issue of conversation, she acted upon it. In the months following the shock, when she opened her eyes fully to her loss of Franklin's heart, she decided that she would not spend the rest of her life pining away in unrequited love. She saw no realistic chance of finding a new husband who would suit her better and behave as tenderly as she desired. Instead Eleanor embarked on the courageous experiment to seek fulfillment and personal satisfaction with her given circumstances, depending solely on a drastic change of her pursuits.

By the time Eleanor wrote her autobiographies of 1937 and 1949, her self-directed metamorphosis had ended in triumph. She had become a different, happier person after shifting gears in 1920. Service to her immediate family moved to second place in her efforts when she began to devote her time and talents to a career of her own. But how was Eleanor to explain a transformation visible to all, both in 1937 when she described her life as First Lady and later (in 1949) when she described it as a widow? She found immediate sympathy and approval from her readers and pundits when she gave the reason for her division of her life between the conventional young Eleanor and the independent mature Eleanor. She declared that she had to liberate herself from subjugation by a domineering mother-in-law who inhibited her growth as a personality.

Eleanor obviously convinced herself of the negative impact of Sara on her development. She ignored the fact that the chronology of her estrangement from a long-loved mother-in-law did not match the sequence of events marking her emancipation from the traditional bonds that tied a woman to marriage and motherhood. In September 1918, and again two years later, Eleanor had been pushed to respond to Franklin's actions—not because she no longer accepted his mother's authority, but because she could not count anymore on being first in her husband's heart. She needed other ways to find self-fulfillment. Eleanor's inability to talk about Lucy, the real thorn in her side, made it impossible to be open about the one-time shock that had moved her to become a new person.

Eleanor not only controlled her tongue, forbidding herself to tell others how Lucy Mercer had damaged Franklin's attachment to her. Her disgust with her husband's infidelity also closed her mind to the fact that her discovery of her failure as a wife, as she saw it, had led her directly to the pursuit of new ways to find satisfaction and contentment.

It took Eleanor twenty-five years to open up to anybody about the hurt she held hidden inside her. Only two years before her husband's death, she finally revealed to her young friend and protégé Joseph P. Lash the pain Lucy had caused her. By this time she could trust her assistant and later biographer as her faithful partisan. Lash nurtured strong reservations toward both Eleanor's husband and her mother-in-law. He recalled that during a brief first encounter with Sara, shortly before her death, he was stunned by her similarity to her son—no compliment to either of them. Eleanor was protective of her young friend and his political opinions. To her great anger, FDR had initiated an FBI report on Joseph Lash's leftist leanings and his travel with the First Lady.

In his best-selling book of 1971 *Eleanor and Franklin*, Lash quoted Eleanor's letter to him of October 23, 1943, which disclosed her "discovery of the romance between her husband and her social secretary, Lucy Page Mercer." According to a later conversation with Lash about FDR's return to New York in September 1918, "Eleanor took care of his mail, and in the course of doing so she came upon

Lucy's letters." Lash was first to publish Eleanor's distress at the irrefutable proof of her husband's devotion to Lucy. He also was first to share her confession that "the bottom dropped out of my own particular world, and I faced myself, my surroundings, my world, honestly for the first time. I really grew up that year."

In Eleanor's painful reappraisal of her relationship with Franklin, there were indeed many problems to be faced. Over the years the differences in their personalities had taken their toll. At the time they met, they confirmed the old adage that opposites attract. But in living together they were pulled apart by the divergence of major character traits and the dissimilarity of many preferences. Franklin was an extrovert, Eleanor an introvert. In contrast to Franklin, Eleanor did not care for sports—such as golf and swimming—and she did not like boat rides or dance parties. Franklin was a collector; Eleanor always felt an urge to discard superfluous possessions.

Over the years Franklin grew more irritated by small conflicts with his wife. He no longer sought Eleanor's presence as eagerly as in the time of their engagement. As a result, Eleanor often craved her husband's company in vain. Contact with women of her age was limited to the wives of Franklin's associates in government. The best friend of her youth, Isabella Selmes Ferguson, was far away much of the time.

Franklin had not been as lonely in his youth in hospitable Hyde Park as the orphaned little Eleanor had been in isolating Tivoli. Her Grandmother Hall did not like to entertain guests. Sara Roosevelt, on the other hand, was hospitality itself. She kept her boy Franklin as close to his Delano cousins Warren and Muriel as if they were his brother and sister. Their neighbor's daughter Mary Newbold at Bellefield was as constant a companion of Franklin as Frances, the daughter of Sara's good friend Grace Kuhn on Campobello. The Rogers boys, Franklin's schoolmates, remained his brotherly friends. As a young adult, FDR always had a friend nearby on the golf course and at his luncheon table. He went on sailing adventures with Eleanor's brother Hall instead of joining her on walks around the cliffs of Campobello. In Washington he invited his cousin Polly Delano along on official trips when he could have traveled alone with his wife.

* * *

In the early years of their marriage, Eleanor did not openly vent her disappointment with her husband. Even looking back on her youth in her late writings, she presented Franklin at his best.

Other men she loved—her father, her son Elliott, and her second son-in-law John Boettiger—also profited from her generosity. Eleanor forgave them for disappointing her because they filled her heart with great warmth. Franklin made it harder than any other man to keep up her goodwill toward him. Her uncertainty about his feelings for her went back to their getting acquainted.

As early as November 1903, Eleanor had doubted whether Franklin loved her as much as she loved him. Her touching confession in a letter to her fiancé, telling him, "I pray so earnestly that my love may bring you all the joy that yours has brought me," was followed by a blunt "I hope you want me as much as I want you." When she married Franklin in 1905, Eleanor was finally convinced that he would love nobody else. After serving Franklin and their children dutifully for the next thirteen years, Eleanor was devastated when she learned that her devotion had rested on a false premise.

It was little comfort that Franklin's closeness to Lucy Mercer had been brief and platonic. Eleanor knew Lucy well. Her rival radiated purity and chastity, instilled in her upbringing by devout nuns. It had been her very serenity, her calm of the soul, that had brought about a true meeting of hearts with Franklin. Thriving behind her back, their chaste love was more troubling than any common extramarital affair. Eleanor had learned in the world around her that sexual attraction tends to be transitory. After all, she acknowledged, men have their temptations and women have their moods.

Eleanor knew that Lucy met the highest standards set by Elizabeth Barrett Browning, Eleanor's most trusted authority in matters of the heart. The poet had praised the lofty realms of love beyond sexual temptation. She demanded a love "for life, for death," acting out the demands of a love song of faithfulness in which "no other is left in the rhythm." Franklin and Eleanor shared their generation's obsession with Elizabeth Browning's *Sonnets from the Portuguese*. In sonnet number 131, the poetess ranks virtuous love high among alternative answers to the question "How do I love thee?" When she continued, "Let me count the ways." Lucy's way of chaste loving appeared in a lofty context. It fit the poem's category of lovers who professed, "I love thee freely, as men strive for Right; / I love thee purely, as they turn from Praise."

Eleanor put pure love of the spirit—her very own preserve—above the physical love she detested. In her eyes Franklin's choice of Lucy as his soul mate was absolutely intolerable. It invaded her most sacred emotional territory. Eleanor realized that she could not match Lucy's calm disposition, her ability to relax and refresh Franklin when he got tense. She saw herself fulfill the opposite function in Franklin's life, when she challenged him as "a spur" in her husband's side.

Long before Eleanor tried as First Lady to promote her own political agenda by prodding her husband, close relatives had noticed that her marriage had lost its luster. It was lacking the *délicieux,* as Eleanor's cousin Corinne Roosevelt Robinson put it. Eleanor herself tried in vain to retain the romantic perceptions of an ideal marriage that she had cherished in her youth. Even in old age, when she could not help but acknowledge the upset Lucy had caused her, she would not provide details. Her confidants, Joseph Lash and later David Gurewitsch, were too much in fond awe of the great lady to ask what exactly happened on or after September 20, 1918.

Where facts about Eleanor's marital crisis were hard to come by, rumor and speculation rushed in to fill the gap. Gossips were frustrated by Franklin and Lucy's immediate relatives, who formed a solid phalanx of silence. The Roosevelts and Delanos had dealt successfully with past family scandals in the same fashion. As a disciple of the puritanical headmaster Endicott Peabody at Groton, young Franklin solemnly took the side of the men in a family scandal caused by his aunt Kassie Delano Robbins. In an act of bold transgression against the commandments of church and society, the sister of FDR's mother had won the love of her married pastor Price Collier. Franklin joined his great uncle Frank Delano and his uncle Warren Delano III in condemning Kassie's moral laxity. FDR's mother Sara and his grandmother Katie Delano were more tolerant.

Seven years later, in 1900, Franklin had been equally harsh in denouncing the culprit in a Roosevelt family scandal. Taddy, the son of his half brother James Roosevelt Roosevelt, Jr., had lived with and married a woman from New York's red light district. FDR never forgave Taddy for tainting the Roosevelt image.

In 1918, when Franklin himself violated basic Victorian rules, he carefully avoided compromising the Roosevelt family reputation. FDR had made little effort to hide his infatuation with Lucy in the summers of 1916 and 1917, favoring her at society balls and taking her on drives in the countryside. But he broke off all contact with Lucy when he realized how much pain he was causing his wife. He was shocked to see how much damage the rumor mills could do to a man's reputation.

RIVALS' LEGENDS

The revelation of Lucy's exchange of letters with Franklin apparently caused little commotion within the family. No trace of a single word about any unpleasantness in family relations can be found in the papers of Franklin and Eleanor or Sara and Lucy. The tone of their letters and diary entries was as calm as ever. The Delano relatives in Washington and the secretary of the navy, Josephus Daniels, could be trusted to keep the Lucy episode under wraps. Only the gossipy Alice Longworth had to be watched. She might prevent grass from growing over the faint traces of Franklin and Lucy's friendship.

The Hyde Park Roosevelts gave no sign to outsiders of being disturbed in their usual concord. For all to see, Eleanor nursed Franklin faithfully to recovery from grave illness. Three months after his return from overseas, at the end of 1918, Franklin went back to Europe, this time with his wife. Sara was as supportive of her loved ones as ever. According to Sara's diary, she sent huge baskets of vegetables and chicken from Hyde Park to Eleanor's kitchen in Washington as a sign of her affection. She asked Jenny Delano to relieve Eleanor from hostess duties at Thanksgiving and found a nurse to help Eleanor handle the children's flu in December. On November 21, 1918, Eleanor wrote to Sara, "Dearest Mama . . . You are our angel to help us with Sallie's dinner, but of course you always are more generous than any other I know." She added, "[A] thousand thanks for getting the chiffon cloth."

Only decades later the void of sensational news about the Hyde Park Roosevelts from the fall of 1918 was filled with hearsay. Uncharitable cousins from the Oyster Bay side of the clan did not hesitate to resort to fabrication. If Franklin had remained a conventional, run-of-the-mill New York lawyer, he would not have aroused his relatives' ire. Envy caused Theodore Roosevelt's daughters, niece, and nephew to disregard the ethics of their class. It was a violation of unwritten society laws—and decidedly in poor taste—to dwell on a cavalier misstep like an extramarital summer flirtation, but Franklin's rise to high office left him vulnerable to jealous attacks. Character assassination in important parlors was the ladies' powerful weapon on the political battlefield. Rivalry prompted FDR's Oyster Bay cousins to milk the Lucy Mercer episode for all it was worth. Their interpretation of events turned a discreet and innocent friendship into a salacious scandal. They have misled history buffs to the present day.

Alice Longworth and her cousins used the opportunity to denigrate the rise of FDR, the political upstart they resented. He had challenged the political ambitions of Theodore Roosevelt's heirs—the designated "Crown Prince," Theodore Roosevelt, Jr., and the president's nephew Theodore Robinson. The older generation, represented by the Olympian president and his dignified sisters Anna Cowles and Corinne Robinson, would never have stooped to such low practices.

"We behaved terribly," Alice herself recalled in old age. "There we were—*the* Roosevelts—hubris up to the eyebrows, *beyond* the eyebrows, and then who should come sailing down the river but Nemesis in the person of Franklin. We were out. Run over. . . . My brother Ted had been brought up by my father to follow in his footsteps . . . and then to see Franklin follow in those same footsteps with large Democratic shoes on was just too terrible to contemplate."

Alice's cousin Corinney, Corinne Roosevelt Robinson's daughter, eagerly joined the family crusade against Franklin. She was married to Joseph Alsop, who was on the lookout for his own political opportunities in Connecticut. Corinney rooted with special vigor for her brother Theodore Robinson, who had competed with his cousin Franklin in Albany since 1910.

Although Auntie Bye's only son Sheffield Cowles, Jr., had profited from FDR's patronage in Washington, he chimed in with the family ladies in their diatribes against FDR and his mother. Sheffield served as a witness of FDR's inappropriate behavior when he was quoted in

1982 by Joseph Alsop, their cousin through marriage. Sheffield insisted on having seen Franklin and Lucy together in and out of Washington, "often, I used to think, too often."

The year 1958 provided a first push for wide dissemination of the myths about Lucy and Franklin, spread by the Oyster Bay relatives. Theodore Roosevelt's biographer Hermann Hagedorn had extensively interviewed Sheffield and other members of Teddy's family about their attitude toward the Hyde Park competition. When Hagedorn's work found acclaim, the old apocryphal stories gained even more credibility. Their version of Franklin's straying was now petrified forever in apparently sound recollections of eyewitnesses. Ladies' vague tittle-tattle over cups of tea in 1918 and 1919 had become Oyster Bay family lore. The legend, believed to be solid fact by its creators, had taken on a life of its own. It was handed down for decades by writers who thought they had found a reliable source for their interpretation of the Hyde Park Roosevelts' behavior in a delicate situation.

In 1971 the Oyster Bay ladies' guesses about what took place behind closed doors at 47–49 East 65th Street in late September 1918 were transcribed with remarkable caution into quotable phrases by Joseph Lash. He was declared "ferociously partisan" to Eleanor by her cousin Joseph Alsop. At the end of the chapter entitled "Trial by Fire" in his book *Eleanor and Franklin*, Lash inserted many a "may" and "might." Summing up the hearsay he had gathered about Lucy Mercer, Lash gave new weight to the gossip from half a century earlier by mixing it with his own assumptions. He claimed that "she [Eleanor] was prepared to give her husband his freedom, she told him, if after thinking over what the consequences might be for the children he still wanted to end their marriage."

According to Lash, Franklin soon discovered that divorce might have disagreeable consequences, in addition to the effect upon the children. Lash hid behind rumors when he continued cautiously, "Sara was said to have applied pressure with the threat to cut him off if he did not give up Lucy. If Franklin was in any doubt about what a divorce might do to his political career, Howe [Louis Howe, FDR's secretary and adviser] was there to enlighten him. Lucy, a devout Catholic, drew back at the prospect of marriage to a divorced man with five children. Eleanor gave him a choice—if he did not break off with Lucy, she would insist on a divorce. Franklin and Lucy agreed never to see each other again."

* * *

These oft-quoted fundamental conclusions of action by the main characters in the drama of Franklin and Eleanor's marital crisis were based solely on the views of Joseph Lash. He did not draw a line between his own conjectures of the situation and a distinct quote from Eleanor, gained in conversations with her. He summed up in a few words how he saw Eleanor's predicament. "Having borne him six children, she was now being discarded for a younger, prettier, gayer woman."

Actually, nobody—certainly not Lash—knew what Lucy wrote in the letters to Franklin that Eleanor read in September 1918. There is no indication, before or after this date, that Franklin intended to "discard" his wife. Lucy never would have consented to such a move. The Roosevelt historian Bernard Asbell warned against reading more into Lucy's letters to Franklin than the facts warrant. Since Lucy's letters were destroyed, he cautioned, we were left "with no clue to how ardent they were as love letters; all we know is Eleanor's reaction to them." Asbell gave to consider that "Eleanor, whose emotions are fragile, may have overreacted to what the letters said."

No written exchange within the Roosevelt family suggests that any of Lash's quoted statements were ever actually pronounced in the fall of 1918. Nobody knows whether either Franklin or Lucy ever promised Eleanor not to see each other again. Jonathan Daniels had his doubts. He preceded with "supposedly" the statement that Franklin "ended forever his relations with Lucy Mercer to whom actually he was to be attached by ties of deep and unbroken affection to the day he died."

In spite of Daniels's skepticism, the story of Franklin's promise to Eleanor in 1918 is firmly established in Roosevelt biographies. It is always combined with the reproach that Franklin broke a solemn promise when he reached out to Lucy again and again, from 1926 to 1941. It is certain, however, that the knowledge about such a promise was not spread by Eleanor. She did not talk about Lucy ever, with minor exceptions in old age. This was her way to control the damage done by Lucy.

Joseph Lash had none of Eleanor's inhibitions. He played a decisive role in the propagation of the idea of Franklin's promise. Maybe the assumption of its existence was his own creation, or maybe it was first conceived by the female members of Theodore Roosevelt's clan. They encouraged each other in embellishing the meager facts they knew about Lucy. Joseph Alsop had such gossip sessions in mind when he remarked about his grandmother, Corinne Roosevelt Robinson, that she "loved a good story."

With or without a promise, it was undeniable that Eleanor's awareness of Franklin and Lucy's friendship precluded any further contact between them behind her back. Besides, the bonds that had grown in a few brief months of their association in the summer of 1917 were not expected to last into the future. Franklin knew all the while that Lucy's principles, even more than the rules of her church, were insurmountable obstacles to marriage. Lucy's attitude made a moot question out of Eleanor's alleged willingness to give Franklin "his freedom." Only in the mind of Joseph Lash, inspired by the meandering flights of fancy in the parlors of the Oyster Bay Roosevelts, had images of Eleanor's choice in the matter appeared. It was not Lash but Jonathan Daniels who provided proof of Lucy's hopelessness for a future of her love by quoting Lucy's confidante, her North Carolina cousin Elizabeth Henderson Cotten. Lucy had cried on her shoulder about the misery of a love that never had a chance for fulfillment.

Lash superimposed his dramatic view, adopted from FDR's rivals, over a bland picture of the real situation of the Hyde Park Roosevelts in the fall of 1918. His version of Eleanor dealing with her husband's misstep was filled with his own indignant view of the way his benefactress should have countered the wrong done to her. Lash's musings left many questions unanswered. If Franklin had accepted Eleanor's alleged offer of "freedom" by getting a divorce, FDR could have seen Lucy at any time thereafter without scruples. Did Lash really expect Eleanor to stand her ground and unleash a divorce scandal if Franklin refused to break off all contact with Lucy? It was not in Eleanor's interest to threaten Franklin with public disgrace. He would have needed to earn a substantial salary to pay alimony and child support. Eleanor's Oyster Bay relatives might have derived some satisfaction from seeing their Hyde Park rivals humiliated by a divorce trial. However, they all knew Eleanor well enough to realize that she was in no mood for a public showdown, or even just for an angry family debate, in September 1918. She had an urgent task at hand: she had to help make the sick Franklin well again.

Circumstances indicated that Eleanor was sad and depressed rather than defiant when she found out what had been going on behind her back. By going to court, suing her husband for adultery, she would have caused a sensation. A scandal would have hurt her as much as Franklin. At the time adultery was a cause for divorce in New York State. If Eleanor had sued, she would have been at a loss providing proof for Franklin's infidelity. She had no concrete evidence apart from what she read in Lucy's letters. Even in the unlikely event that the letters hinted at unseemly intimacy, Eleanor would have to explain her right to confiscate documents that did not belong to her. A mere friendship between her husband and a society lady would raise eyebrows at best. Yet would it cause a judge to grant a divorce? Concepts like no-fault divorce, alienation of affection, and irreconcilable differences were still far in the future.

Obviously, Eleanor wished fervently that Franklin would cut all ties with Lucy forever. At the moment there was little opportunity to express this wish forcefully at the bedside of a feverish patient. There is no record in any form of Eleanor's venting such alleged demands, but Eleanor's reaction and her subsequent action—changing her way of life as a consequence of having been betrayed—is richly documented.

The story of what followed after Eleanor's shocking discovery on September 20, 1918, as it was told by Lash, implied that Franklin and Lucy saw each other at least once more in order to finalize their relationship. It is difficult to visualize Eleanor standing by calmly while they met for such a discussion. Besides, FDR was in Hyde Park and Lucy in Washington. He was still weak. It is improbable that he could have mustered the strength for more than a farewell note to Lucy.

Alice Longworth herself told her biographer in 1981, "I don't think one can have any idea of how horrendous even the *idea* of divorce was in those days." By the time Joseph Lash enjoyed Eleanor's motherly friendship in the 1930s, divorce had become commonplace. Joseph Lash himself was waiting anxiously for the divorce of Gertrude Wenzel Pratt (known as "Trude"), the woman he loved, whom he wanted to marry as soon as possible. Taking for granted that divorce was preceded by unfaithfulness, Lash believed as a matter of course that Franklin and Lucy had slept together.

Lash first offered—but then rejected—opinions differing from his own when he quoted Mrs. Lyman Cotten, the daughter-in-law of Lucy's cousin and intimate Elizabeth Henderson Cotten of North Carolina. The younger Mrs. Cotten's comments, based on what she remembered of events long past, refer to the time around 1918. Elizabeth Cotten told Jonathan Daniels for inclusion in his 1968 book, "She and Franklin were very much in love with each other." Mrs. Cotten added, "I know that marriage would have taken place . . . but as Lucy said to us, 'Eleanor was not willing to step aside.' "

* * *

Joseph Lash contradicted her. "Mrs. Cotten is incorrect," he asserted, "not in her impression of what Lucy may have told her, but as to the facts." He continued:

> *Franklin may have told Lucy that Eleanor would not give him a divorce, but this was not the story as Eleanor's friends heard it or as Auntie Corinne heard it from Cousin Susie or as Alice Longworth heard it from Auntie Corinne. "I remember one day I was having fun with Auntie Corinne," Alice said; "I was doing imitations of Eleanor, and Auntie Corinne looked at me and said, "Never forget, Alice, Eleanor offered Franklin his freedom." And I said, "But, darling, that's what I've wanted to know about all these years. Tell." And so she said, "Yes, there was a family conference and they talked it over and finally decided it affected the children and there was Lucy Mercer, a Catholic, and so it was called off.*

It is amazing how such loose talk about what he said and what she said could serve as the basis of serious biographical discussion. Alice Longworth was neither an impartial nor a reliable witness to something that happened when she was not present. Lash based his interpretation of the aftermath of September 20 on what Alice believed to have heard from her Aunt Corinne. Alice was basically in a better position than Joseph Lash to pass judgment on the relationship of Franklin and Lucy. She knew Lucy well and had a more accurate conception of Washington society and its morals than Joseph Lash, who belonged to the postwar generation. He could have been Eleanor's son, and he came from a lower-ranking social background than the ladies he evaluated.

A closer look at the Hyde Park family's mood in the fall of 1918, at the time when Eleanor made her upsetting discovery, rules out any theatrical outbursts. Offers of divorce did not fit into the subdued atmosphere of sickrooms. Eleanor and Sara's anguish was not to be aired in soap opera–style confrontations. Can anybody imagine Eleanor making a scene at her incapacitated husband's bedside? Even if she had been less sensitive and considerate, it would have been unproductive to criticize Franklin while illness made him a shadow of his usual self.

Franklin knew, of course, what his wife was bound to find while she was "taking care of his mail." It is not impossible that the smooth debater approached the painful subject in his own disarming way as soon as he had his wits together again. He would have been physically strong enough for such a confession only by the time he was alone with Eleanor in Washington during the second half of October 1918.

Before late fall vengeful negotiations about divorce with a man too weak to sit up would have been out of the question. It was easier for all affected members of the family to just let life quietly run its course, without adding nerve-racking drama. On top of these deterrents of an open exchange between the spouses, new hurdles appeared by the time Franklin felt somewhat better and could even play a little golf. Overnight Eleanor had been inundated by a new formidable task—having to nurse five children over heavy bouts of influenza. Barely recovered from stress as a caregiver, Eleanor then had to prepare for two months of absence overseas. Overwhelmed by heavy pressure day after day, she continued to be in a poor shape to bargain with Franklin about his "freedom."

While Eleanor's Oyster Bay cousins knew how rumors of divorce could hurt a candidate for elective office, they also were well aware that divorce and alimony were not an acceptable option for a young society matron of thirty-four with five young children. Eleanor had little money of her own. Her once generous trust fund had been shrinking under the overly conservative management of her god-mother's husband Henry Parish. She had not been brought up to support herself and make a living.

FDR, on his part, did not have to listen to Louis Howe to understand that a politician who dared to file for a divorce would be condemned right away for such an offense against the prevalent moral code. He would be "terminating a career." With these words Jonathan Daniels, son of Josephus Daniels, described his father's absolute intolerance of flawed marital behavior. The elder Daniels tolerated no ethical slips, even in his immediate family. While he served as secretary of the navy, he still fulfilled his obligations as the owner of a daily newspaper back home. "Shortly before his own brother-in-law divorced his wife to marry another woman," his son Jonathan observed, Josephus Daniels "declined to let him continue as the business manager" of his publication.

*   *   *

Franklin was realistic enough to acknowledge that his wife's discovery of his attachment to Lucy meant its irrevocable end. To accept this fact, he needed neither a word of admonition from his political mentor Louis Howe nor a warning from his straitlaced boss at the Department of the Navy. He certainly did not need even a whisper of reproach from his mother. Sara had impressed on him since 1916 that he must not stray from the path of devotion to his lovely wife. Sara had proved in word and deed how fond she was of Eleanor, her son's unsurpassed "helpmeet." Above all, to love and be loved by her grandchildren was the essence of Sara's existence. She would have given her last cent for them and would have defended their happiness to her last breath.

If Sara ever heard her Oyster Bay cousins' insinuation that her threat "to cut him off" prompted Franklin to stay with Eleanor, she would have responded with laughter of disbelief. Threats were not her style. It was unthinkable that she would ever leave her son in genteel poverty; her unconditional love for him was beyond censure by pocketbook. Besides, she knew from early on that she had no chance of prevailing against Franklin's "Dutch" stubbornness.

Another oft-quoted assumption of the Oyster Bay ladies is at least as questionable as the alleged disinheritance of Franklin by his mother. Giving their imaginations free rein, they came up with a family conference of the Hyde Park Roosevelts in response to the problems caused by Lucy Mercer. They allegedly got together and "talked it over." Alice later called it "a family conclave, presided over by Cousin Sally [sic]." This is pure fabrication. The only family reunion that actually took place during that critical time was the happy, fondly remembered Thanksgiving dinner at Warren and Jennie Walters Delano's New York City residence. The vision of a family conference serving as a tribunal might have been conceivable for the large Theodore Roosevelt clan, composed of a dozen cousins within call. It was definitely not applicable to the trio of Franklin, Eleanor, and Sara. While each of them had a different reason to be sad, none of them had a taste for a confrontation. The mistress of Hyde Park, trying desperately to keep her sick son "quiet," would have hated to upset him. Letters from Sara to Franklin in the fall of 1918 show the same tenderness toward him as ever before. The family could not afford controversy. They needed all their strength for moving on.

The chorus of presumptuous voices, formed by Alice and her clan, brazenly did Franklin, Eleanor, and Sara's thinking for them. To this day their dramatic explanations have drowned out other, more low-key recollections. According to FDR's daughter Anna, her elderly cousin Susie Parish told her about Lucy Mercer in 1923. The seventeen-year-old girl learned that "Father had a romance with 'another woman' during World War I in Washington; that many people had talked about it at the time and that it was all very hard on my mother; but that there had never been any question of a divorce and the 'talk' had quickly died."

While Franklin, Eleanor, and Sara avoided providing material for "talk," they gave a few indirect indications of changes in behavior at the time after Lucy's letters were discovered. Eleanor tried to overcome her distaste for parties. She aimed to follow Sara's advice to be less serious and tense in her husband's company.

Franklin clearly wanted to make amends for the sorrow he caused. On a Sunday in November 1918, Eleanor informed Sara that he made a tangible effort to change his inconsiderate ways. "Franklin played golf yesterday afternoon & plays again this p.m.," Eleanor reported. "But he went to church [with me] last Sunday & goes again to-day, which I know is a great sacrifice to please me!" Eleanor implied that the real test of Franklin's new commitment, to increase the amount of time he spent with her, was yet to come. She sensed new competition for his hours of leisure when "he received a notice 2 days ago that he'd been made a vestryman which was a fearful shock & I hope he will decline."

Wondering how long Franklin's remorse would last, Eleanor was disappointed by a lack of intensity in Sara's censure of her son. Always sanguine and optimistic about her boy, Sara was inclined to take her daughter-in-law's suffering too lightly. Eleanor understood it was only natural that a mother would forgive her son's transgression more readily than his wife would. The loss of Sara's letters of the time makes it impossible to ascertain how sympathetic she was to Eleanor's long-lasting reaction to her husband's straying.

It was only Sara's failing health that revealed how deeply she was affected by the heartbreak around her. She had held up remarkably well under the strain of her demanding volunteer work for the Red Cross, as well as the constant commotion of five lively grandchildren in her care. When fall arrived in October, Sara suddenly caved in. She felt weak and broke out in a rash. In a striking parallel to Franklin's tendency to succumb to hives under emotional stress, Sara gave evidence of upset by a skin disorder.

* * *

However well concealed the tensions in the core of the family were for outsiders, they showed between the lines in the tone of Eleanor's letters to Sara. They were no longer destroyed but were preserved again after Eleanor's birthday on October 11. Yet the former warmth of Eleanor's affection for her mother-in-law was not recaptured in her new period of communication with Sara. The exuberant expression of love and gratitude that marked Eleanor's writing to Sara in the spring and summer of 1918 had disappeared. Instead of addressing her mother-in-law as "My darling Mummy," she now started out with a "Dearest Mama." She signed off simply with "much love" or "devotedly" rather than "ever loving."

Quite obviously, Sara had done something to temper her daughter-in-law's warm feelings for her. It would have been in character if Sara had suggested to Eleanor kindly but firmly that she would be better off if she could brush aside the humiliation she had suffered in September. Sara might have advised Eleanor in her letters that were destroyed to bury the past and try to win back Franklin's heart. Sara's reaction to adversity was always more robust than her daughter-in-law's sensitive response to offense. Whether Sara said it bluntly in letters, or whether she just hinted orally that it might be wise to forgive, Eleanor was bound to be hurt by such trivialization of an affront that violated her most sacred feelings. A generation gap opened between Eleanor and Sara at this time that widened in the years to come.

Sara always expected her daughter-in-law to count her blessings. After all, Eleanor had a wonderful, healthy, large family. She resided in a spacious home in the capital, at the center of a vibrant social life. Eleanor could at any time relax in a beautiful country home at Hyde Park. She was her own mistress in her "cottage by the sea."

A wise mother in her mid-sixties, Sara had difficulties communicating to her starry-eyed daughter-in-law that a flawless marriage was an illusion. Marital happiness demanded constant adjustment. While Sara accepted wholeheartedly the strict ethical code of the Delanos, also holding husbands to their marital vows, she acknowledged that a Victorian double standard was still in the air. It excused a man's indiscretion but demanded absolute fidelity from the wife. Eleanor, later the bold proponent of equal rights for women, was uncompromising on this point even in her thirties. She dared to differ from her peers' traditional views that favored men.

Sara had tried to prevent the sorrow Franklin caused her daughter-in-law. Once the marital disturbance had blown over, she was quite sure that it was in the interest of both spouses to move on and build a brighter future together.

Sara underestimated the emotional impact of Lucy's appearance in their midst in the minds of both Franklin and Eleanor. FDR's two-year preoccupation with Lucy had left a deep imprint on his heart. What looked like a lark of summer fun to casual observers had been a meeting of kindred souls. Franklin could rely on Lucy's even, sunny temperament, never troubled by moods. Her readiness to listen sympathetically to the outpouring of his joys and sorrows, without interjecting her own concerns, had been a source of inner peace for Franklin.

With her receptive antennae for the sentiments of others, Eleanor accurately appraised the magnitude of Lucy's advantages over her. The fear that she might lose again in the struggle for Franklin's heart would keep Eleanor anxious for the rest of his life. She would not apply the down-to-earth recommendations of conventional wisdom to ease her plight. She was not able to attribute her husband's straying to the general unreliability of men. Joseph Lash quoted Eleanor as confessing that she "never again had the feeling that she came first" with FDR after she realized what Lucy meant for her husband.

Eleanor's belief in ideal love exposed her to pangs of jealousy until she became a widow. While FDR lived she found compensation for the disappointments in her private life in the prerogatives of her position as the president's "Missus." She was gratified by the general admiration for her service as First Lady and by her ability to use the White House as her own bully pulpit.

At the emotionally lowest time of her life, in 1918 and 1919, Eleanor was close to the end of the phase when she derived her main satisfaction in life from fulfilling her wifely duties. She managed FDR's household, raised his children, and did what she could to promote his career. At the same time, she had already decided that she and Franklin would never again be sweethearts.

Her son James was painfully honest in his evaluation of the change in his parents' relationship brought about by Lucy. He called his mother and father business partners, living as husband and wife only "for the sake of appearances." Franklin and Eleanor's "armed truce" endured "to the day he died," James asserted, "despite several occasions I was to observe in which he in one way or other held out his arms to mother and she flatly refused to enter his embrace." As the veteran of a string of marriages, Jimmy questioned whether sticking with his wife had been the right choice for his father. He mused, "Years ago, a divorce was enough to destroy a man's political career . . . but I can't help wondering if my father might not have been an even better president if he'd permitted himself a happier private life."

After 1918 Franklin's happiness depended indeed on his wife's ability to forgive and forget. Later she admitted freely, "I have the memory of an elephant. I can forgive, but I cannot forget." David Gurewitsch—her physician and confidant in old age—added poignantly, "If you can't forget, you don't forgive."

Eleanor's attitude toward her husband and mother-in-law hardened only gradually. Even while Eleanor's emotional wounds afflicted by Franklin and Sara were still fresh, she continued to ask Sara for favors. She still longed to be with her at Hyde Park and wrote Sara on November 1, 1918, "I can hardly wait to get home."

1919: LUCY'S LASTING SPELL

In 1918 Christmas at Hyde Park was not as cheerful as usual. Every member of the family was coping in his or her own way with worries about Franklin and Eleanor's impending departure for Europe. It has been suggested that Sara had a hand in the secretary of the navy's directive to include Mrs. Franklin Roosevelt in the trip overseas. Sara did indeed set high hopes on Franklin and Eleanor sailing to Europe together. She would never forget the miracle of travel with James on their honeymoon in Europe, when respect and affection for her husband had turned into everlasting love.

In any case, Mr. Daniels had already acted as Sara wished. On Christmas Eve 1918, Mr. Daniels's diary listed simply "Mrs. James Roosevelt." It would have been fitting for Sara to express her appreciation to the secretary before his office closed for the holidays; she owed him thanks for being alert to the troubles in his deputy's marriage. Franklin's boss had puzzled the family with a cryptic remark in November at an engagement luncheon for Sallie Collier. It showed Sara and Eleanor that he understood their plight when he said, "No woman marries the man she really marries."

Secretary Daniels's prescription for healing the pain in the Roosevelts' marriage had its risks. The couple had stayed at arm's length for three months since the exposure of Franklin's indiscretion. Barely reconciled, the spouses were hardly ready for the radical cure prescribed by Daniels. They faced being thrown together closely for twenty-four hours a day on a long trip. The intimacy of narrow ships' cabins was bound to revive Eleanor's fear of the sea and marital incompatibilities, now intensified by her vision of herself as a wronged wife.

Eleanor shared her worries with Sara. She might fail again, she foresaw, persisting as a good sailor in the Delanos' parlance and succumbing to seasickness. She could only "hope all the children will be well & nothing happens while I'm gone." She summed up her distaste of the journey. "I never hated to do anything so much. . . . It is rather a horrid world I think!" Sara tried to encourage Eleanor to relax and make up her mind to have a good time abroad. As often before, Sara tried to build up her daughter-in-law's self-confidence. "Susie says 'Eleanor is an angel,' " Sara quoted Mrs. Parish in one of the letters she wrote to her daughter-in-law overseas, "and I agreed with her and said an angel with a heart and a mind."

By 1919 Eleanor was still perturbed by the feeling that Franklin had not torn himself away from Lucy. While Eleanor praised FDR's skill in his demobilization negotiations with the French and English governments over war matérial, she made no effort to hide her personal disappointment. Once again Franklin was avoiding her company. He pursued his social pastimes by himself, just as he had in the bad old days in Washington.

Eleanor aired her complaints in letters to Sara in a breathless fashion, not pausing for commas. She told Sara that Martin Archer-Shee—the British husband of Frances Pell, FDR's childhood friend at Campobello—had invited her and Franklin to "dine with them [in London] next Tuesday, and to-morrow we go down for lunch at least F. does and I shall go if I can induce him to let me!" Next she wrote, "F. and I were to go and pay calls together at 4 on Lady Gertrude [Foljambe] etc., but he insisted on taking my temperature and discovered it was over 100 and wouldn't let me go out. I was furious for I don't feel ill, it is just my old cough for the pleurisy is all gone and staying in does no good. However, here am I and he has gone to call and he dines tonight with Mrs. Copley Hewitt and he made me back out to my rage."

Franklin failed to show his wife that he wanted and needed her. Blinded by his own sorrow at being cut off from Lucy, he refused to see that his demonstrative love might do wonders to improve his wife's health. Her respiratory problems had become chronic.

Eleanor was as vulnerable in her soul as she was sturdy in her body, but the physical consequences of the emotional harm caused by her husband's attachment to another woman now became apparent. Its long-lasting effect on Eleanor's condition would appear only far down the road, in her fatal illness—a long-dormant tuberculosis destroying her bone marrow.

The symptoms of pleurisy plagued Eleanor first when she was in London in 1919. Mrs. Cyril Martineau, Aunt Kassie's daughter Muriel Delano Robbins, cared for her fondly. This was little comfort for Eleanor, who felt abandoned by her husband. He was forever away, in Brussels and on the Rhine, gone with the excuse that "Ladies are not welcomed . . . in the occupied part of Germany." Eleanor sought relief in writing to Sara. She had to admit that she "had to be pretty careful." She was always tired, with "a touch of 'flu.' "

Sara was more alarmed by the manifestations of her illness than Eleanor herself. In their circle the term "pleurisy" was a general term for any affliction in the area of the lungs. There was a "dry" and a "wet" pleurisy, either of which could be accompanied by a chronic low temperature and a persistent cough. In general, flu and pneumonia were openly discussed by the afflicted and their caregivers but the dreaded word "tuberculosis" was not said out loud. Only at the very end of Eleanor's life, when her physician and friend Dr. David Gurewitsch had difficulty finding the cause for her failing health, did his final diagnosis of Eleanor's troubles point to tuberculosis of the bone marrow. He put his finger on a condition that had a tendency of going dormant. In Eleanor's case it did not reappear over the course of four decades. Veiled by her vitality in half a lifetime of energetic action, it surfaced again as part of the frailties of old age. Although Eleanor's disease had first appeared in 1919, a possible psychosomatic component was not in line with medical thinking in 1962.

*   *   *

Eleanor was still weak and depressed when she returned home from Paris and fell into Sara's arms at the end of February 1919. In the diary she kept for a short time in 1919 at Sara's suggestion, she confessed earlier in the month on February 5, "I get no bliss, I suppose it must be the result of planning!" Sara declared Eleanor to be much thinner and more drawn than she had been before the trip. Eleanor was grateful to her mother-in-law for the fortifying supplements she received regularly from Hyde Park. "Many thanks for the tonic which came today," Eleanor wrote on March 2, on the first of twenty-five pages of letters she addressed to Sara during that month. She added, "I really feel very well so don't worry!"

Sara, turned sixty-five by now, was not easily placated. She had reason to worry. Instead of providing a springboard for renewed tenderness and intimacy, Eleanor's overseas journey had pushed romance further back in her marriage. Her relations with her husband were now solely ruled by dictates of necessity rather than promptings of the heart. Eleanor's former outlet for nervous tension, exhaustive service in auxiliary organizations, had dried up with the end of World War I. There was more time for brooding about Franklin and Lucy.

In the knowledge that she was not alone in her predicament, Eleanor tried to find comfort in other lives. She meditated in front of a bronze sculpture by Augustus Saint-Gaudens, popularly known as *Grief*. The monument of a hooded woman in Rock Creek Cemetery marked the grave of the wife of Henry Adams. Clover Adams had enjoyed a brilliant social and intellectual life as the celebrated hostess of a Washington celebrity. In despair at her husband's neglect, Clover killed herself by swallowing photographic acid. Henry Adams had openly put his wife second to "a lovely creature," the wife of Senator James Donald Cameron. Adams had regretted in a letter to Elizabeth Cameron that he could not express fully enough "the extent to which I am yours."

Clover Adams belonged to the generation of Eleanor's mother. She struggled with suicidal tendencies for years and was ill prepared for humiliations by her husband. Her statue in the cemetery personified Eleanor's pain and underscored the striking parallels in Eleanor's mind between Clover's troubles and her own. There had been no sexual consummation of the extramarital affair in either case, yet the anguish at having been betrayed by their husbands' shift to another love was equally devastating for both women. When Eleanor died she had lines written by Cecil Spring-Rice, inspired by the Adams statue, at her bedside. They read, "O tranquil eyes that look so calmly down / Upon a world of passion and of lies!"

In the same place, Eleanor had kept a clipping of Virginia Moore's poem "Psyche." Marked in her own hand with the year 1918, it started out, "The soul that has believed / And is deceived / Thinks nothing for a while, / All thoughts are vile."

Eleanor could only express her woes indirectly, even in letters to her old friend Isabella Selmes Ferguson. Absorbed by a discussion of her health problems, unable to reveal the deeper cause of her distress, Eleanor hinted on July 11, 1919, at the gloomy background of her relatively "idle if at times somewhat trying life." She timed the beginning of her trials precisely, stating, "This past year has rather got the better of me." It was "so full of all kinds of things that I still have a breathless, hunted feeling about it." Eleanor needed time to get control of herself. She remained forever allergic to anything that reminded her of Lucy Mercer. Jonathan Daniels noted that Eleanor did not like to hear him mention his wife because Mrs. Daniels also happened to be called Lucy. As a southern lady and a reverent proponent of her faith, Lucy Mercer remained a strong factor in Eleanor's unease with the South and the Catholic Church.

* * *

In questions of religion, the appearance of the Catholic Lucy Mercer in the Episcopalian Roosevelts' home added a new dimension to the family's ties to different denominations. Lucy had been taught by studying her family history to be open and flexible in her reaction to the beliefs of others. Her mother Minnie Tunis, a convert to Catholicism, had rooted Lucy firmly in the Roman Catholic Church. Her father Carroll Mercer had been born into the Mercer's Episcopalian tradition, but had been raised by his Catholic grandmother Sally Spriggs Carroll. When Lucy fell in love with Franklin Roosevelt, she accepted and respected without reservation the Protestant beliefs instilled in him by his mother. Much later, in the year of his death, Lucy was surprised to discover that the Russian Orthodox form of Christianity represented by her new friend Elizabeth Shoumatoff, harmonized with her own Roman Catholic convictions.

Even though Lucy never tried to proselytize, in the long run she had a strong effect on the feelings of Franklin and Eleanor in matters of faith. FDR's friendship with Lucy softened his conception of Catholicism but hardened Eleanor's stance against the Roman

Catholic Church. Franklin's love for Lucy, and his respect for her devotion to her church, strengthened his tolerance toward other faiths, diverging from the Protestantism of his childhood. The intensity of his liberal approach to different forms of religious belief grew parallel to his mother's changes in the acceptance of ever-wider circles of creeds. Sara, born a Unitarian, married to a formerly Dutch Reformed gentleman turned Episcopalian, matured in her embrace of all faiths.

In 1891, as a young mother, Sara felt strongly about employing a Protestant lady among the native speakers of French who were eligible governesses for her son. Her choice, Mademoiselle Jeanne Sandoz from Calvinist Switzerland, represented for Franklin yet another version of Protestantism.

By 1925 Sara had further widened the horizons of her worship. On a trip to Rome with her granddaughter Anna, Sara lit a candle in a Catholic church. She prayed for her paralyzed son in front of a *Piëta*, a life-size sculpture of Mary with her broken son in her arms. Later Sara also opened her heart to Judaism. Her biographer Rita Halle Kleeman, who eventually became as close to Sara as a daughter, arranged an invitation for her to celebrate the Sabbath with Judge Greenspan's family. Sara was thoroughly captivated by her religious adventure, extolled Jewish spirituality, and established warm ties to New York's Jewish community. Its members eulogized Sara at her death in 1941 in eloquent condolence letters and praised her as a "virtuous woman."

FDR honored his mother's belief in the blessing of spirituality in a variety of forms by donating a part of her estate, the Roosevelts' twin townhouse on East 65th Street, to Hunter College. As an All Faiths House, its mission was to promote interfaith communication between young people.

The year 1941 was when the president reached out once more to Lucy Rutherfurd, the Catholic in FDR's inner circle whose faith had the most tangible impact on his fate. In Franklin's youth the only place where the boy ever met a group of Catholics was his grandparents' mansion Algonac, staffed with Irish Catholic servants.

In Lucy's experience it was the most aristocratic of her ancestors—the Carrolls of Carrolton—who were proud Catholics with a rich Irish heritage. They distinguished themselves as defenders and beneficiaries of religious freedom in their new country. Religious freedom, the central point of Lucy Mercer's family history, was cherished with equal fervor by FDR. "The conception of Freedom of Religion in the Four Freedoms of the Atlantic Charter was Roosevelt's own," Frances Perkins—the secretary of labor in all of the president's cabinets—stressed. She described how "it was Roosevelt who arranged with the Roman Catholic chaplain aboard the ship [sailing back from Yalta in February 1945] to receive [General Edwin M.] Watson into the Roman Catholic faith." The general, the president's secretary and aide, had a wife who was Catholic. "Roosevelt did not have a profound theological argument about it," Perkins quipped.

Indeed, Franklin never matched Eleanor's theological expertise. Growing up in her Grandmother Hall's residence Oak Terrace in Tivoli, Eleanor read her way through a library filled with books on religion. The atmosphere around her was still reflecting the memory of her late grandfather Valentine G. Hall, Jr., and his passion for theological discussion. To get his fill of it, Valentine had engaged a biblical scholar as his permanent guest.

Eleanor had firm theological principles when she asked Franklin about directions for the religious education of their children. She was disappointed when her husband told her not to worry, as long as the children were raised as good Christians.

In her life as a political activist, on her own as a widow, Eleanor still felt strongly about her denominational identity. She was possibly even more conscious of it after Lucy Mercer, one of the few non-Protestant ladies she knew, had brought her Catholic tenets to bear on the fate of her marriage to Franklin. In her column *My Day*, Eleanor expressed in 1949 her concern about the disregard of the constitution's separation of church and state shown by Cardinal Spellman of New York. She strongly disagreed with the cardinal, who favored federal support of "auxiliary services" (such as school buses) for Catholic schools. He had founded the very kind of Catholic schools for girls that Mrs. Lucy Rutherfurd had attended and promoted.

The cardinal overreached himself in his heated reaction to Mrs. Roosevelt's criticism, and accused her in an open letter of "anti-

Catholicism" and "discrimination," "unworthy of an American mother." A storm of public protest, taking Eleanor's side, forced him to apologize in person at her Val-Kill home. "But the episode left its scars," Joseph Lash noted when he devoted a section of his 1972 book *Eleanor: The Years Alone*, to the feud between the cardinal and former First Lady. Lash considered Mrs. Roosevelt's "distrust of the church as a temporal institution . . . one of her reasons for her strenuous opposition later to John F. Kennedy's bid for the presidential nomination." Apart from her support for Adlai Stevenson, the pointed Catholicism of Kennedy and his family was a decisive factor in Eleanor's partisanship.

Eleanor was apt to feel an instinctive aversion to Jacqueline Kennedy as her opposite in personality and her rival in the public's acclaim. If any First Lady was ever cast in Lucy Mercer Rutherfurd's mold, it was Jacqueline Bouvier Kennedy. Like Lucy, Jackie came from a distinguished Catholic family and enjoyed a superior education in Catholic schools. She was beautiful, graceful, and elegant, with a penchant for fine clothes and an individual style. The similarity of their talents, setting Jackie and Lucy apart from their peers, was especially striking in their ability to create comfortable and aesthetically attractive living spaces. As a single woman, Lucy had built a career on her good taste as an interior decorator. Jackie used the same skills on a higher level. Even before her husband's inauguration, she had her plans as future First Lady ready for refurbishing the White House.

Once the Kennedys met the challenges of living in the White House in style, Eleanor overcame her initial doubts about them. She approved of the new First Lady's "sense of art and history" and did not hold back her advice for the young mother. By 1961, the year before her death, the triumphs of Jacqueline Kennedy—Lucy Rutherfurd's kindred soul—no longer caused the wise old Eleanor Roosevelt any discomfort.

Eleanor outlived Lucy long enough to have her tolerance tested when Lucy's legacy assumed a tangible form. Her stepsons' donation of the Allamuchy Mansion to the sisters of an order on Staten Island led to the establishment of a Catholic school for girls on the grounds of the old Rutherfurd estate.

ELEANOR'S NEW PRIORITIES

Like Eleanor, Franklin would never forget Lucy. His career ambitions around 1920 were not stifled by the disappointments of 1918. Rather, the memories of happy hours in Lucy's company turned out to be a boost for his energies.

FDR moved on confidently to a new chapter in his life, out of touch with Lucy. His successful mission overseas had given a lift to his career. He now had to think of the right steps ahead on his way up in politics. The end of the war in November 1918 made it only a question of time until FDR would regard his position in the Navy Department as a dead end on his way to more promising career goals. Eighteen months had passed between February 1919—when Franklin and Eleanor, with President and Mrs. Wilson, returned from Europe on board the *George Washington*—and August 6, 1920, when FDR formally resigned from the Navy Department. The final chapter of his time as assistant secretary was marked by fluctuations in relations with his boss and by a brush with scandal. It took time and finesse for FDR to limit the damage from reports of sailors' homosexual activities in Newport.

Franklin contentedly left Washington. He had made a name for himself in the capital and was showing great promise as a politician to be reckoned with. Only Washington insiders knew about the past turbulence in his personal life. It left no mark on his public image and he kept its effect on his heart to himself.

There is circumstantial evidence that Franklin sought no new contact with Lucy when he was shamed by Eleanor's reaction to his infatuation with the young woman. He was completely surprised when Lucy got married a year and a half after they cut off any communication. Lucy had asked Lily Polk—the wife of Frank Polk, their common friend in the Roosevelts' Washington circle—to alert Franklin to her plans. According to an eyewitness, Franklin "started like a horse in fear of a hornet" when Lily pronounced the news of Lucy's engagement loud enough to be overheard at a tea party. Eleanor had learned about it too. She shared her relief with Sara when she ended a long, rambling letter of February 14, 1920, with the question "Did you know that Lucy Mercer married Mr. Wintie Rutherfurd two days ago?"

In 1920 not only Lucy's life but Eleanor's own goals would change forever. Eleanor had regarded herself as a failure, unable to fill Franklin's heart. Now she saw a chance to test her abilities as her husband's indispensable aide in politics. Joining him on the campaign trail in his run for vice president—on the ticket with James Madison Cox, the governor of Ohio—she was close to Franklin all day long in an important capacity. As a candidate in the new era of women's suffrage, FDR needed the support of his wife to boost his appeal. Franklin did indeed succeed in quickly building a following. On the other hand, Cox inspired lukewarm enthusiasm even in his own party. At the Democratic National Convention in San Francisco, Cox was nominated only on the forty-fourth ballot.

Cox lost his bid for the presidency to Warren G. Harding by a wide margin, but during the campaign FDR gained in name recognition and confidence. Eleanor herself reaped rich dividends from her husband's new political capital when she stepped out into the public arena for the first time. FDR's campaign manager Louis Howe discovered her potential as a politician in her own right and helped her on her first steps to becoming a highly popular public figure. Her commitment to leave the world a better place began in the 1920s.

*   *   *

Eleanor's new public persona had less and less in common with her former self. She no longer represented a conventional young matron who had diligently filled her role as a dutiful wife and mother. One special day, September 30, 1920, can be singled out as the divide between her past and her future development. It demanded a crucial decision that changed Eleanor's priorities forever. For the first time, she permitted goals outside her family obligations to take precedence over service to her children.

Eleanor had always managed smooth transitions for her five school-children as they moved into new classrooms. In early September 1920 her oldest boy, the twelve-year-old James, had been sent to boarding school at Groton. Attendance at the prominent school was a tradition for a Roosevelt boy, not to be broken because James did not yet feel ready to leave home. On September 2, 1920, Eleanor had sent Sara from Campobello one of her many letters of the time, starting out with "will you" but without ever adding a "please." These brisk requests for practical assistance took Sara's willingness to help for granted. Getting James ready for school, Eleanor asked Sara, "Will you get James a trunk, a napkin ring, more plates, sheets . . . [?]"

In his 1976 memoirs, James remembered his miserable start at Groton. He was filled with resentment toward his parents. Plagued by stomach cramps, he landed in the infirmary in great pain. Too shy "to ask where the bathroom was," he suppressed his natural functions. He described bluntly how "I did what had to be done in my pants or in the bushes." When school officials "asked my parents to take me home for a few days," James recalled, "it was my grandmother, not my mother or father, who came for me."

Eleanor had first decided spontaneously to leave the campaign trail and rush to her son's side. On September 29, 1920, in a hand shaken by the vibrations of a railroad train, Eleanor reported to Sara, "I feel as though I've been gone a year. . . . Your telegram and one from the Rector came and I thought perhaps I had better return from here." She abruptly changed her mind when she received a reassuring wire from Rector Peabody. On September 30 Eleanor was relieved to learn that her mother-in-law had taken "Jamesie" to a doctor in Boston. In Sara's hands her boy was in the best possible care. "There was no cause for anxiety," Eleanor told Sara. "I am going gaily on," Eleanor summed up crisply her decision, reacting in an atypical way to the family emergency.

As in many earlier times of stress, Sara had taken a worry off Eleanor's hands. Wrapped up in political excitement, Eleanor ended her letter, "Franklin has certainly made strides in public speaking & gets enough praise everywhere to turn anyone's head!"

Eleanor had chosen "the better part" in the biblical sense. She had discovered the merits of acting no longer like a Martha, stuck in domestic duties, but rather like a Mary, following the teachings of her master. Eleanor proved to be superbly suited for her new calling. Sara would always help with the children under her direction. Sara would know how to deal with the problem at hand—in one instance during the campaign, a sharp drop in James's grades. Eleanor had traveled with the campaign train all the way to Kentucky when she asked Sara to be firm with James and put pressure on the boy to speed up his return to school. A few months later, on June 25, Sara informed Eleanor sadly, "James' examination marks are so low." Eleanor responded, "Make him work at his lessons by himself every day, so he won't get behind."

LUCY REBORN

In 1920 Eleanor, the unfulfilled housewife and mother, was launched on her way to becoming a freelance professional, a star in public performance. In the same year, Lucy Mercer's fate sent her in the opposite direction.

Lucy, the struggling career woman, was transformed overnight into the adored mother of a family of seven. She did not say how it felt to turn into a new woman. Whatever is known about her state of mind at this juncture can only be deduced from her circumstances, her decisions, and recollections of relatives and acquaintances. By contrast, Eleanor's move to new pursuits can be traced clearly, even though large parts of her correspondence in 1918 with close family were destroyed. A wealth of letters and diaries from the two subsequent years provides a solid basis for reconstructing Eleanor's sentiments as she moved on to new challenges.

Jonathan Daniels provides at least some scant evidence for the reaction of Washington society to new developments in the lives of the Roosevelts and Miss Mercer. Like Eleanor, Lucy found sympathy in her surroundings when her hidden ties to FDR came to light. The women closest to Lucy were sure that the end of contact with her beloved friend was no cause for sadness. It was rather a blessing for Lucy to be liberated from her fixation on Franklin, a married man. She was relieved from feelings of guilt toward Eleanor, her admired employer and personal friend. Her separation from Franklin broke the emotional shackles of a hopeless dream, an illusion that kept her from reaching her true destination.

The common explanation for Lucy's restraint, holding her back from trying to win Franklin as a husband, centered on the power of Catholicism over her decisions. Yet a sober appraisal of Franklin and Lucy's situation in 1918 proves that these speculations were idle. Nevertheless, the steady growth of this myth still resists trimming. From the views of the Oyster Bay Roosevelt ladies to interpretations of biographers a century later, the idea that Lucy gave up marrying a divorced man because of her Catholic beliefs had irresistible appeal.

Even if such a conflict of conscience had never come up, Lucy's boundless devotion to FDR would have swept it aside. It was beside the point that divorce, and the annulment of a previous marriage by high church authorities, was definitely an option at the time. Lucy would have followed an unattached Franklin anywhere, whether she was Catholic or Protestant. It was rather her strong convictions of right and wrong, instilled by the nuns who raised her, that guided Lucy's actions more firmly than the rules of a particular denomination. Her belief in the sanctity of marriage was deeply ingrained in her consciousness. Her integrity was not negotiable and did not permit her to fight for a selfish happiness based upon the unhappiness of others. Lucy honored Franklin's devotion to his "chicks," his fond respect and deeply rooted affection for his wife, and his commitment to his "stars," his destiny guiding him to high public office. Lucy's way of loving was to get out of the way when she brought trouble to the man of her heart.

Lucy's loss of contact with Franklin coincided with the loss of her income as Eleanor's assistant. Fortunately, Lucy could fall back on a safety net. Her well-to-do cousin Elizabeth Henderson Cotten, who had sustained her during the heady days of FDR's most ardent attention, was also a reliable friend in need. After an earlier residence in Washington as the daughter of Congressman John Steele Henderson of North Carolina, Elizabeth had returned to the capital in March 1919 accompanied by her husband Captain Lyman A. Cotten and their young son. Elizabeth was available at the right moment to comfort and assist the forlorn Lucy.

Actually, there was no immediate need for Elizabeth to help Cousin Lucy with money. Lucy's mother Minnie Mercer, buoyed by her recent Carroll inheritance from England, was able to bridge any temporary insolvency. Money was not a pressing concern; rather, it was the specter of a dismal future as a spinster that depressed Lucy and worried her cousin and her mother. Lucy had so much warmth and tenderness to give that would be wasted in a life alone. Besides, Lucy was a woman with few marketable skills. Remaining single meant a sadly restricted life, forever struggling with limited means.

Lucy was again as desperate as she had been once before in her teens. Now in her late twenties, she did not know where to go. Amazingly, a second miracle happened to lift her out of her misery. This time her saving angel was not a close relative, like Agnes Carroll Heussenstamm. Instead an old friend of FDR, who was also a new friend of Lucy, pulled the strings of her fate. Edith Eustis, a Washington socialite, offered Lucy an opportunity to come into her own. As before in 1907, Lucy's fate evoked compassion. Again, it was her exceptionally pleasant and sympathetic personality that gave wings to the mission that lifted Lucy out of her hopelessness. She was urgently needed to help a family in despair. Lucy offered just the right combination of delicate sentiment and practical energy to rescue a desperate widower and six motherless children.

*   *   *

Lucy's benefactor Edith Morton Eustis was as prominent in Washington as Countess Agnes had been in Austria when she took Lucy in tow. Edith was highly respected as a leader in society. She had inspired Eleanor to serve in the Patriotic Economy League. She was admired as a writer. Her romantic novel, entitled *Marion Manning*, was dedicated to her father Levi Parsons Morton, vice president of the United States under Benjamin Harrison. Though Mrs. Eustis never attained the fame as an author that her family friend Edith Wharton enjoyed, she aroused much attention with her story's theme. It played out in many different versions in the Washington of her day. Edith's heroine Marion, the devoted wife of an ambitious young congressman, was shattered when she discovered that her husband loved another woman. Surprisingly, their relationship was saved—at least to all outward appearances—when the wronged wife nursed her unfaithful husband selflessly through a grave illness. Marion finally concluded, "Let God judge us, not short sighted [sic] humanity."

In real life the author did not let her fondness for Eleanor Roosevelt stand in the way of her affection for Franklin's friend Lucy Mercer. Edith knew Lucy as a much admired socialite on the capital's merry-go-round and she had taken Lucy's measure as a fellow guest at Eleanor's dinner table. Edith was even closer to Franklin. She had known him since childhood, when her parents and Franklin's parents frequently socialized as neighbors in the Hudson Valley. On vacations in the Adirondacks and trans-Atlantic crossings, Sara Roosevelt had befriended the Mortons well before Edith's sister Alice Morton became the first wife of Winthrop Rutherfurd in 1902.

The head of the family, Levi Parsons Morton, excelled as a successful banker. But to the Roosevelts he was more than a mere "money bag," as Henry Adams had called him. His second wife Anna, the mother of five stately daughters, was a Livingston. He had gained political prominence as a member of Congress, minister to France, and governor of New York in 1895–1896. The Mortons entertained in style in their own residences in New York and Washington. The jewel in their crown, however, was their estate Ellerslie, located on the Hudson River. The mansion held fond memories for Franklin and Eleanor.

In the fall of 1903, when Sara was encouraging Franklin's interest in Eleanor, she had invited Eleanor and Mary Morton—a sister of Alice and Edith—to her traditional house party following the West Point football game. The Mortons, in turn, invited Franklin and his friend Eleanor right back to their important grand ball at Ellerslie. It gave the tightly chaperoned young couple a rare opportunity to lose themselves in a crowd.

Eleanor had felt uneasy writing a thank you note to Mrs. Morton, a hostess she did not know personally. This was no problem for Franklin. He considered a note unnecessary because he knew the hostess so well. He took for granted that he would be a frequent guest of Edith Morton in Washington, where she ranked high. Her prominent husband, William Corcoran Eustis, was a friend of Lucy Mercer's father as a co-member of the Cave Dwellers Association where the elite met. The famous old Corcoran House on H Street, built by Lucy's ancestor Thomas Swann, once a governor of Maryland, was conveniently located on Franklin's way to his office in the Navy Department. He loved to stop by for brief visits with Edith.

An invitation to Oatlands, the Eustises' estate in the horse country near Leesburg, Virginia, was eagerly sought by everybody who counted in Washington society. Oatlands had been built by Lucy's ancestor George Carter I, a great-grandson of Robert "King" Carter. Edith, an ardent student of Virginia history, was well aware of her estate's links to Lucy's forebears.

Oatlands' splendor was originally created by a Carter heir long before Edith Eustis and her husband acquired the place in 1903. Edith excelled as the caretaker of this jewel in the crown of Virginia's antebellum past. Under her ownership the mansion was kept shining with white Corinthian columns in the front and the back, enhancing the sunny yellow of walls inside and out. She upheld the landscaping lovingly and cared for the magnificent white, red, and English oaks, the select cedars, and the Norwegian spruce. She also preserved the terraces, sloping down the hill below the house since 1810.

These horticultural highlights reflected not only George Carter's vision as a master gardener; they also pointed to the plentiful labor at the planter's disposal. The Oatlands Franklin loved to visit stood out as an example of the gracious Old South that Lucy had come to embody for him. The ghosts of Lucy's ancestors were still whispering in the magnolia trees. Among them Judith Carter stood out with her testimony about her family's men. Judith was the daughter of the "Honble Robert CARTER Esq. / President of Virginia" and the grandmother of George Carter I. Her husband, "the "Hon. Mann Page," lived on in the inscription on his tombstone. It had been "piously erected to his Memory / By His Mournfully Surviving Lady." Living "in the most tender reciprocal affection," the Pages had five sons and one daughter. Mann Page had been the perfect Virginia gentleman, discharging "his publick Trust / with / Candour and Discretion / Truth and Justice." He was no "less eminent in His Private Behaviour / For he was / a tender husband and Indulgent Father . . . to All / Courteous and Benevolent Kind and Affable."

Tucked in the middle of the accolade was praise for Mann Page as "A gentle Master." Being an owner of slaves was as inescapable for Robert Carter's heirs as it was for all landowners of the time. The layout of Oatlands, with its long row of slave cabins adjacent to the owners' residence, reminded visitors like Franklin Roosevelt and Lucy Mercer of the shadow cast over the virtues of Lucy's forebears. Edith Eustis's guests at Oatlands were reminded at every step that "King" Carter had owned a thousand slaves. His wealth was based not only on his skill as a merchant, but also on the toil of men and women in shackles.

*   *   *

Eleanor Roosevelt has a guest room in the Oatlands mansion named after her in honor of her visits. Even her uncompromising rejection of slavery did not diminish her admiration for the place. Oatlands invited comparison with the home of Eleanor's grandmother on her father Elliott's side. She never knew Mittie Bulloch herself, but Mittie's sister and brother-in-law, the Gracies, helped bring up the orphaned Eleanor and her brother Hall. The nickname "Mittie" was a form of "Missie," coined by the "colored folks" on Roswell Plantation north of Atlanta. Roswell was smaller than Oatlands. It lacked parkland and gardens but was as conspicuous as its counterpart in Virginia, with extensive rows of huts for the owners' slaves.

Neither Lucy herself nor her parents or grandparents had been slaveholders. Her father Carroll Mercer had been born on the Cedar Park Plantation at West River, Maryland. Their riches did not last. Four generations of successively poorer planters had preceded him at Cedar Park since the time of John Francis Mercer's wedding to the wealthy Sophia Sprigg in 1785. Their union, which merged the property of two great families, had been the plantation's high point. Only Lucy's great-grandmother Sally Sprigg Carroll reminded her of plantation wealth and refinement in pre–Civil War times.

Among the descendants of old planter families, resentful memories of the South's defeat and humiliation had been underscored by their perceived inequities of Reconstruction. As a sequence to these sentiments, waves of nostalgia for the charms of the Old South washed over American public opinion in periodic intervals. They reached their highest point ever with the enthusiastic reception of Margaret Mitchell's novel *Gone with the Wind* in the 1930s. Long before this accolade to noble and less noble southerners, leaders of public opinion had stood for less judgmental attitudes toward the South. Among them were President Woodrow Wilson and the Roosevelts, both of Oyster Bay and Hyde Park—with the notable exception of First Lady Eleanor Roosevelt. They cautiously advocated reconciliation with the heirs of the Confederacy, rather than stirring up further indignation at the evils of slavery. They admired Lincoln's eloquence condemning the exploitation of "bondsmen" but did not emulate his abolitionist passion. In the Roosevelts' eyes, the Carters and Pages—as well as the Eustises from Louisiana—were to some extent exempt from blame as slave owners because they could not escape the pressure from their peers and from the spirit of their time.

Ever so slowly the accents on Oatlands' distinction changed. Upon Edith Eustis's death in 1964 at the age of ninety, her daughters donated the mansion to the National Trust for Historic Preservation. It is at present not only a lovely place to visit, but also a living classroom for the understanding of slavery by twenty-first century Americans. Offering a picture of both the bright and dark sides of the southern past, the site lends itself to serving as a backdrop for informative seminars. It is easy to imagine how Eleanor and Lucy reacted differently to the stark visual lessons of Oatlands.

Throughout her metamorphosis from Miss Mercer to Mrs. Winthrop Rutherfurd, Lucy would be indebted of Edith Eustis, the sister-in-law of Winthrop Rutherfurd. Her friend and patroness served as her bridge to the whole Rutherfurd family. Many strands of Franklin and Lucy's lives crossed in Edith's world. The man who built the fortune of Edith's husband, his grandfather William W. Corcoran, had been a good friend of William T. Carroll, Lucy's great-grandfather. The Corcoran Gallery of Art, near Pennsylvania Avenue in Washington, remains a testimony to Corcoran's philanthropy. It was originally financed by the fortune William earned in trading tobacco. Two of the three children he had with Louise Amory Morris died young; their youngest child Louise married George Eustis, Jr., an attorney and congressman from Louisiana. The couple's oldest son William, orphaned early, became Edith Morton's husband.

Edith had been a bridesmaid at the brilliant wedding of Consuelo Vanderbilt to the diminutive, sullen Duke of Marlborough. It had cost Consuelo's father William K. Vanderbilt, the brother of the Roosevelts' Hyde Park neighbor Fred Vanderbilt, a dowry of two and a half million dollars to make her a duchess. During her engagement Consuelo had been virtually held prisoner by her mother Alva, a lady "of towering ambition." The girl was to be prevented from escaping with the help of the young American aristocrat she adored—Winthrop Rutherfurd. At the age of seventeen, she fell in love with the handsome Winthrop on a cruise. He had expressed his devotion to Consuelo with "one perfect rose" on her eighteenth birthday.

*   *   *

It took Winthrop almost a decade to recover from his failure to win Consuelo's hand. He was forty when he married Alice Morton, the tallest and best looking of Edith's sisters. Nobody foresaw that the happy union would end in great sadness. When Alice died prematurely in 1917, she left Winthrop a widower with six children. The youngest was only two years old.

Edith's heart went out to her widowed brother-in-law. No hired nurse could fill the role of a new mother. Winty's fate attracted the attention of more than one high-born lady aiming to take Alice's place at his side. They included the divorced Duchess of Valency, one of Edith's and Alice's sisters, now calling herself again Helen Stuyvesant Morton. In spite of her sister Helen's interest in Winthrop, Edith decided that nobody was as well suited as Lucy Mercer to take Alice's place at Winty's side. Lucy was both kindhearted and practical, gentle and firm, thoughtful and well organized. She needed a husband and a place to unfold her gifts as a born mother.

It was not certain, however, whether Lucy would be ready to marry a man she did not know well enough to love. It took an emergency in the widower's immediate family to prompt Lucy to take the decisive step of becoming a supportive guest in the Rutherfurd home. The oldest boy Lewis fell ill and shocked the family with the rapid decline of his health. In spite of clear evidence of a charitable motivation for Lucy's move, the legend is inextinguishable that Lucy started out in her acquaintance with the Rutherfurds in the employ of Winthrop as his children's governess. The error lives on even in the most recent accounts of Lucy and Franklin's relationship. Possibly the myth owes its longevity to lingering memories of the popular musical *The Sound of Music,* telling about a governess in the European Alps who marries her charges' widowed father. The parallels drawn between the musical's heroine and Lucy end with the recognition of Lucy's equality—perhaps superiority—in social rank with her future husband.

Franklin Roosevelt could not help noticing that Lucy's road to matrimony was strikingly similar to that of his mother Sara. Then Sallie Delano, she was twenty-six in 1880 when she reluctantly accepted the hand of the fifty-two-year-old widower James Roosevelt. Sallie was facing a drab future as the aging Miss Delano after her heart had been numbed at twenty by her love for the apprentice architect Stanford White. She had accepted her father's opposition to "Stanny" and yielded to James's persistent courtship for high-minded reasons. James could rescue her brother from a dangerous crisis in his career that threatened his advancement as a promising young executive. The squire of Springwood at Hyde Park was welcomed warmly as a suitor by Sallie's parents. Finally, James could convince Sallie that she was wanted desperately in his heart and in his home.

Lucy Mercer was twenty-nine when she married the fifty-eight-year-old widower Winthrop Chanler Rutherfurd. Torn by doubts whether she should marry a man twice her age, Lucy was swayed by compassion to say yes. Affection and high regard for her husband's noble character came later. It will never be known whether the prodding of Lucy's strong-willed mother played a role in her acceptance of Winty's hand. The encouragement of her confessor might have been more effective. The priest pointed to the ultimate blessing of a life spent in the service of loved ones.

Neither Edith nor Winty would have considered FDR's admiration for Lucy a detriment to her eligibility as the second Mrs. Winthrop Rutherfurd. Lucy's reputation was flawless. Not even Alice Longworth or the gossipy Patten sisters in Eleanor's Red Cross canteen would have dreamed of questioning Lucy's virginity. At their time marriage to a Victorian gentleman such as Winthrop Rutherfurd, bound to rigid codes of conduct, would have been unthinkable if there had been evidence of an affair in the bride's past.

On the contrary, Lucy's demure ways added to her attraction. Besides, the distinction of the Mercer and Carroll family trees would be an asset in its association with the blue-blooded Rutherfurd clan. According to Franklin's cousin Joseph Alsop, "Miss Mercer was another 'who was she,' for her father, Carroll Mercer, was one of the Mercers who gave Mercersburg, Maryland, its name, and the Mercers in turn were closely related to the Carrolls." Apart from her brilliant pedigree, Lucy was distinguished by fine personality traits as the perfect lady—gentle, well educated, principled, and immensely warm and caring. Her relative Elizabeth Henderson testified that "she had a vibrant personality, great strength of character," but that she was no "shrinking violet." With a well-to-do countess as her mentor, Lucy learned how to function as the mistress of a great house. Familiar with the management of a baronial household, Lucy could take over

Alice Morton's responsibilities when the services of housekeepers and governesses would be only second best.

On top of it all, Lucy was an enchanting person. She charmed young and old alike. The aid of matchmakers like Edith Eustis, as she responded to a widower's needs and a young woman's problems, seemed outdated in the new world dawning after World War I. It turned out that such an old-fashioned Victorian scenario still had appeal in the postwar world, especially if it led to a happy end.

* * *

Sara Roosevelt could relate to Winthrop Rutherfurd's eagerness to end three years of loneliness as a widower. James Roosevelt had been just as ready to respond to his friend Bamie Roosevelt's matchmaking when she introduced him to Sallie Delano four years after the death of his first wife Rebecca Howland. Becky had left James with Rosy, one adult son. Winthrop Rutherfurd was overwhelmed as a single father with responsibility for six young children.

Like James Roosevelt, Winthrop Rutherfurd had many fine qualities that made him desirable as a husband. Long after James had thanked Bamie for her successful intercession with Sallie Delano, Bamie hinted that she regretted having rejected James's earlier advances to herself.

When Edith recommended her brother-in-law Winthrop as a suitor for Lucy, she could point to a long list of assets that Winty brought into a marriage. He surpassed the Mortons and Roosevelts in social prestige. He could count high-ranking statesmen among his ancestors—from Peter Stuyvesant, the first governor of New York, to John Winthrop, the first governor of Massachusetts. The family had excelled with men of superior intelligence. Winty's father Lewis Morris Rutherfurd had been a law partner of William H. Seward, Abraham Lincoln's secretary of state. Lewis studied science at the University of Heidelberg in the 1860s and won renown as an astronomer with his photographs of the moon.

Morris's wife, Winthrop's mother Margaret Stuyvesant Chanler, was a good friend of Sara Roosevelt. She was generally admired as "uncommonly beautiful." Margaret's brother John Winthrop was married to another Margaret: Margaret Astor Ward. She brought more fame and fortune to her new in-laws, including her nephew

Winthrop Rutherfurd. Margaret Astor Ward Chanler was a direct heiress of the immense fortune of her grandfather, William Backhouse Astor. Margaret's aunt Laura Astor was the wife of Franklin Hughes Delano, FDR's great-uncle and namesake. Laura's grandfather John Jacob Astor was so pleased with the match linking him to the Delanos that he gave the bride $200,000 in trust as a wedding present. Laura's father William Backhouse Astor favored the young Franklin Hughes Delano with another present: a mansion surrounded by a lush farm. It made them William's immediate neighbors. The Delanos' estate Steen Valetje was directly adjacent to Rokeby, the legendary Astor family seat high above the Hudson.

Many fond memories of FDR's youth, which had been handed down by his great-aunt Laura Astor Delano to his mother's brother Warren Delano III, were inseparable from "Steen." It was at Steen where the eighteen-year-old Eleanor had boldly arrived uninvited early in July 1903, traveling south from her Grandmother Hall's mansion Oak Terrace in Tivoli. Eleanor could not wait to see Franklin again. His mother had just recently helped her become more closely acquainted with the attractive Harvard man at three Hyde Park house parties.

Young Franklin loved mornings on horseback at Steen in a cavalcade of Delano cousins. The lively Laura, named after her great-aunt Laura Astor, was—and remained—his favorite cousin. As "Polly," she would be with him on the last day of his life in Warm Springs, Georgia, in the same room with the widowed Lucy Rutherfurd.

There was no end to family relations and meetings in person that linked the Rutherfurds and the Roosevelts by way of the Astors and Delanos. Sara knew all about Miss Mercer's new connections when Lucy became a member of the Rutherfurd clan. In Sara's eyes there was, however, one big difference between the aristocrats from the North and South: the Roosevelts and Rutherfurds on the one hand, and the Mercers on the other. In the 1920s Lucy's ancestral fortunes and estates were only a historical memory; Winthrop Rutherfurd, however, was still in full control of the money and land he had inherited. Winty was a gentleman farmer, like James Roosevelt, but he operated on a much larger scale and with a much larger budget. Furthermore, Winty was not tied down by business obligations in

New York City like FDR's father. The Rutherfurd heir was wealthy enough to concentrate on his hobbies, such as the breeding of fox terriers.

Beyond the material goods he had to offer, Winty Rutherfurd had powerful appeal as a man. Even Lucy's much younger niece, Lucy Mercer Blundon, was dazzled by his charm and extraordinary good looks and raved about him until the end of her life. Winty had presence; he was elegant, eloquent, and ageless. If FDR and his father James appeared to Lucy as models of English country gentlemen, Winthrop had an edge over them. He was more intimately familiar with their lifestyle than any Roosevelt. He had spent an important part of his youth with an uncle in England who imbued him with the graciousness and formality of the upper class.

Winthrop was captivating and mature. He offered a safe haven after the storms in Lucy's parental home. In Lucy's subconscious powerful impressions from her youth worked in his favor. The heroines of Lucy's school years in Vienna, her role models among the Daughters of the Divine Redeemer, had distinguished themselves from other charitable orders by a special form of service. They had come to the aid of fathers and their children who had been deprived of a mother's care by her illness or death. There were rich rewards on earth and in heaven for such acts of charity.

* * *

Back on August 1, 1880, James Roosevelt had brushed off indignantly in a letter to "my dear Miss Bamie" some matrons' parlor talk that dared to find fault in his rush to the altar with a much younger woman. A generation later Winthrop Rutherfurd also rejected critics who challenged his swift action, leading to marriage with Lucy. The ceremony took place on February 12, 1920, in the home of his new sister-in-law Violetta Marbury. Lucy's warmth and courage in the recent crisis, coping with the serious illness of Winty's oldest son Lewis Morton, had woven her into the family's fabric. The wedding, only a few days after Lewis died of pneumonia, sealed an established covenant.

Vio's marriage in 1919 added to the currents that pushed Lucy toward matrimony. Lucy had always lived in synergy with her only sister. Vio's choice of a distinguished husband set a high bar, a standard for Lucy to match. Dr. William B. Marbury, the physician Vio assisted on the front lines during the war, appeared as an ideal suitor. In a delightful coincidence, four other wartime nurses of Vio's acquaintance also married the doctors with whom they worked overseas. Like her grandmother and namesake Violetta Lansdale, Vio was united with a man who combined a respected old name in Maryland with the prestige of a physician.

Dr. Marbury was no provincial. After being licensed in Virginia in 1909, he had been invited to accompany the entrepreneur Joseph Leiter on a trip around the world. Joseph's father Levi Leiter had taken the millions he made as a Chicago meat packer to a life of leisure in Washington. He became a friend of Henry Adams and married his daughter Mary Victoria to George Curzon, later appointed viceroy of India.

While Vio's marriage to Dr. Marbury tied her to Washington, Lucy became less sedentary as Mrs. Rutherfurd. She gladly adopted her husband's habit of residing alternately at their countryseat in Allamuchy, New Jersey, their winter quarters in Aiken, South Carolina, and their homes in New York and Washington. Lucy's wedding day itself foreshadowed a lifetime shaped exclusively by the demands of her immediate family. There was no pomp and circumstance. A minimum of tradition was upheld with a wedding cake, mentioned favorably by an eleven-year-old guest, Lyman Atkinson Cotten, Jr., from North Carolina. He expressed sympathy for his beautiful cousin Lucy, giving herself to an "old and ugly man." Lyman's mother Elizabeth Henderson Cotten looked at the princely groom with kinder eyes. She stressed that Lucy married him "*not* for money but because she felt he needed her."

Jonathan Daniels called the wedding "a quiet event treated quietly. On February 13, the *Washington Post* reported, 'Mrs. Carroll Mercer announces the marriage of her daughter, Lucy Page, to Mr. Winthrop Rutherfurd of New York. The ceremony took place yesterday morning at the home of Dr. and Mrs. William B. Marbury, the latter a sister of the bride. On account of deep mourning only the immediate families were present.' "

The decision to get married a few days after the heartbreaking death of the oldest son of the house was unusual for both the bride and the groom. Winty cried out for an immediate wedding, giving him a rock to cling to among crashing waves of mourning. The loss of his heir had torn wide open the wound caused by the death of his wife Alice three years earlier. Lucy, the angel sent to uphold him in his despair, was to be merged with the family as its new mother in a crucible of pain and sorrow.

Both emotional and practical considerations demanded Lucy's immediate change in status from "Miss Mercer" to "Mrs. Rutherfurd." Lucy was no longer a transient guest in the house. From now on she was forever the firmly anchored heart of a home.

PART TWO

LUCY AS MRS. WINTHROP RUTHERFURD

The picture reflects the glum mood of the Roosevelt family after the marital crises provoked by Franklin's other love came to a head in 1919. Eleanor looks dejected; her mother-in-law puts a comforting hand on her knee. Franklin is noncompliant and faces the camera with a mix of defiance and resignation, while the children are visibly uneasy. Courtesy of the Franklin D. Roosevelt Presidential Library and Museum, Hyde Park, New York.

This portrait of Lucy's husband Winthrop Rutherfurd
was painted after their marriage in 1920.

Ridgeley Hall in Aiken, South Carolina, was the Rutherfurds'
major residence.

In Aiken Lucy's stepdaughter Alice Rutherfurd engaged the
society portraitist Madame Elizabeth Shoumatoff
to paint Lucy, her beloved stepmother.

Lucy's daughter Barbara was introduced to society at a dinner dance in New York on November 22, 1940. Winthrop Rutherfurd, not well enough to be present, had a friend take his place in the receiving line. The debutante was wearing an aquamarine on a pendant, a gift from her mother's friend FDR.

On September 1, 1944, FDR and his entourage were Lucy's guests at her mansion in Allamuchy, New Jersey. She had inherited from her husband upon his death in the spring of that year.

The impeccable great lady, Mrs. Winthrop Rutherford, shows strands of gray in her hair at the time of her last farewell to the president at his retreat—the Little White House in Warm Springs, Georgia.

After FDR died Lucy had only three more years to enjoy her grandchildren before she died in 1948.

The last photograph of FDR was taken by Nicholas Robbins, the photographer in Lucy's party, at Warm Springs a few days before the president's death on April 12, 1945.

At the wedding of her daughter Barbara, Lucy stands beside her stepdaughter Alice surrounded by her stepsons Winthrop, Jr., and Hugo (left) and Guy and John (right).

Lucy's famous subdued smile was still warm and pleasant two years
before her death.

CHAPTER 7

ELEANOR, FRANKLIN, AND LUCY IN NEW ORBITS

ELEANOR'S DEFINING FRIENDSHIPS

The years 1918 and 1919, when Eleanor's awareness of Lucy's rule over Franklin's heart made her miserable, ushered in a time when the goals and attitudes of both spouses shifted. Lucy too became a new person as the currents of her life carried her away from Franklin.

There began another act in the drama showing how Franklin, Eleanor, and Lucy influenced each other's fate. When the curtain went up in 1920, the new scene presented a changed Eleanor. She put more distance between herself and her husband and mother-in-law, and even between herself and her children. The gradual shift in her interests, whereabouts, and daily activities peaked in 1925 and 1926. Starting in 1921, Eleanor promoted the aims of the League of Women Voters as a member of its board. She moved on to work in associations such as the Women's Trade Union League and the Women's Division of the New York State Democratic Committee.

The leaders of these organizations soon became more than comrades in arms. Eleanor never had a sister but her new friends filled this void. She accepted Esther Lape as an affectionate intellectual guide. A college teacher and journalist admired for her brilliant mind,

Esther lived in Greenwich Village with Elizabeth Read, a woman of many talents. The jurist of the feminist group, Elizabeth taught Eleanor the legal basics of their cause. In 1922 Esther and Elizabeth introduced Eleanor to Nancy Cook and Marion Dickerman, two activist women who were equally devoted to each other. Eleanor was first charmed by the boyish friskiness of the curly-haired Nancy. Not long afterward she learned to appreciate the solid qualities of the responsible and reliable Marion, six years younger than Nancy. Eleanor's fast-growing attachment to Nancy and Marion put an end to her family's monopoly over her heart, opening her up to form other warm relationships with women and men from outside her family circle. For Eleanor, Nancy and Marion became family; their symbiotic triangular connection would last for fifteen years. It shaped Eleanor's personality, even before she moved in with them under one roof at Val-Kill cottage.

From 1922 on Eleanor saw less and less of her husband and she no longer sought the company of her mother-in-law. Her youngest boy John was now six, of school age. Together with his four older brothers, Johnnie was used to constant attention and assistance from his grandmother in Hyde Park. Sara took him to doctors' offices and worried about his grades in school. Sara had more time for him and his siblings than their busy mother. Eleanor's main home and center of activities was now her townhouse at 47 East 65th Street in New York City.

Deep in her heart, throughout days filled with exciting new demands, Eleanor was still irked by the discovery of Lucy's hold on Franklin's feelings. It served as a reminder that she needed to rebuild her self-respect. Lucy had taught her the hard way that she had to live without being dependent on the emotional rewards of her service as a wife and mother. She had to be a winner in other ways than being first in a man's heart.

To a great extent, Eleanor's shift of gears paralleled her husband's altered course. In the long run, the most brutal change in Franklin's life reduced their time together more drastically than did his chronic absences from his family on Washington's golf courses. The disaster of a polio attack was unexpected. Franklin's mother compared it to being hit by lightning out of a blue sky.

POLIO!

It began on August 11, 1921. When Franklin climbed out of bed at his and Eleanor's summer home on Campobello Island, his legs gave way under him. Never again would he able to stand by himself unassisted. Two local doctors were unable to explain the sudden paralysis and the loss of motor functions. Finally, Eleanor's appeal to FDR's uncle Fred Delano—who had been so good to her in 1917—brought a renowned orthopedic surgeon from Harvard to Franklin's bedside. On August 25 Dr. Robert Lovett declared as "perfectly clear" that the patient had contracted poliomyelitis.

Franklin was stunned, seeking refuge in disbelief of what was in store for him. Eleanor's position as a wife was again put into question. Her recent adjustments to a new marital situation were dwarfed by the need to face the fact that she had lost her upbeat, easygoing husband of sixteen years. His illness eventually made a more complex man out of him. Franklin's affliction further filled Eleanor with fear that her children were in danger, possibly caught in one of the rampant polio epidemics. Her trepidation was not unfounded. In retrospect it seems clear that the viral infection that incapacitated her thirty-nine-year-old athletic husband had struck him on a joyous occasion—at a gathering of children.

After resigning from his post in the Navy Department, and his unsuccessful run for the vice presidency, Franklin resumed his career as a lawyer. To add more human interest to his dry work, he supported public service organizations. His chairmanship of the Greater New York Council of the Boy Scouts of America provided him with much satisfaction. The roots of the Boy Scout movement in England appealed to him. He shared its ideals of patriotism, military discipline, and Christian values and felt congenial toward the movement's founder, Sir Robert Baden-Powell.

On July 28, 1921, FDR went to Bear Mountain State Park, south of Hyde Park, to preside at the ceremonies of the quadrennial National Scout Jamboree, a ten-day gathering of thousands of scouts and their leaders from around the country. Towering Bear Mountain, the site of several Boy Scout camps, looked down across the Hudson River on some of the happiest scenes of Franklin's early years. The round green peak formed the scenic background for Algonac, the Delanos' family seat and Franklin's beloved second home.

The jamboree on Bear Mountain offered many opportunities for exposure to the most feared infectious disease of the time. In a crowd of susceptible young people, nobody could tell which boy carried the dangerous virus, likely without showing any symptoms himself. Franklin could have caught the disease just by wiping his face after shaking hands with an infected scout. During the critical incubation period, when FDR's body fought the invading virus, his immune system was impaired by overexertion. Franklin's style as a father, modeled after his cousin Theodore Roosevelt's famous "strenuous life," led to a frequent overtaxing of his strength.

Two tiring weeks came to a peak on August 10, the last day Franklin spent firmly on his feet. Instead of taking it easy in a deck chair, "Father" acted as a model of toughness for his boys. He led the kids on beating out a brush fire with pine boughs. Then he jogged with them to a swim in a warm lake, followed by a jump into the icy waters of the Bay of Fundy. Back home Franklin was too exhausted to remove his swimsuit. He resisted the urge to go to bed and collapsed on a chair, reading his mail in a cold wind. The next day Franklin woke up an invalid, changed in body and possibly in mind as well.

Some biographers have contested Eleanor's observation that the trials of battling his paralysis made Franklin a more serious, considerate, and responsible person. But there was no question that he became more introspective. Long periods of waiting for care are the lot of the physically afflicted. The endless days and years spent by FDR in pursuit of healing transformed his lifestyle. No longer constantly active, he was pushed into periods of quiet contemplation. For the first time, Franklin had leisure to ponder his life, his marriage, the dictates of his heart, and the challenges of his career goals. During the seven years out of the public eye following 1921, he looked inward and he looked back. Only in November 1928 did his election as governor encourage him to again focus on the present and the future. Once more politics became the essence of his life.

FRANKLIN SEEKS WARM WATERS

After the Roosevelts moved from Campobello to their townhouse in Manhattan in the fall of 1921, the winter of 1922 turned into a nightmare for the whole family. Worse than the physical pain was FDR's inner struggle, his refusal to accept the finality of being disabled. Eleanor's career plans were threatened because of her husband's illness. She was suddenly indispensable as his nurse. Her designs for a future as a political activist, teacher, and writer were relegated to the back burner.

Yet Eleanor's future turned out not to be as hopeless as she feared. As soon as spring arrived, Franklin moved away from New York. He first went to Hyde Park, under the care of his mother, then to New England for medical treatments. Next Franklin's discovery of the benefit of warm waters in Florida and Georgia gave Eleanor the freedom to do as she pleased. Unexpectedly, she was relieved of her duties as a wife and had more time than ever to build a professional life for herself.

Eleanor could not foresee these developments in the stressful months following her husband's polio attack. Though Eleanor liked to say that nursing was her original calling, it was trying to perform basic bedside procedures for a husband with whom she was no longer intimate.

Louis Howe's residence in the Roosevelts' townhouse during this time was a great comfort for Eleanor. The savvy political strategist kept both Eleanor and Franklin connected with political developments outside their confinement on East 65th Street. However, Louis occupied a room of his own—adding to the overcrowding of the place—and lack of space became a trial for all the occupants. The nerve-wracking situation was resolved only when winter ended and Franklin's mother could open up her Hyde Park house for the summer. As soon as she could, she took her son in.

Louis Howe continued to serve as FDR's faithful liaison to the world of politics during the seven years between 1921 and 1928, when his boss stayed out of the spotlight. The retreat of his boss into solitude meant that Howe could not do much for the future of FDR's career as a statesman—except for a few weeks in 1924, when Franklin mustered enough strength to attend the Democratic National Convention. He was encouraged by the accolades that greeted his powerful rhetoric. He made a lasting impression with his nomination of Al Smith, the governor of New York, for president of the United States.

The convention was encouraging for Franklin, but also strenuous. The interlude showed him that he still had to concentrate all his efforts on improving his physical condition. He resumed his struggle for rehabilitation, begun at Hyde Park in the spring and fall of 1922 and continued there in the fall of 1923. The availability of the Astors' heated swimming pool on their Rhinebeck estate was beneficial but infrequent. Franklin had to look for exercise by swimming in warm water farther south. He explored what Florida had to offer in the spring and summer of 1923, and again in the spring of 1924 and 1925. Finally, in 1924 he found his haven in Warm Springs, Georgia. It served him as a spa, retreat, and southern home until the end of his life.

With his changes of residence, Franklin left not only his wife behind but also his mother. If the ladies could not or would not visit for any length of time in Florida or Georgia, they could not see him. It has been counted that FDR spent 116 of the 208 weeks between January 1925 and December 1928 away from home. Eleanor resided with him for four of these weeks, Sara for two (not counting the summer vacations and numerous weekends she spent with her son in Hyde Park). But during the same time, the congenial Missy—FDR's devoted secretary, Marguerite LeHand—was his live-in companion for 110 weeks.

Although Missy's personal attachment and thoughtful care were a blessing for Franklin, she did not fill all his thoughts. In hours of contemplation on his sickbed, in endless therapy sessions, and during rest after aquatic exercises, Franklin's wandering mind led him away from the present. He later followed up on his musings with old moves, trying to bridge the gap that now separated him from Lucy, the woman who had taught him a new way of loving. His natural inclination to seek pleasant thoughts guided him to reminisce about happy cruises on the *Sylph* in the summer of 1917.

* * *

Franklin's enjoyment of life aboard ships suggested staying on a houseboat as the best place to recuperate. He liked to say that water had done him in and that water would make him well again. The icy water of the Bay of Fundy had hurt him; the warm water of the American South would heal. In 1923 his first choice as the place of a cure was Florida's Atlantic coast. The relaxed atmosphere on his rented houseboat *Weona II* suited him so well that in 1924 he and his Harvard companion John Lawrence bought a better houseboat. Named *Larooco,* a shortened combination of the names of the owners (Lawrence, Roosevelt & Co.), this home on the water served the sailor in Franklin to perfection.

While Franklin's friends were thrilled to accept invitations to be his guests aboard, Eleanor was less enthusiastic. FDR's new casual style of lolling about the deck in his pajamas displeased her. She did not share his love for the unspoiled, raw nature of shipboard life. Eleanor was still averse to setting foot on a rocking vessel, risking seasickness with every step. When she overcame her fears and visited Franklin on his houseboat, she was caught in another net of aversion—her dislike of the geographic particularities of the South. Eleanor's recent painful experience with a southern lady in Washington might have made her especially allergic to the ambience of the region. She was uneasy in the "eerie and menacing" nights off the Florida shore. When she fled to fresher air on the boat's deck, floods of citronella oil would not keep the mosquitoes away.

At first Eleanor's visits were hardly more than brief courtesy calls, but in March 1925 she spent ten days with Franklin on his houseboat anchored off Long Key. She wanted to celebrate their twentieth wedding anniversary together. This time life aboard ship was made more palatable for Eleanor by political conversations with the Roosevelts' friend Henry Morgenthau. Games of cards with Louis Howe helped pass the time. Trips to Florida satisfied Eleanor's sense of duty as a wife. Like Franklin, she was anxious to keep up appearances of an intact marriage. Eleanor was glad to see that Missy LeHand was willing and able to assume the primary responsibilities as FDR's caregiver.

There was no jealousy mixed with Eleanor's appreciation of Missy's service. Eleanor knew that the affection linking Missy and Franklin was not as alarming as his involvement with Lucy Mercer. While Missy adored her boss, and he basked in the warmth of her devotion, a divisive barrier kept the two apart. Differences in age, social background, and emotional disposition separated Franklin and the young woman he called "child."

Relieved of guilt about sins of omission in her obligations as a wife, Eleanor could safely travel back north to the embrace of her friends and the company of her brother Hall's relatives in New York. She gladly resumed the rounds of speeches and lectures, as well as the dinners and luncheons with important associates that determined her standing in the ranks of the political elite. She maintained regular contact with Franklin by corresponding with him, but the content of her letters touched only the surface of her experiences. The endearments in the couple's exchanges were routine, the feelings expressed impersonal. Once more Eleanor did not preserve the bulk of her husband's letters from this time. In surviving fragments of their correspondence, phrases like "I miss you very much," salutations like "Dearest Honey," and sign-offs such as "Devotedly" flowed as easily out of their pens as they did in the days when Eleanor was on Campobello and Franklin was in Washington. Neither of them opened up about their innermost feelings. While Franklin and Eleanor drifted further apart, they carefully cultivated the formal bonds that held them together.

Just as Eleanor was happy with her sisterly friends, Franklin enjoyed the company of old and new buddies. He was by no means lonely. Nigel Law was long back in England but his successor in Franklin's affection, Livingston Davis, filled an ever-larger role as FDR's number one confidant. Livy was discreet and loyal. During the crucial years of his friend's infatuation with Lucy Mercer, he had carefully avoided mentioning FDR's ties to the young lady in his diary. In intimate chats on the *Larooco,* Franklin opened up to Livy. He did not have to hide the fact that he still thought of Lucy. Both he and Livy knew that his longing for any new attachment was more hopeless than ever. Lucy was out of reach as a distant great lady and the happy mother of a large family. It is not known whether Franklin pushed Livy—or whether his faithful friend volunteered—to find out in person whether Lucy still had fond feelings for her old skipper on the *Sylph*.

LUCY'S GRAND NORTHERN HOME: ALLAMUCHY

Franklin's change of pace, from a hectic life to one of leisure, appears to have allowed more room in his thoughts for memories of Lucy. At the same time, Franklin was at a loss trying to visualize her state of mind in her new circumstances. He could not imagine that Lucy might simply not have the time to think of him. Before Livy enlightened him about Lucy's heavy family obligations, Franklin could not realize that she had been plunged into an all-absorbing situation unlike anything she had experienced during the time he knew her. Gone forever were the frustrations of a solitary young woman in enforced idleness, with a disagreeable mother as her main companion. In Lucy's new life of abundance, she was inundated by constant demands on her attention. Somebody wanted something from her all day long—whether it was her husband, her five children, or one of the governesses, housekeepers, gardeners, and maids now under her direction.

Lucy had taken a big risk, marrying a man almost three decades her senior. Livy put an end to guesses how the marriage worked out when he went to visit the Rutherfurds and reported to Franklin that Lucy had made the right decision. She was content in her life with Winthrop. Lucy's motherly friend Elizabeth Henderson Cotten, in Chapel Hill, North Carolina, agreed with Livy's impression. Elizabeth continued to be the relative most familiar with Lucy's circumstances. She told Lucy's chronicler Jonathan Daniels that Winty "and Lucy came at least twice a year to see me—going south and returning." Elizabeth held a high opinion of Lucy's husband. "He was an interesting man," she described Winty. "One never thought of age concerning him. Romantic love was over for Lucy—perhaps for him. It never comes twice. But they loved each other sincerely, and were very congenial."

Lucy endeared herself to her husband with many fine qualities. She combined a sunny, affectionate disposition with a strong sense of duty. Her charm and vitality were matched by practical talents. Lucy proved herself as a model homemaker. She managed her large staff with intelligence and kindness. Lucy's way of captivating her new husband's heart in a short time invited comparison with FDR's mother as a new bride. In a strikingly similar situation, Sallie Delano became the great love of James Roosevelt's life. In both cases the affectionate respect of the young wives for their much older spouses grew into deeper feelings within a few months. Being loved fervently by their husbands, Sara Roosevelt and Lucy Rutherfurd radiated back the warmth they received.

Immediately after the wedding in Washington, Winthrop had taken his bride to Allamuchy. The Rutherfurd homestead was situated outside a small village in northwestern New Jersey. Here Lucy found everything that Franklin had told her about the Roosevelts' Hyde Park estate, but on a much larger scale. Her husband was a gentleman farmer, like FDR and his father James. Unlike James, Winthrop did not have to pursue business interests that demanded regular commutes to New York City. He was independently wealthy. His eight thousand acres and five farms in Allamuchy dwarfed Hyde Park's one-farm operation. The proportions of Winty's possessions put him at an advantage over Franklin, whose perennial ambition to round up his land holdings to a thousand acres was hard to fulfill.

The Rutherfurds' Allamuchy was not as conveniently linked by train to New York City as the Roosevelts' Hyde Park. Used to the whirl of big cities from Washington to Vienna, Lucy was now stuck in "the sticks." Until now she had never been north of Philadelphia, the area she knew from her preteen years as a boarder at the Holy Child Academy. For the first time, she had a taste of the long northern winters. She was amazed to find the small lake in front of the Allamuchy mansion frozen solid. The palatial house had needed a mistress for three years, since the death of Alice Morton Rutherfurd. The grieving Winthrop had closed his mind to maintenance and the small touches that make a house a home. Lucy had her hands full making the Rutherfurd mansion comfortable again.

She had no time to regret that she had missed out on the birthright of high-class brides in her circle. She had not been whisked away to an overseas honeymoon of many months' duration—like her mother Minna, Franklin's mother Sara, and his wife Eleanor. Instead Lucy found herself immersed right away in a heavy load of domestic chores.

*   *   *

Adjusting to surroundings she had not shaped herself, Lucy began to understand what it meant to be a second wife. She was a proud daughter of the South. Her predecessor Alice Morton had been a Yankee rooted in the Hudson Valley. Allamuchy, in the corner of New Jersey that borders Pennsylvania and New York State, was separated only by the Pocono Mountains from the scenes of Alice's childhood.

The forty-room mansion on the northern shore of Allamuchy Pond was built in 1903, the year after Alice Morton's wedding to Winthrop Chanler Rutherfurd. It fit the large dimensions of Ellerslie, his wife's parental home near Rhinebeck, New York. But the Rutherfurds' red brick building at Allamuchy had no equivalent among the traditional Hudson Valley mansions of FDR's youth. It was newer, erected in the architectural style of English Jacobean countryseats, and evoked different associations in Winthrop and Lucy's mind. It bore an uncanny resemblance to the handsome school building where Lucy had been instructed as a little girl by the sisters of the Holy Child Academy. For the Anglophile Winthrop, it mattered that his mansion was a smaller version of Sandringham, a favorite retreat of the queen of England.

The Allamuchy residence was not the first grandiose seat of the Rutherfurd clan in New Jersey, and Winthrop was not the only heir to the Rutherfurd fortune. When John Rutherfurd—the family's founding father—died in 1871, he was the largest landowner in New Jersey. Even after the State of New Jersey assumed ownership of a large portion of Rutherfurd land and turned it into Allamuchy Mountain State Park, sizable parcels remained in the hands of the Rutherfurd heirs.

Winthrop's first cousin Morris Rutherfurd, two years his junior, became a very rich man as a tycoon in the railroad business. He excelled as the vice president and general manager of the Lehigh and Hudson River Valley Railway Company. One of its stations, the Allamuchy Freight House Depot (as it is still called), was the site of FDR's historic stopover in September 1944, when he paid a call on the widowed Lucy at her Allamuchy mansion.

The depot was carefully restored by the local community and was added to the National Register of Historic Places in 2002. All that is left of the Rutherfurds' original homestead, called Tranquillity, is a gate and fragments of stonewalls that are now completely hidden by lush young maples, growing in the middle of an older forest. The mansion was so thoroughly destroyed by fire that rebuilding it was out of the question. It now takes a guide to find its mysterious ruins in the wilderness. Charles A. Fineran, Jr., Allamuchy's current local historian, pointed out to me that the old homestead's name survives in the contemporary Tranquillity Farms, a large, prosperous business that attracts sizable crowds to its informative public events.

In 1920, when Lucy Mercer Rutherfurd first came to Allamuchy as the estate's new mistress, her husband's farm manager was responsible for the property's maintenance and profitability. Lucy did not have to worry about it. She enjoyed the large, well-kept park with sheep grazing in the distance and the flower garden nearby, where she reserved a patch for roses she tended herself.

Lucy was gladly accepted at Allamuchy in her position as the lady of the manor. She held the reins of the baronial household firmly and efficiently. Her staff appreciated her as much for her warm heart as for her organizational expertise. Word spread fast about one of her characteristic acts of kindness: inundated in her own homegrown produce, Lucy still knew what to do when she passed by a roadside stand with a tired vendor. The old lady was depressed, stuck with a mountain of vegetables and flowers at the end of the day. She was tremendously relieved when Mrs. Rutherfurd bought all her goods, allowing her to go home.

CHALLENGES OF AIKEN, SOUTH CAROLINA

Like James and Sara Roosevelt, Winthrop and Lucy Rutherfurd moved in a steady yearly cycle between their northern and southern quarters. From early childhood Franklin was used to switching from comfortable Hyde Park to the more Spartan Campobello Island for the hot months of summer.

Lucy Rutherfurd was offered even more changes of residence. Apart from her country mansion in New Jersey, Lucy could choose between elegant houses in both New York City and Washington, but none of them made her feel as much at home as her place in the South—in Aiken. The resort was located in South Carolina close to Augusta, Georgia, just over the state line. The community's name was derived from William Aiken, Sr. As president of the South Carolina Canal and Rail Road Company, he had opened up the small town as a station on his steam engine line, inviting vacationers to spend the winter in its balmy climate.

Surrounded by pine forests and agricultural land, Aiken was a pleasant place to live. Wide streets linked parks full of "wintergreen" trees, as evergreens were called. The town earned its reputation as society's "Newport of the South" from its roster of prominent residents. The heirs of the Gilded Age built impressive mansions in Aiken, setting a pattern for exclusive, high-class living. The town retained its aura of Victorian refinement in a surprising revival after the First World War.

Two chroniclers preserved the ambience of this anachronistic enclave of bygone pretension. In a long-forgotten book, Harry Worcester Smith paid homage in 1931 to many important residents of Aiken, listed in *Who's Who*. Names of members of America's upper crust dominated the pages of his *Life and Sport in Aiken: And Those Who Made It*. Next to H. W. Smith, Emily L. Bull Cooper captured the Aiken mystique best in a biography called *Eulalie*, which traced the influence of Mrs. Julian Salley—who called herself somewhat presumptuously Lucy Rutherfurd's best friend in Aiken. She was a socialite and real estate agent who pulled many strings behind the scenes. Eulalie Chaffee Salley ruled the town as the provider of the homes and everything inside that Aiken's winter residents needed. According to her ads, they only had to bring their toothbrush. As a dealer in art and antiques, she also "aided FDR in his varied collecting."

Eulalie idolized Lucy. She had a higher opinion of Lucy's exceptional qualities than Aiken's chronicler Harry Worcester Smith. In his eyes Mr. and Mrs. Winthrop Rutherfurd were just another distinguished couple—among many others who—had established Aiken's fame. Winthrop Rutherfurd of Allamuchy, New Jersey, had put down roots in Aiken before he was widowed, living in a big house next to the renowned Calico Cottage. When his house burned down, "[H]e erected on its foundation the stately fireproof mansion called 'Ridgeley Hall.'" Smith noted that the large building contained fourteen bedrooms and baths. It was separated from Berrie Road by well-landscaped grounds and profited from its closeness to the prestigious Palmetto Golf Club.

Lucy saw to it that the interior of Ridgeley Hall was as attractive as its grounds. The time had finally come when she could use her good taste in furnishing her own home. Lucy's mother had made a name for herself in Washington society by turning the Mercer residence into a showcase for the latest trends in high living. Justly proud of her reputation as an artistic interior decorator, Minnie Mercer assembled a collection of pictures of the rooms she designed. When she was forced to make a living from her talents, the photos promoted her career as a consultant for the affluent ladies of her acquaintance.

In her looks and temperament, Minna's daughter Lucy took after her father. But she inherited her mother's talent as an interior decorator. While Lucy no longer had to use her expertise to support herself, she still took pride in her artistic abilities. She too compiled an intriguing photo album with pictures of rooms she furnished; they were worlds apart from her mother's heavy Victorian creations in dark woods. There were no more carved elephant heads at the foot of the staircase. Lucy's living rooms, dominated by light-colored chintzes, were more comfortable and cheerful than anything in her parents' home. They radiated harmony with the world around them, both in the urban elegance of the social rooms and in the casual atmosphere created by rustic plaid textiles in the family rooms.

*   *   *

In FDR's experience Lucy's ambition—excelling as a homemaker, providing comfort and visual pleasure for her loved ones—set her apart from his wife. Eleanor considered discerning interior decorating a superfluous luxury. She was proud of losing not a minute when she set up a new residence after a move. Her last picture had to be hung within twenty-four hours after settling in. Sensible, practical, and efficient, Eleanor resented the efforts of her mother-in-law to embellish the look of new quarters.

Lucy was more like Sara than Eleanor in choosing her priorities as the lady of the house. As a decorator, Lucy had much competition in Aiken. The Rutherfurds' place offered its visitors many aesthetic treats. However, it was not an invitation to Ridgeley Hall but to the mansion *Mon Repos* that was "most sought for in Aiken." Mr. Smith, the *arbiter elegantiorum* of the vacation colony, was awed by the villa's owner Thomas Hitchcock. The gentleman at the top of Aiken's ranks was the eleventh of his line and a graduate of Oxford. Hitch-cock derived his high social position from his closeness to Charles Anderson Dana of the *Sun*, New York City's daily newspaper. As a re-sult, he stood out as "a leading figure in Metropolitan Society and fi-nance." But what counted even more in Aiken was Mr. Hitchcock's "serious interest in sports," which was especially meritorious be-cause he had acquired it in England.

It was *de rigeur* in Aiken to belong to at least one of its traditional categories of sportsmen or sportswomen. There was a wide variety of sports to choose from. Smith mentioned drag hunting, steeple-chases, and thoroughbred racing at the track. Excelling at polo was more highly esteemed than driving a four-in-hand. Together with turkey hunters, crack shots at dove drives and quail hunts were most admired. The participants in these exclusive "sports" were automati-cally "in." Smith contrasted them somewhat condescendingly with the rest of Aiken society. He declared that many of those who were struggling for recognition may "come for their health and others for the air, but not many for loafing."

Winthrop Rutherford's reputation as a good golfer linked him se-curely to the leading groups of Aiken's society. The Rutherfurds knew when to take part in important events. A photograph of the couple in elegant attire shows them as spectators at a horse race. While Winthrop was not actively involved in Aiken's equestrian cul-ture, he stood out with his gentlemanly hobby of breeding fox terri-ers. He was not overly ambitious in his efforts. Neither Winty nor Lucy were jockeying for a high-ranking position among their peers. First of all, they found much pleasure in each other's company. Sec-ond, they were responsible parents, raising six children to become well-educated and successful adults, worthy of their forebears.

When Lucy Rutherfurd was newly married, she differed in decisive ways from other ladies of her class. She did not follow in the foot-steps of her mother, Minnie Mercer, who scanned the society pages for favorable mention of her social standing. Neither did Lucy share the ambition of Franklin's mother. Sara always recorded in her diary when she had the privilege to "walk in with the host" as the most honored guest at big dinners.

Although Lucy had been much in demand at Washington society parties for her spirited conversation, she did not share Eleanor's pride in the high intellectual level of talk at her dinner table. Lucy voluntarily disqualified herself from leadership in Aiken society. She was sure of herself and was not competitive. Lucy just wanted to be a good wife and mother.

Besides, Lucy was considered "arrived" in Aiken society without any effort on her part. Her aristocratic ancestry and her husband's connections were enough to set her apart from her peers. Moreover, Winty was close to the ruling queen of Aiken, Mrs. Thomas Hitchcock, the former Louise Eustis. He was like family for Aiken's equivalent of a First Lady. The fame of Louise, the mistress of *Mon Repos,* surpassed even that of her husband. Louise was the role model and trendsetter for Aiken's ladies. The *New York Times* praised her as "a polo enthusiast, famous horsewoman, and philanthropist." Her life was summed up in her eulogy "All Aiken is a Memorial to Mrs. Hitchcock."

Mrs. Hitchcock's sister-in-law Edith, the wife of her brother Billy Eustis, was her equal as a regal, wealthy, and intelligent leader of the social circle around her. This was the same Edith Morton Eustis of Washington who played a decisive role in the fate of Lucy Mercer. As the sister of Winty's first wife Alice, Edith Eustis cut a wide swath. Lucy had been too young to witness the marriage of Louise Hitchcock's parents, Louisiana Congressman George Eustis, Jr., and Louise Morris Corcoran, the daughter of Washington's celebrated William W. Corcoran. Their wedding had been an unforgettable event in the District of Columbia. The Eustis children, William, George, and Louise, were orphaned early. When William married Edith Morton and Louise married Thomas Hitchcock, two *grande dame*s began their rule in society.

*   *   *

There was no end to counting family ties between the social elite of Washington and Aiken. The architect Julian Peabody, who had designed Ridgeley Hall, was married to Thomas and Louise Hitchcock's daughter Celestine. In the 1920s American high society was still tightly knit. It filled Aiken not only with associates of the Eustises and Rutherfords, but also with the wealthiest of the Roosevelts. Aiken was familiar to FDR from reports of his half-brother Rosy and those of relatives of Rosy's wife Helen Schermerhorn Astor. They fit as seamlessly into the resort's top layer as another guest of Aiken, Edmund Rogers—FDR's next-door neighbor and close companion during his childhood in Hyde Park. The Roosevelts and Astors represented New York and the Hudson Valley in Aiken. The Hitchcocks maintained their family roots up north in Westbury, Long Island.

Lucy formed her own friendships in Aiken independently of family connections. Her dearest friends were chosen for their personal qualities; it was coincidental that they happened to be the wives of prominent entrepreneurs. George H. Mead of Dayton, Ohio, was a tycoon in the paper industry, working as president of the Mead Corporation. Lucy's closeness to FDR, and her assurance that George Mead could be trusted, would eventually raise him to prominence.

In 1936 and 1937, Mead appeared in FDR's official "Day-by-Day Chronology" as chairman of the president's Business Advisory Council. In 1943 he served as a member of the president's Business War Group, symbolic of FDR's effort to keep the business world involved in his strategy. The Meads' personal bonds with Lucy would outlive George's service in the capital. Lucy told only the Meads about her stay in Warm Springs before the president's death. The following year, in 1946, the Meads offered their own place to the widowed Lucy for the wedding of her daughter Barbara.

Lucy's attachment to the Kittredges was as much a part of her continued contacts with FDR as her friendship with the Meads. Benjamin Rufus Kittredge, from Peekskill, New York, had transformed an abandoned rice plantation in South Carolina into Charleston's popular Cypress Gardens. His acquisition of seven thousand acres in Putnam County, New York, in 1910 gave him the power to make or break FDR's plans for what is now the Taconic Parkway. In the late 1920s, Lucy had a hard time easing Franklin's difficult negotiations with Kittredge. Kittredge's wife Bessie was more accommodating as a friend. In the summer of 1945, she accompanied Lucy on a difficult mission of mourning—trying to get access to the president's grave in Hyde Park.

Apart from casual get-togethers with the Meads and the Kittredges, Lucy also entertained formally, in line with the rest of her circle. Though she was well equipped to organize big parties, she did not aim to become one of Aiken's celebrated hostesses. Lucy preferred to make use of the experiences of her youth in other ways. As a student in a demanding teacher-training program in Vienna, Lucy was well rounded in what would now be called the liberal arts. She had learned the basic rules of teaching, from the elementary "three R's" to college-level courses. Her new family presented her with ample opportunities to use her expertise. Guy, the youngest of her stepsons, born on September 11, 1915, had just reached school age when Lucy became the family's mother. Her oldest stepson John needed guidance on the threshold to higher education. Lucy was well qualified to watch over the schooling of her stepchildren in Aiken's private schools—a prep school for boys and the Fermata School for girls—but beyond that level the advice of her old friend Franklin would be invaluable.

It is unlikely that Lucy ever had time to teach her stepchildren herself. At least she felt competent to choose the right governesses for them—preferably native French speakers like FDR's beloved governess. Sara Roosevelt had selected Mademoiselle Sandoz as Franklin's governess because of her pedagogical talent and her command of several languages. Like Sara, Lucy also promoted her children's fluency in foreign languages. Since Winthrop Rutherfurd was far superior to James Roosevelt in his mastery of European tongues, everybody in the Rutherfurd family could converse in French. If Winty and Lucy did not want to be understood by their children, they would communicate in German or Italian.

*   *   *

Sara had just one son to engage her maternal energies. Lucy, on the other hand, managed to give each of her five stepchildren so much individual attention that they all felt like only children. It was to be expected that Lucy's biological daughter Barbara enjoyed a special status as "the Smallest." She was adored not only by her parents but also by her five older siblings. Barbara was born on June 14, 1922, in the second year of her parents' marriage. Forty years earlier, on January 31, 1882, Franklin Roosevelt had been born after Sara had been married for one year and four months.

In the 1960s an outrageous rumor surfaced when it became known that President Franklin Roosevelt had been exceptionally fond of Barbara Rutherfurd and had called himself her "Godfather."

These whisperings were grist for the mill of those who believed in the old myth that Lucy had been FDR's mistress. They surmised that Barbara was Franklin's biological daughter. The rumor became so persistent that Jonathan Daniels felt the need to refute it in his writings. Even Daniels's wife thought that Lucy Rutherfurd's child "was FDR's also." Daniels marveled at this absurd speculation "in defiance of all laws of biology." In 1967, in a correspondence between Daniels and his historian friend Frank Freidel at Harvard, both men expressed utter astonishment at this ridiculous view of FDR.

Obviously, Lucy and Franklin never dreamed of getting together in the fall of 1921. FDR was absorbed by overwhelming health problems after his polio attack; Lucy was struggling to fill her new role as Mrs. Rutherfurd. The old friends were completely sealed off from each other. In an interview with Joseph Lash, FDR's daughter Anna exclaimed emphatically, "I'm damn sure after she [Lucy] was married they didn't see each other."

The rise of such mind-boggling miscalculations was to a great extent the result of the total silence observed by Lucy and her daughter Barbara about their connection to FDR. Anna Roosevelt Boettiger agreed with their silence. On August 19, 1977, Anna's widower Dr. James Halsted approached Barbara Knowles about the problem they shared: unwelcome media attention recalling Lucy's closeness to FDR. He suggested that two letters from Lucy to the president should be preserved in the presidential library but kept inaccessible for fifty years. Mrs. Knowles expressed her approval in a beautifully written reply to Dr. Halsted on October 30, 1977. She closed her letter, "All my family & I are very opposed to publicity—I have tried to avoid all written or verbal contact with the various authors & reporters who want to know 'my side of the story.' It is a great abhorrence to my half brothers & me all the crude implications that have been printed by people trying to cash in."

Mrs. Knowles's horror at the thought of having her "words twisted" by journalists could not alter the fact that her family's ties to President Roosevelt made them historical figures in their own right. In the long run, her secretiveness encouraged writers to invent stories about FDR and Lucy that created sensations where there were none.

Toward the end of her life, Mrs. Knowles opened up a trifle to Jon Meacham, a writer she chose carefully for his integrity and professional prominence. Lucy herself never wavered from her own policy of wiping out all traces of her love for FDR. Having been hurt as a vulnerable young woman in 1918 by the exposure of a very personal matter, she joined Franklin—who had his own reasons for discretion—in protecting their privacy from prying eyes and minds at all times.

CHAPTER 8

FRANKLIN REACHES OUT TO LUCY, 1926-1928

FDR'S STUNNING MOVE

By 1926 Franklin and Lucy had become strangers to each other. Both needed all their strength to master the challenges at hand. Lucy's own little daughter was now four years old. What in the world could have moved Franklin Delano Roosevelt to seek a new, unexpected connection with a friend who had moved out of his life almost a decade earlier? Lucy had brought much turbulence into his closest relationships. He should have been glad that she was out of his life.

The amazing fact that FDR reached out to Lucy again for no obvious reason is central to the interpretation of Franklin and Lucy's relationship. Without this initiative Franklin's attentions to Lucy in 1917–1918 would be memorable only in their unsettling effect on Eleanor. By opening a second chapter of Lucy's involvement in his life, he revealed a side of his personality that resisted interpretation by outsiders. It did not fit FDR's image as a steely leader that the voice of his heart had more power over him than the dictates of his rational self. Contrary to many psychological analyses of FDR that described him as cunning, cold, and distant, he proved that he could love with abandon, without calculation. It is clear in retrospect that Franklin attested by his actions—rather than by words—that the love of his life was Lucy Mercer Rutherfurd.

If Franklin had not been moved by an inner voice, why would it suddenly occur to him to send an emissary to Lucy? Why start a correspondence with a happily married lady in North Carolina? Had a promise not to see each other again expired? FDR never hinted at such a pledge; it seems to have existed only in the imagination of his envious Oyster Bay Roosevelt relatives. It is not easy to answer the question of what could have prompted Franklin's sudden effort to reinstate long-discontinued ties with Lucy. For those who only knew the pragmatic side of his disposition, his step was a mystery.

ANNA

A close look at Franklin's frame of mind in 1925–1926 offers some clues. These years had brought about changes in his personal life that left empty spaces in his heart. FDR's old male friends Lathrop Brown and Livingston Davis were no longer constant companions. His mother still stayed close and supported him, yet Franklin needed to compensate for painful emotional losses. The two most important women in his life shifted away from him. Anna, his only daughter, got married. His wife Eleanor decamped from his beloved homestead at Hyde Park to a nearby home of her own at Val-Kill.

Anna had always cherished her good times with her father. He was more fun than her serious mother. She favored him even though he had disappointed her twice, just at the time when she was undergoing the rites of passage from a girl to a young lady. Anna told Bernard Asbell, the author closest to being her biographer, how inseparably her life was intertwined with that of her father. She had agreed to study agriculture at Cornell only because she wanted to become his partner, providing much-needed hands-on help in managing farm and forest in Hyde Park.

FDR himself had more conventional ideas for Anna's present and future. She resented his old-fashioned views, showing that he still "belonged to *that* generation" obeying Victorian rules. To Anna's chagrin even her unconventional mother believed in outdated customs. "These are the most complicated and fascinating creatures, both these parents of mine," Anna complained to Asbell. "Because in many ways they never gave up form. . . . Things were done in a certain way. . . . I was informed that I had to come out in society and I died." It was Anna's mother who made her go to Newport for Tennis Week and "stay with her cousin Susie Parish who was really Old Guard."

Anna's father disappointed her when she begged him to support her rebellion. "He'd just say, 'That's up to Granny and Mother. You settle all this with them.'" Tennis Week turned out better for Anna than she expected. During her stay with Cousin Susie, she experienced a second, even more painful disillusionment caused by her father. Susie opened Anna's eyes to "this woman named Lucy Mercer almost running off with Father." When her mother deepened the shock a year later, confirming that there had been a crisis in her marriage, the young woman was raging mad at FDR for causing her mother such grief.

Thirty years later Anna concluded, "I got married when I did because I wanted to get out." Biographers routinely interpreted Anna's decision as the result of her disgust at difficulties between Sara and Eleanor. Anna's second son, John Boettiger, Jr., saw it differently. In his view the tension between Anna's mother and grandmother "must have served as a convenient mask for her less conscious—and probably more frightening—experience of serious tension between her parents."

*   *   *

Sara took great care indeed to suppress her dislike of Eleanor's metamorphosis from an old-fashioned "good" wife to a self-reliant professional woman. Eleanor was correct when she sensed basic disapproval behind her mother-in-law's constant praise for her. While these discords were kept below the surface, the growing chasm between Anna's father and mother could not be hidden from family nearby. An adult daughter, forced to watch the human frailties of her parents, could not help but be disturbed. The revelation of the "near wreckage" of their marriage by Lucy Mercer made Anna notice "a coldness, a deadness in her parents' dealings with each other." It made sense to Anna that "Mother was now building—for *herself*—a cottage more than a mile away from the Big House at Hyde Park, in the woods on the other side of Route 9, along a stream called Val-Kill."

It was hard for Anna to accept the painful changes in her parental home. From now on Eleanor would spend more time with her friends Nancy and Marion than with Franklin. Anna knew her mother's associates well. She had met them regularly at Hyde Park, when six or seven of them enjoyed a weekend in the country as her grandmother Sara's houseguests. By June 1925 Anna saw this pleasant pattern disintegrate. The architect Henry J. Toombs, a cousin of her mother's intimate friend Caroline O'Day, began to dominate the conversation at Springwood's dinner table. He had been entrusted with building a cottage for Eleanor at Val-Kill and shared his plans with the family.

Anna noticed Marion Dickerman's stress on the fact that this was not Eleanor's project. Rather, it had been Franklin's idea. As Marion's host, FDR had picked up eagerly on his wife's regret at the thought that the end of summer would also mean the end of her hospitality for her friends as Sara's guests. Sara's routine, her move to the city for the winter after closing the Big House, would deprive Eleanor's companions of their customary weekend retreat at Hyde Park. "Aren't you girls silly?" FDR had asked. He gave to consider that he owned the land at their favorite picnic site by a small stream north of the mansion. He added, "Why shouldn't you three have a cottage here of your own, so you could come and go as you please?"

Anna was sold on the idea of a new cottage close by when she learned that its grounds would include a swimming pool for her father. She was pleasantly surprised by her father's zeal in making his plans materialize. His involvement permitted him to indulge in his secret passion as an amateur architect and builder. FDR bragged to Anna about having saved more than four thousand dollars with his suggestions. "Your Pa is some little contractor," FDR wrote proudly in his letter to her of July 20, 1925.

Anna was duly impressed, but at the same time puzzled. Why was her father so eager to get her mother out of the Big House, the place that was home for both of them? Wouldn't Eleanor miss the wide park with its beautiful old trees, and the little round tea table outside on the lawn with its gorgeous view down to the river? After all, the crowded townhouse of the Roosevelts on East 65th Street did not invite a husband and wife to spend harmonious hours together. It rather served as a convenient overnight retreat for subsequent days of business in the city.

It was chilling for Anna to realize that her mother looked forward to the time when she would live away from her father. Eleanor would no longer make up for a hectic workweek in New York by relaxing on a long weekend devoted to her husband and children. Anna dreaded the prospect of no longer finding all the family together on leisurely Sundays at the Big House.

Wasn't it even worse that Franklin didn't show a trace of possessiveness of his wife? He didn't seem to mind the loss of Eleanor's company. He didn't care if he saw less of her and talked less to her. Instead he looked on placidly while Eleanor spent her free time with intimate friends, the "girls" he approved of without jealousy. It was little comfort that Anna's parents agreed on the necessity of her mother's presence in the Big House at official events. These occasions were now rare during the hiatus in FDR's political engagement.

As always, Eleanor was unsurpassed in her graciousness, welcoming important guests at her husband's side. Anna was glad that her mother would continue to demonstrate the Roosevelts' marital concord to the outside world as people expected to see it. Outsiders would be kept in the dark about the sad truth that the intimacy of Anna's parents in their day-to-day living together had suffered when Eleanor moved out from under her husband's roof.

Eleanor had brought a favorable reputation as an unselfish wife and mother with her from Washington. People took a good marriage of FDR and Eleanor for granted. Their lack of perception of what was really going on, and their lack of awareness of the changes in the couple's relationship, were of little importance while FDR was a private citizen. When he returned to public life as governor and president, admiration for Eleanor's eye-opening accomplishments outside her personal life took precedence in media stories about the first family.

*   *   *

Anna's father appeared less disturbed by her mother's demonstration of independence in a home of her own, than the nineteen-year old girl herself. Father had been away a lot too. He had drifted gradually out of his emotional ties to his wife. He had been separated from Eleanor by the demands of his rehabilitation since 1922, and then by his stays in Florida and on his houseboat. In 1925, when he had to come to terms with the shift in his wife's affection to two congenial women (Nancy and Marion), he faced a vacuum in his feelings. His marriage no longer provided the satisfactions of loving and being loved. His heart cried out to have the gap filled.

Nobody knows whether FDR felt liberated or guilty in 1926 when he suddenly and unexpectedly reached out to Lucy with a letter. Obviously, he had to hide his move from Eleanor. In spite of his new distance from her, geographically and in spirit, Franklin knew what he owed his wife. She had given him the many children he craved. She had been his dutiful helpmeet in health and illness. There was much to be admired and respected in a lady who was his opposite in many ways, but could be relied on as his faithful comrade in arms.

Franklin hesitated for years before he took the risk of upsetting Eleanor again by renewed contact with a rival to whom she was sensitive to the point of being allergic. Much has been said about FDR's attachment to Lucy behind his wife's back as proof of his inborn deviousness and predilection for secrecy. Actually, he just stubbornly followed the course he had chosen. With an intensity comparable to that in 1903 when he told his mother that he could not help himself and had to marry Eleanor right away, he now demonstrated that he could not help himself but had to ask Lucy to share his life once more.

Circumstances made it easy for FDR to communicate again with Lucy without hurting Eleanor's feelings. Lucy was far away, in places unknown to his wife in South Carolina and the New Jersey countryside. Eleanor was preoccupied with building a freelance career, constantly coming and going. Absorbed by her travels and the need to uphold her public persona, her visits home became more and more sporadic.

Anna had been alarmed by the chasms in her parents' marriage well before she turned twenty in 1926. As the years went by, she observed the consequences of her mother's decision to limit her family obligations. Anna understood her grandmother's dismay at the changes in Eleanor's priorities. Always intent on protecting the Roosevelts' public image, Sara felt acutely embarrassed by the present unusual situation. Outsiders would wonder why Eleanor, the mother of five children with a ten-year-old boy as the youngest, would retreat from her husband without being divorced. They would question her teaching position at the Todhunter School, which restricted Eleanor's movements to New York City. She raised eyebrows by living in a separate home with two single ladies. It was strange that the land for her new residence by herself was a gift from her husband. Dealing with such controversial thoughts, Sara added on for her own consideration that her daughter-in-law's new home was her own financial responsibility. Eleanor's work outside the home had always been emotionally rewarding. From now on her teaching and writing was needed to cover new expenses.

Worried about Eleanor, Sara looked upon Franklin's long absences in Georgia with mixed feelings. Her son was certainly far enough away from the complications of the Roosevelts' family life at Hyde Park to gain in peace of mind. Sara tried to stress the positive side of the situation with cheerful letters to Warm Springs. According to her reports to Franklin, relations between the Big House and "the Cottage" were just fine. They flourished with constant visits back and forth. On April 2, 1926, Sara told her son, "Eleanor has the boys [Johnnie and Franklin, Jr.], but they came over for some hours today and tomorrow they lunch here. We three are invited for supper tomorrow at the cottage and they all lunch here on Sunday. Eleanor is so happy over there that she looks well and plump, don't tell her, it is very becoming."

A decade later Anna realized that Sara's benign view of the situation was a deliberate act of will. Anna looked in vain for mention of the Val-Kill cottage in *Gracious Lady*, Sara's authorized biography, written by her friend Rita Halle Kleeman. There was not one word in the book about Springwood's important spin-off.

LIVY DAVIS: FRANKLIN'S EMISSARY TO LUCY

In the late spring of 1926, Franklin was only too glad to hear from his mother that everything was working out fine at home. His new distance from Eleanor, engineered with his own zeal and her consent, made it easier to think back to Lucy. It was pleasant to dwell on memories of the lady whose company he had sought so eagerly in 1917.

When Franklin's reminiscing turned into longing, he found nothing but hurdles on his way to establishing even the most casual contact with Lucy. She was contentedly married to a proud and prominent husband who adored her. Winthrop could be expected to guard his monopoly of her attention with a vengeance. It has long been assumed that Mr. Rutherfurd's love for Lucy was too possessive to allow any mention of Franklin Delano Roosevelt in his house. This was not the case, as FDR's newly accessible letters to Mrs. Rutherfurd from the 1920s show. Winty was too secure to mind a former admirer of his wife once more paying homage to her. Mr. Rutherfurd certainly had reservations about Mr. Roosevelt, if only because he was a staunch Republican and Franklin was a leading Democrat. Still, there was no objection when Lucy received mail from FDR in her husband's house. She was completely open about her continued interest in an old friend. For Winty it was enough that Edith Morton Eustis, the sister of his first wife, vouched for the innocence of their longstanding bond.

In Aiken Mrs. Eulalia Salley was talking without inhibition about the integrity of Lucy and Franklin's acquaintance. She was a force in shaping public opinion in her community. Her words carried weight when she insisted, "Of course he was in love with her. So was every man who knew Lucy." In this benign climate, Winthrop Rutherfurd was flattered rather than jealous at the renewed attention that an important gentleman devoted to his wife. Winty was in favor of hosting Livingston Davis, Lucy's acquaintance from her days as Miss Mercer. His guest was an interesting gentleman of class who knew Washington high society inside and out at the time when he belonged to Lucy's wartime circle in the capital. Livy's value as an informative and entertaining guest was enhanced by his friendship with Franklin Roosevelt, who had distinguished himself as the assistant secretary of the navy and a candidate for vice president in 1920.

Winty's curiosity, piqued by Livy's visit, was fed anew when FDR himself wrote to Lucy at Aiken. The correspondence between Franklin and Lucy in the 1920s was clearly more voluminous than it appears from its remnants. Its first known fragment, dated May 22, 1926, was written in Hyde Park. It is obvious that Franklin had both Winty and Lucy in mind as its readers. Franklin stressed the impersonal character of his letter by including a copy of his recent talk to the alumni of Milton Academy, near Boston, entitled "Whither Bound." "I hope this little book may interest you," he offered as an introduction. Then he referred to his friend Livy, the Rutherfurds' recent visitor, "It was so nice to hear about you all at Aiken from Livy Davis." A year later Lucy said in her first preserved letter to Franklin from Aiken, dated April 16, 1927, "I was interested to hear a little about you and your projects from Livy Davis who was here."

Livingston Davis, FDR's close friend since his student days, was a smart choice as his emissary to the Rutherfurds. He was perfect as his agent for reestablishing contact with Lucy. Livy, the smooth, cosmopolitan financier, fit well into Aiken society. As a man who made a good living by following events on the stock exchange, he was bound to be respected by Winty. This very reason made him anathema to Eleanor. Livy is seen in the Roosevelt literature mainly through Eleanor's eyes, in her critical view of him as her husband's drinking companion. She resented that he encouraged Franklin to stay up until the wee hours and waste his time in clubs. Eleanor rightly sensed her opposite in Livy, who sought and found fun wherever he went. She distrusted him as a major crony in Franklin's convivial group, centered in the British embassy around Nigel Law and Lucy Mercer.

Unkind observers called Livy Franklin's Sancho Panza. This was an insult for Livy, who considered himself an intellectual—not a follower but an equal in a team of two close friends. Growing up a world traveler like FDR, Livy made nine trips to Europe before going to Harvard. He not only played hard but also worked hard as Franklin's assistant in the Navy Department from 1917 to 1919. A diligent writer, he served as FDR's historian on inspection trips overseas. Livy had been FDR's main golfing partner on courses near and far, including the prestigious Essex County Country Club. As Franklin's favorite sailing companion, he accompanied him on countless journeys. Back in 1908 Livy had faced grave danger when FDR's boat, the *Half Moon*, capsized during a vicious storm off the coast of Nova Scotia. He admired his friend's absolute fearlessness at the helm. Eleanor, left behind on Campobello with toddler Anna, could not complain about the risk her husband took. Her brother Hall was aboard as Franklin's companion in an adventure for men only.

When FDR was crushed by polio, the faithful Livy stood by his incapacitated friend and helped him disembark from his train from

Campobello in New York. Livy remained the embodiment of Frank-lin's undiminished zest for life. As a successful broker in Boston, he "made money without really trying." Sara was delighted to have him at hand when Franklin received his first leg braces from Dr. Lovett in Boston in 1922. She stressed that it was so "nice to be near nice Livy."

As soon as FDR moved to his houseboat in Florida, Livingston Davis and Mr. and Mrs. Henry de Rham became his favorite guests on the *Larooco*. Livy was a mainstay in its fast-changing roster of pas-sengers in 1924, 1925, and again in 1926. It was his loss too when a hurricane destroyed the boat, ending the informal lifestyle that suited both friends so well.

If Lucy Mercer Rutherfurd continued to be interested in the un-folding of Franklin Roosevelt's fate, she could not have found a bet-ter source of information than Livy Davis. Once Lucy entertained Livy as a guest in her house, his first-hand acquaintance with the Ruther-furds turned him into an ideal detective for Franklin. Livy could eas-ily find out whether Franklin's letters to Lucy would be appropriate and welcome.

FDR AS FATHER–IN–LAW

It took FDR by surprise how early his children confronted him with the joys and sorrows of their own romances. "Anna as you know is to be married June 5th," read Franklin's most important message to Lucy on May 22, 1926. Lucy would appreciate what it meant to him. Not so long ago, FDR had been struggling himself to find his equilib-rium in affairs of the heart. He was only forty-four when Anna, his oldest child, married at the age of twenty. He expressed his shock at finding himself a father-in-law in a letter to Lucy, exclaiming, "Doesn't that sound ancient!"

Anna had been a little girl of seven when Lucy became acquainted with her at the Roosevelts' residence in Washington. Five years later, in February 1918 when Anna was twelve, she was unhappy in her up-scale private school. She would not have been present when Eleanor asked her former secretary Lucy to lunch at her house after a morn-ing of working together. By 1926 Anna had turned into a spirited bride, golden-haired and full of straightforward charm. Her proud fa-ther told Lucy, "I wish you knew the child, she is really a dear fine person." Sara had just described Anna to Franklin as "cheerful, jolly, funny & pretty." FDR's wish that Lucy would meet and appreciate the adult Anna pointed far into the future. It finally came true almost two decades later, in 1944 and 1945.

Franklin could write in a relaxed and happy vein about Anna because the love between daughter and father proved stronger than their differences. Franklin was forgiven for failing Anna in her rebellion against Tennis Week, and for failing Eleanor with the Lucy Mercer episode. Nothing stood in the way of their affection for each other when Anna paid a farewell visit as a single daughter to her father in Warm Springs. She arrived by herself on May 8, 1926, just two weeks before FDR returned to Hyde Park. He invited his mother to come along too but Sara tactfully declined. "I really want dreadfully to go," she replied, but "I have a feeling that I better not do it." The warm glow cast by the rare closeness of father and daughter, just by themselves, is reflected in Franklin's lines to Lucy of May 22.

Anna had been elated by her father's ready acceptance of the man she had chosen as her husband. It was important to FDR that Lucy knew how much Anna's fiancé pleased him. His favorable comment on Anna's choice sheds new light on a hushed-up chapter in the Roosevelt family chronicles. Commenting on Anna's romance, Franklin stated firmly, "I am happy too in Curtis Dall the new son-in-law." FDR's fondness for Curt was buried in silence by the family after Anna's marriage, when the young financier fell victim to the shocks caused by the stock market crash in 1929.

Anna's first love and marriage remained a taboo subject for many years. It was excluded from *FDR: His Personal Letters* as well as from subsequent biographies. When Anna left her first husband after seven years of marriage, at the beginning of FDR's first term, Curtis Bean Dall was erased from the family's records. Eleanor barely mentioned his name in her autobiography. She never explained why she "could not stand" the young investment broker. It was part of her political credo that she did not think highly of Curtis's line of work. Furthermore, the conservative banker withstood the efforts of Louis Howe to pull him politically to the left. It was no surprise that Eleanor encouraged Anna when she began to turn against her husband. Only a generation later, Anna Eleanor Roosevelt Seagraves—Curt and Anna's daughter—shed light on the situation. Ellie contrasted

Eleanor's aversion to her father Curt, the solid but undemonstrative provider, with Eleanor's enthusiastic promotion of Anna's second husband, the honey-tongued journalist John Boettiger.

FDR's friendly view of Curt, his first son-in-law, put him in opposition to yet another one of Eleanor's views. Franklin's approval of Curt, shared happily with Lucy, went back to his first meeting with Anna's suitor. The handsome, patriotic balloonist of World War I was likeable as a sportsman and outdoors enthusiast. He was quick witted, too. In a first conversation, when Curt asked for Anna's hand, FDR could not resist teasing the young man. Curt promptly called his bluff when FDR jokingly pretended that he had never heard of Yale, Curt's university. Unfazed, his son-in-law-to-be coolly reminded him that he must have heard that Yale recently defeated Harvard on the football field.

Decades later Curtis's own memoirs, now long forgotten, stressed that he and FDR "hit it off" in the first hour of their acquaintance. Curtis treasured forever the affectionate letters he received from his father-in-law, both before and after Anna divorced him. During the bitter years of Curt's rejection by his ex-wife and his former mother-in-law, the president's warmth continued. It meant much to Curt to be congratulated for his wartime promotion to colonel by the former father-in-law he adored.

*   *   *

Livy Davis might have hinted to Lucy that Eleanor was opposed to Anna's marriage, while Franklin and his mother Sara welcomed it warmly. Like FDR, Sara stood by Curtis even after Anna cast him out of her life. Sara insisted that he had a right to see his children after the divorce and invited him to Hyde Park together with her great-grandchildren—Anna Eleanor Roosevelt Dall, known as "Sistie," and Curtis Roosevelt Dall, nicknamed "Buzz." In 1938, when Curt decided to remarry, Sara asked her former grandson-in-law to bring by his second wife, the beautiful Katherine Miller Leas, for a visit at Hyde Park.

FDR took pleasure in announcing to Lucy that "great preparations are in progress for the wedding." It was not the mother of the bride but her grandmother who shouldered the work and expense for the first wedding of a Roosevelt daughter at Springwood in Hyde Park.

Livy Davis, a witness to all important events in Franklin's life since his student days, could see that Anna's romance of 1925 and 1926 had much in common with her parents' road to their engagement in 1903. Sara was instrumental both times. She had brought Eleanor close to Franklin by inviting her first to Hyde Park house parties, then to Campobello. In the summer of 1925, after a trip to Italy with Sara, Anna also discovered Curt at the Hyde Park house parties she had begged her grandmother to give for her friends. The girl was at a loss how to decide between several suitors.

Sara's third party, celebrating the New Year in 1926, finally inspired Anna to make up her mind. She wanted Curtis and she wanted him fast. The Roosevelt and Delano relatives applauded Anna's haste to get her "young man." Betty Roosevelt, the wife of FDR's half brother Rosy, sent her congratulations from Bermuda on January 27, along with the comment "It is a good thing he is 10 years older than she is, he will have a steadying influence over her."

Anna's parents helped but little with the festivities in the bride's honor. In February Eleanor had paid a brief visit to Franklin in Warm Springs. Back home she was preoccupied with professional obligations and settling into her new residence at Val-Kill. Sara took care of the younger boys, Johnnie and Franklin, Jr., and proudly hosted the big engagement parties for Anna and Curt. She reported to her son that the dinner for family was "very gay and jolly" even though Eleanor "had work to do." Sara was consoled with her daughter-in-law when "she came in about 9.30, and all enjoyed her."

Lucy would understand FDR's elation at the first great wedding of his children's generation. He loved to uphold family traditions in formal nuptials and was delighted to learn that the Reverend Dr. Peabody would officiate. Winning the rector of Groton for Roosevelt weddings was a coup, a custom that had been started by FDR himself. In 1926 it was Anna's brother Jimmy who walked her down the aisle at St. James' Episcopal Church in her father's place. Anna carried a large bridal bouquet of lilies of the valley—the same flowers her mother had carried at her wedding in New York on March 17, 1905.

The wedding of Franklin and Eleanor had been a modest affair compared with the opulent event staged by Anna's grandmother. A special train carried a big crowd of relatives from New York to Hyde

Park. As a bride, Eleanor had kept track of 340 wedding presents. Anna counted up to four hundred presents on her own list and left the recording of eighty more to her mother. A modern bride in a knee-length bridal gown, Anna preferred receiving money to yet another silver tray. She marked Mrs. Fred W. Vanderbilt's $600.00 check "for rug."

FRANKLIN AND LUCY RECONNECT

FDR took pains to mention Anna's wedding in an impersonal fashion in his letters to Lucy. He was careful not to slip into an intimate personal mode. Altogether he kept the format of his messages to Lucy pointedly detached. Their tone was reserved, suitable in anyone's eyes. Lucy's husband could not possibly take offense.

Only FDR's first letter had been written on Hyde Park stationery. The second and third letters, of September and December 1927, presented him as vice president of the Fidelity and Deposit Company of Maryland in New York City. The last of the series, sent in May 1928, was written on letterhead from the Indianapolis Athletic Club.

Appearing as a New York representative of the Fidelity and Deposit Company of Maryland, a large security-bonding concern, boosted FDR's credentials in Aiken. The resort in Georgia stood out as a citadel of big city banking, with prominent bankers from all over the country as vacationers. For Lucy, Franklin's association with this financial institution had a special meaning. It was rooted in Maryland and had ties to her Carroll relatives. Franklin himself never confirmed his family's assumption that he owed his position to his kinship with Jenny Walters Delano. Jenny, his aunt, was the daughter of William Walters, Baltimore's prominent railroad tycoon. It was Jonathan Daniels who noted that it was not the Delanos who helped FDR secure his job with Fidelity. FDR himself pointed to support from a different quarter. To win his position, he "did claim Charles Carroll of Carrollton and [he] asked Senator Radcliffe to tell his Maryland Catholic friends."

The former U.S. Senator George L. P. Radcliffe was a good Democrat. He was on the board of Fidelity and Deposit on January 1, 1921, when FDR secured his twenty-five-thousand-dollar-per-year job with the firm. His new regular source of revenue was an absolute necessity for the financial survival of Franklin and Eleanor. FDR's income in the years after his public service in Washington had been more than modest. Radcliffe supported Franklin's appointment with the argument that FDR was worth his salary from Fidelity because of his connections in New York.

Franklin's standing with the financial elite, like the Morgans, was indeed impressive. It went back to his father and had been cultivated by his widowed mother. When Radcliffe "was told that there was no hope of F. & D. getting" a security bond with a seventy-five-thousand-dollar premium placed by J. P. Morgan & Company, he "went to Franklin D.'s office and gave him the facts. Franklin D. picked up the telephone called Mr. Morgan, got him to the 'phone and talked to him on a first name basis and F. & D. got the business."

FDR's assistant, the Catholic Willam Hassett, remembered in his 1958 book that Catholic connections had been instrumental in his boss's entry into the world of banking. He told about Van Lear Black, FDR's longtime sailing companion, who was publisher of the *Baltimore Sun* and a bridge to Cardinal Gibbons of Baltimore. The "venerable churchman," as Hassett called him, supplied another voice, supporting FDR's assignment at Fidelity. He had grown fond of Franklin as undersecretary of the navy, addressed him as "my boy," and liked to meet him for lunch.

In his later correspondence with Lucy, FDR expressed feelings of guilt that he did not do enough for the Fidelity Company. This confession was as personal as he permitted himself to be in his letters to Lucy. All of FDR's handwritten letters to Lucy ended with a noncommittal "I hope all goes well with you" or "I hope all of you are well." Franklin signed them with his full name underneath a "Very Sincerely Yours" or "Sincerely Yours." Only a one-line postscript with the words "my belated 'many many happy returns of the day'" hints at an earlier closeness—when he had celebrated Lucy's birthday on April 26.

Franklin never touched more than briefly on his own personal problems. He did not dwell on the pain he still felt in his legs and on the treatments he underwent in Marion, Massachusetts. Yet he never failed to give Lucy an exact schedule of his prospective whereabouts. He obviously had to be sure that she knew where to send return mail. Franklin let on that he cherished her family news. He appreciated her practical advice, like her referral to a good dentist. Aware of the weak points of Lucy's health, he cautiously expressed his concern. As an aside, he would gently press on, in a safely avuncular tone, "You say nothing about yourself—It means I hope that you have been well—really well."

HEADACHES OVER WARM SPRINGS

FDR was careful not to appear as too intimate a friend of Lucy. He did not refer to any of their past times together on the *Sylph* or in his office. Instead he chose to report on his charitable projects. They represented a clear-cut common ground, to be shared between correspondents of equal social standing. The Rutherfurds belonged to the same crowd as the Roosevelts. They too adhered to the credo of noblesse oblige that Sara Roosevelt had instilled so eagerly in her son Franklin.

FDR casually mentioned his longtime service on major Boy Scout committees, pointing discreetly to his leadership in an institution that promoted his ethical values. His work for the Boy Scouts—his favorite good cause—was now centered in New York City, more distant during the months spent in Georgia. But his new residence in Warm Springs called for other charitable endeavors, exciting enough to fill long passages in his letters to Lucy. One of them started out, "I think you may be interested to know of my latest venture. I have bought Georgia Warm Springs on the instalment [sic] plan!'" He stressed that the benefit of the mineral waters at the springs was not limited to improving his own health and rehabilitation; it had the potential to serve the common good. Franklin was convinced that it had "great possibilities for the treatment of infantile paralysis—they have never had any doctor here in the past." This had changed, Franklin wrote optimistically, when the results of a medical experiment with thirty patients were in. "[W]e shall . . . take care of a lot more cases—and as there are over 100,000 children & others who need treatment it might do so much good."

A year later, in April 1927, Lucy shared with Franklin her own thoughts of how to assure the financial success of the Warm Springs medical establishment. FDR acknowledged her suggestions in a long letter of September 15. He felt that perhaps the fashionable treatments mentioned by Lucy would be "the thing to do to make a 'health resort' a panacea for every variety of ailment & that Warm Springs would become more quickly notorious if I were to adopt the idea." By this time, however, financial worries—rather than plans for the introduction of the latest spa innovations—dominated FDR's reports about Warm Springs. He hoped for Lucy's understanding in his enforced change from an idealistic, self-appointed philanthropist to a budget-conscious, down-to-earth businessman.

"The greater part of the country is in the midst of another epidemic of infantile paralysis," FDR warned, at the same time reassuring Lucy that the contagious region was "not I think out near Allamuchy." As a result, he said, "We have 40 patients at Warm Springs & many more applications than we have money to take care of." Franklin bared his soul with unusual candor, confessing his inadequacy in dealing with the financial side of his venture. He was more self-deprecating in writing to Lucy than he was in his letters to his mother and his wife.

> The "campaign" for funds progresses slowly. It seems to take weeks to beg even a few thousand dollars & I loathe the thought of this begging & will never succeed as professional money raiser—If in the next few years I can put the Warm Springs treatment on a permanent & satisfactory basis I shall never again let my enthusiasm run away with me—but shall settle down into a life of leisure! But by this time it will probably be the Poor House.

By sharing his financial unease with Lucy, Franklin included her in his closest circle of female advisers. Debating the wisdom of his commitment to Warm Springs, he used as his sounding board the three women in his life he respected most. The letters containing Lucy's reaction to FDR's soul-searching have not survived. It can be deduced that FDR knew he could count on Lucy's unconditional support of his ideals as surely as he could rely on the indulgence of his mother. He had high regard for the caution of his judicious wife, even though Eleanor's letters expressed a veiled criticism.

On May 4, 1926, just prior to the date of FDR's first known letter to Lucy, Eleanor had warned her husband, "I know you love creative work, my only feeling is that Georgia is somewhat distant for you to keep in touch with what is really a big undertaking. One cannot, it seems to me, have *vital* interests in widely divided places." In the same breath, she told Franklin, "Don't be discouraged by me." She explained that she herself "just couldn't do it . . . because I'm old and rather overwhelmed." Eleanor referred to nearby tasks, including support of her Val-Kill friend Nancy Cook in her bold plans to found a furniture factory.

Franklin was creative indeed as he directed his energies to the development of Warm Springs. He knew from experience that his wife might be more puzzled than impressed by his eagerness to prove himself once again as the family's master builder. He described not to Eleanor but to Lucy why it was "great fun" to have new, affordable cottages built at Warm Springs under his direction.

* * *

Receiving mixed signals from his wife to go ahead in Georgia, Franklin placed all the more hope in the moral support of Lucy and hands-on assistance from his mother. He had told Sara right after he acquired Warm Springs, "I want you to take a great interest in it, for I feel you can help me with many suggestions and the place properly run will not only do a great deal of good but will prove financially successful."

Sara quickly put her own worries about Franklin's risks behind her. She visited him at Warm Springs and even had her own cottage built there. FDR found warm words of thanks for his mother. "I miss you a lot and I don't have to tell you how I loved having you here, and I know you were really interested."

Sara put her money where her heart was. She told Franklin later that year that "a cheque for $50,000 for shares in your new venture" was taken "out of my legacy from dear Aunt Annie." It is well known that FDR's half brother Rosy left him one hundred thousand dollars in his will when he died on May 7, 1927, four months before Franklin confessed his financial headaches to Lucy. The equivalent of more than one million in today's dollars was more than welcome. None of FDR's biographies mention that the death of his mother's sister Annie Delano Hitch on March 6, 1926, provided another sorely needed windfall. Franklin was Annie's favorite nephew, a secret substitute for her own only boy who had died as an infant in China. The fifty thousand dollars that Annie left to FDR was taken out of his mother's share, meaning that Sara consequently received a third less than her siblings. Nevertheless, Sara even devoted a sizable portion of her remaining legacy of fifty thousand dollars to prop up FDR's shaky financial plans for Warm Springs's renaissance.

Spurred on by her axiom "If it helps Franklin," Sara also persuaded her brother Fred Delano and her sister Kassie Delano Collier to drum up donations. Uncle Fred liked Franklin's praise of the resort's altitude, which made it "cool enough even in summer," and requested more promotional materials. Sara's sister Kassie used her residence at affluent Tuxedo Park as a platform to win over "some of our rich friends who are suffering from nervous prosperity," as FDR described them with characteristic mockery. Underneath his irony he was sincerely glad that "the Tuxedo meeting was such a success" for the Warm Springs Foundation.

While FDR was canvassing his family to keep his project afloat, he inserted an element of inquiry in the frequent mention of the subject in letters to Lucy. The well-to-do Mrs. Winthrop Rutherfurd certainly had the potential to become a part of his fundraising network. Lucy had as much access to rich friends in Aiken, South Carolina, as Kassie had in Tuxedo Park, New York. It is not known whether Lucy acted on Franklin's hints. If she did, it was done with utmost discretion. Lucy was always wary of provoking second thoughts in her husband's perception of her standing with Franklin. It would have aroused suspicion if she invested great sums in FDR's enterprise.

Clearly, Lucy was suffering from a low in energy when she wrote Franklin on April 16, 1927. She had lost the vitality of her youth and showed signs of a frailty that gradually became more pronounced. At the time she pulled all her strength together after a miserable winter that had taxed the reserves of her health.

Whether she was well or not, Lucy was kept busy with preparations for the Rutherfurds' "first extended family jaunt." Her five teenage stepchildren were excited about spending a summer in Europe. Lucy's daughter Barbara, just five years old, looked forward to a great adventure. A large family with six lively children, covering a wide range of age and interests, commanded all of Lucy's energy. Her organizational talent was essential for the success of travel with a crowd of children. Lucy looked on the trip as an investment in a tranquil future, because it would "get it out of their system for several years to come."

FDR's response to Lucy's account of her life as a mother of six is not known. He was bound to be pleased—he loved to think along with her and liked the commotion of large families. At least one of his letters to Lucy during this time seems to have been lost. It is known, however, that Franklin was glad to receive Lucy's congratulations when his daughter Anna made him a grandfather. Livy Davis had again served as the messenger between Lucy and Franklin. Livy had made a good impression at Aiken with his wit and ability to entertain. Invited once more by Winty and Lucy Rutherfurd, Livy happily told his hosts that a new generation of Roosevelts was on its way. Lucy had a hard time coping with the changes in her friend's life. She was still puzzled when she wrote Franklin, "I hear that you are a grandfather."

FDR was only forty-five. His youngest son Johnnie had just turned eleven when Anna's daughter (Anna Eleanor Roosevelt Dall) was born on March 25, 1926. In the previous year, as a new father-in-law, Franklin had called himself "ancient." Now Lucy hedged a little, confessing, "I do not know exactly just what one's feelings are on that question."

Lucy was still in the middle of things as the busy mother of young children. She could not visualize herself as a grandparent and hesitated to imagine Franklin, the energetic man under fifty, as a patriarch. When she wrote Franklin again aboard the SS *Belgenland* on July 2, Lucy was preoccupied with her main job—keeping six excited children happy. They loved every hour of the trip, she wrote, "and it is a great pleasure for me to find them all entertained without having to lift a finger."

LUCY AND FRANKLIN'S CONCERNS

Lucy's letters to Franklin show that she also extended her strong mothering instincts to her friend. As well as she could, she tried to assist him in practical ways. She had never seen FDR in a wheelchair but she visualized his special needs vividly. When she watched the sister of her friend Bessie Kittredge use a folding wheelchair, she thought of FDR and suggested that he might get one for himself. It would enable him to travel overseas, maybe on French trains, with Eleanor at his side. Four years later, in 1931, FDR did indeed travel to Europe in a wheelchair. He was not accompanied by his wife but by his son Elliott, on a mission of mercy to his mother's bedside in a Paris hospital. Sara had been stricken with pneumonia during a visit by her sister Dora Forbes.

This trip happened after Lucy's greatest worry about Franklin's well-being had materialized. He was now in his third year as governor of New York. Lucy had been proved wrong when she feared that the strain of his new duties would hurt him. FDR's return to public service had not overtaxed his strength, but rather revived his vigor. His mother had reason to be jubilant. She had promoted Franklin's campaign for governor with more determination than the hesitant Eleanor.

Sara's ambition for her son always outdid her worries that he was taking on too much for his advancement. By contrast, Lucy's admiration for her friend's accomplishments was forever secondary to her anxiety about his health and happiness. Even though she could know his frame of mind only from reading his letters, in 1927 Lucy sensed danger for Franklin's well-being. All the way to Paris, in the midst of managing travel and bouts of sickness in her family, Lucy trembled at the prospect of Franklin's return to the arena of political warfare. Her instincts of protective love made her warning prophetic. In July 1927, more than a year before FDR was elected governor, Lucy wrote that she did not want to come back to America "to find you President or Sec'y of State nor yet a physical wreck from too much work for Al Smith or any other potentate!!"

These were the last preserved lines to FDR from Lucy's pen in their correspondence of the 1920s. Two of Franklin's letters to Lucy from 1927 have survived—a long one of September 15 sent to Paris, and a briefer message of December 22 sent to Allamuchy. Both times FDR did not talk at first about himself. He only mentioned as an aside that the Warm Springs treatments were unsurpassed in bringing back the function in his leg muscles. Franklin centered on his concerns about Lucy and her children. He commiserated twice with her little "invalids" and the "hospitally summer" they suffered overseas.

After expressing his sympathy for the Rutherfurd children's trials, FDR came to the main point of his letter. He sought contact with

Lucy because she might be able to help him solve an urgent business problem. This time, he wanted more than Lucy's advice. He wanted her to act on his behalf in his capacity as "Chairman of the Taconic State Park Commission which is to build a parkway north through Putnam County."

An explanatory letter from Franklin, preceding his message to Lucy of December 22, is missing. Lucy had to be alerted to Mr. Kittredge's power as the owner of vast stretches of land in the Hudson Valley. FDR speculated that Mr. Kittredge's wife Bessie, one of Lucy's closest friends in Aiken, might be able to convince her husband to sell part of his land to the state. His consent was essential for the realization of FDR's plans for the construction of the Taconic Parkway. But Mr. Kittredge proved stubborn in his refusal to sell. Lucy had an uphill struggle on her hands, trying to point out the economic advantages of the deal. She argued that the acreage adjoining the prospective parkway would appreciate significantly in value.

FDR's last letter of the known correspondence with Lucy, the only one preserved from the year 1928, started out with his thanks to her for dealing with landowners who obstructed his goals for the parkway. Franklin wished to be seen as a successful, pragmatic businessman by all his acquaintances, especially by the down-to-earth Rutherfurds. He had to persuade Lucy, and likely her husband too, to believe in the feasibility of his plans for an important thoroughfare. They were conceived both for economic and idealistic reasons, mostly benefiting his native upstate New York.

Worries about relatively small local enterprises, such as the building of the Taconic Parkway, would later look to Lucy like idyllic interludes in a life demanding earth-shattering decisions. Franklin's imminent move to the world of leadership frightened Lucy. Her friend sensed her anxiety and toned down the announcement of the changes ahead of him. They appear only on the horizon in Franklin's last known letter to Lucy from the 1920s, half a year before he was elected governor. His lines to Lucy of May 18, 1928, foreshadow the end of the seven-year hiatus in FDR's political career. From 1921 to 1928 he had lived as a private citizen, putting care for his health and service to good causes ahead of more monumental goals. His longing for Lucy had thrived in this self-centered period prior to his return to politics.

FDR indicated now that he was ready to move on. He was not reticent about his restlessness in his position as vice president of an investment company. He told Lucy with the frankness of a long-time intimate friend:

> *I am ending a very strenuous ten days with the*
> *President & other officers of the Fidelity & Deposit Co.—*
> *Toledo, Detroit, Milwaukee, Chicago & St. Louis—one or*
> *two days in each place to look over our branch office &*
> *encourage business—I hate this sort of thing—with lunch-*
> *eons and dinners & receptions—but I had to do it as I*
> *have done little these past few years to earn my salary—*
> *and I need the latter! I get to N.Y. on Monday or will be*
> *there (except weekends at H.P.) till I leave for the Hous-*
> *ton Convention on June 19th—I am stopping off at*
> *Warm Springs on the way home for a couple of days.*

When Franklin told Lucy what to expect in the next few months, he tried to assuage her worries about his return to politics with a double, not-too-convincing "I hope." "The convention will be a terrific week" he announced, adding in brackets "(not longer I hope) & I fear I am in for the nomination speech again—but it is all over I hope for a comparatively quiet summer—Smith will almost certainly be nominated & will make a strong run, though of course the country is normally strongly Republican."

When FDR wrote his mother after the Houston convention on July 14, 1928, "I have declined the National Chairmanship, and will decline the nomination for Governor," he still seemed to express his belief in an uneventful future for himself. Sara read correctly between the lines that her son's dormant urge to answer his real calling had been awakened. Franklin mentioned contentedly that there had been "a lot of really nice editorials" applauding his speeches at the convention.

Like Sara, Lucy was aware of Franklin's deepest wishes, hidden in the depth of his heart. They upset her more than they upset his mother. Lucy's anxiety was matched only by the fears of Franklin's devoted secretary Missy LeHand. She too anticipated nervously that FDR would be nominated for governor of New York after his successful step into the spotlight at Houston. Missy revealed the depth of her feelings for her boss when she opposed the prospect with a theatrical threat: "Don't you dare to accept!"

The response to FDR's options from the most important voice near him, that of his wife, was more muted and detached. Eleanor was convinced that Franklin would serve the common good better than any other candidate. She was not so sure about her own role in a new scenario and had mixed feelings about becoming New York State's First Lady. Her husband's rise to political prominence would endanger her own hard-won professional independence. Eleanor was thriving in her new career as a teacher at the Todhunter School and was pleased by her promotion to associate principal. Staff duties, starting on October 2, 1928, cut short her attendance at the state Democratic convention in Rochester. In spite of her misgivings, Eleanor "finally was persuaded to get F.D.R. on the ticket," as Elliott Roosevelt noted in an annotation in *FDR: His Personal Letters*. Elliott stressed the importance of Eleanor's role in dispelling her husband's doubts about shifting gears in 1928.

Behind the scenes FDR's gradual change of mind about running for governor was to a great extent influenced by his mother's strong views in favor of his move. Well aware that the public voicing of a mother's ambition meant the kiss of death in politics, Sara disguised her dreams carefully in coy language. They had surfaced already in the spring of 1928. In March she let Franklin know in a letter to Warm Springs that two of her friends, Mrs. Morgan and Mrs. Fairchild, had told her at the tea table that they were "both longing to vote for you! (of course for President)." If that was to come true, his mother assured him, she would emigrate. Of course she could not fool her son with her fake modesty, pretending not to be able to stand the Roosevelt family's rise to grandeur.

Sara took issue with cautious friends who opposed FDR's inclination to step into the political ring, among them even Louis Howe. Her biographer Rita Halle Kleeman recorded Sara's firm belief that her son "would never consent to remain quietly at Warm Springs." She "felt that his duties as Governor would be no more arduous than his work in his law office and in the Fidelity and Deposit Company."

Sara took her happy excitement about the new prospects for her son on an overseas journey. In July, in a letter from a spa at Vittel near the Vosges Mountains in France, she passed along to Franklin the compliments of "Mr. B. Baruch" for "your fine speech." Spending the rest of the summer on Campobello, Sara even joined her politically savvy daughter-in-law as a freelance campaigner. The very private Sara Roosevelt took her son by surprise with her report of September 26. "I have been working hard for the Governor here and in Lubec and on the ferry. You would admire my eloquence!"

Franklin was touched by the devotion of his seventy-four-year-old mother. "I loved your letters," he replied. It seems that the warmth of attachment between mother and son reached a new intensity, while Franklin's feelings for Lucy cooled somewhat. Meanwhile Sara worked out a plan to ease Franklin smoothly into high office. She was ready on October 2, immediately after "Eleanor telephoned me . . . that you have to run for the Governorship." Sara sympathized only briefly with the "*self* sacrifice" it would demand. The old Delano spirit of prevailing against the odds got the better of her when she wowed, "*If* you run I do not want you to be defeated!"

Sara called her offer of support "*really private.*" First, she would make up from her own purse for the loss of income FDR would suffer as governor. Second, she would arrange for Franklin to get one thousand dollars a month by renting his townhouse at 49 East 65th Street for him. She would move its present occupants—his daughter Anna and her husband Curtis Dall—next door into her own place at number 47.

In the same spirit as her grandmother Sara, Anna pushed her father to do what both knew he really wanted. He thoroughly enjoyed being prodded. In the hot summer of 1928, the Dalls found a cool escape from the city at Dandruff-on-the-Knob, a cottage owned by Curt's friend Freddy Warburg. A telegram from Warm Springs with the news that FDR was pondering a run for governor culminated in the question "What do you think about it?" It reached the young couple after a tennis match. Anna replied immediately, "Think it is a great idea. . . . Will do everything possible to help you and the cause." FDR's pleased reaction ("Your wire received. You ought to be spanked") marked the beginning of the special relationship with her father that made Anna an ally of Lucy Rutherfurd in 1944 and 1945.

Sara heard every speech her son made on her radio in Hyde Park. On November 7 Sara and Franklin motored together to Hyde Park's town hall to vote. That night neither Eleanor nor Anna joined Sara in her suspenseful vigil as she followed the election results from the Roosevelt headquarters in New York's Biltmore Hotel. Only Frances Perkins, later secretary of labor in FDR's cabinet, stayed at Sara's side until four in the morning. Together they celebrated his unlikely victory in what was otherwise a Republican year.

THE GOVERNOR WATCHES OVER LUCY

Even before FDR was elected president, he discreetly used his leverage as governor of New York to protect and aid his old friend Mrs. Rutherfurd. This was not to be expected. FDR's wife Eleanor, his mother Sara, and his daughter Anna were now the most active women in his orbit, surpassed in daily cooperation only by his secretary Missy LeHand. Franklin's sails were filled with the winds of success; he was running at full speed toward a promising political future. Every look back appeared a waste of emotional resources.

Indeed, there seemed to be no room left in FDR's personal world for old ties. Livy Davis, his reliable contact with Lucy Rutherfurd, had faded from the picture. Divorced since the early 1920s, Livy had remarried. FDR told his mother on August 29, 1927, that instead of attending Livy's wedding to Georgia Appleton at Bar Harbor, he could only have lunch with the newlyweds. Altogether, Franklin's time with his faithful friend was running out. In 1929 FDR still assured his "dear old Liv" that "being Governor is nothing in comparison" to being chosen grand marshal for the Harvard commencement. "I expect to call on you a million times before commencement," Franklin wrote Livy. "Come to Albany if you can, any time."

Livy never followed up on the invitation, and when he offered to assist a prospective writer of FDR's biography, the governor took a dim view of the project. This would be FDR's own preserve. He had "deferred serious writing," he told Livy, "until the 50th reunion of the Class of 1904," when he "may have more leisure." But by 1954 both the old classmates were no longer alive. In January 1932 Livy Davis shot himself in the woodshed of his Boston estate. He left Franklin one thousand dollars in his will, "in grateful remembrance of joyful comradeship."

Livy's death was a part of the disintegration of Franklin's links to the past. His circle of friends from the war years in Washington was falling apart. Following his divorce in 1922, the British diplomat Nigel Law had married his old love Anastasia, Lady Cheetham, in London in May 1929. Law continued to exchange Christmas greetings with FDR but regretted after 1933 that he was "never able to accept his invitation to stay with him at the White House." Whereas both Livy and Nigel Law ceased to play a role in Franklin's life, Lucy remained as a permanent link to his pre-World War I social circle in Washington. Franklin was now back in a leading position, having risen high above the station of his old friends. In spite of all that had changed, Franklin began to think back more frequently to Lucy in the mid-1920s, and Lucy too found times in her new hectic life that brought back memories of Franklin.

A strange but telling incident showed that in the early 1930s, possibly while he was still in Albany, FDR held a protective hand over Mrs. Winthrop Rutherfurd. In 1966 Roosevelt's bodyguard, Sergeant Earl Miller, explained the connection in a long letter to a friend. FDR had thought highly of Miller's abilities ever since they became acquainted on his overseas tour in 1918. As governor, when he ordered Miller to protect his wife, FDR was confident that he would also keep Eleanor safe on her inspection tours of state prisons.

FDR must have counted on the former state trooper's absolute discretion when he assigned him to watch over Mrs. Winthrop Rutherfurd. Lucy saw it as her Christian duty to visit prisons in Georgia and Florida. In line with her principle to erase any written evidence of her personal life in general, and of her good works in particular, Lucy left no record of this self-imposed service. It is in character, however, that Lucy obeyed the imperatives of her faith to feed the hungry, clothe the naked, and visit the imprisoned.

The unusual order to guard an out-of-state friend of the governor was a delicate matter for Miller. He was boundlessly devoted to Eleanor, whom he referred to as "the lady." The burning of Eleanor and Earl Miller's correspondence led to much speculation about the degree of their mutual attraction. While it is unlikely that Miller was aware of Mrs. Rutherfurd's true place in the affections of the governor, he knew that she had been in the employment of his lady. Miller passionately took Mrs. Roosevelt's side in what he sensed to be a competitive situation.

In Miller's condescending evaluation of Mrs. Rutherfurd, he called her a copycat who sounded "like her former boss." Miller admitted that Lucy was "quite the 'all-out' worker & giver of her time and money to many underprivileged." Nevertheless, he saw her mainly as a pampered rich woman. He did not know that she had struggled in her youth and that her efforts on behalf of the weak and needy had deep roots. Long before Lucy admired Eleanor Roosevelt, she had found role models for selfless service in the sisters who taught her in Vienna.

While it is not known how Lucy thanked Franklin for providing her with protection on a precarious mission, it was no secret that she did not hesitate to call on the governor when her sister needed help. When Violetta Marbury's son Carroll died of leukemia in 1932 at the age of twelve, Vio was denied her wish to have the boy buried in his grandfather Carroll Mercer's grave at Arlington National Cemetery. FDR's first intervention on Lucy's behalf, countermanding a bureaucratic dictate, was immediately successful. Johnny Carroll Marbury was granted a place of burial near the grave of his mother's father.

Although FDR maintained only sporadic contact with Lucy when he moved up to the White House and faced the challenges of his First Hundred Days as president, he could at least assure her presence at his inauguration. Though Lucy would be there incognito, he knew that her applause was part of the crowd's cheering. Franklin's invitations to Mrs. Rutherfurd were only possible with the cooperation of his assistant. In her unselfish devotion to "FD," Missy LeHand willingly accepted that Mrs. Rutherfurd occupied a special place in her boss's heart.

CHAPTER 9

LUCY AND THE PRESIDENT

HER HUSBAND'S "WILLING SLAVE"

For the years after 1928, there are no documents available to supplement the fragmentary correspondence between Franklin and Lucy from the prior two-year period. FDR was preoccupied with the demands of the offices of governor and president. By 1933 Lucy too had little room in her life for thinking back to the love of her youth. She was fully engaged by two obligations. First, she had to fill the position of a *grande dame* of Aiken in a way fitting a Rutherfurd's social rank. Second, and more importantly, she had to grow into her role as a primary caregiver, serving her husband's declining health as a full-time occupation. Gradually but persistently, working as a nurse took more and more of Lucy's time until she was completely absorbed by her duties at her husband's bedside.

Whatever Lucy may have recorded about this period is lost. The void is filled to some extent by the testimony of vivid impressions that Lucy's commitment made on her friends. Among them Eulalie Salley stood out in her attachment to Lucy, in her understanding of FDR's role in her life, and as witness to Lucy's gallant response to the challenges of the 1930s and 1940s (demanding extreme unselfishness). Eulalie was remarkably successful in transferring detailed memories of Lucy to a writer, Emily Bull Cooper. In the form of a biography of Eulalie, the book appeared in two editions.

Eulalie, Aiken society's center of communication, had grown rich supplying its residents with whatever they needed for their homes and gardens. As the town's top real estate agent, she knew more than anybody else about the over 150 millionaires who could be counted in town in a single season.

Eulalie's designation of Lucy Mercer Rutherfurd as her "best friend" seems a tad self-congratulatory. After all, the only preserved piece of correspondence between them is centered on landscaping business. Other, more personal letters might have been lost. The copy of Emily L. Bull's *Eulalie* that Mrs. Salley gave to Lucy's daughter Barbara Rutherfurd Knowles is dedicated "To my very precious baby and her lovely husband & babies—Love, The Saint." This was the name given Eulalie by Winthrop, when he decreed that Lucy and Eulalie continue their relationship on a first-name basis. Later Lucy too was generally declared a saint.

"Why in the hell don't you call her Lucy?" Winty demanded after a short acquaintance of the two ladies. "She is too beautiful. I'll always call her Mrs. Rutherfurd," Eulalie protested. "Well, I have a name for you," Lucy interjected. "I shall call you Saint." She used this affectionate address until she died and her daughter Barbara continued the tradition.

The Rutherfurds and Salleys entertained each other. Apparently, Lucy liked Eulalie's husband Julian. The attorney was one of her many admirers in Aiken. Julian did not think much of his wife's distinction as a successful campaigner for women's rights in the 1920s. On the other hand, Eulalie complained that he spent too little time with her and that "[the] law was his mistress."

When Mrs. Salley was interviewed by the *National Observer* in 1966, she was more effusive than ever about the sentiments Lucy evoked among Aiken's men. "I don't doubt for a minute that Mr. Roosevelt was in love with her," Eulalie insisted. "My own husband was madly in love with her, himself, and would have gladly left me to marry her." He "kissed her every time she came to our house. All the husbands did." It was amazing that "all the women in Aiken who knew her were remarkably free of feminine envy of Lucy Rutherfurd's beauty." Eulalie stressed that "we were flattered, not jealous, because we knew there was nothing scandalous in all their feelings."

Julian Salley called Lucy "one of the few women he ever knew who looked even more beautiful as you got closer to her." Everybody agreed. "It was a beauty the artist and photographer did not catch. Her beauty was in her expression and in her graceful manner." Eulalie added that "she was blue-eyed and brown-haired, with skin the color of milk. . . . She wore no make-up . . . and she had such a lovely mouth."

Lucy was no flirt; this was one of the keys to her popularity in Aiken. General opinion centered on the verdict that "Mrs. Rutherfurd is remembered here as an old-fashioned kind of wife, with a single-minded devotion to her marriage." All Aiken shared Mrs. Salley's indignation toward Jonathan Daniels, who dared to offer hints of a romance in his description of FDR and Lucy Rutherfurd's relationship. All Aiken believed that Lucy's perfection as a wife "would have made infidelity, even with an old love who had become President of the United States, simply unthinkable."

*   *   *

While Lucy, Aiken's "wonderful lady," was beyond reproach, her husband's rough language cast a shadow over his image. His reputation did not do justice to his good looks, to his "keen sense of humor, and a brilliant mind." The Rutherfurds' family portraitist, Madame Elizabeth Shoumatoff, came to a similar conclusion in 1937. The artist was awed by Mr. Rutherfurd in spite of his advanced years. He "was one of the handsomest men I have ever painted, and certainly one of the most aristocratic. He looked like an English peer, with his chiseled features, sharp eyes, and a sarcastic expression around his mouth." He "vaguely resembled FDR. Lucy, at one time, admitted that herself."

Winthrop's similarity to FDR ended when he opened his mouth. Lucy warned Madame Shoumatoff that "he did not hesitate in saying sharp things." This trait became more pronounced as Winthrop's health deteriorated. He "was often cross because of a paralysis that plagued him." Eulalie noted. She explained, "To many, he was gruff, but to her [Lucy], never. He was truly a gentleman of the old school."

Eulalie would not suffer any man ordering her around, but allowed Winty to do it because she appreciated the kind heart under his rough shell. When he asked Eulalie to come by and she turned him down, Mr. Rutherfurd snapped, "I didn't issue you an invitation! I gave you a command. Now get over here!" Curiously, Eulalie obeyed and was greeted with a package and the proclamation "Happy birthday!" When Eulalie objected, "[I]t's not my birthday," Winty retorted, "Dammit! If I say it's your birthday, it's your birthday." Eulalie's breath was taken away when she found in the package a fine silver teapot engraved with her initials.

Winty's cursing was shocking enough to be remembered verbatim. A typical situation arose when Lucy, the perfectionist interior decorator, requested carpeting on the steps to the mansion's second floor. Winty raged and threatened to secure his sons' opposition to the project. Eulalie tried to calm him down with the argument that Lucy really wanted the carpet badly and suggested, "Why don't you let me get an estimate for you?" "Goddamn it!" Winty exploded. "You know I'm going to let Lucy have anything she wants, but I ought to at least be able to swear a little bit over it."

Eulalie insisted that Lucy's husband was "the meanest man I ever saw," adding in the same breath, "but I'd give anything to have a man look at me the way he looks at you." Lucy's reply "Yes, he does love me, doesn't he?" made Eulalie angry. "You're a slave," she shot at her. Lucy smiled and replied sweetly, "Yes, but a willing one." Eulalie had put her finger on a critical aspect of Lucy's relationship with her husband. Unlimited willingness to serve, and absolute submission to her husband's interests, was Lucy's way of dealing with her domestic "slave driver." It empowered Lucy to master awkward situations that might appear unacceptable to outsiders.

Emancipated friends like Eulalie Salley resented Winty's dictates only mildly. In spite of being a proud feminist, Eulalie obeyed Lucy's husband without a murmur when he decreed, "Go downstairs and you and Lucy have lunch in the dining room and then go for a drive. But have her back by three o'clock." Later he told Eulalie, "No matter how ill I get, you must spend every Thursday with Lucy."

She did. Every Thursday Eulalie had lunch with Lucy. After the meal they went on a carriage ride together. It was touching to see how much Lucy, kept at Winty's side in the house all day, enjoyed the outdoors. She could not take her eyes away from the beauty of the wild dogwood around Aiken. Another trait of character, besides Eulalie's love of nature, endeared her even more to Lucy. She enjoyed Eulalie's company because she was an intelligent partner in conversations—not only about feminism but about politics, the national news, and Washington society.

As long as Winty could dictate the rules, he remained jealous of "anybody who took up Lucy's time and love." Even his daughter Barbara was not to disturb her parents' togetherness. If an unwelcome visitor interfered with Winty's monopoly on Lucy's presence, he would simply snap, "Call the maid and get her out of here."

Eulalie disapproved of Winty's order that Lucy have all her meals on a tray by his bedside. As soon as he was no longer well enough to go to the dining room downstairs, Lucy was to live upstairs. In an age when well-to-do people routinely hired a live-in private nurse for a sick family member, Winthrop Rutherfurd's nurse would have had little to do. Lucy's self-imposed role as her husband's all-around caregiver permitted no substitution. This kind of submission was unheard of in her circle. Lucy's extreme devotion to her husband began to raise eyebrows.

* * *

The testimony of Barbara Rutherfurd's best friend confirmed that Eulalie was not exaggerating when she stressed Lucy's subservience to her husband. Pam, now Mrs. LeBoutillier of Westbury, Long Island, spoke animatedly about the good times she spent in Barbara's company during their teenage years in the mid-1930s. On many days the girls would come indoors at Ridgeley Hall, hungry from play in the garden, and find a message hanging from the railing of the staircase. It told them to help themselves to goodies in the refrigerator. Lucy could not accommodate the girls herself because she was absorbed by her obligations upstairs. Barbara accepted the situation without question; Pam didn't mind either. She had a lot of fun at the Rutherfurds' place. Barbara could offer a special attraction to the girls she befriended: an array of tall and handsome older half brothers. They invited crushes from a distance. It was a great sport for the girls to hide behind hedges and giggle wildly when the young men went by.

Winty was in the center of all reports that FDR received about Lucy in the 1930s and early 1940s. There was obviously no room left for any contact between old friends, such as Lucy and Franklin.

Lucy's absolute disregard for her own interests in the service of her husband's gave Franklin pause. Was this how a "good wife" acted? FDR remembered only too well that his own mother decided in his father's favor when she had to choose between devoting her attention to her son or her ailing husband.

In the eyes of Aiken, Lucy Rutherfurd definitely went overboard in making her husband "happy and comfortable." Madame Shoumatoff noted that Lucy never went out in the evenings and "wore clothes that made her look somewhat older, as if deliberately diminishing the thirty years' difference between herself and her husband." The artist felt that Lucy's service for Winty, taking up every minute of the day, "was one of the outstanding features of their life. Everything whirled around him."

Lucy was only in her forties when she sacrificed all personal pleasures to her husband's needs. She actually deserved the title "Saint" more than her down-to-earth friend Eulalie. Lucy's extreme self-denial suggests explanations beyond her gentle and compassionate nature. Ever since the Mother Superior at her convent school had instilled in the young girl a strong belief that "Right *is* Right," Lucy followed the commands of a finely tuned conscience. Did it tell her to compensate for forbidden feelings for another man by showering her husband with extravagant attention?

Nobody will ever know, except her confessor. Aiken's Monsignor George Lewis Smith was in the front line of Lucy Rutherfurd's defenders when rumors of a romantic attachment to Franklin Roosevelt surfaced. The reverend insisted that there was never a clandestine affair. "Everything was out in the open. Of course there was an attraction—she was a beautiful woman."

The Right Reverend Smith had taken Aiken by storm with his dark good looks. Coming from a family of distinction, he was accepted as "born to it." His high-class instincts told him what Aiken expected of him. He knew where to draw a line of restraint at the bridge table. Mastery of the card game counted as much on Aiken's scale of snob appeal as expertise at the racetrack.

Smith was an oft-quoted raconteur, famous for his sense of humor. He once pointedly regretted that he had been fired from the job of praying for good weather at the steeplechase. The great event had taken place in pouring rain. When his successor at the task,

Rabbi Goldberg, could do no better, the monsignor suggested that the track "use a Baptist this year—they're more used to the water."

The jocular priest was sensitive. He had a feeling for the tragic side of his parishioner Lucy's fate. He respected Mrs. Rutherfurd's gallantry and her reticence. He refused an offer of thirty-five hundred dollars for permission to copy a portrait of Lucy in his possession. When Lucy died he accompanied Mrs. Salley to the funeral in Allamuchy.

It is remarkable that Winthrop Rutherfurd displayed no jealousy toward Lucy's countless admirers, from Julian Salley to Monsignor Smith. Winty was absolutely sure that Lucy was committed solely to him. He did not find anything objectionable in the stiff letters that FDR sent to his house. He took any man's admiration for Lucy as a compliment for himself.

*   *   *

In 1933 Winty must have approved of Lucy's acceptance of the new president's invitation to his inauguration. Only an unusual event could pull Lucy away from his side, even for a short time. It is possible that Lucy told Winty that she had to travel to Washington to visit her sister, Violetta Marbury. Violetta, her husband, and her three children were exempt from Winty's ban on intruders into the magic circle of his family's seclusion. It was formed by his four sons and his daughter Alice—with little Barbara, "the Smallest," in its center as everybody's darling.

The Marburys were an important part of the Rutherfurds' summers at Allamuchy. They adjusted to Winty's formality without reservation. Vio's daughter Lucy Mercer Marbury still remembered in her eighties that the whole family appeared in evening dress at dinner, even on ordinary weekdays. The Allamuchy mansion was only a few minutes' walk downhill from Stone Cottage, the vacation home built by Winty specifically for Lucy's Marbury relatives. Stone Cottage was adjacent to the handsome fieldstone chapel erected by Winty for family worship on Sundays.

Winthrop Rutherfurd's Catholicism was intense, but it was as recent in his family history as Lucy's strong beliefs. As Miss Mercer, she had adopted her mother Minna's conversion to the Catholic Church with a passion, even though her father Carroll was an Episcopalian.

Adherence to the same denomination formed a strong bond between Lucy and Winty. It was not Lucy, however, but Winty's first wife
Alice Morton who had the Rutherfurds' own house of worship built.
Their chapel was stately enough to accommodate a sizable congregation. In the 1930s the picturesque place served on weekdays as a favorite location for the Marbury children to play with their little
cousin Barbara Rutherfurd.

Lucy and Violetta's mother—Winty's mother-in-law Minnie Mercer—was a regular houseguest at Allamuchy. She did not always fit
smoothly into the family idyll. There is a record from 1934 that mentions Mrs. Minna Mercer's visits to Allamuchy in the summer, and to
Aiken in the winter. In spring and fall, Minna migrated between
suites at her favorite hotels in New York and Washington. This much-
enjoyed peripatetic life ended when Minnie had to be moved to a
"sanatorium," the term used for her home for the aged. Although the
Waverley was conveniently located in Rockville, Maryland, Minna herself did not think so. She detested her new residence because it was
too far away from her friends in the capital. She always liked to be
close to the government. Though Minna had every reason to be
grateful for Vio and Lucy's splendid marriages, she still engaged in
her old sport of fighting for increases of her own tiny pension as the
widow of an incapacitated veteran.

The old Mrs. Carroll Mercer cherished her role as a link to the maternal nobility of Lucy's biological daughter. Minna sent her visiting
card to Miss Barbara Rutherfurd along with a memento from her own
childhood. She explained in a remarkably decorative hand that the
enclosed ribbons were "hung on the back . . . laid under my chin to
look grown up! *Your* gt. grandmother was much amused I wanted to
look like her. She was very beautiful." Minna, signing as "Granny,"
hoped "it may please you to keep for your grandchildren." On another occasion Minna sent Barbara a small heirloom of valuable old
lace, made in France. It came from a christening robe owned by
"your precious Mummy." Unfortunately, it was "ripped apart for use
by your Aunt Vio—and this is the only piece left," Minna wrote Barbara.

Aunt Vio's daughter, Mrs. Lucy Mercer Blundon, remembered her
grandmother vividly. She told me with a chuckle how Minna's recurrent visits with the Rutherfurds came to an abrupt end. Minnie Mercer

and Winty Rutherfurd were too much alike in their fiery temperament. As a rule, Lucy could keep the conversation at her dinner table
low key. She had a hard time at it when Minnie visited. The opinion-
ated old lady could introduce an edge into any subject.

One day, when Winty picked an argument and forcefully contradicted his mother-in-law, the formerly polite exchange got out of
control. To Lucy's horror the old lion and lioness began to growl at
each other. Winty was sharper in debate than Minna. When the formidable matron found herself outmaneuvered, she played a dangerous trump card. She put her son-in-law in his place, reminding him
that he was a year older than she herself, his wife's mother. Minna
was born in 1863, Winty in 1862.

Minnie's arrow hit home. Accustomed to ignoring the fact that
Lucy was almost thirty years his junior and could have been his
daughter, Winty was speechless at the tactless remark. The old lady's
triumph did not last long. In the long run, she was the loser when
her son-in-law declared her *persona non grata* in his house. Never
again would Minne be welcome under his roof.

From here on Lucy and Vio divided the responsibility for their
mother's care along clear-cut lines. The Rutherfurds would provide
financial help for Minna and the Marburys would keep her entertained with visits from her grandchildren.

ADMIRATION FROM A DISTANCE

The transition from the 1930s to the 1940s was marked for Lucy by
the accelerated breakdown of her husband's health. After years of
slow decline, the end of Winty's struggle to stay alive was clearly in
sight. Lucy would be a widow before long. By this time the stress of
relentless caregiving had noticeably diminished Lucy's own vitality.

Lucy's frailty provided a new reason for her to envy Franklin's
wife. Since her youth Eleanor's emotional vulnerability was balanced
by her solid physical condition and tireless energy. When the possi-
bility of marriage first appeared on Franklin's horizon, his mother
had been concerned about the fragility of Franklin's first great love,
Alice Sohier. After Franklin and Alice split up for this very reason,
with Franklin sharing his mother's concerns, Sara regarded Eleanor's
physical strength as a crucial asset and eagerly prepared the way for

Franklin's engagement to the nineteen-year-old girl. Her daughter-in-law would fulfill all her hopes, bearing six children—five of whom lived. As First Lady and as a widow, a tireless activist on her own for seventeen years, Eleanor amazed her friends with her ability to work hard after only five or six hours of sleep at night. Accustomed to vibrant health, it was especially hard on Eleanor to be tied down for a few weeks by pleurisy in London in 1919. She was, of course, not aware that this brief illness would remain latent in her body and contribute to her death in 1962.

While Lucy gave birth to just one child, and did not work outside the home, she had to be mindful of her physical limitations. In group pictures with her family, it is not her forceful presence but rather her gentle radiance that makes Lucy the center of her circle. In 1927 FDR had worried whether Lucy was *really* well. She always subordinated her own troubles to the troubles of loved ones. As Franklin's guest in Georgia in 1944 and 1945, she needed special consideration from the president's cousins because she was considered "not well."

Lucy's strength gradually waned. She did not live to see Eleanor prove her stamina in the years after Franklin's death. But even if Lucy had witnessed Eleanor's rise to heroic stature in her battles for social justice and human dignity, she could not have adored her more than she did in her youth. Lucy never aimed beyond her role as a subordinate friend of Eleanor. She continued to look up to Eleanor when she became the great lady's social equal in her middle years, as the wife of a rich and prominent man. In Aiken Lucy found herself alone with her admiration for Eleanor in an environment full of hate and ridicule for the Roosevelts.

Now more than ever, Lucy forcefully expressed her veneration for a woman who was her opposite in personality in many ways. In the ultraconservative citadel of rich Republicans in Aiken, it took courage to stand up for a First Lady whose political agenda was more radical than that of her husband. Lucy not only "never said an unkind word about Eleanor Roosevelt," she also did not permit any disparagement of the First Lady by others. When "Eulalie made some remark about her [Eleanor] looking like a hippopotamus . . . she [Lucy] quickly stopped her, demanding, "You mustn't say anything [bad] about her." At the dinner table, "Lucy cut the conversation short" when one of the guests made a nasty quip about Eleanor's looks.

Lucy put the critic sharply in her place. She closed the topic by insisting that Mrs. Roosevelt "knows more about dress than any woman I know."

Lucy gladly declared Eleanor superior to herself even in the field of good taste, her own domain. Mainly, she was awed by Eleanor as a pioneer who set an example for women's accomplishments outside the home. Lucy herself had no similar ambition. Rather, she filled the traditional role of the southern lady to perfection. As a model wife and mother, she was a match for any other *grande dame* of her social circle. Beyond this sphere Lucy towered over her peers with her superior understanding of politics. Her friendship with Franklin and Eleanor had taught her to evaluate politicians realistically and to constantly sharpen her political judgment. When Lucy worked in the Navy Department during the First World War, listening attentively to FDR's discourses on domestic and foreign policy, she had formed a solid basis for evaluating day-to-day political developments. After being married, Lucy felt handicapped by the irregular news service at the secluded places where she lived. She complained from Allamuchy, "Newspapers arrive a day late here, which is trying, and radio reception [is] the worst in the world, which is even more trying."

*   *   *

Lucy always tried to be up to date on current affairs. She took a keen interest in the public's praise for Franklin as governor of New York and closely watched the unfolding of the president's New Deal. She later followed his wartime decisions even more eagerly. A collection of newspaper clippings among Lucy's memorabilia shows that she was not only an attentive reader of the news, but also an ever-alert fan of FDR—uplifted by any expression of approval she considered her friend's due. On November 1, 1932, she cut out a letter to the editor in the *New York Times* lauding the governor's speeches for being free from cant and hypocrisy, and for the persistency of his arguments.

Lucy was well qualified to classify the top industrialists she knew from the dinner circuit in New Jersey and Aiken by the degree of their partisanship for FDR. "There seems to be more sympathy with the administration for a backing up of its foreign policy," Lucy noted. "Yesterday I was told that Eugene Grace [then the president of Bethlehem Steel] is now completely loyal to the administration and that Bethlehem Steel has several million dollars in defense orders." She offered Franklin, if "you care to know about loyalty I can easily find out. He has always seemed to me clever. Nonetheless, I wouldn't trust him around the corner."

Relying on Lucy's judgment, the president later chose George Mead of the Mead Corporation as one of his major wartime business advisers. She had recommended Mead earlier because she felt "he might be a help to you in some capacity as an ironer-outer of sorts." Lucy suggested that Franklin ask Harry Hopkins "to bring him [Mead] to lunch with you sometime, when you are alone. He has high ideals and seems to be headed always in the right direction." Mead also had the right friends. He told Lucy that for a long time he had shared "the same office with Sidney Hillman, an admirable and v.[ery] fine man" and a prominent labor union leader. Though Lucy called George Mead's wife "a great friend of mine," she did not hesitate to warn FDR against Harold Talbott, one of Mrs. Mead's brothers. She believed Talbott, chairman of North American Aviation, to be "quite poisonous."

It was bold of Lucy to take such strong stands for or against the president's prospective associates. FDR received similar advice all the time from Eleanor. Surprisingly, he took Lucy's judgment about candidates for high positions as seriously as the opinions of his politically astute wife. Franklin obviously trusted Lucy fully because he knew that she was not pursuing any self-serving political goals. She was thinking about his problems purely along the lines of his own interest.

Franklin appreciated Lucy's independence from her surroundings and admired her courage in openly taking his side. It required a special effort on her part—not only to stand against her social circle, but also to battle her own conscience at the same time. Quite obviously, she tried to make up for her guilt, preserving her love for Franklin in the depth of her heart instead of eradicating it for her husband's sake. Now she had to overcome guilt as the wife of a stout Republican. How could she justify betraying Winty's political party by spying for FDR and serving as his adviser?

Lucy had years to solve these conflicts within her heart while she looked after Winty with total devotion. While she was glued to her husband's bedside, she still found ways for keeping up with what was going on in the world, in order to assist Franklin whenever the need arose. In the thirteen years between 1928 and 1941, when she and Franklin heard little from each other, Lucy had to constantly sort out her position in the lives of two men. Though she and Franklin seemed to live on different planets, they did not grow apart and heard enough about each other to keep up their mutual admiration from a distance. When the time came for an active renewal of their friendship, Franklin and Lucy were ready—especially since the ties of their marriages had weakened.

ELEANOR AND MISSY: FDR'S TWO "WIVES"

There was a wide gulf between the public's perception of the president's marriage and the immediate family's close-up view of it. Franklin was eager to consolidate the public image of the president and First Lady as a team with superbly coordinated interests. They obviously worked well together to mutual advantage. Eleanor created her own power base as a leader among women in the Democratic party while she made a name for herself as a publicist. She was highly motivated, always on the go. Visible all over the country, she made up for the president's limited mobility. Eleanor's designation as her handicapped husband's "eyes and ears" was utterly convincing. Her omnipresence in the public eye suited her temperament perfectly.

Franklin, acting from the top platform of the White House, could provide a springboard for Eleanor on the way to fame. Given free rein by her husband to set her own goals, Eleanor went from being a modestly paid teacher and administrator at the Todhunter School to a much-sought-after, highly paid lecturer and journalist. With her idealistic drive and political acumen, she perfectly complemented Franklin's relatively cautious, pragmatic approach to political problems.

By 1936 Eleanor's journalist friend Lorena Hickok had launched her on a new and brilliant career as a columnist. Eleanor's *My Day* columns, filled with reports of her daily activities inside and outside the White House, appeared in newspapers all over the country until her death in 1962. Eleanor's professional success arrived at a critical point in her marriage. Lorena recoiled in horror when Eleanor revealed that she was toying with the idea of divorce and gave her a pep talk about her husband's merits. Eleanor would have to put up with him, if only for the country's sake.

Eleanor's uncle Theodore Roosevelt had told his young cousin FDR at the time of their wedding that the ability of a married couple to remain lovers was more crucial to their happiness than any political triumph. Even winning the presidency was no match for it. This happiness had been denied Franklin and Eleanor. They tried to make up for the lack of ardor in their marriage with attachments to devoted associates and intimate friends. However, an emptiness remained in their lives that even their extraordinary success as working partners could not mask. By contrast, the regal and bright Edith Carow brought different assets to her married life with Theodore Roosevelt. Edith lacked her niece Eleanor's political brilliance but provided an island of security and calm amid Theodore's turbulent existence, forever winning his absolute devotion.

Reaching out to Lucy in intervals, Franklin revealed how much he longed for the harmony and peace that he associated with her presence. During his first two presidential terms, absorbed by his struggle to pull the country out of the Depression, he denied himself the luxury of catering to his emotional needs. Missy LeHand's affection for him had to suffice, offering the warmth and fun that he missed in his wife's company. But FDR's relationship with his personal secretary was basically burdened by differences in their backgrounds and tastes that were never overcome, in spite of many years of being together every day. Although FDR was sincerely grateful for his secretary's caring, and although he enjoyed exchanging gay banter with her, he could not return Missy's total commitment to him. He called her "Child" and never shared his innermost thoughts with her. This was a privilege he reserved for Lucy.

FDR had always chosen his favorites from a narrow social circle—Alice Sohier, Eleanor, Daisy Suckley, Lucy Mercer, Lathrop Brown, and Livy Davis all came from distinguished families. Eleanor was more egalitarian in her choice of friends. As First Lady in the Albany statehouse and later in the White House, she preferred friends from backgrounds other than her own. Her bodyguard Earl Miller, her biographer Joseph Lash, and the journalist Lorena Hickok were prime examples. Eleanor grew much closer to them than Franklin ever did to Missy.

The down-to-earth, ever-reliable Missy was settled firmly in FDR's life throughout the changes in his health and occupation from the 1920s until June 1941, when she had her first stroke. By comparison, the aristocratic Lucy Rutherfurd was not a tangible presence in FDR's days during the same period. She was rather the object of FDR's dreams and longing, tied to him only by a thin line of correspondence.

DAISY SUCKLEY: CLOSEST COMPANION

Franklin's mother saw that her sociable son needed more company that suited his wit and his high-class ways. Sara found what she was looking for in Margaret Suckley, a distant cousin and lady belonging to the Hudson Valley gentry. Called Daisy in her circle, Margaret was well educated and able to share Franklin's everyday experiences. Eleanor had limited her own contact with Franklin mainly to political concerns. Sara herself was more preoccupied than ever as a hands-on grandmother and great-grandmother. Besides, Sara took her public relations duties as "First Mother" seriously.

Margaret Suckley fulfilled Sara's expectations as a desirable companion for her son. The young woman was congenial to Franklin and made him feel less lonely as he worked hard at his rehabilitation from the onslaught of polio. Margaret was just the right age as a friend, a little younger than Franklin. Her primness and lack of glamour precluded any new complications in FDR's love life.

In the spring of 1922, Sara issued Daisy the first of many invitations to tea with Franklin in Hyde Park. He was struggling every day with exhausting exercises, using crutches to help navigate the tree-lined road between the mansion and the entry gate on Albany Post Road. His paralysis from the previous summer had left deep marks on his once-even disposition. Daisy was eager to cheer him up. She had taken a liking to her handsome sixth-degree cousin since meeting him in 1910 at one of the famous New Year's parties given by the family of Archibald Rogers, the Roosevelts' neighbors. Crumwold, their massive mansion, was a fortress of a building in Romanesque style. Daisy's own home, Wilderstein, was more gracious. Hidden in the woods near Rhinebeck, upstream on the Hudson, the villa was a Victorian architect's dream come true. Remodeled as a Queen Anne mansion in 1888, it charmed visitors with its turrets, multiple gables, and colorful gingerbread woodwork. To this day the Suckleys' homestead remains a gem in the string of landmarks in FDR's beloved home region.

If Franklin took close notice of Daisy's circumstances, he would have discovered that her life paralleled Lucy Mercer's fate in many ways. Both Daisy and Lucy were born in opulence in 1891. Both their families had suffered a decisive blow to their fortunes in the financial crash of 1893. Daisy's father, Robert Bowne Suckley, had taken his family to Switzerland for ten years in order to ensure an affordable upper-class education for his children. Lucy too had attended a superior school overseas as a result of her parents' insolvency. But Daisy Suckley had been able to return to her childhood home, Wilderstein, while Lucy spent her mid-twenties in a rented apartment in Washington. Trapped in genteel poverty, both Daisy and Lucy chose a modest but dignified way of supporting themselves. Daisy became the paid companion of an old aunt, Mrs. Woodbury G. Langdon; Lucy, eight months younger than Daisy, worked with her mother as an interior decorator and held a part-time job as Mrs. Franklin Roosevelt's social secretary.

Thoughtful and sympathetic, Daisy was good at entertaining people. A meticulous keeper of records, Daisy entrusted to her diary how much she enjoyed Mrs. James Roosevelt's charge to distract Franklin from his woes. As Geoffrey Ward said of FDR in his preface to his volume of Daisy's letters and diaries, "He had come home to Springwood an invalid . . . and his wife Eleanor was already busy elsewhere, seeing to the care of their five children, pursuing causes of her own, trying to keep the Roosevelt name alive in the political world."

Eleanor's detachment contributed to Franklin's urge to reach out anew to Daisy in 1933. As president, he had to cope with a new form of loneliness created by the distance and awe of associates now far below him in status. Eleanor welcomed his choice of Daisy as a companion and correspondent. Daisy was no threat to her self-esteem. Eleanor's secretary Malvina Thompson called her "rather mousy." A relative described Daisy as "adamantly opposed to sex." Miss Suckley dressed in a way that made her look older than she was.

Franklin didn't mind her being "dowdy" and "retiring." He was comfortable with her; she belonged to his crowd. Daisy was intelligent but unassuming, loyal, and visibly more and more taken with him. She expressed freely how she was captivated by his wit and awed by his leadership. Daisy flattered Franklin with her gratitude for being allowed to share his leisure time. Their close companionship began with a phone call from FDR on August 1, 1933. He invited her to tea on August 5, together with her aunt and his mother. Two days later he took Daisy by herself on a drive through the woods around Hyde Park. It was a significant compliment to Daisy to be chauffeured by the president in his personal automobile, one that was specially equipped with hand-controlled devices to make up for the handicap of his lame legs.

Daisy had a right to be elated at being the only passenger on the many long drives she took in the countryside with the president at the wheel. Even though she did not know it, she was the third lady to be singled out by Franklin with this proof of his affection. He had been twenty-two in 1904, during the time of his not-yet-official engagement to Eleanor, when he was recognized by his godmother Nelly Blodgett. He was driving an open car, gazing fondly at Eleanor by his side. Franklin thoroughly enjoyed outsmarting the tight chaperoning system of his class. He wanted to enjoy private conversations with Eleanor, the girl he was going to marry.

Thirteen years later, in 1917, Alice Roosevelt Longworth teased Franklin when he had been observed in a similar situation. He had been seen by Alice's acquaintances driving alone with Lucy Mercer at his side, far out in the country. Franklin refused to be embarrassed at being caught and laughed off cousin Alice's reproach.

*   *   *

A generation later, as a married man seeking privacy on a drive with a single woman in the 1930s, Franklin was even more nonchalant about being watched. As president, he was well aware that the White House was a glass house where nothing could be hidden from the public. Nobody dared to censure the president anyway when he went on joyrides with Miss Suckley during weekends at Hyde Park. Again, as on his excursions with Miss Roosevelt in 1904 and with Miss Mercer in 1917, it was not the destination of the trip—with its potential for a clandestine get-together—that seemed to call for an explanation. The question in the air was rather why Franklin enjoyed so much such innocent pleasures as a ride in the country with a lady friend.

Miss Suckley's company enhanced FDR's joy at demonstrating that he was his own master. As in the two preceding similar episodes, his outings were made great fun by the thrill of a successful escape. Franklin, the Harvard man, had slipped away triumphantly from Eleanor's chaperones. As a young government official, he showed his indifference to gossips who speculated about his relationship to Lucy Mercer. Now he fled with Daisy at his side, shaking off the pursuing Secret Service cars by winding his way through narrow lanes in a terrain he had explored since boyhood.

Daisy felt honored by every bit of secrecy Franklin shared with her. With deep emotion she called a scenic spot "our hill," a place where they had been touched by common fondness for their native landscape. Daisy participated in Franklin's planning for a secluded cottage in the woods, "a small place to go" whenever he felt pressed by "the mob." Like Missy, Daisy imagined herself as the mistress of Hilltop Cottage. It was disappointing that nothing ever came of these dreams. Although the cottage was finished in 1939, Franklin used it only sporadically in the daytime. If he ever spent a night under its roof, it was not recorded.

As in the 1920s, when Franklin sought solace in regular contact with Lucy Rutherfurd through the mail, he now tried to ensure that a letter from Daisy was waiting for him wherever he went. Just as the informal, undated piece of blue paper from the 1920s—preserved by the Rutherfurd family—that lists in Franklin's hand the places and days where he expected to find mail from Lucy, waiting for him as he traveled, Daisy mentions in a letter to Franklin the same type of memo. Daisy told FDR, "[Y]our mother said you had given her your P.O. list." Actually, Franklin had given his friend a much more detailed itinerary than he gave his mother. It contained meticulous instructions, indicating which mail pouch to catch. Franklin not only loved to receive a personal letter every day, he also enjoyed writing one as

LUCY AND THE PRESIDENT   263

part of his daily routine. In a way these letters took the place of a journal. Sadly, the bulk of them is lost. Their major recipients destroyed Franklin's letters deliberately—Eleanor in 1937 and Lucy in 1945. It is a boon for presidential history that Daisy did not follow suit. She kept Franklin's letters carefully and tucked them away in a suitcase under her bed. In another stroke of luck for future biographers, a prominent historian of FDR's personal life, Geoffrey Ward, took over the scholarly evaluation of these letters after Daisy died at the age of one hundred in 1991. The thirty-eight letters from Franklin to Daisy—edited by Ward and partly published in his book *Closest Companion*—are proof of FDR's diligence as a correspondent, even while he was pressed by important official duties.

Franklin's letters are detailed and sincere enough to permit an in-depth appraisal of his feelings for Daisy. They convey the importance of Daisy's role for the president's emotional well-being. He relished the opportunity to exchange information, both relevant and trivial, with a friend like Daisy whom he could trust. It was fun to address a recipient who would appreciate his witticisms. FDR's fondness for Daisy, and his anticipation of her presence, shine between the lines of his simple reports of daily events.

FDR's letters also show clearly the limits of his emotional involvement with Daisy. There was no suppressed passion in his reaching out to her, no gratification of erotic impulses. On the contrary, an avuncular kindness often permeates passages that Daisy might have wished to be more romantic. With a touch of fatherly indulgence, Franklin occasionally addressed her as "Child," in the same spirit that permeated his affection for Missy LeHand, his secretary and personal aide. With Daisy there was another adult "Child" in Franklin's orbit, precious to him but not enough to make him reciprocate the adoration extended to him. Unselfish concern for the happiness of his lady-child was especially endearing in one of Franklin's diary-type letters to Daisy that said, "I truly want you to . . . perhaps some day find just the right kind of 'Gentle Man' who will take very good care of you."

FDR's feeling of responsibility for Daisy showed most tangible results when her aunt and employer Mrs. Langdon died. She left Daisy stranded without a regular income. Franklin proved at a critical time that he made no empty promise when he told Daisy on August 3,

1941, "Save any problems for the broad shoulders of . . . F." Now he acted as her *deus ex machina* and offered her a dream job. On October 1, 1941, Daisy started happily as archivist at FDR's brand-new presidential library in Hyde Park. Her salary of one thousand dollars per year would cover all necessities.

By this time the chain of Franklin's regular get-togethers with Daisy had already been broken. In the summer of 1939, Daisy was relegated to the sidelines of the all-important visit by England's king and queen to Hyde Park. In all of 1940, just one letter from Franklin to Daisy survived but none from Daisy to him. There remains just a sprinkling of correspondence between them from May to August 1941. After that an everlasting bond with Daisy remained in her famous present for Franklin, his beloved Scottish terrier Fala.

COMING OUT

The year 1941 was when Lucy moved back circumspectly into Franklin's life. Lucy's husband Winty and their daughter Barbara were instrumental in pulling her from the seclusion of her caregiver's role into the commotion of big cities. Winty, close to eighty and incapacitated, needed Lucy as his emissary in Washington to negotiate his admission to a top hospital. Barbara, going on eighteen, called for her mother's organizational talents to prepare for her coming-out party in New York City.

Barbara was ready to enter the world of the class into which she was born. The cards announcing Barbara's coming-out dinner dance on Friday, November 22, 1940, directed the guests to Hampshire House, 150 Central Park South. The invitations were issued in the name of Mr. and Mrs. Winthrop Rutherfurd, but only one of Barbara's parents—her mother—appeared in the pages of the luxurious photo album illustrating the event. It included a reception, the dinner, and dancing to live music. Everybody knew that Barbara's father was too sick to preside. It was Barbara's good fortune that her mother was perfectly capable of introducing her to society by herself.

The attractive, gracious debutante, resplendent in a shimmering satin evening gown, was the image of her father. She had inherited his dark hair, his strong eyebrows, his tall, athletic build, and his strong jaw. Her mother, her hair carefully waved, was still beautiful.

She had become only slightly heavier as she approached fifty. Discreetly adorned with simple jewelry and a few orchids, she gladly put to use her long-dormant skills for directing social events. Finally, Lucy could experience vicariously as a mother what she had missed as a daughter. When she and her sister came of age, neither of her parents had been able to host coming-out parties for their two daughters. In 1940 the Winthrop and Lucy Rutherfurd could invest large amounts of money and good taste in a picture-book party in honor of their youngest daughter. There were no Mercers or Carrolls among the forty guests, but the Rutherfurds and Stuyvesants were well represented.

Most of the older, distinguished gentlemen at the party could be expected to be Republicans. They would not have suspected that the most prominent Democrat in the country, the man labeled a traitor to his class, had left a memo of his friendship at the event honoring Barbara Rutherfurd. The debutante's most important piece of jewelry, the focal point of her attire, was a present from President Franklin Roosevelt. Mrs. Rutherfurd wore a conventional string of pearls, but Miss Rutherfurd's striking necklace attracted all the attention. A large, square aquamarine on a gold chain was framed exquisitely by the tulle top of Barbara's gown. The aquamarine, later fashioned into a ring, is owned to this day by Barbara's descendants. The circumstances of FDR's present to Lucy's daughter remain cryptic.

It is certain that Lucy's daughter Barbara was dear to Franklin's heart. It is puzzling, however, why FDR chose to express his affection for the girl by calling himself her godfather. After he met Barbara in 1941, FDR always signed his congratulatory birthday telegrams with the word "Godfather." If FDR did not simply appropriate this title for himself, if he had actually been assigned this position prior to Barbara's christening in 1922, all the exchanges that followed between Lucy and Franklin would be cast in a different light.

LUCY MEETS FRANKLIN FACE TO FACE

Lucy's joy at seeing her daughter shine as a debutante was soon overshadowed by sadness. Winty's condition grew worse. A stroke in the early spring of 1941 was followed by a second, disabling stroke at the beginning of June. In her despair Lucy turned to FDR, her powerful friend. She needed the president's connections in order to have her husband admitted to Walter Reed Hospital in the capital, where he would get the best possible medical treatment. Winty could hardly speak anymore, nor could he move his right arm. Lucy's stayed in Washington to ensure that her husband would be seen by the best specialists. But although her visit was dominated by anguish, it was made unforgettable by a magic moment.

On June 5, 1941, Lucy thanked Franklin in person for his intervention on behalf of her husband. They saw each other again, face to face for the first time in twenty-three years. It is not known whether FDR left Hyde Park on June 3 specifically for Lucy's sake, to be in Washington in time to meet her. In any case, it was again Lucy and Franklin's old patroness from 1917 and 1918—Winty's first sister-in-law Edith Eustis—who acted as the appropriate escort on Lucy's way to the president's White House study. During the day of Lucy's visit, Franklin made two heartbreaking visits to the sickbed of Missy Le-Hand. On the eve of his encounter with Lucy, Missy had suffered the first of the strokes that would end her life. The White House Usher's Log states that on June 5 he was in the company of "Mrs. Johnson."

Lucy's Secret Service code name also protected her identity in telephone conversations. Chats on the phone were more discreet than letters in the years when Lucy was tied down as her husband's caregiver. They also proved to be the most private way for old friends to stay in touch. For Lucy and Franklin, being able to converse in French added an extra layer of protection to their privacy.

In cooperation with Marguerite LeHand, Louise Hachmeister was the most effective guardian angel of the president's contact with Mrs. Rutherfurd. As the chief operator of the White House switchboard, Louise ranked high in FDR's regard. When the wartime White House was eventually moved to Hyde Park, the president decreed that Miss Hachmeister would be honored with the occupancy of the master bedroom in the Vanderbilt mansion, which had been taken over by his staff in 1940 after being donated to the National Park Service by the Vanderbilts' heiress Mrs. Van Alen. FDR himself had suggested the donation. He teased "Hackie" that nothing would do in the palatial residence but black nightgowns of the kind Mrs. Vanderbilt used to wear to match her black pearls.

Louise Hachmeister was recognized as a genius in her line of work. She could remember the voices of all callers in the president's orbit and could connect Mrs. Rutherfurd directly with him, as he requested. Louise was one of the accomplices in the silent conspiracy of those who welcomed every bit of warmth in their boss's stressful life. They approved of the president's friendship with a lovely lady of great dignity, but observed secrecy out of respect for the First Lady.

The quiet phase of Lucy's life, filled with clear-cut obligations in South Carolina and New Jersey, came to an end when she met Franklin again in person. It became obvious that the slow-burning flame of their love had been rekindled. But before they could begin to direct more attention to each other, they had to deal with painful shifts in the lives of the dearest around them. In June 1941, when Franklin lost the help of Missy LeHand, his mother also suffered a stroke that was relatively light but warned of her impending failing. She died on September 7, two weeks before her eighty-seventh birthday. Sara had been the major pillar of Franklin's inner balance, his oldest and most dependable source of love and support.

After Sara died Franklin tried to fill the silence around him with new voices. Margaret Suckley's time was now occupied by her work in the library. In her place attractive royal ladies, refugees from Europe, appeared in the president's surroundings. Martha, the crown princess of Norway, stood out among them as especially attractive, first in the eyes of the president's mother.

Sara, always fascinated by bearers of crowns, had been star-struck by the beautiful and regal refugee from Hitler's invasion of Norway in 1940. FDR welcomed his mother's hospitality for the émigrés in Hyde Park before he took them under the government's wing at the White House. Besides Martha of Norway, FDR's favorite was Queen Wilhelmina of the Netherlands and her daughter, Princess Juliana. Even Austria's former Empress Zita lent interest and sparkle to the president's leisure hours. European royalty filled Sara's guest book with exalted names that she had once invoked with awe in her student years in Hanover.

*   *   *

Eleanor did not take offense at FDR's personal attachment to the Norwegian princess. She did not mind its flirtatious overtones and was content that it was carried out under the nose of Martha's husband and her three children. The First Lady did not see much of the royals because she was traveling. She stayed overnight more frequently away from home than in her suite at the White House. She shrugged off Princess Martha, who obviously adored Franklin, as the most recent "worshipper at his shrine." This had been Eleanor's name for potential voters—ladies fawning over her husband during the 1920 election campaign. Later Eleanor discussed Franklin's need to be admired with her old friend Joseph Lash, who was always open to criticism of the president. Eleanor deplored that for Franklin "there was always a Martha for relaxation and for the non-ending pleasure of having an admiring audience for every breath."

Eleanor despised what she later called "uncritical love." After Sara's death the only other female besides his wife in Franklin's immediate family, his daughter Anna, was her father's greatest champion. Her love for him was unconditional, even though it was by no means uncritical. It could not unfold as Anna wished because she lived too far away from Washington—on the West Coast in Seattle— with her second husband John Boettiger.

Franklin's distance from Anna lost some of its sharp edge when a new, enchanting equivalent of a young daughter turned up in Washington. The president was delighted with his first daughter-in-law. James's wife Betsey Cushing was an aristocrat in her own right. Her father was a prince in the field of medicine, a celebrity as a brain surgeon. The president and the famous man's daughter charmed each other. For Eleanor's taste Betsey came to be a little too closely integrated in Franklin's world when she took over some of the duties of the First Lady. Eleanor especially resented Betsey's interference in her own privilege to decide the seating of guests at official dinners. It was a relief for Eleanor when James divorced Betsey unceremoniously, ending a brief marriage, Franklin was all the more upset at the loss of Betsey, a source of warmth and fun on lonely evenings. In 1941 Anna could not yet move to fill the vacuum of affection around the president.

Eleanor did not know that Franklin's old love, rightly regarded by her as her only serious rival, was about to re-enter her husband's life. In hindsight it appeared providential that Lucy Rutherfurd resurfaced in the months following Franklin's most severe losses in companionship.

Lucy too had arrived at a junction in her life where she needed new emotional and practical support. Franklin understood. His use of presidential power for Lucy's sake in the weeks after they saw each other again followed the pattern of previous years. The president's standard question "How can I help?" was met by Lucy's perennial answer "Please help my family." FDR's response was as prompt and enthusiastic as ever. While he was not at ease expressing his love with words, Franklin was a model of loving by action. He had been able to secure admission for Lucy's husband into the best possible hospital. He had shown his affection for Lucy's daughter Barbara, treating her truly like a goddaughter. Now the time had arrived when he could contribute to the advancement of Lucy's stepsons. FDR loved the chance to integrate himself ever more warmly in the Rutherfurd family by assisting its heirs. For the four boys, the president—the father of four sons of similar ages—represented a younger substitute for their own old and impaired father. Putting to use a lawyer's training, FDR was well qualified to act as the boys' knowledgeable guide in career questions. As commander in chief, he had unsurpassed leverage to help with the boys' military careers.

Britain was holding out as the last bastion of democracy in a region overrun by Hitler's blitzkrieg. Though Winthrop Rutherfurd and Franklin Roosevelt were divided by party lines, they agreed on questions of foreign policy. Both were ardent Anglophiles, ready for any sacrifice to rescue England. On January 6, 1941, in his famous Four Freedoms speech, the president formally announced his Lend-Lease plan to supply American war matériel to the hard-pressed nation. It was signed into law on March 11, 1941.

The Rutherfurd sons were in the vanguard of young Americans putting on uniforms, eager to go to war. FDR acted immediately on their behalf. On June 9, 1941, only four days after his meeting with Lucy, the president received a White House memo in response to his "recent inquiry regarding possible appointment of Mr. John P. Rutherfurd in the Supply Corps Reserve." While mobilization quotas were "about filled," the president was told that "S & A would be glad indeed to get an additional number of young men like John Rutherfurd, who have accounting experience."

*   *   *

The president's successful move on behalf of Ensign John P. Rutherfurd, Lucy's second-oldest surviving stepson, led to increased family contacts that were enjoyed by both sides. Going properly through channels, John sent his thank you note to the president by way of General Watson. John politely expressed his appreciation to the general for "steering me through the devious ways of Washington. For an Army 'yard-bird' it was quite an experience." John's letter of thanks to the president was even more effusive. He glowed, "It was awfully nice of you to see me in Washington, and Mother and I especially enjoyed your notation . . . about my case." John ended by regretting that the world was "in a terrible mess, but I know you'll bring us through."

Franklin was especially pleased when John's military transfers brought Lucy's stepson together with his daughter Anna. The president himself had established the connection by asking her over the phone to be nice to John Rutherfurd. Anna reported back to Grace Tully, her father's assistant, on January 13, 1942:

> *I have forwarded the piece of mail to John Rutherford [sic]. If you get a chance, you might tell Father that he seems like an awfully nice person, was at our house once, and we spent part of New Year's Eve at his house. If Father doesn't already know it, tell him that John is a mere six foot six, broad to match, and therefore quite formidable when practicing a bit of New Year's Eve weaving! His wife and twin boys arrive next month.*

A long letter of July 19, 1942, shows John more relaxed than he was a year earlier in his correspondence with his stepmother's awe-inspiring friend. Apparently, he had been encouraged by the president to send reports about the military build-up he saw to the White House. He apologized for his delay in writing to "let you know what we are doing here at Boeing." The best part of his news was that "the bomber, of which I enclose a picture, is testing very satisfactorily."

The personal side of John's handwritten letter stressed that "again I want to tell you how grateful I am to have been given the opportunity to serve in the type of work in which my training can be of the most use to the tremendous task you are leading us all through." John continued in the family-oriented way FDR cherished. "Have not seen Anna recently," he announced, "—she's away on a fishing trip, and I hope will have some 'big ones' to tell about on her return." John tops the chatty part of his letter with news about the president's son. "A friend of mine just came up from California and reported that John is working hard and is in his usual good form."

In his prompt reply to Ensign Rutherfurd in Seattle, the president added, "My Johnny is furious because he applied for duty on an aircraft carrier and instead was made Supply Officer for four special training destroyers operating out of San Diego—with his own office on shore!" He ends, "I am happy, indeed, that you are getting on so well and that you like the work." The exchange of Rutherfurd and Roosevelt family news ends with FDR's mention of Lucy. "I hear from your Mother that your family has joined you."

John Rutherfurd's older brother, Winthrop, Jr., was also invited to the White House at the end of June 1941. He was asked by the president to return three more times in 1943. John's younger brother Hugo, encouraged by the president's kindness, was gratified when he received the call to active sea duty he had requested. FDR's own physician Vice Admiral Ross McIntire had intervened on Hugo's behalf.

Lucy's youngest stepson Guy was privileged to receive career advice from the president before he requested and received assistance in his military service. Like his brother John, Guy pleased FDR by establishing contact with one of his own sons—Franklin, Jr., the older of the president's two younger boys. In a letter of June 25, 1942, sent from the naval operating base in Newport, Rhode Island, Guy expressed his "deepest appreciation for your help and interest in regard to my getting into the Navy." He added, "At your suggestion I stayed in Charlottesville long enough to get my law degree and then got through the New York Bar Exams. I was so glad to see Franklin there and learn that he had also passed the exams in spite of his being sick."

Lucy, in a letter to Franklin around this time, said in a worried tone, "I hope my other son wrote you to thank you." She recalled that she had launched the president on his mission as Guy's counselor with a wish that "some day I should like to ask your advice about my youngest step-son who is studying law at the University of Virginia, but has one more year. He wonders if it would be more interesting and better training for him to take a job in Washington, perhaps with a political slant to it, or to go immediately into estate work and where his cousin . . . has offered him a job. It seems to me that life in Washington where he could have a house and a garden would be better than life in N.Y. where they say most of the lawyers work themselves to death."

* * *

Ever since the first months of his presidency, FDR had enjoyed showering favors on his own family and friends, especially his Delano relatives. His aunt Kassie's son, his cousin and childhood friend Warren Robbins, had profited most as the president's protégé with his appointment as the envoy extraordinary and minister plenipotentiary to Canada. Now Lucy's stepchildren benefited from FDR's intervention. It arose from a big heart overflowing with the desire to use presidential privilege as a means to make people happy. He also found it reassuring to know personally the officials he appointed, such as Warren Delano. FDR's nepotism allowed him to reap at least a little direct satisfaction from the office that mercilessly consumed all his strength and inherited treasure.

It was a great joy for Franklin to succeed in bringing his and Lucy's children together—and to act as their friend. For Lucy's part she took her time in becoming reacquainted with her old love. She saw Franklin in person only three times in 1941 after their first meeting in June. On August 1 she was alone with him in the White House from 8:40 to 11:00 p.m. On the following day, she stayed after dinner until midnight. Eleanor's absence—not only when she was far away on Campobello—echoed similar situations two and a half decades earlier. On November 9, the day of Franklin and Lucy's next meeting, Eleanor was in New York City. Before Lucy dined with the president, she brought her daughter Barbara along to tea. It was a special pleasure for FDR to have Lucy's daughter included in their revived friendship. His affection for the young girl represented a big step toward his goal to become a part of Lucy's family.

FDR had met Barbara in person only a few days earlier, on October 29, 1941, at a White House luncheon with the president. He was overwhelmed by fondness for the lovely nineteen-year-old and expressed his enthusiasm spontaneously in an informal note to her mother. There was no longer any trace of the stiff formality of his letters to Lucy from the 1920s. This note was the only part of their later correspondence that was written without inhibitions, right from his heart. Franklin started out, skipping a salutation, "The littlest Babs is all that I dreamed—just the dearest thing in the world." Franklin added a unique expression of his feelings with a barely readable "'cept one." He wanted Lucy to hear once more that she was dearer to him than anybody else in the world.

Finding words to express love was not easy for Franklin. He always avoided superlatives while describing emotions. It was all the more remarkable that he ended his note to Lucy with a line unmatched anywhere in his known correspondence; it stood out by itself underneath the text of his message. This time Franklin was dead serious in his confession; he was no longer hiding his feelings behind jokes and clever witty passages. At this moment it is likely that he came closer to baring his soul than on any other occasion. Apparently in response to a question from Lucy about old times together, Franklin burst out, "I do remember the times—so well—*à toujours et toujours.*"

Slipping into French, their language of love, helped Franklin use the magic words "forever and ever." Here was the sentiment that Eleanor craved from Franklin. She had found it elusive ever since he proposed to her and had pushed in vain for more fervor in her suitor's letters. Eleanor later told Joseph Lash that she burned the letters from Franklin's courtship in 1903 and 1904 but left it to him to come up with a reason. At least at the peak of this emotional time, he could have—or should have—promised never-ending devotion.

*   *   *

As in all his close relationships, Franklin was most comfortable in expressing his fondness for Lucy by what he did for her. Meeting her children's needs was his way of telling her how much he cared. He happily took Barbara's first visit as the prelude to many more to come. "We have decided that she will come back very soon," FDR wrote Lucy. Barbara's next known invitation from the president came when he asked her to a dinner with him and Harry Hopkins in December. On another occasion he showed his consideration for Barbara's position as a worker for the Red Cross by inviting her to dine with him and the organization's president. Anything he thought would please or impress Lucy's daughter could be arranged.

In early 1942 FDR had to concentrate on his responsibility as commander in chief of a country involved in a newly declared war. At the peak of stress, Franklin's need for occasional relaxation became more urgent. There was no company as calming as Lucy's. He was grateful for her willingness to spend time with him and to bring Barbara along. The president acted with utmost caution in reaching out to Mrs. Rutherfurd. There were four major reasons for keeping his encounters with her as quiet as possible. First, consideration of Eleanor's feelings was paramount. As in the other Great War, in 1917, Franklin saw Lucy only when Eleanor was not in Washington. Second, the president had to watch out for gossip. It could lead to the kind of political blackmail that John F. Kennedy feared from J. Edgar Hoover as a result of his marital indiscretions.

In addition, it was inopportune to tear a hole into the carefully spun net of illusion that assumed that FDR's marriage was as harmonious and fulfilling as voters liked to believe. The public was not ready to acknowledge that a politically outstanding president and an extraordinary First Lady need not have a flawless relationship as lovers, on top of standing out as a couple of historic achievement.

Finally, the impeccable Mrs. Rutherfurd had previously been hurt by unwelcome public scrutiny of her personal matters. Lucy would never take advantage of the generosity of a husband who had graciously accepted his wife's properly formal contact with Mr. Roosevelt, a friend from her past. After Franklin's death Lucy continued to keep all former ties to him out of the public eye. Her daughter Barbara followed suit.

FDR's strategy was amazingly successful. He spared Eleanor a prolonged replay of the humiliation and sorrow Lucy had caused her twenty years earlier. When Eleanor was newly widowed, and finally found out about the full scope of her husband's sunset romance, she made a point of never saying a word about it. She refrained from mentioning her husband's friendships, just as she stayed away from describing her own personal associations. Wisely, Eleanor warded off suspicion about her secrecy by appearing unusually frank and open about private matters in her autobiographies of 1937 and 1949.

While Winthrop Rutherfurd lived, the president was careful to let Lucy appear in his company only under the pseudonym Mrs. Paul Johnson. Her visits were neither hushed up nor fussed about. The White House log for the 1940s reveals that Franklin and Lucy saw each other at first only after long intervals, but later with increasing frequency. For almost four years, fate granted them only a few hours at a time by themselves, mainly with the assistance of Lucy's sister Vio. More often others were around, as in the old days. Only toward the very end of FDR's life would they stay under the same roof— twice in Georgia, each time for a few days in a row.

In 1942 Lucy saw FDR in the spring and again in October, when Eleanor was in England. Violetta's home on Q Street proved perfect as their meeting ground. Violetta's daughter remembered that there was nothing extraordinary or secretive about the appearance of the president at their door. Everything was completely open and accepted as the cheerful reunion of old friends. Lucy's personal maid Marie had come from Paris to the United States to join the Rutherfurs' large, mainly white staff. Although Marie always enjoyed a respected position among the Rutherfurd's staff, she was no match for the most highly esteemed member of the Mercer sisters' households: Emma, Vio's African-American housekeeper in Washington.

Proudly conscious of the decisive difference between her status and that of her forebears, the house slaves, Emma refused all offers to live in the Marburys' home. Pointedly independent, Emma derived great satisfaction from her irreplaceable role in the Marbury family. She gave all her life to the mistress she loved and admired, as she herself was loved and admired by Mrs. Marbury. The Marburys were Emma's second family. She refused to count the hours of her labors of love. Understanding the feelings of all members of the family, she evaluated correctly the delicate nature of Lucy's attachment to the president. She always answered the door when he was expected and greeted the invalid man with her warmest smile. She felt good about never talking to an outsider about his visits.

FDR was comfortable with Emma. He had learned at home about the preciousness of relationships of employers with their help, like the one between Vio and Emma. His mother Sara not only inspired loyalty but offered absolute loyalty herself. She cared for FDR's ex-governesses as long as they lived, as if they were her daughters.

Emma understood why the president and Mrs. Marbury's sister went for long drives together. An automobile provided a tiny, secluded island of privacy. The president also used his unmarked car occasionally to have his chauffeur bring Lucy from Q Street to the White House. On days when FDR came along with his chauffeur, the sliding glass window that separated the passengers in the back from the driver in the front would be closed. Brief sentimental journeys along familiar routes in the Maryland and Virginia countryside evoked memories of the long-gone days when Franklin himself had been at the wheel.

CHAPTER 10

SUNDOWN SOLACE

LUCY'S "POOR DARLING"

FDR, the wartime president, was seen by Lucy in a light that differed sharply from Eleanor's perception of her husband. Eleanor's old romantic view of the Franklin she adored had long been obscured by his disappointing behavior as a lover. She had become foremost a political reformer and looked upon her husband as a man of power. As president, Franklin controlled the levers that could be manipulated to turn her own idealistic visions of domestic policy into reality.

Lucy saw Franklin from another perspective. She stood in awe of the president's accomplishments without relating them to her own interest. Her heart went out in compassion to a vulnerable man, burdened by the concerns of high office. Lucy referred to Franklin as her "poor darling" in an important lengthy document—a frequently quoted window into her hidden thoughts. It is part of the collection of Lucy's preserved writings and memorabilia guarded by the Rutherfurd Foundation. The document is preceded by a notation from an earlier archivist: "L ltr to F no salutation, no date. Probably 1941 pre Pearl Harbor."

Both the classification and dating of Lucy's document are to be doubted. It does not fit the format of a regular letter. Only a fraction of the text might have been written before Pearl Harbor. Lucy's writings most resemble a diary, or possibly fragmentary notes for a later letter. The first four paragraphs of the document could have been written at different times, in either of Lucy's residences. New Jersey is mentioned in the text; Aiken too is indicated in some places. In the third paragraph, Lucy seems to have been writing at a time when her stepson Guy was a student at the University of Virginia.

The postscript to the document is a full letter in its own right, written much later. Groping with the uncertainties of the postwar world, it reflects the mood of the months close to the end of the war. Lucy describes FDR as thin and tired. She hopes he will get some rest on a big trip coming up—obviously the president's journey to Yalta.

With all its puzzles and imperfections, this piece of writing is invaluable as an opening into the world of Lucy's secret thoughts. Lucy herself felt uneasy about sharing her musings with their object. Nobody appeared worthy to intrude into Franklin's deliberations. Lucy would have felt guilty for taking the president's time with lines "best unwritten and unmailed." She called it "practically criminal" to give Franklin "one more thing to read or think about."

Lucy had to relieve herself of worry by committing it to paper. "Day by day the news becomes increasingly ominous and complex," she agonized. They appeared to bring ever-new threats to Franklin's personal well-being. Lucy modestly hid her own reactions to the world around her by substituting the word "one" for the outspoken "I." "And one sees," she wrote cautiously, "that the responsible heads of the Democracies must indeed be Super men . . . with the power [over] life and death." Franklin, the first among these heads of state, is contrasted with the irresponsible men who surrounded Lucy at Aiken. "Living as we do here," she wrote, "in a community of pleasure seekers, who cannot see further than the glasses in their hands, one is terrified by the lack of vision, or understanding of what is going on in the world."

More revealing than Lucy's comments about her surroundings were her visions of a utopian future, sketched in broad outlines in her postscript. She first joked that she apparently caught the bad cold that kept her housebound on the telephone, referring to another one of FDR's frequent calls while he had respiratory troubles. Thinking out loud in her enforced leisure, Lucy then put into words her dreams of a happier tomorrow. They were of the kind that a woman in love cannot help dreaming, even if there was no hope for them to come true.

* * *

It remains unsaid with whom Lucy expected to share the years after peace was restored. "I suppose now more than ever," Lucy pondered, "one must live each day as it comes, but it helps to have a milestone in sight. And if we have to re-live in a horse and buggy era, it won't break my heart. If only it will be a friendly world. A small house would be a joy, and one could grow vegetables as well as flowers, or instead of . . ." Here Lucy drifts off, shocked by her own boldness, and continues, "[O]h dear there is so much I should like to know." Finally, she addressed Franklin directly, confessing, "[I] have [as] much hope [as] you have, and [there are a] thousand questions one does not like to ask. The old gentleman here . . . says you have a close agreement with Churchill as to what will happen after the war."

Suppressing her fragmentary, self-centered ideas, again using the self-deprecating "one" instead of "I," Lucy resumed her full voice in the message of her postscript. She firmly believed in Franklin's genius as a leader. Paying homage to the man she worshipped, she declared him competent to fill any extraordinary mission.

> *I know one should be proud—very very proud of your greatness—instead of wishing for the soft life of joy and . . . the world shut out. One is proud, and thankful for what you have given to the world and realizes how much more must still be given to this greedy world, which never asks in vain. You have breathed new life into [its] spirit and the fate of all that is good is in your dear blessed and capable hands.*

Lucy described how she looked at a newspaper photograph of FDR clutching a handful of pencils. She regarded it as "pretty wonderful" but found him too thin. He looked like "what my colored man here would call 'tired, tired, till yet.'" Lucy wished, "May the trip rest you. As ever the only thing [I wish] is that all your anxieties go away with you, even your bad throat." Lucy included Barbara in her farewell wishes when she wrote, "The smallest sends you her love." She ended with "Bless you" and "As ever."

It is not known whether Lucy's incoherent writings ever reached Franklin. She might have kept the draft in a drawer, afraid of having revealed too many of her dreams of spending the postwar years with Franklin at her side. Theoretically, there was room for Lucy's fantasies. FDR expected to retire after he had reached his major goal— winning the war. He would have time to write his memoirs and make room for some personal happiness. Both he and Eleanor had made concessions and sacrifices, staying together in service of their mission. Once they succeeded, it appeared not unreasonable that they might yield to Eleanor's wish to go their separate ways. At the end of 1944, FDR was only sixty-two, Lucy fifty-three. Even if his unlikely fourth term would conclude the president's career, both might have decades left for the enjoyment of each other's company.

The dreams that surfaced fleetingly in Lucy's writing might have been spun in consensus with FDR in one of their few hours alone with each other. They could have been carried away by the happiness of being together again after a long separation, but Franklin was too much of a pragmatist to integrate such utopian flights of fancy into his own down-to-earth planning. As the president saw victory approach, and as he conceived the postwar world, his public persona as a great leader took precedence over his private aspirations. He saw his teammate Eleanor at his side on a triumphant tour of England. In FDR's vision of the crowning event of his presidency, Eleanor would wear a becoming new outfit and ride with him through London's cheering crowds.

CONSPIRATORS: LUCY, DAISY, POLLY, AND ANNA

At the time when Daisy Suckely began her work at FDR's presidential library in 1941, she also fulfilled a mission in FDR's private life. In 1942 she mused in her diary, "That big house without his mother seems awfully big and bare—she gave him the personal affection which his friends and secretaries can not do, in the same way—He always was 'my boy,' and he seemed to me often rather pathetic, and hungry for just that kind of thing. His wife is a wonderful person, but she lacks the ability to give him the things his mother gave him. She is away so much, and when she is here she has so many people around—the splendid people who are trying to do good and improve the world, 'uplifters,' the P. calls them—that he can not [sic] relax and really rest."

When Daisy discovered that Franklin longed for the presence of Lucy Mercer Rutherfurd, the secret queen of his heart, she put Lucy first in line to fill the emptiness left by his mother's death. Daisy joined the group of connivers who aided Franklin in his attempt to see Lucy as often as possible. As many scenes described in her diary will show, she supported his renewed pursuit of Lucy without reservation.

In her struggle to keep the president well, Daisy had found a comrade-in-arms in his cousin Laura Delano. Laura, a self-assured extrovert, was opposite in temperament to the reserved and introspective Daisy. Franklin had loved Laura like a sister since childhood, when his mother had brought him together with the children of her brother Warren Delano III as often as she could. Laura grew up quite close to Hyde Park, on the old Franklin Hughes Delano estate Steen Valetje, near Rhinebeck. FDR knew every wrinkle of Laura's past. Her nickname "Polly" originated in her early years when she had lived for awhile on nothing but the popular Apollinaris mineral water. Now in her mid-fiifties, Polly was rich, elegant, maddeningly capricious, and her cousin Franklin's perennial favorite.

Polly took an immediate liking to Lucy when the two ladies met. She pondered whether the gentle Lucy might not have made a better wife for Franklin than the more forceful and high-strung Eleanor. Polly kept the expression of such secret thoughts carefully within the inner circle of the ladies who were the caregivers in the Little White House. All members of FDR's new substitute family subscribed to the mandate of silence about the president. FDR's secretary William Hassett described in detail the tight-lipped atmosphere around the president in wartime. The news "blackout" after 1942 not only kept the more than forty weekend trips of the president from Washington to Hyde Park out of public view. It also helped Franklin and Lucy become more closely reacquainted under the shroud of secrecy that surrounded the president's moves.

FDR's daughter Anna joined the triangle of Daisy, Polly, and Lucy, the guardians of the president's well-being, with special zeal. As his closest kin, Anna could vent her criticism of her father's unhealthy habits with more authority than the other ladies.

Ever since June 1941, when FDR asked Anna to befriend Lucy's stepson John, Anna knew that Lucy had again become a part of her father's life. From 1944 on Anna could renew her acquaintance with Lucy from nearby. She decided not to return to Seattle but to stay on indefinitely in the White House because of her father's poor health, extending her traditional Christmas visit to Washington in 1943 into the New Year.

Joined by her husband John Boettiger, together with "Sistie" and "Buzz" (her children from her first marriage to Curtis Dall), Anna immediately stepped into her role as the president's main social representative. She soon found herself included in the renewed friendship between Franklin and Lucy and approved of it heartily. Her husband worked in the Pentagon and the Boettigers occupied the Lincoln Suite in the White House that had recently been vacated by Harry and Louise Hopkins, their predecessors as FDR's live-in companions and assistants.

Anna was appalled by the insufficient medical attention to her father's clearly visible ailments. When the president finally received a long overdue cardiac examination at the Bethesda Naval Hospital on March 28, 1944, he was diagnosed with dysfunction of his heart and lungs, dangerously high blood pressure, and a general state of exhaustion.

The president's main medical authority, Dr. McIntire, was intent on keeping his patient as active as ever in a reelection year. By contrast, his heart specialist Dr. Howard Bruenn demanded consideration for the patient's health above all political expediency. Facing disagreement among her father's physicians, Anna followed the dictates of common sense. She initiated a badly needed revision of FDR's artery-clogging diet of bacon, eggs, steak, and sweetbreads, tried to enforce Dr. Bruenn's orders to reduce his smoking from twenty to ten cigarettes a day, and warned her father to go easy on the cocktails in his "children's hour." Best of all, she brought laughter and light into his lonely days.

*   *   *

Anna needed help for her difficult assignment and appreciated the efforts of relatives and friends who had tried to improve her father's lot before she came to his rescue. Among them Anna's cousin Polly had been close to her all her life. Daisy inspired respect as a professional and a longtime companion of FDR. Anna had known and liked Lucy Mercer as friendly and cheerful since her childhood in Washington. She now she discovered a mature and experienced family mother in Lucy Rutherfurd, a congenial soul who held the key to her father's contentment.

On March 19, 1944, death relieved Lucy's husband Winthrop from long suffering. The time had come when Lucy finally felt free to direct herself fully and fondly to Franklin. On March 26, her seventh day as a widow, Lucy met FDR on his home ground in his beloved Hyde Park.

She no longer needed a cover. From then on "Mrs. Paul Johnson" turned into Mrs. Winthrop Rutherfurd. Lucy appeared openly in the president's entourage, often accompanied by one of her children. FDR's friends took immediate notice. Bernard Baruch, the longtime adviser to many presidents and an admirer of both Franklin and Eleanor, invited FDR for a recuperative Easter vacation to Hobcaw Barony, his estate on the coast of South Carolina. The president had hardly settled in when he requested that his host ask Mrs. Rutherfurd to join him. On April 28, 1944, Lucy brought two younger Rutherfurds along—her stepdaughter Alice and the wife of a stepson. Mr. Baruch facilitated the three-hundred-mile round trip from Aiken by letting Lucy use his own wartime gasoline ration. He pleased his friend the president by giving Mrs. Rutherfurd the place of honor at the table, at his side.

Lucy's encounter with FDR in the middle of a one-month rest at the Baruchs' retreat was brief but decisive. It confirmed their attraction for each other and ushered in a string of get-togethers in Washington. They could be traced exactly in the president's official logs and were counted carefully by FDR's biographers. Resa Willis quoted Doris Kearns Goodwin, Geoffrey Ward, James Roosevelt, and Anna Roosevelt as sources for her numbers of FDR and Lucy's meetings in public surroundings. They tallied more than a dozen visits that Lucy paid to the president in the White House over the course of nine months. On one occasion (July 7, 1944) Lucy and the president were spending a weekend together at the White House when FDR was surprised by his son Franklin, Jr., who burst into his office unexpectedly. The president explained that it was not a stranger but rather an old friend who was massaging his legs.

In an unpublished article on Lucy Mercer, FDR's daughter Anna explained how she organized Lucy's frequent invitations to the White House at her father's request. All of FDR's children and friends supported Anna's decision to orchestrate her father's meetings with Mrs. Rutherfurd behind her mother's back. By then Anna had overcome the upheavals of her own secret love affair of just a decade earlier. On the campaign trail with her father, Anna experienced the excitement of falling in love again. John Boettiger, the exuberantly romantic journalist, made her first husband Curtis Dall appear especially bland in comparison. Anna reacted differently from her parents when they had to decide in 1918 how to deal with the intrusion of Lucy Mercer into their marriage. They chose to live with their problems and stuck to their marriage; Anna obtained a divorce and moved on to a second spouse. But when Anna's marriage to John Boettiger did not live up to its promise (and after his death), she found a third husband in Dr. James Halsted in 1952.

No longer as starry-eyed as in her youth, in 1944 a more pragmatic Anna sympathized with both her father and her mother. Deception about FDR's friendship with Lucy seemed the only way to minimize hurt for Eleanor. Likewise, the middle-aged ladies keeping FDR company in Georgia were defensive and apologetic about shielding Eleanor from news of Lucy's encounters with Franklin but were absolutely sure they were doing the right thing. Daisy and Polly agreed that human kindness toward the president, as well the need to protect Eleanor from specters of the past, justified their compartmentalized thinking. They insisted that FDR's innocent rendezvous with Lucy, clandestine only from Eleanor's perspective, were the best medicine imaginable for the president's heart.

A historic day stood out as a high point of these visits. The liberation of Paris from German occupation on August 23, 1944, was celebrated by the president and his daughter Anna at a special tea party on the South Portico. It included Lucy Rutherfurd, her daughter Barbara, and her stepson John.

* * *

Shortly afterward, on September 1, 1944, the president's private train—running from Washington to Hyde Park—was switched over from its customary B & O route to the Lehigh and Hudson River Valley Railway line. The change would permit a stopover at Lucy's estate. The Rutherfurd mansion at Allamuchy, a perfect replica of a noble English country house, was bound to have special appeal to FDR. Winthrop had chosen the red brick royal retreat at Sandringham as the model for his summer residence at Allamuchy. Its magnificent setting was spoiled only after Lucy's death, when Interstate 80 was built within walking distance north of the mansion. Heavy traffic on the superhighway now separates the estate's main building from its auxiliary structures, including the Rutherfurds' chapel and Stone Cottage, their guesthouse.

At the time of FDR's visit, however, Allamuchy's peace and rural seclusion were still intact. The estate's park and gardens were immaculately groomed. In happy anticipation Lucy had the mansion polished squeaky clean for his arrival. When a servant grumbled, "You'd think the president was coming," the lady of the house replied brightly, "He is."

The lovely setting of Lucy's countryseat was similar to the surroundings of FDR's favorite English great mansion, the Cholmeleys' Easton Hall in Lincolnshire. He never forgot how enchanted he was with the place as a Harvard man in 1903. Lucy's Allamuchy residence had its own special charm. Instead of being bordered by a small trout stream, like its English counterpart, the Rutherfurd mansion was adorned by a larger body of quiet water. A gently terraced lawn descended to a small lake, framed by weeping willows. The interior of the mansion—with its huge fireplaces, massive doors, and gracious bay windows—recalled the ambience of a castle. It was similar in character to rooms in the historic Belvoir castle, owned by the Cholmeleys' peers and neighbors. As a visitor to Belvoir on a side trip from Easton Hall, Franklin had admired the ancestral seat of the dukes of Rutland. He was proud to have met the contemporary duke in person.

Allamuchy, where everything was very English, appealed to Franklin inside and out. It dwarfed his parental home in Hyde Park. Springwood was less spacious and more old-fashioned in comparison. It was amazing to realize that Lucy, who had lived in a small Washington apartment in 1918, was now the *chatelaine* of a monumental mansion.

Daisy Suckley, the leading member of the president's entourage at Lucy's luncheon on September 1, could not take her eyes from the hostess. She decided that Lucy deserved the constancy of the president's feelings. She called her "a lovely person, full of charm, and with beauty of character shining in her face; no wonder the Pres. has cherished her friendship all these years." Looking back on the visit, Daisy described it as "centering around Mrs. Rutherfurd, who becomes more lovely as one thinks about her—The whole thing was out of a book—a complete setting for a novel, with all the characters at that lunch table if one counts the absent husbands and wives[,] etc."

* * *

The most conspicuously absent wife was Eleanor. She would be spared the description of such joyous occasions. There was no lack of excuses for keeping them secret. From Anna's perspective her mother, in denial of the menace presented by her husband's illness, had removed herself to her professional world, resembling another star. She now lived exclusively for the realization of her own idealistic goals. Eleanor herself did nothing to dispel the impression that she had delegated her wifely obligations to substitutes.

Two of Eleanor's letters to her longtime friend Esther Lape— dated November 15 and 19, 1944—serve as proof of her own special view of her role in the president's life. Lucy's claims on Franklin's heart can only be understood as the result of her awareness that his wife had given up her proprietary interest in his well-being. Eleanor declared that she had opted out of being her husband's caregiver in favor of her professional advancement. She would leave staying at her husband's side to other women. Eleanor stated frankly that she no longer felt tied to him by bonds of love; even the bonds of duty were fraying. In the first letter, she wrote:

Maybe I'd do the most useful job if I just became a "good wife" & waited on F.D.R. Anna has been doing all of it that Margaret Suckley does not do but she can't go on doing it. If I did I'd lose value in some ways because I'd no longer have outside contacts. I'd hate it but I'd soon get accustomed to it. It is funny how hard it is to be honest with yourself & not be swayed by your own wishes, isn't it?

In her second letter to Esther, the realization that she had deceived herself diminished Eleanor's self-respect. "I find it hard to know sometime[s] whether I am being honest with myself [because] so much of life is play acting, it becomes so natural!" As part of her uncompromising self-examination, Eleanor corrected Esther's assumption that love still played a role in her relationship with Franklin. "There is little or no surface friction," she assured her old friend. But she could not be "a good wife" because "there is no fundamental love to draw on, just respect & affection."

As a rule, Eleanor was harder on herself than any friend or relative could be. This time Daisy could barely suppress her indignation at Eleanor's failure to take charge of her sick husband. In Daisy's eyes lack of love was no reason for a wife to let the preservation of valuable outside contacts stand in the way of waiting on him.

Daisy could not understand why FDR had not been warned against getting chilly in his open car after he had been diagnosed with pneumonia. "That is where a member of the family should be with him all the time, to watch over him." Daisy expected Eleanor to protect her husband instead of adding to his burdens. On July 1 she observed in her diary that at 6:15 p.m. "The P. felt tired and listless. He said he would like to go on the sofa in the library & go to sleep for a half hour, but he couldn't because the room would be full of people—Mrs. R. bringing some newspaper women to dine, 11 in all—The P. wondering how he can 'escape' afterwards!"

By Thanksgiving Daisy had taken over many previously neglected family obligations for FDR. After Franklin and Eleanor "had their lunch alone—a remarkable occurrence!" the president requested that Daisy come to his aid. A holiday visit from his cousins, Miss Ellie

Roosevelt and her widowed sister Grace Walton Clark, was coming up soon. The women were daughters of FDR's Uncle John from Rosedale, his relatively small estate south of Hyde Park. Daisy was indignant about their neglect. "No one pays any attention to them since Mrs. James R. died," Daisy complained. She pointed out, "Mrs. R. 'hasn't the time' to bother about them—a strange inconsistency in a woman whose every thought is to help her fellow man."

* * *

While Eleanor called for more criticism, Lucy Rutherfurd gained in Daisy's respect. Even though Daisy took pride in keeping the president relaxed and in good cheer, she conceded that Lucy's company was best for Franklin. His old friend's presence was the ultimate balm for his lonely soul. Daisy and Polly felt even more strongly about Lucy's beneficial influence on the president's condition when they hosted Lucy themselves. Their party had left Washington for the Little White House in Warm Springs on November 27. Lucy and Barbara Rutherfurd joined them a few days later on December 1. Daisy decided that Barbara, then twenty-two, looked rather serious; she was very tall and too thin for Daisy's taste. She granted that the girl was quite pretty, though she did not compare to her mother in beauty of face and soul. Lucy was in a class by herself. Daisy declared Lucy's "sweetest expression" irresistible. She embraced her from then on without a shred of envy as an ally in her battle for Franklin's survival.

There was "so little one can do." Daisy was grateful that she and Lucy "understand each other perfectly" because they shared deep concern for FDR. "She has worried & does worry, terribly, about him, and has felt for years that he has been terribly lonely." The two women "got to the point of literally weeping on each other's shoulder & we kissed each other." For her part Lucy warmly welcomed "dear little Margaret," who had helped Anna relieve her father's sense of abandonment. She had heard from a friend of Harry Hopkins "that there were evenings after evenings when Franklin was left entirely alone."

The president savored every moment of Lucy's visit. Enthused by his role as a host, he made her old-fashioned stronger than Lucy wanted. He ignored her protestations—after all, she said, she had not accepted a drink until she was fifty years old. She did not like Barbara to drink either. FDR knew very well what occasion Lucy had in mind. He had talked her into sharing one of his mixed drinks just after her fiftieth birthday in April 1941. Prior to that time, Lucy had not budged from the strict principles of abstinence instilled in her by nuns during her formative years. She abided by their rules even while living in Aiken's punch bowl circuit. Finally, in the spring of 1941, upset by Winty's strokes and exhilarated by seeing Franklin again after more than twenty years, she was amenable to taking part in his traditional happy hour rituals.

At Warm Springs Lucy was delighted when FDR took her, together with other guests, on invigorating drives in his big car. The December air was brisk. Everybody was bundled up in furs—Lucy next to the president, Daisy "half hidden" in the corner next to her. Polly occupied one of the small collapsible seats next to Monty, one of Daisy's cousins. The dog Fala, Daisy's present to Franklin, sat in front with the chauffeur. Guest beds were scarce in the Little White House, so Monty shared Mrs. James Roosevelt's little cottage with FDR's physician Dr. Bruenn. Polly and Daisy had cleared their rooms for the Rutherfurd ladies and moved to the guesthouse.

Franklin felt "let down" when Lucy left on December 3. Pouring rain added to his depression. Polly took the dogs out in Daisy's Sears, Roebuck raincoat and her half rubbers. A "tea" party for local friends, with Polly in charge, was to brighten the drab scene. Glasses and bottles were set up on a long table. When Daisy questioned him about them, the president answered, "If I gave them tea, they would never come again."

Polly too had to part with Franklin on December 11, when she left to tend to business in New York City. After Daisy took over her room and bath, only recently occupied by Lucy, she felt outright "luxurious." It was a "privilege to be really taking care of F.D.R. for a whole week" all by herself. Lucy and Daisy stayed in touch through the mail.

On December 17 Daisy "hated to leave the little house, with its cheerful fire burning day & night." She considered herself "a lucky, lucky person" for having been allowed to wait on the president for three weeks but stepped aside immediately when he had another chance to be with Lucy. "It will be lovely to see her again," Daisy looked forward to the interlude. Mrs. Rutherfurd came aboard on a train stop in Atlanta, having been invited for the trip to Washington. "I have left her with the Pres., so they can have a little talk without an audience," Daisy said tactfully. She expected to be useful again in the near future. Before leaving Warm Springs, the president had been spreading good news. "He is planning to come down in the spring, & says he will bring Polly & me again. It is so wonderful that he wants me."

* * *

Back in the White House for the Christmas season, Daisy willingly yielded her superior position to the president's family. She had "quite a talk with Anna about her father's health." She disapproved strongly of FDR's son Elliott. He had been sheepish about introducing yet another new wife, the actress Faye Emerson, and his father had been visibly annoyed. When the first trying meeting was over, Daisy wrote rebelliously in her diary, "But why F.D.R. has to have these *family* things, on top of everything else—I don't know."

Daisy, however, did not let go of Franklin altogether. After the Christmas festivities in Hyde Park, the president agreed to visit her home at Wilderstein on December 28. She had lined up Lenny, a highly recommended Italian masseur from New York, for a two-hour treatment of FDR's legs. The president accepted the massage gallantly and made time for more of them in spite of his overwhelming schedule. On January 12, 1945, Lucy Rutherfurd and the masseur took the train to Hyde Park for a brief visit. "Lucy goes down on the 3.27 from Pksie. [Poughkeepsie] & Lenny arrives for a treatment at 4," Daisy explained.

Such refreshing interludes eased the burdens of January. They were fast consuming the energy the president had gathered at Warm Springs. Daisy complained that FDR had no daytime rest in the week leading up to his fourth inauguration on January 20, 1945. Two days earlier she had moved out of her White House quarters to make room for the grandchildren. Daisy soon felt superfluous, "a little de trop," at the boisterous family reunion and faded into the background with other fans of the president—specifically, the Norwegian royals Princess Martha and her husband Prince Olav. The White House usher could differentiate built-in authority from newly acquired rank. He sought out Daisy to start the inaugural luncheon.

With the journey to the Yalta Conference looming, the president's birthday party was moved up to the evening after the inauguration. Champagne glasses were raised for a dozen toasts, one of them "to the absent ones." The president's mother came to mind. A few of his close friends thought of a special lady staying on Q Street with her sister Violetta. Daisy had visited Lucy Rutherfurd immediately after the ceremony to tell her "all about the 'inside' which she could not see from the lawn."

In a long diary entry dated January 22, the day of the president's hectic departure for Yalta, Daisy wrote, "He doesn't relish this trip at all—thinks it will be very wearing, & feels that he will have to be so much on the alert, in the conversations with Uncle Joe [Stalin] & W.S.C. [Churchill]." Daisy "just hated to leave him." She clung to two comforting thoughts. First, it was "so wonderful that Anna can be with the Pres., and to be of such help to him." Second, he had decided on March 28 as the date for his departure to Warm Springs, one month after his return from his meeting with Stalin and Churchill. Again, Lucy stayed in touch with Daisy by exchanging long letters. Lucy's fond epistle of February 9 showed to what extent the two women had become comrades-in-arms in the battle to extend Franklin's life.

Franklin took his longing for Lucy with him on the journey. He told Anna that Lucy was on his mind when the USS *Quincy* passed the shore of Virginia. He had explored the world of Lucy's ancestors in the summer of 1917, during stopovers on the voyage of the *Sylph*. "That's where Lucy's family used to live," he explained to Anna. "That's where they had their plantation."

When FDR was safely home, he topped Daisy's happy anticipation with even better news. She wrote in her journal, "F. is asking Polly & me to go with him to the San Francisco Conference [the United Nations Conference on International Organization, at which the UN was founded] in April—How can such exciting things to be happening to us all the time?" Polly was less optimistic. To her Franklin looked "really ill—thin & worn" and she "didn't think he would live to go to the San Francisco Conference." Contrary to her assessment, Franklin spread new hope a week later. He looked better and proved that he could still bounce back in a remarkable manner.

FDR'S BELOVED GUEST

By Easter Sunday, April 1, the president was settled in Warm Springs. To Polly and Daisy's surprise, he joined them, "very spick & span in a light grey suit," on their drive to church. Spring brightened the countryside with profusely blooming dogwood and filled it with the perfume of yellow azaleas. Franklin's caregivers, depressed by the president's rapidly deteriorating condition, were grateful for the season's boost to their spirit. They tried to halt his disastrous weight loss by adding a favorite comfort food from his childhood to his meals. Franklin's special "gruel" was his mother's invention. Sara used to stir the outer shavings of cooked corn on the cob into a little melted butter, then mix them with scrapings of the layer underneath, dissolved in warm milk.

Nostalgia spiced Franklin's bland treat. It was tied to an odd little ritual that Daisy Suckley found embarrassing. She regarded it as significant enough to be included in her diary, but then changed her mind and made a halfhearted attempt to hide it by drawing lines through her sentences.

The routine started as soon as Arthur, the president's valet, left for the night. "I get the gruel," Daisy reported, "& Polly & I take it to him. I sit on the edge of the bed & he 'puts on an act:' he is too weak to raise his head, his hands are weak, he must be fed! So I proceed with a tea spoon & he loves it!" Only a moment before, "he had been sitting up reading a detective story." After Franklin took half his gruel, he smoked a cigarette and talked seriously about the San Francisco conference. He looked forward to the founding of the United Nations with great hope, expecting an important step forward toward world peace. To Daisy's surprise, he "then relapsed into babyhood for the rest of the gruel—& then I kissed him good night & left him relaxed & laughing."

Daisy tried to explain. "On paper it sounds too silly for words, and it is silly—but he's very funny and laughs at himself for us." Polly saw a genetic Delano trait in Franklin's antics. "All the men in [my] family are like that," she told Daisy. "And those who have accomplished most in the world can be the silliest & funniest!" The nightly show had merit as a "great safety valve for a man to whom the whole world turns."

The strange little ceremony made sense as the playful evasion of a weary man yearning for the solace of a mother's care. FDR continued taking his cups of gruel but stopped the evening ritual as soon as Lucy Rutherfurd arrived for a visit on April 9. She was scheduled to stay until the following Saturday. Like a young man in eager pursuit, Franklin went out of his way to lay eyes on Lucy as soon as possible. It was a long drive from Aiken to Warm Springs, more than two hundred miles over narrow country roads. Starting out by way of Augusta in eastern Georgia, Lucy's party had to cross the whole state to get to the spa north of Columbus, not far from the Alabama border. FDR decided that he would meet Lucy partway, in the town of Macon— some forty miles east of Warm Springs. To the chagrin of both Franklin and Lucy, it did not work out as planned. On a bright afternoon, FDR waited in vain at the appointed place.

Among many accounts of the end of the president's life, the frustrations of this day were described most vividly by Lucy's two traveling companions, Nicholas Robbins and Elizabeth Shoumatoff. Madame Shoumatoff published *FDR's Unfinished Portrait: A Memoir* in 1990, long after the portrait was painted. By contrast, the Roosevelt historian Bernard Asbell interviewed Elizabeth's assistant, Mr. Robbins, shortly after the historic trip to Warm Springs. Traveling on April 9, 1945, with Madame Shoumatoff at the wheel of her Cadillac convertible, Mr. Robbins was sitting contentedly in the back seat. He was immediately captivated by the lady sitting beside Madame. Mrs. Winthrop Rutherfurd, he told his interviewer, was enchanting and possessed "distinguished beauty of face."

Asbell introduced the narrator of his story as a short, thin gentleman in his late fifties. Mr. Robbins used a pince-nez, hiding "sleepy gray eyes under great tufts of eyebrow and a bald dome. When he spoke, it was in a high, gentle voice and with the strained effort of making himself understood through a seemingly ineradicable Russian accent." The judge in charge at Nicholas Kotzubensky's naturalization had advised him to shorten his name to Kobbins. When Nicholas's Russian-style handwriting caused "Kobbins" to be read as "Robbins," he accepted the change for good.

Nicholas had owned considerable property in Crimea but lost his fortune during the Russian Revolution. The Avinoffs, Elizabeth's distinguished parental family, had preceded him as emigrants from Russia to the United States. Mr. Robbins made a name for himself in his new country as the master of a highly specialized craft, called reproduction photography. He could replicate oil paintings in photographs that were uncannily close to the original. Madame Shoumatoff brought him along to Warm Springs for simpler tasks. Since his time for the sittings would be extremely limited, she wanted Robbins to speed up her work as a portraitist by taking photographs of President Roosevelt in various poses.

*   *   *

Elizabeth Shoumatoff was a perceptive observer of Lucy's attachment to FDR. She had known the Rutherfurds ever since Alice Rutherfurd engaged her to paint her stepmother in 1937. The family amazed her. "I can say truly, I have seldom seen a mother more beloved and respected than was Lucy by her stepchildren," Elizabeth professed. At first she refused to believe that Mrs. Rutherfurd was Alice's stepmother. As she grew closer to the family, however, she found their amity irresistible. Husband and wife were absolutely devoted to each other. Their youngest daughter Barbara was everybody's favorite. Elizabeth was instantly at ease in their tranquil world.

Upon meeting Lucy, Elizabeth had seen her mainly as "very tall, like the rest of the family, exquisitely lovely and gracious." The artist noted later that Lucy "impressed you not so much by her striking appearance as by the shining quality of her features, particularly in her smile."

In the spring of 1943, Elizabeth Shoumatoff had hesitated when Mrs. Rutherfurd inquired whether she would do a portrait of the president that had been requested by FDR himself as a present for Lucy's daughter Barbara. A committed Republican, Mrs. Shoumatoff was strongly prejudiced against the president. She finally agreed to paint him at the White House only because Lucy, now a close friend, wanted it so badly. To her surprise the president made good on his promise to invite her to Hyde Park a few months later, by the middle of July 1943. He courted his portraitist so sincerely at a luncheon, followed by a tour of his home and grounds, that Elizabeth surrendered completely to his charm.

FDR was pleased with Mrs. Shoumatoff's small watercolor depicting him with his navy cape. He was comfortable with the artist in spite of her Republican convictions. Joking back and forth, Elizabeth became one of the select few who were able to help the president relax.

Two years later, in 1945, it no longer seemed so strange that Elizabeth Shoumatoff was again in demand by FDR. She recalled that Mrs. Rutherfurd brought up the president's wish to have a new portrait of himself painted right after her return to Washington in March. "There was somebody who asked very much about you," Lucy had told Mrs. Shoumatoff in a low voice, speaking in the far end of her Aiken living room so she couldn't be overheard. "He seems very anxious to have his portrait done now." When the artist protested that the last pictures of the president looked "ghastly" in his poor health, Lucy urged, in an even lower tone, "If this portrait is painted, it should not be postponed."

Madame Shoumatoff remembered Lucy's next call three days after Easter. "She telephoned to say it was all arranged. The president was at Warm Springs ready and waiting." The prospect did not suit the artist in New York at all. She had given up smoking for Lent and continued her sacrifice after Easter. The withdrawal made her irritable. A lack of gasoline coupons was Madame Shoumatoff's final excuse to back out from the trip south. It was her last attempt to turn down the unwelcome invitation to Georgia, which included a detour to pick up Lucy in Aiken. Madame's objection was brushed aside; the president could certainly help out with gas coupons. Elizabeth finally yielded, mainly because she was so fond of FDR and Lucy. When she met Mrs. Rutherfurd in Aiken, she found her "quite excited about the trip."

After a good night's rest, the three travelers were to leave after lunch, meet the president in Macon at four o'clock, and be in Warm Springs for dinner. It was Mr. Robbins's fault that the plan did not work out because he delayed the journey even before it started. In spite of the efforts of Grace Tully, the president's secretary, it had been difficult to get his security clearance. Now the photographer put the brakes on again. Sitting in the back of Madame Shoumatoff's Cadillac with a stack of maps on his lap, he failed miserably as a navigator. Madame noted tartly that he was gazing more at Lucy than at the road.

The artist regretted later that she did not preserve a letter from Nicholas Robbins in which he confessed that he "really got carried away" when he met Lucy. "It was the most elaborate eulogy to her, and on several pages he wrote how deeply he was impressed by her spiritual and physical beauty."

Mr. Robbins's fascination with Mrs. Rutherfurd did her little good. As a result, her travel party arrived at Macon "way after four o'clock." Feeling guilty about being late, Lucy was nervous when there was no trace of the presidential car. After the three travelers drove on "for quite a while," Lucy tried to make a joke of her disappointment. Powdering her nose, she gave a theatrical sigh and pronounced solemnly, "Nobody loves us, nobody cares for us." Believing the opposite in her heart, Lucy was finally rewarded just as the sun was setting and the warm day gave way to a cool night.

In the hamlet of Greenville, near Warm Springs, Madame Shoumatoff "noticed, by a corner drugstore, several cars and quite a crowd gathered around them. We drove up and there in an open car was FDR himself, in his navy cape, drinking Coca-Cola! We pulled to the curb. Lucy and I got out of the car. The expression of joy on FDR's face upon seeing Lucy made all the more striking the change I saw in him since painting him in 1943. My first thought was: How could I make a portrait of such a sick man?"

Daisy Suckley was equally touched as she watched Franklin's face light up the very moment he saw Lucy. Together with the Scottie Fala, Daisy moved willingly to the front seat. Inside Madame shivered without her coat, "while Lucy, seated next to the president and his navy cape, was warm and happy. FDR said that he had gone to Macon, but after waiting a while decided to make one more attempt at meeting us and went to the village close by."

*   *   *

As soon as the motorcade—consisting of the president's car, the Secret Service vehicle, and the visitors' Cadillac—arrived at the Little White House in the crisp April night, Mr. Robbins was sent off to the hotel in Warm Springs. Lucy and the artist were taken to the guest cottage, about a hundred feet away from the main building. Lucy, always alert to decorating styles, noted how well the flowered chintz patterns of the curtains fit her light and airy room. Elizabeth Shoumatoff's room was attractive in a more rustic fashion.

When the two ladies walked to the president's quarters, they found him seated by the fireplace. The card table, his writing place in the daytime, had been turned into a bar. Madame enjoyed an old-fashioned before dinner. She was fascinated by Laura Delano, the only "exotic-looking" person in the room. Next to the inconspicuous Daisy and the distinguished Lucy, Laura's profile, "as beautiful as a cameo," was set off by her brightly colored blue hair and her striking dinner pajamas.

FDR was in high spirits. He joked about the rhyming of "Aiken" and "Macon," which reminded him of Winston Churchill's clever "Let's not falter twixt Malta and Yalta." Holding his four lady companions spellbound with frank appraisals of the famous men he had met recently, he described a banquet held in honor of King Ibn Saud of Saudi Arabia. He marveled at "Winnie's" constant craving for a glass of Scotch. Asked whether he liked Stalin, FDR replied, "Yes; he was quite a jolly fellow. But I am convinced he poisoned his wife! They seemed to be quite a nice crowd of people, except for a few sinister faces appearing here and there."

Elizabeth was astonished by the president's openness with guests he obviously trusted not to quote him. It was understandable that he shared his personal observations with Laura, Margaret, and Lucy—he had been close to them for decades—but she could not understand why he was not more cautious in her presence. After all, she had been a complete stranger until they met just two years earlier. Madame Shoumatoff, now called "Shoumie" by the president, soon had proof that FDR regarded Lucy's friends as his friends too. He accepted Elizabeth into his inner circle without reservation. There was a precedent for such a relationship. Franklin understood perfectly when Lucy explained to him that her inner connection to Elizabeth went beyond the customary familiarity between a portraitist and his or her subject.

Lucy made FDR think back to his second winter at Harvard. His mother, widowed in December 1900, had opened a new chapter in her life after spending long years as her invalid husband's caregiver. She moved into her friend Grace Kuhn's house at 36 Commonwealth

Avenue in downtown Boston and tried to make up for what she had missed. Boston, the citadel of the fine arts, offered a fast return to her long-neglected interests in art and music.

The artist chosen by Sara for her own portrait became a good personal friend. On the day before Christmas Eve 1902, Sara took Franklin to Prince Pierre Troubetzkoy's studio in the city. Franklin had not seen the painter's portrait of his mother and was thrilled to receive it as a Christmas present. While Sara was only moderately successful in her effort to kindle in her son her own enthusiasm for the arts, Franklin soon shared his mother's personal fondness for the portraitist. Sara would also turn Eleanor into a fan of the painter and of his sculptor brother, Prince Paul Troubetzkoy. The Russian-born princes occupied the same position for the Roosevelts at Hyde Park that Elizabeth Shoumatoff assumed for the Rutherfurds at Aiken.

Many of Shoumie's prominent clients—such as the Mellons, Fricks, and Firestones—had befriended their portraitist. Surpassing them in personal magnetism, Lucy won Elizabeth's heart for good. The artist's grouchy assistant, Nicholas Robbins, rode into Georgia's Little White House on the coattails of general affection for Lucy and Elizabeth. As many times earlier, Lucy's smile had worked its magic as a catalyst of goodwill all around.

A born photographer, Robbins knew all about the power of a smile. Yet he had a hard time catching the elusive beauty of Lucy's smile on camera. At midday on April 10, after the president had finished signing the papers submitted by William Hassett, Mr. Robbins was put to the test. He was asked to take three photographs of the president as a prelude to the painting of his portrait. "When they were done, Mr. Roosevelt asked if he would take a picture of Mrs. Rutherfurd. Robbins engaged her in conversation until her blue-gray eyes were lit by a certain quality of reserved warmth he had come to admire.

"I have seen two smiles like that in my life," Robbins later recalled. "One was on Leonardo da Vinci's 'Mona Lisa'; the other was Mrs. Rutherfurd's." Mr. Robbins's comment started a misleading myth. Lucy's alleged Mona Lisa smile would become her trademark in many Roosevelt biographies. So little was known about her character that her subdued smile had to serve as a substitute for more important traits. Lacking other cues, biographers interpreted Lucy's smile as the key to understanding a supposedly mysterious temptress who had lured FDR into her net.

Nothing could have been further from the truth. Lucy Mercer Rutherfurd was no Mona Lisa. There is nothing comparable to Lucy's "reserved warmth" in the most famous face in the Louvre. Leonardo's masterpiece caught the enigmatic, cunning smile of an erotically charged young beauty. Renaissance Florence was known for its loose morals and the beguiling mystery in the Mona Lisa's facial expression seemed to indicate that she was one of many temptresses living in Florence in 1503. But any sexually provocative stance was foreign to Lucy. Her smile hid her vulnerability. It came from "a really unselfish, understanding heart," as Elizabeth Shoumatoff described it, and it served as a shield against a world full of hurt. It was the mirror of a "most idealistic, almost naive mind."

* * *

FDR did Lucy a favor when he asked Nicholas Robbins to create a photographic portrait of her. Lucy was a private person to a fault, not vain enough to have many pictures taken of herself. Ordinarily, Mrs. Rutherfurd only agreed to appear in family pictures. When her association with FDR became public knowledge after her death, writers looked in vain for a characteristic picture of Lucy. The only widely printed photo of Miss Mercer in the Roosevelt literature shows her in her twenties, distinctly unlovely. A large black hat hides a bland face, void of expression. In 1968 *Life* magazine finally published a more distinct likeness—Elizabeth Shoumatoff's delicate watercolor of Mrs. Rutherfurd, painted as a society lady in 1937. It showed Lucy as an exquisite beauty but did not reveal Lucy's personal characteristics as well as Nicholas Robbins's photographic study of April 1945. This picture too had its shortcomings. Lucy's face was tense; she was consumed by worry about her friend's poor condition.

On many other points, Robbin's image of Lucy was apt to remind Franklin of Pierre Troubetzkoy's portrait of his widowed mother. Both Sara and Lucy wore their black mourning dresses with dignity and grace. Both were beautiful, carefully coiffed, and posing with deliberate concentration. Sara, only forty-six, wore a black chiffon dress with a bright décolletage but unadorned by jewelry. Lucy, approaching her fifty-fourth birthday, showed first strands of gray around the temples. Her black dress underlined her somber mood. Lucy never tried to look younger than she was and did not hesitate to complete her formal attire with a matronly lorgnette, dangling on a cord from her neck into her lap. Two strands of pearls remained inconspicuous inside a scalloped neckline. While Sara looked thoughtful, Lucy bravely tried to force a hint of a smile. Both of them shared the poise of a great lady—erect, regal, and serene.

Before Lucy's picture was taken, she spent a restless night. In the morning she bared her soul to her friend Elizabeth. Lucy knew what it meant to nurse a fatally sick husband. She now felt strongly that the president needed more high-quality medical care. She suggested that one or two well-trained male nurses, on call around the clock, should not only assist him with his braces but make his life altogether a little easier.

Exasperated by worry and frustration, Lucy sought comfort in God's guidance. She was grateful for a devout friend nearby. Elizabeth Shoumatoff professed her strong religious faith more openly than Lucy, but Lucy too obeyed its dictates all throughout her life. Their spirituality formed a powerful bond in a "wonderful friendship that grew as the years went by." Elizabeth recognized a true Christian spirit in Lucy. She was astonished to discover that "in all our religious talks, I never once sensed a difference in our creeds—she being Roman Catholic, and I Russian Orthodox. In her presence, you always felt uplifted and inspired for the best."

When Elizabeth read the day's "word" from her religious magazine to Lucy on April 10, "she knew how I relied on the help from above in my work, and understood me." Composed in spite of their inner turmoil, the friends entered the sunny Little White House exactly at noon. To their surprise they found the president outside on the terrace. Miss Tully had suggested that his new place might be better for the painting. Madame Shoumatoff disagreed strongly but did not say a word. "I did not have the heart to move him inside," she recalled. "[He] was sitting in a comfortable armchair, gay and at ease." The artist simply started preliminary sketching and arranged the details for the work ahead. She called for FDR's famous navy cape, which had added distinction to her portrait in 1943. The roll of paper in the president's hand was the program for the Jefferson Day dinners, held annually by Democratic organizations around the country.

The president was working on his speech for the occasion, to be delivered over the radio on April 13. The address ended with his oft-quoted words "The only limit to our realization of tomorrow will be our doubts of today. Let us move forward with strong and active faith." FDR explained that the rolled-up program in the portrait would stand in for the United Nations charter, the document now foremost on his mind.

The president was joking with Lucy when their luncheon guest arrived. Leighton McCarthy, a former U.S. minister to Canada, had built a house in Warm Springs to be near his son, afflicted by polio. FDR had high respect for Leighton, his associate of many years. Daisy Suckley was attracted to him as a charming and interesting man. In December the ambassador had invited the president as his special guest to help celebrate his seventy-fifth birthday. Daisy noted that McCarthy had "taken a great fancy to Polly & is planning '12 mile walks' with her." Lunching with FDR on April 10, the ambassador was all ears for Polly. Elizabeth observed that "the president exchanged smiles with Mr. McCarthy" when Polly interrupted a discussion of the prospective end of the war with the question "What about Japan?" Both men knew that Otohiko Matsukata, a Japanese nobleman and FDR's classmate at Harvard, had been the love of Polly's youth. His parents vetoed a marriage because Laura Delano was not good enough for their son. Ironically, Polly's parents also felt that their daughter's Japanese suitor was not good enough for the Delanos. Snobbery from both sides left Polly unmarried for life.

*   *   *

FDR's luncheon lasted until four o'clock, when Lucy finally had a chance to look at Shoumie's first sketches. All the ladies agreed on a plain background for the portrait. At five o'clock FDR emerged from a nap to take Lucy and Fala on his customary afternoon drive. They headed for the panoramic vista at Dowdell's Knob, where they loved the peaceful view into Pine Mountain Valley. Two miles south of Warm Springs, the lookout on top of a rock had special significance for the president. It was part of a scenic piece of land he had purchased, made accessible by a road built with his own money. Soothed by the fragrance of warm pine needles, Franklin and Lucy "sat in the sun, talking, for over an hour." Daisy added that FDR came back with good color on his face from the sun. Lucy told her friend Shoumie that Franklin was planning to take her on a drive in his little Ford by himself.

That night the president went to bed early. On the next day, April 11, he appeared at noon, "very smiling and handsome in a double breasted grey-blue suit and crimson tie." Mr. Robbins took more pictures. He was made nervous by the distinct impression that Mr. Hassett did not approve of his activities.

The honeymoon of goodwill for Mrs. Rutherfurd's party of three was running out. Ever since the visitors arrived, the president's entourage had been grumbling under their breath about the disruption of their usual routine. By now the guests had worn out their welcome even more. William Hassett and Daisy Suckley did not like the challenge to their monopoly on caring for the president. FDR's obvious delight with the three recent intruders did not ease the pain of competition. Madame Shoumatoff was indignant when she read later that Hassett complained about her allegedly bossy ways. "He implied," Elizabeth wrote, "that I was a nuisance, that I was measuring the president's nose, which I never do, but fundamentally he was concerned that I was tiring the president with my painting."

Daisy had mixed feelings about Lucy's presence at the Little White House. She expressed them in her diary but also indicated to Lucy directly that she should stay more in the background. On the morning of April 11, Daisy could not guess how sensitive their guest was to such criticism. Lucy was still shaken by her conversation of the past hour, when she had opened up to Elizabeth as never before. She had shown her friend a picture of Franklin in his thirties, which he had given her on the previous day, that had overwhelmed Lucy with old memories of hours spent in his company in the Washington of her youth. At this point it was a relief for Lucy that she could pour out her heart to a new friend, talking freely about Franklin and herself. She recaptured the depth of their feeling for each other and described how it became increasingly intense. Lucy knew, she told Elizabeth, that she and FDR must part "since she [Eleanor] would not consider a divorce."

Right after this heartbreaking session with Elizabeth, Daisy "had another long talk with Lucy." She repeated that the doctor had just said to Franklin, "Keep lazy, Sir!" Once more she appealed to Lucy to cooperate. "So today should be pretty quiet," Daisy concluded, "though Sec. Morgenthau comes for dinner."

In September of the previous year, when the president offered formal condolences to Lucy in her Allamuchy mansion, Daisy had marveled at the way their hostess gained in loveliness as they became more closely acquainted. While she had since become a fond friend of Lucy, Daisy's feelings for Franklin came first. She did not hesitate to warn Lucy about causing too much commotion in the Little White House.

Fortunately, FDR was not aware of these ripples under the tranquil surface. He noted with a chuckle how beautifully he managed the "four women on his hands." Grace Tully was approaching the professional perfection of her predecessor Missy LeHand. Lucy and Franklin's cousins Polly and Daisy were a picture of harmony, knitting and crocheting together on the sofa. Occasionally, they had brief disagreements. Daisy grew defensive when Lucy made suggestions for improving Franklin's diet. It sounded like a reproach when Lucy recommended that dextrin, a nutritional supplement, be added to his meals. She had brought it along because it had helped her husband gain weight.

Daisy felt that it was not up to Lucy to comment on Franklin's health regimen. Besides, Lucy should not have distracted him at a time when he was concentrating on military strategy that would affect the course of history. It was mind boggling and awe inspiring for Daisy to watch that he had "the whole western front in Europe in his head [and] knows exactly where each army is at any moment. He says he has to, for sometimes he has to make decisions about operations." Bill Hassett shared Daisy's misgivings. He had to admit, though, that the president worked on happily "despite the handicap of the artist's continued interference."

*   *   *

On the afternoon of April 11, when Daisy was invited to join the president and Lucy on his afternoon drive, her appraisal of FDR's friend softened. She appreciated that Lucy was "so sweet with Franklin— No wonder he loves to have her around." Daisy tried bravely to overcome her possessive streak, mixed with a little jealousy. She admired Lucy's tender gesture of putting her sweater over Franklin's knees when the air turned chilly. Lucy was always thinking of the little things, she conceded, "which make so much difference."

Daisy pointed to the gulf that separated Lucy and Eleanor. Franklin and Eleanor's relationship had cooled since the time of Lucy and Eleanor's first acquaintance, when a more conventional Eleanor had fussed about Franklin's health. At eighteen Eleanor had rebelled against Franklin's teasing about her "grandmotherly" concern for his welfare. Eleanor had never experienced a grandmother's tenderness and might have missed the compliment in FDR's remark. After her estrangement from her husband in her thirties, Eleanor came to look upon his mother's solicitous attitude as a form of domination. She was disgusted when Sara called Franklin back from the door to remind him to take his rubber overshoes. In her strong disapproval of Sara's pampering, Eleanor refused to acknowledge that Franklin enjoyed it thoroughly. Now in his sixties, he looked for motherly warmth in the women he chose to have around in Warm Springs. He was sobered by his wife's disregard for his physical condition. Eleanor "simply wasn't interested in physiology," as Geoffrey Ward put it. In her eyes "illness could always be conquered by will and determination; her husband was merely tired."

The more perceptive Lucy had a strong urge to keep her hand constantly on Franklin's pulse. After her husband died, Lucy shifted all her motherly concerns to Franklin. She no longer resisted his efforts to see her as often as possible. By 1945 they needed each other more than ever. Lucy lifted the spirits of a lonely and stressed man. On his part Franklin was invaluable for the widowed Lucy, assisting her with his practical experience and legal expertise. Lucy lacked guidance as the sole guardian of a large family and the heiress of a formidable estate.

Though Daisy admired Lucy's tender little gestures to make Franklin comfortable, she felt that Lucy did not think enough of the big things in Franklin's life. She had a hard time suppressing doubts about the unselfishness of her new friend and began to question whether Lucy was really good for "the P.," as she referred to FDR. Was Lucy truly as self-denying in her love for Franklin as she herself was? Daisy started out in her diary, "Lucy is such a lovely person." On the other hand, "she seems so very immature—like a character out of a book. She has led such a protected life with her husband, who was much older than herself, always living on a high scale, that she knows little about life. Now, she faces a very different future . . . entirely alone. Also, she isn't very well and that makes it more difficult to face life & make decisions." Daisy continued:

> *F says she has so many problems & difficulties that she brings to him. She has no other person like him—a friend of such long standing—to whom to go for the kind of sympathetic understanding which he always gives—I cannot blame her, but at the same time, I can't help feeling that she should face her own life & not put too much of its difficulties on his shoulders.—But, I must add, that he is always happy when he feels he is helping others & making others happy.*

Daisy could not deny that Franklin was deeply gratified in his role as a mentor, expressing with his advice how much he cared for Lucy. She failed to respect the stoic side of Lucy's character that kept her from indulging in self-pity and seeking the sympathy of her friends for the difficult years in her past. Daisy's criticism of Eleanor's lack of sensitivity for Franklin's needs had been muted by her compassion for the hardships in Eleanor's early years.

Lucy had suffered a worse fate than Eleanor without talking about it. Like Eleanor, Lucy had lost her childhood home when her parents separated. Lucy too had been left in the care of relatives, but on top of these trials she had felt the sting of being penniless. Polly, Daisy, and Eleanor could not imagine Lucy's predicament because they had never faced real poverty. (Even though Daisy had no regular income until FDR appointed her a librarian at his Presidential Library, she always had a roof over her head with her ancestral Wilderstein. Lucy, on the other hand, was homeless and penniless after her parents went bankrupt in her early teens.) Eleanor had been emotionally unfulfilled as a conventional society matron and built up resentments about being immersed for a decade in childbearing and childrearing. At the same time, Lucy—having to work for a living in her twenties—faced more tangible problems. While the Roosevelt ladies had resided in substantial homes all their lives, the young Lucy struggled in her twenties to scrape together thirty-five dollars a month for her mother's rented apartment in Washington.

Eleanor had the good fortune of marrying the man of her heart and being blessed with a large, rewarding family. Lucy, on the other hand, had suffered the consequences of falling in love with a married man and declined opportunities to get married. As Mrs. Winthrop Rutherfurd, she was finally relieved of financial worries. But Daisy never realized the price Lucy paid for her affluence, living for many years as the caregiver of a sick husband confined to his bedroom and isolated from the outside world.

*   *   *

Daisy had strong opinions in her appraisal of other women devoted to Franklin's care. Even though she respected both Eleanor and Lucy, she declared that these two important ladies in Franklin's life were not measuring up to her own standards. Daisy could truly say that she always put FDR ahead of her own interests. Franklin's mother Sara was the only other person in FDR's life who made all her decisions dependent on one condition: taking any step only "if it helps Franklin."

Like Sara, Lucy excelled as a model homemaker, wife, and mother. After all, these qualities were expected from a lady in her era. Eleanor dared to be different. She won distinction outside the home as a successful politician, teacher, journalist, and lecturer. She had her own independent income, her own separate home, her own set of dedicated friends, and her own standing in the public eye. Ever since she found her own path in the 1920s, Eleanor honed her intellectual skills in a way that neither Sara nor Lucy could match.

While Lucy admired Eleanor's exceptional qualities, she dismissed herself as intellectually inferior. This was not necessarily what others thought of her, but it was caused by the feeling that she did not measure up to her own high standards of what a smart woman can accomplish. She learned at school in Vienna from highly educated teachers that women can match men in academic pursuits, but she was not ambitious. In February 1945, depressed by Franklin's fading vitality and in poor health herself, Lucy wrote Daisy a self-deprecating letter, calling herself the world's worst correspondent. She regretted that great sorrow had left her "with a tremendous incapacity or fear of thinking." Widowhood had overwhelmed her with so many decisions that she felt incapable of judging anything. She found it "difficult to think anything through." She "could scrub this little house from garret to cellar," Lucy vowed, "but my own desk frightens me."

In her distress Lucy lost her perspective. None of the ladies in the Little White House made her feel intellectually inferior. It was true that Lucy was better at listening than at holding forth with her own ideas, but she was not a passive listener. Lucy was better educated and better informed about world affairs than the average society lady in her circle. She endeared herself to Franklin as a knowledgeable partner in conversation. In the 1920s she corresponded with him about prominent politicians such as Al Smith, a fellow Catholic and a candidate for the presidency. In 1945 she could share with gusto dinner table evaluations of Stalin and Churchill.

Witnesses of Lucy's conversations with Franklin, especially his daughter Anna, were impressed with the caliber of her questions. She was not just sitting silently at the president's feet, looking at him adoringly. Rather, Lucy responded eagerly to Franklin's report on the challenges of his day. She recognized the priority of FDR's hopes for the founding of the United Nations. She took in every word when he talked to her about "what he regarded as the real problems facing the world now." Elizabeth Shoumatoff never forgot how Lucy "appeared deeply moved" when she told her of "a most wonderful talk [in which] the president spoke about world affairs, the past and the future in the most inspiring way."

Lucy was sincerely grateful for the privilege of being the president's confidante. She kept every word to herself when FDR spoke about his past efforts and his visions for the future. In April 1945 Madame Shoumatoff was eager to learn what the president told Lucy about the latest political developments, but Lucy would never repeat what he said. Violetta Marbury, Lucy's sister, remembered similar frustrations. Lucy would return to Q Street from long White House visits with the president, overwhelmed by what she had learned from FDR as he thought out loud about his strategies. She would be glowing with admiration for her friend but had too much respect for him to commit any indiscretion. If anybody had learned to be reticent, it was Lucy. Franklin appreciated her reticence and rewarded it with his trust.

The years were long past when Eleanor had filled the role of Franklin's most highly valued listener. By now Eleanor had her own agenda and knew that she could speak eloquently for herself. Indeed, she expected her husband to listen to her. On May 28, 1943, after Winston Churchill observed how Franklin adjusted to the First Lady's style of activism, he set down his thoughts about Franklin and Eleanor in a letter to his wife. Starting out fondly "My darling Clementine," Winston reported, "Mrs. Roosevelt, however[,] was away practically all the time, and I think she was offended at the President not telling her until few hours before I arrived of what was pouring down on her. He does not tell her the secrets because she is always making speeches & writing articles & he is afraid she might forget what was secret & what was not." His letter ended, more affectionately than Franklin's notes to Eleanor, "With many kisses & tender love your ever loving husband W."

MERCIFUL PARTING

FDR's letters to his "Missus," as he liked to refer to his wife, lacked the tenderness Eleanor craved. Henry Morgenthau, Jr., was one of the president's associates who had a feeling for the weak points of his marriage. The secretary of the treasury arrived at the Little White House on April 11. His personal ties to the president went back to the previous generation. FDR's mother had learned valuable lessons in foreign policy at the dinner table of his father, Henry Morgenthau, Sr. Elinor, the wife of Henry Morgenthau, Jr., had won the First Lady's heart as her frequent riding companion in Rock Creek Park.

In the Little White House, dinner with the secretary on April 11 began at seven o'clock. Lucy followed the conversation closely. She had been primed to understand the importance of this conference of the three world leaders; its aftermath was still tangible. Even a large bowl of Stalin's caviar could not ease the initially tense mood of the dinner party. In addition to the fate of the world, personal worries also affected the mood of the diners. Morgenthau worried about his wife Elinor, who had suffered a heart attack and was being treated for thrombosis. FDR had his own concerns. He had just heard from Anna that her little son Johnny was still very sick; his glandular infection would not abate. Earlier his illness had kept Anna at the boy's side and prevented her from coming to Warm Springs.

Gradually, the dinner conversation "picked up momentum as Roosevelt and Morgenthau began recalling different amusing and entertaining incidents about Churchill." Madame Shoumatoff observed that Lucy "was looking especially happy and animated that night." As always, she sat on the president's right "and he seemed constantly to address himself to her."

At the end of the dinner, after the guests from Washington left, the president's party relaxed and entertained each other telling ghost stories. The president was so exhilarated that he, "like a little boy, asked to stay up longer" after Dr. Bruenn arrived for his evening visit. Everybody finally retired but Lucy was too restless to relax. Once more she hardly slept at all. She had been kept awake by worry about Franklin, she told Elizabeth on the morning of April 12.

It was another beautiful day. The president looked cheerful. He was full of energy, working on the morning mail at his card table. His portraitist was pleased with his exceptionally good color. "That gray look had disappeared," she observed. After lunch FDR enjoyed his gruel, which was now served to him at various times of day. Daisy recalled that he said, "Wouldn't it be strange if this gruel should be the one thing to put weight on me!" Everything seemed as calm as ever. The president signed papers while Shoumie worked on his portrait. He was facing Lucy and Daisy, who were crocheting on the sofa, talking and sometimes exchanging remarks with the president.

In an uncanny symbolic coincidence, Franklin's mother seemed to send a greeting to her son in this fateful hour. On May 9, 1880, Sara Delano had paid her first visit to Hyde Park at the invitation of her future husband James Roosevelt. The way she gathered roses from the Springwood garden, and arranged them beautifully in a shallow bowl, became part of her image. The incident was forever linked to Roosevelt family lore. As the mistress of Springwood, Sara created a rose garden as its center. This was the place where FDR asked to be laid to rest.

Polly Delano had learned from her Aunt Sara the art of presenting roses at their best. Warm Springs, where roses flourished, lent itself to using her skill. Graceful ceramic bowls, brought back by the De-lanos from China, were ubiquitous wherever members of the family lived. On April 12, 1945, Polly offered Franklin the sight of such a bowl of roses when he looked up from his card table as she entered the room.

His delight lasted only a few seconds. At the very moment, the president suddenly slumped over. Daisy heard him say in a low voice, "I have a terrific pain in the back of my neck." With her friends' assistance, she carried him to his bed, opened his collar and tie, and held his right hand. Polly was on his left, fanning him and testing his heart. Lucy waved camphor under his nose, as she had done many times to revive her husband.

Dr. Bruenn took over within minutes but the patient never re-gained consciousness. It fell to Polly, "as the one everybody looks to next to the Pres.," to telephone Eleanor and alert her about the emergency. "F.'s breathing became very heavy & labored," Daisy re-membered. "I had the distinct feeling that this was the beginning of the end." It also meant the end of their stay at Warm Springs for Franklin's substitute family—those nearest to him in place of his wife and daughter. Lucy, the light of his last days, vanished first from the scene, leaving hastily with her retinue for Aiken, South Carolina.

The drama of FDR's death has been told in many versions. Some of them implied that Lucy had to be ousted from Warm Springs. This is pure speculation. Mrs. Rutherfurd was the kind of lady who would rather leave too early than too late. Franklin was still living when she gave her travel companions the signal for departure. She knew that the time was up and that she could no longer be of help. FDR's fam-ily, remote while he was alive, would take possession of him in death.

Just four months earlier, when Lucy ended her previous visit at the Little White House on December 3, 1944, she had been escorted out of town by FDR himself as his honored guest. He had accompa-nied her to the small settlement of Talbotton, twenty-five miles east of Warm Springs. From Talbotton a major road took her home to Aiken by way of Macon and Augusta.

*　*　*

On April 12, 1945, Lucy left in stealth. She had turned into an embar-rassment for the president's staff. Her name was only whispered. Bill

Hassett erased his frequent references to Lucy's presence from his diary. Only a misleading footnote about Mrs. Rutherfurd was left in his 1958 book *Off the Record with F.D.R., 1942–1945*, a detailed account of the president's last years. Some of the Roosevelts' longtime servants, however, were not ready to shift allegiances so abruptly. Lizzie, a senior maid who did not hesitate to speak her mind, had praised Eleanor for hiring colored help. In Warm Springs, however, she had grown attached to Lucy. In her despair at the sudden death of her beloved boss, she found comfort in the thought that the president died while resting his eyes on a beautiful woman.

For most members of FDR's entourage, Lucy's formerly open visit turned into a secret within minutes. Frank Allcorn, the mayor of Warm Springs, had invited the president to a barbecue on the afternoon of April 12 and prepared the Brunswick stew he liked so much. FDR had accepted for 4:30 p.m. with the proviso that Mrs. Winthrop Rutherfurd be placed on the guest list.

When the time came for the party, the president was on his deathbed. His Secret Service men combed the neighborhood, searching for Mr. Robbins. They ordered him out of the pool at the hotel in Warm Springs and put him hastily in the car with Madame Shoumatoff and Mrs. Rutherfurd. Mr. Robbins was incensed at the way he was treated. He only began to understand when the travelers stopped at a public telephone. Their call to the Little White House was brief. They were told that the president had died.

Close to the corner where FDR met Lucy when she arrived just four days earlier, she asked Elizabeth to slow down. In brief commemoration Lucy tried to control her emotions. Franklin had always been forced to part with her after brief encounters, before he was ready to let her go. Their last leave taking had been different. Lucy's heart would be bruised forever by having seen him collapse without warning, only an arm's length away from her. Yet Lucy had strong inner resources and could rely on her faith during the storms of life. A mark in Lucy's prayer book pointed to Psalm 145. She quoted a favorite hymn containing the passage "The Lord is gracious, and full of compassion." In the same place, she had singled out her comfort in Verse 9: "The Lord is good to all." The passage went on, warning that God has not promised "joy without sorrow, peace without pain." The refrain reassured, "But God hath promised strength for the day, rest for the labor, light for the way; grace for the trials, help from above."

Lucy's acceptance of God's will, instilled in her in her youth, opened her eyes to the merciful aspects of her friend's death. Unlike her husband, who had died a long, slow death, Franklin had been spared all but a few seconds of pain and passed in the peace that only love close by can give. Franklin's pursuit of her when he was in his mid-thirties, and again when he was in his early sixties, had always been bittersweet, overshadowed by the inevitability of the next adieu. This time they did not have to say good-bye.

Driving on, immersed in thought, Lucy and her party lost their way. They stopped somewhere in the dark to call Aiken. Pam Tower, Barbara Rutherfurd's intimate friend, told me on a visit to her home in Long Island that Lucy—in a state of shock and dead tired—did not arrive home until midnight. Pam (now Mrs. LeBoutillier) still remembered vividly in 2008, at the age of eighty-six, what happened in Aiken on that fateful night after FDR's death.

She recalled that it was a butler, Daniel, who threw the Meads' garden party into disarray with the news that the president had died. The sudden surprise shook Lucy's friends to the core. Barbara Rutherfurd, a guest at the party with her friend Pam, turned white and red. Utter confusion followed. Lucy had told only the Meads about her invitation to Warm Springs. In the general consternation, nobody took action except Pam.

First of all, Lucy had to be escorted home from her rest stop in the middle of nowhere. Barbara went on the mission in Pam's Mercedes, an old car with a canvas top. Pam was now without a ride but expected to be invited by Lucy's good friends the Kittredges to stay with them. She was disappointed: they were too disturbed to think about her and turned the girl out into the night. She finally found a ride home with other friends.

By the time Lucy was back in Aiken, it was midnight. She was exhausted but safe. Only later she learned that Polly Delano had given up her room at the Little White House for Eleanor. Daisy cleared her quarters for "whoever might come down with her." Both moved into the guesthouse just vacated by Lucy and Shoumie. From then on every move Polly and Daisy made was "for the last time." They yielded instantly to the members of the family who had left FDR for many months in their care. To outsiders, ignorant of the circumstances, it looked as if FDR's guests had usurped the family's privileges.

The postlude to Franklin and Lucy's relationship evolved on two parallel levels. In the three years she had left, Lucy never ceased looking back to the days when FDR had called her close to him and lifted her onto the sidelines of his personal history. At the same time, Eleanor totally eclipsed the memory of Lucy and her appeal for Franklin. The president's widow stepped boldly into the future, making history with her own courage in fighting for equality and social justice, inspiring generations after her with new respect for human dignity.

EPILOGUE

TWO WIDOWS

ELEANOR'S STAR RISES

FDR's sudden death was more of a surprise for Eleanor than it was for Lucy. In denial about the seriousness of his condition, Eleanor was not prepared for tragedy when she arrived as the keynote speaker at a charity event at Washington's Sulgrave Club on April 12. A phone call from Dr. McIntire (the president's physician) warned her that Franklin had fainted, but he told her not to be alarmed. After the end of her talk, as Eleanor listened to a piano recital, an urgent call from press secretary Steve Early asked for her immediate return to the White House. She wrote later that she politely "went back to the party" and said her goodbyes but "knew down in the heart that something dreadful had happened."

By the time she arrived in Warm Springs, shortly before midnight, Eleanor was dressed in black. She had already fulfilled the immediate official functions of a bereaved First Lady. Next she had to face the personal side of the shock of Franklin's death. She had misjudged the urgency of her obligations to her husband. Franklin had needed more of her "waiting on him" as a "good wife" than she had been ready to admit. Worst of all, Eleanor's old nemesis Lucy Mercer had taken her place in the hour of his death. For years, behind her back, Lucy had provided the caring love Franklin craved. It had been

Eleanor's own daughter Anna who understood her father's need and prepared the way for Lucy's presence in her father's lonely life.

The repetition of the trauma caused once before by Lucy was stunning. On September 20, 1918, Lucy's letters to Franklin opened Eleanor's eyes to the problems in her marriage and she suffered a hard blow to her self-esteem. After twenty-seven years of healing, the wound was torn open again on April 12, 1945. Once more Eleanor faced the limits of her impact on her husband's existence. She had to abandon the illusion that she could shape it to fit her own expectations.

Eleanor was given little time to cope with the hurt. A few quiet minutes alone with her dead husband in his bedroom only served to make her bitterness more intense. The mourners in the parlor assumed that the new widow would emerge from the death chamber dissolved in tears. It was bewildering that Eleanor reappeared dry-eyed, calm, somber, and in full control of herself. Looking at her dead husband's face failed to soften Eleanor's heart; instead it led to a painful reappraisal of her own feelings after forty years of marriage. The death of Franklin's mother had forced Eleanor to submit to a similar self-examination. On September 7, 1941, Eleanor tried to find clues for her attitude toward her mother-in-law by gazing at the deceased woman's face. She concluded that she saw things in it that she had missed while Sara was alive.

In 1920 the passing of another mother figure, Eleanor's grandmother Mary Hall, had also provoked more thought than emotion. Eleanor regretted the waste of human potential that she saw in Mary's old-fashioned Victorian life, which affected her all the more since she begun testing the rewards of following her own interests outside the family.

On yet another sad occasion, when her brother Hall died shortly after Sara, Eleanor was deeply immersed in grief. It was tragic how Hall's high intellectual promise was cut short by the same addiction to alcohol that had ruined Eleanor's father. The sobbing Eleanor, shaken by the fate of the little brother she had once mothered, found comfort in her husband's compassionate embrace. It was a rare moment of warmth, uniting spouses who were living complementary but frequently parallel lives.

At Franklin's death four years later, nobody was at hand to assist Eleanor in coping with bitter emotions. Eleanor's biographers accused Laura, her cousin by marriage, of aggravating her pain. On the night of April 12, on one of the most grueling days of Eleanor's life, Laura lost no time telling Eleanor about Lucy's prominence in Franklin's last days. Although FDR's biographers censured her, it was Laura's obligation to make Eleanor understand the situation as soon as possible. Before the First Lady arrived in Warm Springs, nobody at the Little White House had questioned Laura's authority. She was in charge as Franklin's closest relative on the spot.

Since childhood FDR had favored his cousin, and Eleanor appreciated the faithful support she herself had received from Laura since 1904. At that time FDR's fiancée, barely twenty years old, had been relieved when she was welcomed cordially into the Delano family. A few years later, Laura had helped Eleanor on Campobello as a babysitter. She had been a good champion of the wife of the assistant secretary of the navy during a trying inspection trip to New Orleans. Eleanor's last letter to Franklin, dated April 8, 1945, had ended, "Give my love to Laura & Margaret & I'm glad they'll be along on the trip to San Francisco."

After FDR's death Laura stayed in close touch with his widow. Eleanor told her friend Elinor Morgenthau what fun it was to take "all the children to Laura's for a swim and supper." William Turner Levy, a great admirer and biographer of the "Extraordinary Lady" in her old age, stressed the mutual pleasure in comings and goings between Eleanor's Val-Kill cottage and the residence of Miss Laura Delano in Rhinebeck.

*   *   *

In 1945 Laura witnessed the innocence, beauty, and healing power of Lucy's company for Franklin. She trusted Eleanor's magnanimity. Besides, the down-to-earth Laura argued that Eleanor would learn sooner or later from others about Lucy's role in Franklin's last years.

Eleanor was hit hard by Laura's revelations. Forced for a second time since 1918 to appraise her marriage realistically, she was indignant about the "handmaidens'" acceptance of Lucy as Franklin's favorite. Eleanor felt insulted by the willingness of her daughter Anna to take her father's side. Even more disturbing was the fact that Daisy and Laura, the other two conspirators in the defense of FDR's welfare, felt likewise The three women defended themselves vigorously—with more righteousness than apology—about encouraging Lucy's second entry into Franklin's life, insisting on the innocence of the relationship and vowing that "nothing inappropriate" had happened.

Nevertheless, FDR's staff braced itself for the First Lady's anger. Steve Early, the president's press secretary, warned William Hassett, "Bill, there's hell to pay. Mrs. Roosevelt knows that Mrs. Rutherfurd was here." Anna exclaimed, "Boy, am I in the doghouse" when her mother's wrath descended upon her. Eleanor's wrath soon faded, however, when mother and daughter quickly made peace. In the long run, Eleanor grew fonder of her daughter than ever. She was full of sympathy for Anna who had been deserted, betrayed, and financially hurt by John Boettiger. The romantic lover who became her second husband also disappointed his mother-in-law. She had enjoyed being called by John his "LL," standing for "Lovely Lady." More than ever Anna depended on her mother's emotional and financial support, just as Eleanor's self-regard was tied to her daughter's devotion.

Eventually, it became irrelevant whether Laura and Anna had wronged Eleanor. It was more essential for Eleanor's peace of mind that she reconciled her own feelings for Franklin. It had definitely been her husband who was the principal offender, reaching out to Lucy again and again. Why had he betrayed his marital vows to love no other? After all, Anna had only responded to her father's wishes when she invited "an old friend" to dine with him in the White House. It was Franklin who had been eager to assist Lucy's children, and who had invited Lucy to be his Thanksgiving 1944 and Easter 1945 guest at Warm Springs.

Now he was dead, unable to respond to Eleanor's reproaches. The problem was especially acute since the accused was not an ordinary man. He was a national hero, worshipped by millions. Eleanor's own professional future depended in many ways on the quality of his public image.

Eleanor reconciled her memory of her husband with a bold leap over the shadow of her own victimhood. She had dealt in the same way with a parallel problem when she wrote about her father, half a century after Elliott Roosevelt had succumbed to excessive drinking. In spite of her disappointments, Eleanor painted attractive posthumous portraits of both her father and her husband. She left the men's painful behavior in the dark and focused instead on the ways in which they had benefited her. Her father's transgressions, under the influence of alcohol, were canceled by the warmth of his love for her. Her husband's unfaithfulness was balanced by the interesting and rewarding life he had provided for her at the side of an exceptional man.

Franklin's determination to keep his attachment to Lucy out of the public eye made it easy for Eleanor to exclude it from her discussion of personal matters. Only her daughter Anna knew how unhappy she was about Franklin's love for another woman. Anna shared with Joseph Lash that "to the day she died Mother resented LM." She was deeply impressed by her mother's confession that the realization that "l[ucy]m[ercer] was there when Father had his stroke was devastating." Anna testified that her father "had a meaningful relationship with this gal." She called Lucy Mercer a *"grande dame*, tall, statuesque—with an obviously regal carriage—a very handsome woman. As far as emotions were concerned, she was Father's emotion for life."

Anna thought that her mother was able "to accomplish so much after Father died" because she "learned to talk about the things that troubled her." There was one exception to Eleanor's openness: she could not talk freely about her upset over her rival Lucy. She kept even her confidantes in the dark, including Stella, Lady Reading, founder of the Women's Voluntary Service in England, and her old friend Esther Lape. Trying to erase Lucy's name from her life meant that Eleanor could not fully explain her relationship to Franklin in retrospect. Her reticence was partly caused by her Victorian upbringing. It became imperative when Eleanor's status as a popular public figure demanded that she present an attractive picture of herself to her followers.

The general silence of the main actors in the drama of FDR's life and death was officially broken in 1949, when Grace Tully mentioned Lucy Rutherfurd briefly and matter-of-factly in her book *F.D.R., My Boss*. In the same year, Eleanor brought out her second autobiography under the title *This I Remember*. Her first memoir *This Is My Story*, published in 1937, was a chronological account of the challenges of her youth. Her new book—written as a widow—was to a great extent an apologia, a defense against hostile observers like the columnist Westbrook Pegler. Eleanor deflected attacks on her abilities as a mother by pointing to the hazards of living in the White House. She did not deny that the four sons she had raised appeared undisciplined and that they provoked a succession of scandals as they went through multiple divorces. Blaming their behavior on their circumstances, Eleanor argued that they had been spoiled both by their upbringing in the White House and by her indulgent mother-in-law.

* * *

Next Eleanor warded off criticism of "the large sums I was able to earn through radio and writing" by declaring that she spent her wealth on promoting good causes. She did not mention, of course, that she needed to bail out her daughter and her sons—especially James—with substantial payments for alimonies and debts. Eleanor could come to the rescue of her children because she did indeed make a lot of money as an exceptionally successful career woman. On January 1, 1937, *Ladies' Home Journal* paid Eleanor fifty thousand dollars for the serialization of her first autobiography. By comparison, Eleanor's son-in-law John Boettiger was paid thirty thousand dollars per year to serve as publisher of William Randolph Hearst's *Seattle Post-Intelligencer*.

In her seventeen years alone, from 1945 to 1962, when Eleanor became a legendary figure of awe-inspiring qualities, she wrote hundreds of pages about herself. Only one of these pages hinted at her marital discontent. In a brief passage, Eleanor provided an in-depth analysis of her marriage as she saw it.

Eleanor's failure to be at her husband's side when he died baffled her admirers. She now stated that consideration for her husband had been the reason she encouraged Franklin's cousins Laura Delano and Margaret Suckley to accompany FDR to Warm Springs at Easter in 1945. She explained, "I knew that they would not bother him as I should have by discussing questions of state; he would be allowed to get a real rest and yet would have companionship—and that was what I felt he most needed."

Lucy, the company Franklin wanted most, was not mentioned even though insiders knew about her decisive role in keeping the president content. Instead Eleanor noted on page 349 of her 351-page autobiography that "much further back I had had to face certain difficulties until I decided to accept the fact that a man must be what he is." She obviously referred to her husband when she continued, "All human beings have failings, all human beings have needs and temptations and stresses." Eleanor had shown in other writings that she accepted—if reluctantly—the double standard that excused men but held women responsible for marital unfaithfulness. In her view FDR had surrendered to the ever-looming temptations of seductresses, who encouraged men to stray from their promises by engaging them in extramarital relationships. It is questionable whether Eleanor's diagnosis of her husband's missteps did justice to the nature of Franklin and Lucy's friendship, When Eleanor filed away their relationship as a traditional, typically fleeting affair, she ignored Lucy's lasting hold on Franklin's heart as his soul mate. Assuming that Franklin could be seduced as easily as Eleanor allowed, Lucy's monopolizing of Franklin's feelings would have kept other, more aggressive temptresses at bay. Lucy had made Franklin betray his marital trust, but at the same time she had prevented him from falling for more dangerous "temptations" (always referred to in the plural) that could have destroyed Eleanor's precarious marriage.

Eleanor's analysis, based on the assumption that Lucy was Franklin's mistress, overlooked a crucial fact. If sexual attraction had been the main tie between Franklin and Lucy, he would not have pushed for a renewal of their attachment eight years after they separated. Franklin's paralysis and Lucy's absolute commitment to her husband ruled out any trysts.

However Eleanor interpreted Franklin's unfaithfulness, she took Franklin's offense forever to heart. She would have felt wronged by any kind of romantic longing of her husband behind her back, whether it was platonic or not. She learned to be more philosophical in her conclusions as time went by and expressed them beautifully when she said, "[M]en and women who live together through long years get to know one another's failings; but they also come to know what is worthy of respect and admiration in those they live with and in themselves."

Millions of admirers loved Eleanor for her positive attitude in adversity. She was forgiven for her selective memory that interfered with chronological accuracy. Eleanor put her public interests ahead of her duties as a wife and mother long before 1945. She actually started to satisfy her professional priorities in 1920, after Lucy and Franklin had made her feel inadequate as a wife. At that time her mother-in-law and her children's governess, Elsbeth Connochie, took care of her two youngest children—Franklin, Jr., and John, just six and four years old. When John entered Groton in 1934, his mother the First Lady was already recognized as a writer and speaker. Yet Eleanor wrote in 1949, "When the last child went to boarding school I began to want to do things on my own, to use my own mind and abilities for my own aims."

Eleanor came closer to describing the complexity of her marriage when she stated indirectly that all was not well with it. Her husband "might have been happier with a wife who was completely uncritical," she mused. "That I was never able to be, and he had to find it in other people."

*   *   *

Relatives like Alice Longworth, Laura Delano, and even Eleanor's own sons James and Elliott agreed that FDR was not married to a woman who made him perfectly happy. They cited other reasons than Eleanor for the flaws in her marriage. While Eleanor mainly blamed her readiness to criticize her husband for the lack of warmth in their life together, the Oyster Bay Roosevelt aunts of Eleanor had observed that the *délicieux,* the delicate tenderness, was missing in the couple's relationship. Their initial delight with each other had cooled fast—right on their honeymoon. Part of the disappointment of initial hopes was rooted in temperamental differences. Franklin was used to being admired, while he himself was not inclined to express the exuberant admiration that Eleanor needed to thrive. She too "had to find in other people" what Franklin did not provide.

Eleanor drew deep satisfaction from the adoration showered on her by her fans, especially by her friends. She cut the ties to three emancipated women (Nancy, Marion, and Lorena) earlier than they wanted. The friendships with three male admirers ran out more gradually—the affections of her bodyguard Earl Miller, her biographer Joseph Lash, her physician David Gurewitch, and her old age companion William Levy never faded. The enthusiastic admiration of her friends eased Eleanor's perennial pain of not having been loved enough in her childhood. Franklin had the opposite problem. He had been addicted to praise since his childhood. He had charmed everybody down to the last kitchen maid at Hyde Park, and he expected the women he loved to follow suit. His wife soon pinpointed his shortcomings. On the other hand, the unceasing tributes to his special personality paid by his mother and his friend Lucy filled a need for Franklin.

Franklin's mother Sara had made a special point of declaring that her love "for her own" included constructive criticism. Lucy herself, regarded as uncritical by Eleanor, found fault with Franklin for harboring political ambitions that were detrimental to his health.

In high office Franklin resented Eleanor's nagging about political causes that aroused her passion and made her demand support from the president. She readily admitted that she could be hard on her husband in the pursuit of her progressive projects and wrote in her second autobiography, "I think I sometimes acted as a spur, even though the spurring was not always wanted or welcome." Franklin's doctors felt that this spurring was bad for his health, to the point of advising him to stay away from the stress caused by his wife.

Jonathan Daniels put it more gently when he observed that Eleanor's political activism put her at a disadvantage in her rivalry with Lucy. He granted the president a right to enjoy his gentle friend's presence because he "had need of grace, love of beauty, and a need for a company that was not always on the militant march."

If anybody was to blame for the incompatibility in Franklin's marriage, it was his mother Sara. Contrary to the prevailing view that Sara opposed Franklin's marriage to Eleanor, a close examination of events in the summer of 1903 shows that Sara actually promoted their union. Together with her close friends Anna Cowles and Corinne Robinson, sisters of former president Theodore Roosevelt, she successfully maneuvered Franklin into awareness of what Eleanor had to offer as a wife and helpmate. In her eyes Eleanor gave promise to become the healthy mother of many children. As the niece of President Theodore Roosevelt, she would bring Franklin close to the White House, where Sara always thought he belonged.

At Thanksgiving 1903, three months after Sara recommended Eleanor for a visit with her brother Warren Delano III, the arbiter of Delano marriages, she was taken aback by Franklin's premature proposal of marriage. Eleanor had just turned nineteen, and Franklin (only twenty-one) had not finished law school. Sara suffered another shock when the young couple's honeymoon revealed grave differences in the temperament and the preferences of bride and groom.

Unlike Eleanor, Lucy had the same talent as Franklin's mother for keeping him comfortable in a cocoon of warmth. She cared about every aspect of his health, from his need for rest to a healthful diet. Like Sara, Lucy was an optimist. Franklin could count on Lucy's sunny disposition. Contrary to Eleanor, she knew no moods, was always ready to laugh at his jokes, and loved fun.

*   *   *

On the other hand, Eleanor had reason to nurture grievances about Franklin's shortcomings as a lover and husband. He certainly had been lacking in patience with an insecure young wife when she made a deliberate effort to become more sportive and more tolerant of the parties he enjoyed. He failed to carry over the attention of a suitor into the routine of married life. When Eleanor succumbed to what she called her "Griselda" moods, Franklin avoided her instead of trying to cheer her. He had barely restrained himself from telling her to "snap out of it" when she suffered attacks of depression. He had adopted only too willingly the Victorian habits of his peers who neglected their wives and children, spending their leisure time in clubs, on the golf course, and on sailboats with male companions.

While Franklin's behavior was old-fashioned, Eleanor was ahead of her time with her misgivings about Victorian ways She championed the dawning of a new age in marital relationships, marked by equality and cooperation of the spouses. She asked for tenderness from a husband toward his wife, in place of traditional male assertiveness.

Franklin and Eleanor fell short of making a success of their marriage as perennial lovers. As Eleanor saw it in hindsight, they rather "made a mess" of their young lives. It was their good fortune, and a historic gain for the nation, that they found a new anchor for closeness in their thinking about the common good after their feelings for each other had faded. They were a brilliant success as partners in political leadership. When Eleanor's role as the president's helpmate came to an end with Franklin's death, she amazed the world by unfolding talents as a politician and humanitarian that had been overshadowed in the past by a husband who excelled in both roles.

By 1949, when Eleanor lifted a corner of the shroud of secrecy that had covered the problems in her private life, she was already safely established in the public's admiration. Long gone were the days of her early widowhood, when she tried to ward off reporters with a tart "The story is over." In the following years, "it was common for her to receive in a normal week over one hundred requests for public appearances."

Since January 1946 Eleanor had served in London as one of five U.S. delegates to the meetings of the United Nations General Assembly. Because she felt that she lacked the necessary experience, Eleanor had accepted President Truman's appointment to the impressive position with "fear and trembling."

She need not have worried. She quickly distinguished herself as a creative contributor to the drafting of the Universal Declaration of Human Rights. She transferred to the international stage the ethical authority she had gained in more than twenty years in the domestic political arena. Her personal correspondence with citizens in need made her well loved nationwide. Eleanor's advocacy for the African-American contralto Marian Anderson became a twofold symbol of her courage: it served as an example for taking a stand on women's rights and insisting on racial equality. Near the end of her life, President John Kennedy appointed Eleanor head of his Commission on the Status of Women. Eleanor's cup was overflowing with honors.

Eleanor outlived Lucy by twenty-one years, dying in 1962 at the age of 78. She was just seven years older than her rival but survived her by fourteen years. Eleanor's way of dealing with Lucy's relationship with Franklin had been effective in retrospect. Her cousin Joseph Alsop stressed that "until the very last years of her life, Eleanor Roosevelt pretended for the record that there had been no such relationship." Using Franklin's letters to her as proof, she tried to convince Professor Frank Freidel—a foremost authority on FDR's life—that her hold on Franklin's heart had not been broken by Lucy in 1917. Shaping the Roosevelts' image for posterity, Eleanor had the last word.

LUCY'S SUN SETS

In the spring of 1945—shortly before the end of World War II— Eleanor moved into the center of the spotlight when she inherited the political legacy of FDR, the most powerful man on earth. At the same time, Lucy mourned in seclusion. She sank into oblivion from her exalted position as the president's best-loved companion; with him gone she could no longer serve her beloved friend. She could only commit her admiration for Franklin's greatness to paper, write a few letters about his grandeur, and return to her obligations as the matriarch of her family.

A casual note on Allamuchy stationery, jotted down in Lucy's hand with many abbreviations, might have served to collect her thoughts before she sent them on to Anna. It read, "A supremely great American & one of the towering figures of world history.—It is difficult to adjust to a world without him. His bitterest enemies have been shocked into a realization—or a half realization of his greatness—If ever in the history of mankind any one gave his life to its service— Franklin Roosevelt did." Lucy was still used to thinking about Franklin in French and she was too modest to speak about herself as "I," preferring to use the French *on* for the English "one." *On aurait voulu le voir achever cette tâche de géant qu'il affrontait avec tante de souriante grandeur* ("One [or I] would have wanted him [to live long enough] to see the completion of his giant task, which he approached with such cheerful grandeur"). Lucy put random thoughts on paper before using them in a letter.

Writing to Anna on May 9, Lucy expressed the same sentiments in a more structured form. "The world has lost one of the greatest men that ever lived—to me—the greatest. He towers above them all—effortlessly—& even those who opposed him seem shocked into the admission of his greatness. Now he is at peace—but he knew even before the end—that the task was well done."

Even before Anna and Lucy reconnected after FDR's death, Eleanor approached Lucy in a surprise move. She sent her a gift, a picture of FDR. If a note was attached, it was lost. On May 2, 1945, Lucy responded with a letter of thanks and condolence. This exchange represented the first direct contact between the two ladies in almost thirty years. The last known written communication between Lucy and Eleanor dated from the end of summer in 1917. After all the emotional turmoil that had separated them for decades, it is remarkable that the tone of Lucy's address to Eleanor had hardly changed. Lucy started now out with "Dear Eleanor" instead of "My dear Mrs. Roosevelt." As before, Lucy ended her epistle with "Affectionately." She signed off as Lucy Rutherfurd instead of Lucy Mercer, but still assured Eleanor of her devotion "as always." Most strikingly, Lucy extended the same warm respect to Eleanor as she had in her youth. In 1945 Eleanor was still "the mistress of the situation," just as she had been in 1917.

Lucy came right to the point when she wrote, "Margaret Suckley has written me that you gave her the little water color of Franklin by Mme. Shoumatoff to send me. . . . Thank you so very much—you must know that it will be treasured always."

After a long period of silence from both sides, Lucy had to touch upon some personal issues that stood between her and FDR's widow. It was to be expected that she would defend herself against Eleanor's grievances toward her. Lucy could have stressed that it was Franklin who had approached her first in 1916–1917, and again after eight years of separation by starting a correspondence in 1926. Instead she presented herself as a supplicant who had appealed to the president's charity. Humbly, like a schoolgirl caught neglecting a duty, Lucy apologized. "I have wanted to write you for a long time to tell you that I had seen Franklin and of his great kindness about my husband when he was desperately ill in Washington, & of how helpful he [Franklin] was too, to his [Winthrop's] boys." Aiken's *grande dame*, the advocate of the First Lady against her detractors, was sincere when she assured Eleanor, "I hope very much that I might see you again."

Lucy expressed her condolences to the widowed Eleanor with great candor. She frankly confessed that she envied Eleanor. "I can't tell you how deeply I feel for you and how constantly I think of your sorrow," Lucy maintained. "You—whom I have always felt to be the most blessed and privileged of women—must now feel immeasurable grief and pain." By 1945, while Lucy had caught up with Eleanor in social rank and in stature as a family matriarch, she still stood in awe of Eleanor as a superior person. "I send you—as I find it impossible not to—my love and my deep sympathy," Lucy ended modestly.

A pale penciled "ans" in a corner of Lucy's letter indicates that Eleanor answered it, together with her replies to many other condolences. The disappearance of Eleanor's acknowledgment is probably no great loss. Eleanor had neither the time nor the inclination to confront the delicate matters hinted at in Lucy's letter. Her gesture of sending Lucy the portrait of FDR, painted by Madame Shoumatoff in the White House, was gracious enough without a message. Eleanor could have used the picture herself. Her friend in old age, the Reverend William Turner Levy, noted at a visit to Mrs. Roosevelt's Val-Kill cottage that a reproduction of a Shoumatoff portrait of FDR hung in a place of honor above a sofa. It was hanging alongside a framed memorial tribute to the president by the Irish poet Lord Dunsany. The arrangement showed that Eleanor had cleansed her husband's image from the shadows of the wrong he did to her. Her attitude toward him had switched to a mode of hero-worship that was not far removed from Lucy's adulation of her husband. Franklin was all hers in death. Eleanor had prevailed for good over her rival.

*   *   *

Daisy, now exclusively referred to as Margaret by her friends, appeared in a new light to Lucy after she served as intermediary for Eleanor's gift. The sisterly fondness between the two women, formed by their shared adoration of FDR, proved beneficial for both of them in the long run. The Margaret Suckley papers, kept in her family's historic mansion Wilderstein, in the woods near Rhinebeck on the Hudson, show the depth of Margaret's and Lucy's continued friendship. Margaret tried to ease Lucy's sadness by giving her photographs from Franklin's world—including his retreat at Top Cottage, near Hyde Park, and his second home in Georgia. "I love having the one from Warm Springs," Lucy wrote with her thanks in a letter to her friend, "though they make the pain in one's heart even sharper."

Lucy was glad to assist Margaret in her work as an archivist at the Franklin D. Roosevelt Library. Margaret, for her part, was impressed with Lucy's detailed knowledge of FDR's activities in World War I. Lucy agonized about the whereabouts of the diary she knew Franklin had kept during his secret mission for the navy to England and France in 1918. Her correspondence with Franklin during these weeks had been lively. It appears that his letters to Lucy were more extensive than his messages to his wife and his mother, who longed day after day for mail from Franklin.

If Lucy was glad to cooperate with Margaret Suckley in preserving FDR's heritage, she derived even more pleasure from becoming a special friend of Franklin's daughter Anna. Lucy and Anna were brought together ever more closely in mourning, in their common fate of loving and having been loved by FDR. Taking the initiative, Anna unexpectedly called Lucy late at night in early May 1945. Anna wanted Lucy to know that her acts of loving care for the president were not forgotten. This was exactly what the depressed Lucy needed to hear. Deeply moved, she wrote Anna, "I did not know that it was in me just now to be so glad to hear the sound of any voice—and to hear you laugh—was beyond words wonderful."

No ordinary letter of condolence could have touched Anna's heart as much as Lucy's lines of May 9, 1945, written two days after the surrender of Germany. Nobody was as sensitive as Lucy in appraising the happiness father and daughter had given each other. It never came easy to Lucy to express her feelings in writing. Now grief gave wings to her words.

> *I had not written before for many reasons, but you were constantly in my thoughts & with very loving and heart torn sympathy & I was following every step of the way. This blow must be crushing to you—to all of you—but I know that you meant more to your Father than any one and that makes it closer & harder to bear. It must be an endless comfort to you that you were able to be with him so much this past year. Every second of the day you must*

*be conscious of the void and emptiness, where there has
always been—all through your life—the strength of his
beloved presence—so filled with loving understanding,
so ready to guide and to help. I love to think of his very
great pride in you.*

Lucy's detailed description of Franklin's admiration for Anna
showed how close father and daughter were to each other. They also
revealed that Franklin poured out his heart to Lucy without his usual
reserve. He had become dependent on Lucy as his sounding board,
eager to see the reflection of his thoughts and actions in Lucy's eyes.
Anna was especially moved by Franklin's praise of her talents as a
traveling companion. Lucy remembered:

*He told me so often & with such feeling of all that you
had meant of joy & comfort on the trip to Yalta. He said
you had been so extraordinary & what difference it
made to have you. He told me of your charm and your
tact—& of how everyone loved you. He told how capable
you were & how you forgot nothing & and of the little
typewritten chits he would find at his place at the beginning or end of the day—reminding him of all the little or
big things that he was to do. I hope he told you these
things—but sometimes one doesn't. In any case you
must have known—words were not needed between
you.*

Behind Franklin's enthusiastic account loomed the fact that the
president had rejected Eleanor's request to accompany him to Yalta
and had chosen Anna instead. His decision raises a question about
the historic journey. Would Eleanor have subordinated her own
political concerns to her husband's agenda as selflessly as his daughter did?

The answer to this question was not for Lucy to ponder. Her
strong urge to stay in her place, outside the divide that separated relatives from friends, once again kept her within limits. Lucy remembered all the more fondly that FDR himself had wanted her to
befriend Anna. She quoted a passage from his letter to her of May 22,

1926, written in Warm Springs. In his first move to reconnect with Lucy, he raved about his only daughter, about to be married. Two decades later Lucy let Anna share her way of mourning Franklin when she began, "I have been reading over some very old letters of his, and in one he says: 'Anna is a dear fine person—I wish so much that you knew her'—Well, now we do know one another—and it is a great joy to me & I think he was happy this past year that it was so."

Franklin had been right in expecting that Lucy and Anna would become fond of each other. Both were open to the sunny and funny side of things, which he himself constantly sought in order to relax. "And through it all one hears his ringing laugh," Lucy recalled, "& one thinks of all the ridiculous things he used to say—& do—& enjoy." Lucy could not regard herself as an outsider in Franklin's life; she was intimately tied to its ups and downs. It was her privilege to touch in conversation whatever she wanted, even delicate topics "that are sacred."

Anna kept Lucy's lines close to her bed as long as she lived. They confirmed Lucy's impact on her beloved father's welfare. Anna's daughter Sistie and her younger son Johnny commented on the importance of Lucy's letter for their mother. They saw Lucy's presence in many places of their family's destiny. Together with Anna, Lucy had been a source of joy for Franklin. Anna was reassured that she had done the right thing in 1944 when she promoted Lucy's companionship with her father in the face of her mother's likely disapproval.

*   *   *

A month after Lucy made Anna happy with her long letter, Anna helped Lucy fulfill an urgent wish. She wanted to visit Franklin's grave in his mother's rose garden in Hyde Park. It was still closed to the public, but Lucy was confident that her card of admission with Anna's signature would let her pass through security.

Warm weather had brought Lucy north to Allamuchy. Looking for someone to accompany her on a trip to Hyde Park to visit Franklin's grave in his mother's rose garden, Lucy found a perfect escort in her old friend from Aiken, Bessie Kittredge. Bessie remembered Lucy's intervention with her husband on FDR's behalf when he needed a part of the Kittredges' land to carry out his plans for the layout of the Taconic State Parkway. Mrs. Kittredge had followed FDR's rise to president with a sense of special closeness. She was a friend of a friend of the great man.

Lucy hoped that she and her companion could "slide in and out again without being a burden to anyone" at FDR's grave site. She was taken aback when the guards on the Roosevelt grounds asked for Mrs. Franklin Roosevelt's signature on Mrs. Rutherfurd's card of admission. Fortunately, Lucy could call on Miss Suckley—at work in the archive close by—to rescue her in an awkward situation. The guards accepted the authority of Margaret's boss, Mr. Palmer, the new superintendent of the library. Eventually, Margaret wrote in her daybook, "[T]he ladies had got safely away!"

Lucy took her initial failure to visit Franklin's grave deeply to heart and apologized profusely to Margaret in a letter of June 19, 1945. "It distresses me that you were given so much trouble by my descent upon you. . . . I am sorry that you were held up all down the line in your work and by the guards." Shaken by a day of overwhelming emotions, Lucy continued, "I loved seeing you, however, and thank you for making it all [as] easy as possible, in difficult circumstances for all. The memory will be with me always."

Margaret tried to comfort Lucy by inviting her to her home at Wilderstein. Lucy was grateful for "your very great thoughtfulness on asking me to stay," but she was not yet strong enough to accept. Sadly, she told Margaret, "You know how much I should like to and someday perhaps I may be able to ask you if you will have me, but you, who know all the facts, will understand that just now I do not feel I should go."

Lucy sought comfort in a return invitation, asking Margaret Suckley to visit her. "On the other hand," Lucy suggested, "I should love to have you come here and will you let me know what the possibilities are. I could pick you up in New York and bring you here and return you to N.Y. again." Thinking back to Margaret's first visit at Allamuchy as a member of Franklin's entourage only nine months earlier, Lucy inquired "about the RR on which you traveled last year, but there are no passengers trains on it." A stopover at Allamuchy had been easy to arrange for the president's private train. It was impossible for Lucy, an ordinary citizen.

The timing of Margaret's proposed visit to Allamuchy was as difficult as its logistics. "Must it be a weekend or could you come in the

middle of the week?" Lucy asked. She had not forgotten the re-
straints of a working woman, now far back in her past. "What about
the 4th of July weekend?" she inquired as her last hope.

Lucy's own calendar did not offer much leeway either. She would
have proposed "this next week, but then there is a family wedding at
which I should really put in an appearance." In her old jocular vein,
Lucy added, "I suppose though a convenient attack of almost anything, bronchitis or a grippy cold would be most welcomed!"

Lucy Rutherfurd never visited Wilderstein, nor did Margaret Suckley ever visit Allamuchy. Now that she had lost the love of her life,
Lucy returned to her main calling as the matriarch of the Winthrop
Rutherfurd clan. She sensibly downsized her surroundings. Ridgeley
Hall at Aiken, the baronial place where she had built a new life for
Winty and herself, had become too large. As a widow, she also might
have found it too full of memories. She decided to move into a
smaller house, called Tip Top Too. It was still big enough for visits
from Lucy's step-grandchildren, the main light of her life. The shortcomings of Lucy's new place became apparent only when her social
life picked up momentum with her daughter Barbara's engagement.
Her "Godfather," the president, would have been electrified by the
news. For the first time in years, he had not been able to send his traditional telegram to Barbara on her birthday in June.

It was again early April, two years after FDR's death, when Lucy
found both happiness and sadness in the marriage of her daughter.
Barbara's fiancé, Robert Knowles, Jr., came from a prominent Boston
family. He could count a great poet, Henry Wadsworth Longfellow,
among his ancestors and excelled as a distinguished sportsman on
the golf course. Lucy was relieved of the main stress of preparing the
wedding, announced for April 8, 1947, by her good friends Mr. and
Mrs. George H. Mead. Pictures of the ceremony, taken in the Meads'
garden at Aiken, show the mother of the bride in a youthful floral
dress. She looked as serene as ever, though her distinctive smile had
grown fainter. The emotional strain of the last two years had left its
mark.

Distinguished as the senior lady of the party by wearing a little
hat, Lucy appeared frail. Barbara stood at the center of the family
portrait, wearing a traditional bridal gown with a veil and a floral
wreath on her head. Surrounded by her siblings, Lucy's stepdaugh-

ter Alice towered queenly over the assembly. The groom and the four Rutherfurd stepsons presented a stunning display of tall good looks.

*   *   *

Barbara's life with her new husband put Lucy at a greater distance from her daughter. Her only other close relative, her sister, stayed on nearby in Washington. Vio, Lucy's long-loved shield against loneliness, turned out to be no longer the customary pillar of strength for her sister. She rather needed help herself during bouts of depression. It was telling that neither Vio nor her husband William Marbury appeared in the pictures of Barbara's wedding at Aiken.

Vio had been her sister's guardian angel at the time of Lucy's rendezvous with the man she loved. Her house on Q Street had been a respectable meeting place for Lucy and the president. Vio had been a witness to Lucy's restraint when she met FDR again in person. She admired how her sister took care not to overstep the proper limits of a friendship. It was obvious that neither Lucy nor Franklin ever gave lasting thought to leaving their marriage partners.

It was an irony of fate that Vio suffered the consequences of less principled behavior in her own family when her husband surrendered to a temptress who wrecked their marriage. Vio's generosity toward a desperate relative, combined with her trust in her husband's integrity, led to disaster. The end of World War II had washed ashore in the United States a homeless refugee from Austria, an aristocratic, attractive woman of Vio's age. She had divorced her Austrian husband, a baron, and lost all her property in the turmoil of war. It was the same Marguerite Pennington who had been like a sister to Vio and Lucy when they were under their cousin Agnes Carroll Heussenstamm's care in Austria. The fun times from forty years earlier, at the beginning of the century, were reenacted in tragedy after World War II. It hurt to look at the lighthearted memories in Violetta's album and remember the carefree times when the three girls would romp on the grounds of the villa near the Danube.

Full of compassion, Vio took Marguerite into her home on Q Street when she stood at her door, penniless, without a roof over her head. Inconceivably, Marguerite abused Vio's hospitality without scruple. Throwing herself into the arms of her host, Dr. Marbury, she turned him against his wife. Put under great pressure by Marguerite,

he divorced Vio and married his houseguest. When Marguerite became the second Mrs. Marbury, the situation of the newlyweds in the
capital became untenable. They moved far away to New Mexico. "My
mother had many friends in Washington," Vio's daughter Mrs. Blundon commented drily.

Violetta could not live with the heartbreak and humiliation. Lucy
saw the danger in her sister's misery and invited her to her new
home in Aiken, but she could not watch over her every minute.
When Lucy had to leave for the day on November 11, 1947, Vio went
into her sister's bedroom, took a small revolver from the drawer in
the nightstand, and shot herself in the head in her sister's garden.

Vio's tragic death hit Lucy right in the heart. She was made to feel
even more alone a few weeks later, on Christmas Day 1947, when her
mother died in the Waverly sanatorium in Maryland. Lucy could not
mourn together with her sister and had to tackle all practical matters
by herself, including the return of Minnie Mercer's last pension
check to the Veterans Administration. Lucy was devastated. She had
lost a sister who had been a defining part of her life, a leader in her
youth, and her rock in years of hopelessness and poverty. Vio had
been at Lucy's side when they lost their parental home, and again a
generation later when she lost her husband Winty and her friend
Franklin. Vio's grisly end put major decisions in Lucy's life in a new
light.

Dr. Marbury's betrayal called another marital crisis to mind. It occurred almost thirty years earlier, when Franklin Roosevelt had to
come to grips with his wife's anguish over Lucy's intrusion into his
heart. How differently the characters had behaved then in a similar
drama. In all her sorrow, the redoubtable Eleanor persevered after
the discovery of a rival. She triumphed in the long run, having mustered the courage to change her life and herself. In the end her transformation from a home-oriented matron to a professional woman
proved immensely gratifying. Franklin was rewarded too for re-
nouncing his impulse to follow the dictates of his heart. Remaining
with his sometimes difficult wife, he ended up with an unsurpassed
teammate in her years as First Lady.

Most likely Lucy had to practice even more self-denial than Eleanor and Franklin did. In 1918 she could have selfishly pressed her advantage of being first in Franklin's heart. Yet instead of feeling sorry

for herself, making scenes, begging to be married, and pulling the strings of seduction, Lucy obeyed the voice of her conscience. She put an end to the triangle situation by marrying another man.

Unexpectedly, six years later Lucy was given another chance to fill the emotional needs of her friend. When Franklin initiated a correspondence with her, Lucy never wavered in her absolute commitment to her husband. She responded with reserve to FDR's letters after he pulled her once more into his life. Only later did she learn that Eleanor had moved out from under his roof and that Anna had been married in 1926.

Lucy permitted a new closeness to Franklin in the 1940s only after the bonds of her marriage had been cut by her husband's fatal illness. The opposite of Marguerite, who drove her cousin Vio's husband to adultery, Lucy always tried to minimize the visible results of her friendship with Franklin. She did not mind that its footprints were soon covered by the dust of change. Lucy was glad to be forgotten fast. In June 1945 she shocked Elizabeth Shoumatoff with the remark that she had burned all of FDR's letters. Lucy shrugged off her friend's warning that her destruction of concrete evidence would invite unwelcome rumors.

*   *   *

Madame's prediction came true. Tall tales soon filled the gap left by Lucy's reticence. FDR's visit to Lucy at Allamuchy on September 1, 1944, was a historical fact that spawned many legends, some of which are still alive. In 2007 friends of the Rutherfurds still believed that Franklin had also visited Lucy in Aiken, at Ridgeley Hall. Aiken's rumor mill ground out one unbelievable story after another. Longtime residents of Aiken laid out in precise detail the logistics of FDR's alleged stay or stays in Aiken. According to eyewitnesses, they insist, FDR's private train docked directly behind the Willcox Inn for incognito overnight sojourns. In this illusionary view, Ridgeley Hall was well prepared to host the president's visit. Even though the elevator from the first to the second floor was obviously built to accommodate Winthrop, the incapacitated master of the mansion, local Aiken citizens fantasized that it carried the crippled president upstairs.

As a mysterious widow—beautiful, rich, and romantically linked to a great president—Lucy captured the imagination of many writers.

In order to make her come alive as a seductress, proof had to be invented where facts were missing. A classic example of such an apocryphal story, handed on without question from one biographer to the next, was created in 1985 in *FDR: A Biography*.

Although the author was not able to spell the name of his witness correctly, his flights of fancy—imagining scenes that never happened—prompted writers after him to move over these tales into their own books on the Roosevelts. "According to Lucy Mercer herself, the love affair was consummated," he started out. "Soon after FDR's death in 1945, Betsy [sic] Cushing, who had divorced James Roosevelt and married John Hay Whitney, went to stay with friends in Aiken, South Carolina." The report overlooked the fact that Mrs. Jock Whitney did not spell her name "Betsy" but rather "Betsey," and that James Roosevelt had left her rather than the other way around. FDR had fondly called the green-eyed beauty "Bets" when she was his daughter-in-law. She brought laughter and elegance to his pre-dinner cocktail hours. He told her father, the famous brain surgeon Harvey Cushing in Boston, that "Betsey is about 100%!"

Betsey Cushing Roosevelt Whitney needed no invitation from friends to visit Aiken. She owned property in the resort that had belonged to her family for two generations. Her husband's grandfather William C. Whitney had invested heavily in Aiken woodlands, race-horse stables, and mansions. On her trips to Aiken, Betsey had ample opportunity to see Lucy. Franklin's cousin Joseph Alsop reported that Lucy had confided in Betsey, telling her "that although she loved Winthrop Rutherfurd, and owed him much, Franklin Roosevelt had none the less been the love of her life." There is no such verification of the following story, vaguely ascribed to the time from May to June 1945.

According to the author relating the episode, Betsey had last seen FDR at his fourth inauguration in January. Her daughters Sara and Kate were among the thirteen grandchildren who gathered around the president for the occasion. In early 1945 Betsey assisted her husband in settling her mother-in-law's estate. If she had really come to Aiken "soon after FDR's death" in April, Betsey would have found the place deserted. All high society left at the end of the resort's winter season. Lucy too had gone north to Allamuchy for the summer. This was around the time when Lucy was shaken by her visit to FDR's grave site in Hyde Park.

The description of the event in the Rutherfurds' parlor, when Lucy supposedly entertained Mrs. Whitney, borders on the surreal. Allegedly, a portrait of FDR painted by "Mopsy"—the biographer's distortion of Shoumie, Madame Shoumatoff's true nickname—was hanging on the wall. The writer put gloves on Lucy's hands at her own tea table.

> *Betsy [sic] thought at first that Mrs. Rutherfurd was awfully ladylike—she wore white gloves at teatime. But Lucy began to ask embarrassingly personal questions. She wanted to know whether any other woman had had the same physical claim, whether there had ever been, after her departure from the scene, a rival for Franklin's physical love. Betsy found herself unable to respond to Lucy's inquiries, and was relieved when suddenly all the lights in the house went out. It must be Franklin, she thought, annoyed at the line of questioning.*

Lucy did not need to inquire about FDR's personal life; she knew all about it from Franklin himself. She never "departed" from FDR's "scene" because she had never been his mistress. Lucy's granddaughters Lucy and Alice Knowles were incensed at such flights of imagination. In their view Mrs. Winthrop Rutherfurd, the perfect, convent-educated lady, would never have touched a topic like sexual relations at the tea table. Lucy's true attributes of dignity and tact did not at all fit the writer's characterization of the "feminine, seductive, geishalike Lucy Mercer."

The story was absurd but typical in its distortion of the truth. Decades after Lucy's death, there was still no end to similar misrepresentations of her personality. The real Lucy never worried about rivals for FDR's affection and it is hard to imagine that she would fantasize about an imagined rival who dominated the president's sex life. She was preoccupied, challenged by more mundane problems, like decisions about the responsible use of her large inherited estate.

Such down-to-earth matters were of little interest to her biographers. It went unreported that Lucy's heirs honored her memory with a major meaningful donation. On July 7, 1950, they deeded a large "parcel of land with the buildings thereon," in Allamuchy, Warren County, New Jersey, for "the sum of One dollar" to the Congregation of the Daughters of Divine Charity of Staten Island, New York. Their mother superior, M. Melissa Gubiza, accepted the momentous gift gratefully and made it bear fruit, in the spirit of the giver.

The ailing Lucy felt more acutely the physical weakness that Daisy had observed earlier. Lucy had appointed her daughter Barbara Knowles and her stepsons Guy Gerald and Winthrop, Jr., Rutherfurd as executors and trustees of her estate. Two years after Lucy's death, they directed her inheritance into channels that Lucy herself might have chosen as a way to do the most good with her fortune. Practical considerations pointed in the same direction. A formidable tax bill made it questionable whether it was wise to keep the Allamuchy mansion and estate in the family. Located within easy reach of New York City, the property would have brought a high return from a sale to a developer.

*   *   *

It was not so much money, however, as immaterial values that had priority in decisions about the future of Allamuchy. In an act of loving gratitude, Lucy's heirs gave the core of the estate to an institution that would use it to build a Catholic school for girls on the grounds. The donation closed a circle in the life of Lucy Mercer Rutherfurd. As a little girl, she had received a sterling education at the convent school at Sharon Hill near Philadelphia. She had grown up to become a well-informed young woman at the school of the Sisters of the Divine Redeemer in Vienna. The Daughters of Divine Charity on Staten Island belonged to an order with goals similar to its Austrian counterpart: to provide girls with a character-building, academically superior education. The Mother House of the Staten Island Daughters order still stands in Vienna.

Some of the order's sisters who moved as teachers from Staten Island to New Jersey lived in the old Rutherfurd mansion until 2003. Their girls' school, the *Villa Madonna*, was a new, modern building. It faced the road, standing at an angle to the old Rutherfurd mansion and hiding it from public sight. In 2007 the Allamuchy public school system took over the property where nuns had administered Lucy's spiritual legacy for more than half a century. Dr. Timothy Frederiks, then the superintendent of the Allamuchy Township School District, made sure that the school board was aware of the role that their newly acquired property had played in American presidential history.

It fit Lucy's lack of ambition that the school for girls based on her heritage did not bear her name. Lucy left this world without fanfare, without a stir in the society pages. She never recovered from the blow of her sister's suicide. When Lucy's will to live was shattered, the cancer in her blood spread quickly, causing her to suffer from constant fatigue and loss of appetite. Chronic pain was held in check by morphine after her transfer to New York's Memorial Sloan–Kettering Cancer Center. Lucy died on July 31, 1948, only fifty-seven years old. Her friend Eulalie Salley and faithful confessor Monsignor Smith attended her funeral as delegates from Aiken. Lucy's casket, placed in the Rutherfurds' private chapel on the Allamuchy estate, was covered with a blanket of yellow roses that cascaded all the way to the floor. A slab of stone on the grounds of the village cemetery, marked with Lucy's name, matched the stone on the neighboring grave of her husband. Winthrop Rutherfurd, who had died four years earlier, was one of many members of his clan who found their rest here, not far from the ruins of their old Tranquillity homestead.

Lucy's simple burial and remote resting place fit her lack of significance after FDR's death. The attention paid to the end of Lucy's life was worlds apart from the celebration of Eleanor's passing. Before she died on November 7, 1962, fourteen years after Lucy, Eleanor had requested that a private funeral take place first, followed by a public announcement. Yet the "first lady of the world," as President Truman first called her, was too prominent for such modest arrangements. Only one of Eleanor's last wishes was honored—the banning of flowers at her internment. When the funeral procession took her casket to the white marble stone at FDR's grave site in the Hyde Park rose garden, any floral adornment was missing. The whole nation was looking on as Presidents Kennedy, Truman, and Eisenhower and Vice President Johnson headed the throng of mourning family members and dignitaries.

President Kennedy ordered all U.S. flags to be lowered to half-staff. Ten thousand people listened in New York's Cathedral Church of Saint John the Divine to Adlai Stevenson's eulogy at Eleanor's memorial service. Eight days earlier Stevenson had included in his tribute to Eleanor, delivered to the General Assembly of the United Nations, a phrase that became unforgettable: "She would rather light candles than curse the darkness."

If FDR could have witnessed the adulation that his wife received, he would have been immensely gratified. He would have felt vindicated in his decision to promote her self-realization as First Lady, with room also for political goals diverging from his agenda. He was glad to have excused her from the obligations as an ever-available wife and mother, of the kind Lucy represented as Mrs. Rutherfurd. After nursing him over the first stages of his polio attack, Eleanor had no longer been required to be his "helpmeet" in all situations of everyday life—as had been visualized at their engagement in 1903. Eleanor's partisanship on behalf of the weak in society and on the new importance allotted to the observance of human rights surpassed in their idealism Franklin's more pragmatic approach to reach his version of *salus populi* ("the good of the people").

Eleanor's greatness also confirmed Franklin's own vision for the nation's future. FDR was spared the pain of mourning for the two women he singled out to define his life. He did not live to see Eleanor become a historic figure in her own right. He could not share the grief of Lucy's friends in Aiken, who mourned the passing of "a Saint . . . beloved for her goodness and purity by all."

Lucy had filled the role of the biblical Martha, caring tirelessly for the physical and emotional well-being of loved ones around her. She exemplified the blessings inherent in being a wife and mother, a comfort and haven for all whose lives she touched. Franklin had been attracted until his end by her spirit of gentleness and unselfishness. Secretly, he might have longed to be at the receiving end of her gifts as a homemaker and caregiver.

Eleanor, on the other hand, had chosen "the better part"—the one embraced by Mary, Martha's sister, in the biblical story. Rather than serving as a supplier of everyday needs for her family, Mary sat at her master's feet, ready to receive and spread his mission. She rejoiced in following a noble calling. Eleanor went even further than the biblical Mary, the faithful listener to new messages, when she asked others to listen to her. Loving and being loved by mankind, Eleanor became a model for women seeking to enrich their lives with accomplishments outside the home.

Franklin did not have a partner who combined the qualities of Martha and Mary in one person. Still, he was fortunate to experience the best of traditional feminine virtues represented by Lucy, together with the best of creative female energy in the world at large represented by Eleanor. In subsequent generations it has been the goal of many women to succeed both as a professional and as a mother. Franklin's daughter Anna, the assistant editor of a newspaper, took an early step in this direction, foreshadowing women's achievements in the twenty-first century. She combined journalistic work with the obligations of a wife and a mother of three children. If Anna's effort to "have it all" did not lead to all-around happiness, she nonetheless provided a widely visible example of an alternative for women seeking fulfillment outside traditional roles.

Anna was the only Roosevelt left to say after Lucy's death, "It makes me sad that I will not see her again." She summed up Lucy's blessing for her father in just five words. "She was a wonderful person."

NOTES

Author's Note:

The research for this book is based primarily upon unpublished sources. The study's main characters—besides Lucy, FDR, his wife Eleanor, his mother Sara, and his daughter Anna Halsted—were all eager to keep their personal affairs out of public view. Their success in withholding any written evidence of Franklin's devotion to Lucy lends special importance to the circumstantial evidence of his affection. Much of it is provided in unpublished sources. The author is grateful for generously offered access to numerous privately owned documents and pictures illuminating Lucy's life and personality. While they enrich the information gained from interviews and printed sources, they call for special explanatory comments in some of the following entries.

PROLOGUE: WAYS TO DISCOVER LUCY

p. xi **Personal Letters**: Elliott Roosevelt and associates (eds.), *F.D.R.: His Personal Letters*, 4 vols. (New York: Duell, Sloan & Pearce, 1947–1950). Eleanor Roosevelt entrusted her son Elliott with a responsible and lucrative task: to select for publication, and annotate with his own comments, the letters his mother had inherited from her husband. The four volumes covered the years 1905–1945.

p. xi **Alice Sohier** burned all letters she received from Franklin in 1902. Her impact on FDR's development was examined first by Geoffrey C. Ward in *Before the Trumpet: Young Franklin Roosevelt, 1882–1905* (New York, Harper & Row, 1985), his foundational work on Franklin's youth (pp. 252–255, note 16). Franklin shared with Sara his concern about Alice's fragile health after he escorted the girl on October 7, 1902, to a boat taking her to a steamer bound for Europe.

p. xii **Eleanor skimmed over:** Eleanor Roosevelt, *The Autobiography of Eleanor Roosevelt* (New York: Harper & Brothers, 1961), pp. 40–41.

p. xii **Sara introduced the girl**: In a note to her brother Warren Delano III, written on September 6, 1903, from her summer residence at Campobello, SDR was impressed by Eleanor's fine qualities and recommended her as a houseguest. The full text read, "You are to have one of the nicest & most thoughtful & intelligent girls I know to stay with you in Eleanor & I seem to know quite a number of them pretty well, as they are always sweet with me."

p. xiii **write her more often:** ER to FDR, December 3, 1903

p. xiii **"absolutely lost":** ER to FDR, January 18,1904.

p. xiii **Before Eleanor published:** Eleanor Roosevelt, *This Is My Story* (New York: Harper & Brothers, 1937).

p. xiv **She reminded her readers**: ER, *The Autobiography of Eleanor Roosevelt*, p. 41.

p. xv **Joseph Lash did not think so:** Joseph P. Lash, *Eleanor and Franklin: The Story of Their Relationship Based on Eleanor Roosevelt's Private Papers* (New York: W. W. Norton, 1971), p. 101.

p. xv **Apparently, they were destroyed:** Lucy herself told her friend Margaret Suckley at Warm Springs that she destroyed all of FDR's letters after his death. It is not known what happened to Lucy's letters to FDR. Fragments of Franklin and Lucy's correspondence from the 1920s survived and are housed in the Lucy Mercer Rutherfurd File at the FDR Library.

p. xvi **Four of his very formal letters,** inherited by Lucy's granddaughters, were donated to the FDR Library.

p. xvi **the watchful eyes of a lawyer:** Judy Segretti was at the time in charge of the LMR collection, a part of the documents preserved by the Rutherfurd Foundation in Manhattan. They were examined by the author on November 14, 2007.

p. xvii **William D. Hassett,** *Off the Record with F.D.R.: 1942–1945* (New Brunswick, NJ: Rutgers University Press, 1958), p. 34.

p. xviii **Ellie Roosevelt Seagraves** was interviewed by Dr. Thomas Soapes for the FDR Library Oral Interviews Series on February 2, 1978 (p. 33). In Mrs. Seagraves's view, "Franklin Roosevelt and Lucy Mercer were so Victorian, that if they spent an afternoon together it was driving in the country and having tea and holding hands and perhaps a kiss. But she would doubt whether they would, either of them, since Lucy came from a very strict family herself, would [sic] have ever tried to go to a hotel. They both felt too public, and that too much was at stake. That's what my mother's [Anna Roosevelt Halsted's] feeling was. . . . But she felt that they were probably very much in love, but that it was not the consummated kind of thing . . . each had responsibilities, family pride and all the rest of it. Lucy Mercer is another person who's had kind of a bad press, nobody's ever done anything to describe her background or what her outlook was. And I understand that she was a very wonderful person."

The author learned many details about FDR's immediate family directly from Dr. Soapes on a visit at his retirement home in Alexandria, Virginia. The conversation was doubly informative. Dr. Soapes's wife, his former colleague at the FDR Library in Hyde Park, shared the interviewing of FDR's relatives and contributed her own observations.

p. xix **Montague Blundon** wrote this message on a card that is in the author's possession.

p. xix The author learned on an early visit in the Blundons' home that **Ludy Blundon Biddle** received her unusual first name, with a "d" in the middle instead of a "c," after careful deliberation of her parents. They meant to set their daughter apart from "too many Lucy's" in the family.

To meet and consult with Ludy, I accepted her invitation to visit her residence in rural Vermont in the summer of 2007. Earlier I had made the acquaintance of Ludy's brother Montague Blundon in his parents' home in McLean, Virginia. I owe him a major debt of gratitude for his willingness to welcome and support my plans to write a biography of Lucy Mercer, the niece of his grandmother Violetta Mercer Marbury. A physician like his Marbury grandfather, the youngest heir of the Montague Blundon tradition introduced himself as "Tad." He was pleasantly approachable.

p. xx **Yearly journeys to the FDR Library**: I regret that the publication of my larger manuscript, a biography of FDR's mother, did not precede the publication of this book. The manuscript, with the working title *America's Mother*, was donated to the National Archives in 2004 but has remained in its unedited state. My frustrations as an unpublished author have been balanced by the benefit of my studies of Sara Delano Roosevelt as a power behind the scenes for the smaller project of Lucy Mercer Rutherfurd's role in FDR's life.

p. xx **My husband Don Edward Totten** helped me to meet not only the practical but also the scholarly challenges of our travel as historical detectives. He complemented my own background in history, linguistics, and comparative literature with his studies of political science, added to his basic expertise in cultural and historical geography.

p. xxi **Mrs. Pamela LeBoutillier:** Our day with Mrs. LeBoutillier turned out to be well worth the struggle to find her residence in Long Island's backwoods. She extended an invitation for lunch to us at the suggestion of Lucy Knowles, her goddaughter in Aiken, South Carolina. After hours of reminiscing about Lucy Mercer and the Rutherfurds in Aiken in the 1930s, Mrs. LeBoutillier was so animated that she regretted not having invited us to stay overnight.

p. xxi **Our daughter Katherine:** Katherine C. Totten, by training a pianist and a software designer, used her linguistic skills on her exploratory trip to Austria. Among contemporary residents of Melk and Vienna, able to appraise Lucy Mercer's education from 1907 on, Katherine met with Magister Elisabeth Schmid, a retired educator and author of books on parochial girls' schools; Anton Harrer, historian of Melk; and the nuns in charge of the schools at the convent of the Daughters of the Divine Redeemer in Vienna. Katherine talked to Countess Elisabeth Heussenstamm, the heiress of the Count Heussenstamm's estate and legacy, in their historical mansion at Matzleinsdorf (near Melk) and took pictures of her property.

p. xxi **Jonathan Daniels:** Journalist, author, and public servant, Daniels is uncontested as the leading chronicler of Lucy Mercer's world. He stands out with his books *The End of Innocence* (Philadelphia: J. B. Lippincott, 1954), *The Time Between the Wars: Armi-*

stice to Pearl Harbor (Garden City, NY: Doubleday, 1966), and most important *Washington Quadrille: The Dance Beside the Documents* (Garden City, NY: Doubleday 1968). Lucy's relatives, the Blundons in McLean, Virginia, thought highly of Daniels's research concerning Lucy and bought six copies of the important book for their home.

p. xxii **the president's own sons:** The literary feud between James and Elliott Roosevelt was carried out mainly in two books: Elliott Roosevelt and James Brough, *An Untold Story: The Roosevelts of Hyde Park* (New York: G. P. Putnam's Sons, 1973); and James Roosevelt with Bill Libby, *My Parents: A Differing View* (Chicago: Playboy Press, 1976).

James Roosevelt was infuriated by the liberties his younger brother Elliott took with historical facts. Elliott invented corners of his father's private life that did not exist. James was especially incensed at his brother's "dishonesty," faking a knowledge of the Lucy "affair" that Elliott did not possess. On p. 42 of his 1976 book, James reminded his readers that his sister Anna was the only one of the Roosevelt children who knew Lucy Mercer Rutherfurd in person. None of the other siblings was even aware of Lucy's existence when they were young. James wrote, "It is easy now for any one of us to say we were, but it simply isn't the truth." In spite of James's exposure of the untrue flights of Elliott's imagination—or possibly his co-author's unchecked embellishments of Lucy's allure—future writers about Franklin and Lucy repeated many of the myths created by Elliott. A typical accolade to Lucy, celebrating her alleged power of seduction, was concocted by Elliott in 1973 (*Untold Story*, p. 82). In 2004 it was given a place of honor on the dust jacket of Resa Willis's insightful book *FDR and Lucy: Lovers and Friends* (New York: Routledge, 2004). It said about Lucy, "There was a hint of fire in her warm dark eyes." Actually, Lucy had inherited her father's blue-gray eyes.

Ironically, James himself was not immune to the temptation of inserting a sensationalist, apocryphal story into his text to prove that Lucy was indeed his father's mistress. The legend might have been good for the marketing of his book; it certainly made the difference between FDR's plain marital history and James's own complicated love life less striking. James's first marriage to Betsey Cushing in 1930 occurred thirty years earlier than his fourth and last marriage to Mary Winskill in 1960.

p. xxii **Joseph P. Lash**, *Eleanor and Franklin*. In his book *FDR, 1882–1945: A Centenary Remembrance* (New York: Viking, 1982), Joseph Alsop called the book "a short and somewhat biased account of the relationship of FDR and Lucy by Joseph P. Lash, always a ferocious partisan of Mrs. Roosevelt" (pp. 67–68).

p. xxii **Arthur Schlesinger, Jr.**, first expressed his concern in his essay "FDR's Secret Romance," which appeared in the November 1966 issue of the *Ladies' Home Journal* (p. 66).

p. xxii **Anna Roosevelt Halsted's** widower James Halsted, living in Hillsdale, New York, received a letter from Lucy's daughter Barbara Knowles, written in a beautiful hand, dated October 30, 1977. It referred to Anna's concern about unwelcome media attention for FDR's relationship with Lucy Mercer Rutherfurd. Barbara wrote, "It is a very worrisome and ticklish situation—All my family and I are very opposed to publicity—I have tried to avoid all written or verbal contact with the various authors and reporters who want to know 'My side of the story.' It is a great source of sorrow and abhorrence to my half-brothers and me all the crude implications that have been printed by people trying to cash in. I am sure it must have been most upsetting for Anna—whom I greatly admired—Your plan to place two letters presumably from my mother to President Roosevelt at Hyde Park not to be opened for 50 years sounds excellent to me."

p. xxii **Her father's friendship with Lucy:** Joseph P. Lash, *A World of Love: Eleanor Roosevelt and Her Friends, 1943–1962* (Garden City, NY: Doubleday, 1984), p. 183.

p. xxiii **"called sex 'an ordeal' ":** James Roosevelt, *My Parents*, p. 97.

p. xxiii **Joseph Alsop,** *A Centenary Remembrance*, pp. 68–74. Alsop was skeptical of the objectivity of Joseph P. Lash, trusting the impressions from his own personal acquaintance with Franklin and Eleanor more than those of any other fellow writer (*A Centenary Remembrance*, p. 73).

p. xxiv **Resa Willis,** *FDR and Lucy: Lovers and Friends* (New York: Routledge, 2004).

p. xxiv **Joseph E. Persico**, *Franklin and Lucy: President Roosevelt, Mrs. Rutherfurd, and the Other Remarkable Women in His Life* (New York: Random House, 2008).

p. xxv **Marilyn Monroe and Monica Lewinsky:** The eminent Roosevelt historian William E. Leuchtenburg gave the author the opportunity to discuss with him the results of her study of Lucy's role in FDR's life. Leuchtenburg pointed out in his writings that FDR was fortunate to have escaped media publicity that would have exposed his romance with Lucy Mercer to criticism. Other presidents after FDR's time had more difficulty keeping extramarital attachments secret. Dwight Eisenhower's ties to his chauffeur Kay Summersby, John F. Kennedy's affair with Marilyn Monroe, and Bill Clinton's entanglement with Monica Lewinsky were all contained in brief episodes, while FDR's longing for Lucy lasted thirty years. Writing in his book *In the Shadow of FDR: From FDR to Bill Clinton* (Ithaca, NY: Cornell University Press, 1992), William Leuchtenburg made a significant comment about the significance of FDR for the presidents after him. He doubted whether "Franklin Roosevelt, surely one of our greatest presidents, would have survived the scrutiny to which Clinton was subjected (p. 266)." In 1932 FDR did not have to fear any prying into his relationship with Lucy Mercer Rutherfurd. Some eighty years later, in the same situation, FDR would hardly "have made it through today's primary season."

PART ONE: Lucy As Miss Mercer

CHAPTER 1. BORN OF THE BLUEST BLOOD

p. 3 **The photographic portrait of Lucy's mother** was taken in 1898, when Lucy was seven years old.

p. 5 **Lucy's Mother**: Mrs. Carroll Mercer signed her portrait here "Minna Leigh Mercer." Using "Leigh" as a middle name, instead of her maiden name "Tunis," may have been her way of expressing a long-lasting resentment against her mother Caroline Henderson Tunis. She replaced her given first name "Minna" with "Minnie" for long periods of her life, but returned to calling herself "Minna" when she wanted to appear more formal.

p. 5 **The picture from the Mercers' family album** is now more than one hundred twenty years old. Almost all photographs in the Mercers' collection were taken by Lucy's sister Violetta Mercer Marbury. They were inherited by Violetta's daughter Mrs. Lucy Mercer Marbury Blundon of McLean, Virginia. She permitted the author to take them to a graphics studio for reproduction and to use them in her biography of Lucy Mercer.

p. 6 **Lucy's forebears:** Both Lucy and her sister Violetta were active family historians, eager to collect genealogical data and pass them on to their children. Lucy gave her daughter Barbara Rutherfurd her own version of the Mercer family history to study when the girl was twenty, at the time when President Roosevelt declared himself her "Godfather." Two years later, on December 25, 1944, Barbara received as a Christmas present from her mother's sister Violetta Mercer Marbury a self-researched history of their extended family. "Your affectionate aunt," Violetta signed her dedication to Barbara. She presented her with a beautifully handwritten and typed text illustrated with pictures and genealogical charts. She told Barbara, "[W]hen you are old enough to be interested in family history, I will probably be too old to write down what I have learned and collected." The document is divided into seven chapters—Mercer, Carroll, Sprigg, Tunis, Henderson, Johnson, and Earl(e).

pp. 7 **The family tree of Lucy's mother:** The history of the Tunis and Henderson families is based on Violetta's account for Barbara Rutherfurd.

pp. 8 **John Lowell, Jr.** Mrs. Lucy Mercer Marbury Blundon allowed the author to copy the lawyer's reports and letters on one of her visits to the Blundons' home in McLean.

p. 11 **a Washington hostess:** Daniels, *Washington Quadrille*, p. 24.

p. 11 **the Isthmus of Panama:** Daniels, *Washington Quadrille*, p. 23. On this expedition Carroll was briefly suspended from the Navy as "too drunk for duty."

pp .11 **Sarah Carroll:** Research by Violetta Mercer Marbury, family history.

p. 15 **"an elegant old lady"**: Quoted in Daniels, *Washington Quadrille*, p. 25.

p. 16 **"on the arm of the president"**: Quoted in Daniels, *Washington Quadrille*, p. 4.

p. 16 **Countess Esterhazy**: Daniels, *Washington Quadrille*, p. 7.

p. 17 **Mrs. Edith Benham Helm**: Daniels, *Washington Quadrille*, p. 8.

p. 17 **"her young admirers"**: Quoted in Daniels, *Washington Quadrille*, p. 8.

pp. 18 **Mr. Lowell's consent**: Correspondence of attorney Lowell with Minnie Mercer. Mrs. L. M. Blundon's papers.

p. 18 **"Pray for us at church"**: Quoted in Daniels, *Washington Quadrille*, p. 25.

p. 19 **Judge Victor Clay Barringer**: Daniels, *Washington Quadrille*, p. 27.

p. 22 **Cave Dwellers Club**: Daniels, *Washington Quadrille*, p. 29.

p. 22 **Chevy Chase Club**: Daniels, *Washington Quadrille*, p. 29.

p. 22 **"admission to any home"**: Quoted in Daniels, *Washington Quadrille*, pp. 24–25.

p. 23 **skill in interior decorating**: Violetta Mercer Marbury's photo album.

CHAPTER 2. THE SILVER SPOON SLIPS OUT

p. 25 **"the companies of officers and soldiers"**: Carroll Mercer's Pension File.

p. 26 **"a graceful escape"**: Quoted in Daniels, *Washington Quadrille*, p. 31.

p. 27 **Elizabeth Henderson's often-quoted explanation**: Quoted in Daniels, *Washington Quadrille*, p. 34, confirmed orally by Mrs. L. M. Blundon.

p. 27 **Mr. Lowell was determined:** Mrs. L. M. Blundon's papers.

p. 28 **ready for an abrupt change:** Alumnae Address Book, 1873–1917, Archive of the Holy Child Academy at Sharon Hill, Pennsylvania. Telephone interviews (2007/2008): Sister Helena G. Mayer, SHCJ, American Province Archivist, Rosemont, Pennsylvania, October 18 and October 20, 2007.

p. 31 **the Declaration of Independence:** Kate Mason Rowland, *The Life of Charles Carroll of Carrollton, 1737–1832* (New York: G. P. Putnam's Sons, 1898), vol. 1, p. vii.

p. 31 **"the duties of my religion":** Quoted in Rowland, *Life of Charles Carroll*, vol. 2, p. 370.

p. 32 **Holy Child Academy:** The existence of the first public school attended by Lucy Mercer was not known to contemporary Mercer descendants. It is not mentioned in any Roosevelt biography.

Apart from the Alumnae Address Book of the Academy, Lucy Mercer's so-called "signature book" provides information about Lucy's life between ten and twenty years of age. The book, actually a small album consisting of one-page contributions from friends and family, is owned by Lucy's granddaughters Lucy and Alice Knowles of Aiken, South Carolina. The discovery of the initials "E de J" under a few names of the contributors to Lucy's album, translated from the French *Enfants de Jesus* into English "children of Jesus," led to Internet searches and telephone interviews with the archivist of the Society of the Holy Child Jesus.

p. 34 **her "signature book":** Lucy and Alice Knowles's papers.

p. 36–37 **forever be their hero:** Photo album of Mrs. L. M. Blundon.

p. 37 **had deteriorated alarmingly:** Carroll Mercer's Pension File.

p. 37 **"any old way":** Quoted in Daniels, *Washington Quadrille*, p. 100.

p. 39 **"They only had each other":** Interview with Mrs. L. M. Blundon, Memorial Day, 2006, McLean, Virginia.

p. 40 **The Carroll sisters:** Unpublished Heussenstamm family history owned by Countess Elisabeth Heussenstamm, Matzleinsdorf near Melk, Austria; and Jonathan Daniels Papers, Wilson Library, University of North Carolina, Chapel Hill.

The relationship of the Carrolls and the Lees is described in detail in Rowland, *Life of Charles Carroll*, vol. 2, pp. 439–440.

p. 41 **matrimony for the girls:** Interview with Countess Elisabeth Heussenstamm, Matzleinsdorf, Austria, by Katherine C. Totten, 2007,

CHAPTER 3. RESCUE FROM OVERSEAS

p. 49 **the Cholmeleys or Foljambes:** As a houseguest of Sir Hugh and Lady Cholmeley in Lincolnshire, the author could visit country-seats of the English nobility that made a lasting impression on FDR as a Harvard man in 1903—from the Cholmeleys' Easton Hall to the mansions of the Foljambes and the Dukes of Rutland.

p. 51 **Stefan Zweig,** *The World of Yesterday: An Autobiography* (New York: Viking, 1943).

p. 52 **the wedding in Vienna's papal chapel:** Countess Elisabeth Heussenstamm, Family History.

p. 52 **American dowries in Europe:** Hester Dorsey Richardson, *Side-Lights on Maryland History: With Sketches of Early Maryland Families,* 2 vols. (Cambridge, MD: Tidewater Publishers, 1967).

p. 53 *The Clubfellow and Washington Mirror.* Daniels, *Washington Quadrille,* p. 70.

p. 61 **"as well as pedagogy":** Daniels, *Washington Quadrille,* p. 70.

p. 63 **the "three R's":** Eleanor Roosevelt, *Autobiography,* p. 8.

p. 63 **Lucy enjoyed enviable schooling:** Beginning in 2006 information about Lucy's formal education in Austria was gained by correspondence and telephone interviews with contemporary Austrian sources. Anton Harrer, Melk's town historian, quoted from a town almanac—the *Stadtbuch Melk, Daten and Fakten of 1999*. He referred the author to Magister Elisabeth Schmid, a former teacher, administrator, and still active writer. Her book on Melk's convent school for girls, the Privat Maedchenhauptschule, explained the standards and curriculum of the schools founded by the sisters belonging to the

Congregation of the Daughters of the Divine Redeemer, who also taught Lucy Mercer in their convent school in Vieanna. Magister Schmid, using her honorary title of *Hofrat*, arranged a transatlantic interview with Waltraud Haas, a renowned Viennese actress. Mrs. Haas's mother, an alumna of the type of school Lucy Mercer attended, shared fond memories of the academic and practical advancement provided by this prominent parochial school.

The order's contemporary archivist in their motherhouse in Vienna, Sister Sieglinde Zeug, together with a Sister Noberta added more facts about their education programs. In 2007 they requested a donation for their girls' school in Argentina as payment for the material on the order's schools they sent to the author. These books and pictures served as a blueprint for the reconstruction of the principles and values instilled in Lucy Mercer in her formative years overseas.

Among them, a publication by the Archbishop's [of Vienna] Office for Education stood out (especially pp. 24 and 83). It appeared in 2004 under the title *Volksschule Waldkloster Quellenstrasse, Festschrift anlaesslich der Eroeffnung des Neubaus* [Academic discourse on the School in the Forest, in celebration of opening ceremonies for the new building]. Another publication of the order, *Ruf der Zeit* [Call of the times] (Vienna: Archbishop's Office for Education, 1983), yielded facts on pp. 20, 21, 43, and 220. The characterization of Mother Alphonse Maria (born Elisabeth Eppinger), the founder of the order, sheds more light on the ethics transmitted in her schools (pp. 19–22).

p. 64 **a wealthy childless couple:** *Ruf der Zeit*, p. 16. "Nulla salus sine virtute; nulla virtus sine labore" [Nothing good comes without virtue; there is no virtue without work] (*Ruf der Zeit*, p. 220).

p. 65 **"conduct" and "diligence":** Papers of Magister Elisabeth Schmid.

p. 65 **streetcars roll by:** Reported by Katherine C. Totten.

p. 66 **eastern and southern parts of the empire:** *Ruf der Zeit*, p. 43.

p. 68 **their way of loving God:** *Festschrift*, p. 24; Daniels, *Washington Quadrille*, p. 61.

p. 68 **devastating epidemics:** *Ruf der Zeit*, p. 21; *Festschrift*, p. 41.

p. 69 **She would keep house:** *Festschrift*, p. 36.

p. 73 **in her sister's care:** Documents provided by Elisabeth, the contemporary Countess Heussenstamm.

CHAPTER 4. RETURN TO REALITY

p. 75 **Papa Mercer had tried his luck:** Daniels, *Washington Quadrille*, p. 68.

p. 76 **"an inside decorator":** Quoted in Daniels, *Washington Quadrille*, p. 70.

p. 78 **"it is not severe":** SDR to FDR and ER, December 3, 1913.

p. 78 **"I am sure":** SDR to FDR, July 18, 1913, and July 24, 1913.

p. 78 **"three mornings a week":** ER, *This Is My Story*, p. 74.

p. 79 **the hand of Sara Delano:** James Roosevelt to Bamie (Anna Roosevelt), August 1, 1880, Houghton Library, Roosevelt Collection.

p. 79 **summer of 1903:** FDR's A-Line-a-Day diary of July 7, 1903: In code "E. is an Angel." Entry on the day the *Half Moon* broke down.

p. 80 **between May and June 1914:** *Elliott Roosevelt, His Personal Letters,* vol. 2, p. 219; Daniels, *Washington Quadrille*, p. 72.

p. 80–81 ***Thomas Nelson Page:*** *A Memoir of a Virginia Gentleman by His Brother Rosewell Page* (Port Washington, NY: Kennikat Press, 1923), p. 128. President Theodore Roosevelt later appointed Page as U.S. ambassador to Italy.

p. 83 **like Franklin and Eleanor Roosevelt:** FDR reciprocated. Newly settled in Washington, FDR wrote his wife on March 19, 1913, "[T]onight give a dinner for Helen and Lathrop! Going some!" (Elliott Roosevelt, *His Personal Letters*, vol. 2, p. 200).

p. 84–85 **assignment to the United States:** Daniels, *Washington Quadrille*, p. 87.

p. 85 **"the loftiest of British nobility"**: Quoted in Daniels, *Washington Quadrille*, p. 129.

p. 85 **"gaiety and kindliness"**: Quoted in Daniels, *Washington Quadrille*, pp. 88–89.

p. 85 **her son's new best friend:** Daniels, *Washington Quadrille*, p. 105.

p. 87 Frederic Adrian Adams, a contemporary descendant of the banker **Frederic Baldwin Adams, Jr.,** the husband of FDR's cousin Ellen Walters Delano (1884–1976), explained in correspondence with the author the results of his own research of the Delanos' origin in Flanders and the Netherlands. He denied any connection between Philip de la Noye's family and the princes of the Holy Roman Empire. FDR would have been sorely disappointed by the results of Adams's research.

p. 89 **in the brick-and-marble Rosewell mansion:** Richard Channing Moore Page, *Genealogy of the Page Family in Virginia* (Bridgewater, VA: Carrier Company, 1883), p. 56.

p. 89 **"the most affectionate domestic character"**: Quoted in Moore, *Page Genealogy*, p. 76.

p. 90 **happily together ever after:** Moore, *Page Genealogy*, p. 70.

p. 90 **"Mr. Henry Hill"**: Ronald Hoffman with Sally D. Mason, *Princes of Ireland, Planters of Maryland: A Carroll Saga, 1500–1782* (Chapel Hill: University of North Carolina Press, 2000), p. 128.

p. 92 **Margaret Mercer:** Mercer Family History, Lucy and Alice Knowles' papers.

p. 95 **Eleanor's assistant Miss Mercer:** Daniels, *Washington Quadrille*, p. 134,

p. 96 **"extreme innocence and unworldliness"**: ER, *This Is My Story*, p. 109.

p. 96 **"the most beautiful woman in Washington"**: ER, *This Is My Story*, p.1; Daniels, *Washington Quadrille*, p. 33.

p. 96 **Eleanor's *Dinner Book***: FDR Library.

CHAPTER 5. 1917–1918: LUCY AND ELEANOR

p. 102 **"not only wicked but unnecessary":** SDR to FDR, July 31, 1913, and August 5, 1915.

p. 103 **On June 16, 1917:** Daniels, *Washington Quadrille*, p. 114.

p. 104 **than in ball gowns:** Daniels, *Washington Quadrille*, p.119. Jonathan Daniels called the uniforms "awkward."

p. 106 **"but *not* comfy!"** FDR to ER, July 25, 1917.

p. 106 **past of Lucy's family:** Moore, *Page Genealogy*, pp. 98–99.

p. 107 **Nigel Law himself:** Nigel Law to Jonathan Daniels, quoted in Daniels, *Washington Quadrille*, p. 120.

p. 108 **"time off from our duties":** Quoted in Daniels, *Washington Quadrille*, p. 133. Law usually worked from 8:30 a.m. to 2:00 or 3:00 a.m.

p. 109 **"I shall try to improve":** FDR to ER, July 16, 1917.

p. 110 **as "jesting":** Comment by Elliott Roosevelt in *His Personal Letters*, vol. 2, p. 349.

p. 111 **"to crawl away for shame":** Elliott Roosevelt, *His Personal Letters*, vol. 2, p. 350.

p. 112 **"the most lovely person to rush to you":** SDR to FDR, August 10, 1917.

p. 113 **"what you do for him now":** SDR to FDR, undated.

p. 113 **"Saturday, Sept. 2nd":** SDR to FDR, August 13, 1917.

p. 115 **"they are so distressed!"** Lucy Mercer to ER, September 2, 1917.

p. 115 **"pick up if it does at all":** ER to FDR, August 21, 1917.

p. 115 **"quite cross with me":** ER to FDR, September 8, 1917.

p. 116 **"*You* are entirely disconnected":** FDR to ER, September 10, 1917.

p. 116 **In his book *My Parents*:** James Roosevelt added that after

1918 Franklin and Eleanor "had an armed truce." "[D]espite several occasions I was to observe in which he . . . held out his arms to mother and she refused flatly to enter his embrace" (p. 101).

p. 118 **"to make your mother suffer":** Quoted in James Roosevelt, *My Parents*, p. 99.

p. 118 **"I am inexpressibly busy":** FDR to ER, October 10, 1917.

p. 118 **"late into the night":** ER, *Autobiography*, p. 87.

p. 119 **"all to my children":** Mercer Family Memorabilia.

p. 122 **on easy speaking terms with Mr. and Mrs. Daniels:** SDR's Guestbook, November 25–26, 1916, FDR Library.

p. 122 **"some real home life":** SDR to FDR, from Fairhaven, undated.

p. 122 **dated simply Sunday night:** A librarian at the FDR Library added October 14.

p. 122 **To further veil the letter's obvious intent:** Comment by Elliott Roosevelt in *His Personal Letters*, vol. 2, p. 279.

p. 124 **"how different E. is from some of her friends!"** SDR to FDR, August 10, 1917.

p. 124 **"Theodore Roosevelt's celebrated daughter":** Comment by Elliott Roosevelt in *His Personal Letters*, vol. 2, p. 206.

p. 125 **She was still basking in the glow:** I relied heavily on three secondary sources on Alice: Michael Teague, *Mrs. L.: Conversations with Alice Roosevelt Longworth* (Garden City, NY: Doubleday, 1961); James Brough, *Princess Alice: A Biography of Alice Roosevelt Longworth* (Boston: Little, Brown, 1975); and Carol Felsenthal, *Alice Roosevelt Longworth* (New York: G. P. Putnam's Sons, 1988).

p. 126 **Alice was "just giggling":** Felsenthal, *Alice Roosevelt Longworth*, p. 146.

p. 126. **Susan Walker Longworth:** Alice Roosevelt Longworth, *Crowded Hours: Reminiscences of Alice Roosevelt Longworth* (New York: Charles Scribner's Sons, 1933), p. 134.

p. 126 **from Washington's salons to New York's parlors:** Felsenthal, *Alice Roosevelt Longworth*, p. 161.

p. 127 **because he was married to Eleanor:** paraphrased in James Roosevelt, *My Parents*, p. 100.

p. 127 **"I didn't want to *spoil the fun*":** Longworth, *Crowded Hours*, p. 160.

p. 128 **"a lovely boy-meets-girl thing":** Longworth, *Crowded Hours*, p. 158.

p. 129 **"your husband did not wish you to know":** Quoted in Lash, *Eleanor and Franklin*, p. 226.

p. 130 **a chance for fulfillment:** Jonathan Daniels Papers.

p. 131 **"my Nastia" in London:** Daniels, *Washington Quadrille*, pp. 227–228.

CHAPTER 6. HIDDEN ROMANCE, OPEN FALLOUT

p. 142 **travel with the First Lady:** Alsop, *A Centenary Remembrance*, p. 68. Born in 1910, Alsop was a distant cousin of Franklin by marriage. Corinne Roosevelt Robinson, the sister of President Theodore Roosevelt, was Alsop's mother-in-law. Alsop considered Lash "somewhat biased . . . in favor of Mrs. Roosevelt" (*A Centenary Remembrance*, pp. 67–68).

p. 142 **"her social secretary, Lucy Page Mercer":** Quoted in Lash, *Eleanor and Franklin*, p. 226.

p. 144 **"as much as I want you":** ER to FDR, December 6, 1903.

p. 145 **a "spur" in her husband's side:** Eleanor Roosevelt, *This I Remember* (New York: Harper & Brothers, 1949), p. 349.

p. 147 **"too terrible to contemplate":** Longworth, *Crowded Hours*, p. 158.

p. 148 **"I used to think, too often":** Quoted in Geoffrey C. Ward, *A First-Class Temperament: The Emergence of Franklin Roosevelt* (New York: Harper & Row, 1989), p. 366, note 12.

p. 148 **quotable phrases by Joseph Lash:** Lash, *Eleanor and Franklin*, p. 226.

p. 149 **Bernard Asbell warned against:** Bernard Asbell (ed.), *Mother and Daughter: The Letters of Eleanor and Anna Roosevelt* (New York: Coward, McCann & Geoghegan, 1982), p. 26.

p. 150 **she "loved a good story":** Quoted in Alsop, *A Centenary Remembrance*, p. 70, comment on his grandmother Corinne Roosevelt Robinson, the younger sister of President Theodore Roosevelt.

p. 151 **"the *idea* of divorce":** Longworth, *Crowded Hours*, p. 158.

p. 154 **a daily newspaper back home:** Daniels, *Washington Quadrille*, p. 142.

p. 155 **a family conference:** Lash, *Eleanor and Franklin*, p. 227.

p. 155 **"Father had a romance":** Quoted in Asbell, *Mother and Daughter*, p. 40.

p. 156 **"a great sacrifice to please me!"** Quoted in Lash, *Eleanor and Franklin*, p. 228.

p. 156 **"I hope he will decline":** ER to SDR, November 19, 1918.

p. 158 **"she came first":** Joseph Lash, interviews with Anna Halsted, 1966–1968, Lash Papers, FDR Library.

p. 159 **"I cannot forget":** Quoted in Lash, *Eleanor and Franklin*, p. 227.

p. 159 **listed simply "Mrs. James Roosevelt":** Ward, *A First-Class Temperament*, p. 419.

p. 159 **"the man she really marries":** ER to SDR, November 19, 1918.

p. 160 **"a horrid world I think":** ER to SDR, December 16, 1918.

p. 160 **"Eleanor is an angel":** SDR to FDR and ER, January 15, 1919.

p. 160 **"with a heart and a mind":** SDR to ER, undated, 1919.

p. 161 **tuberculosis of the bone marrow:** Peter Collier with David Horowitz, *The Roosevelts: An American Saga* (New York: Simon & Schuster, 1994), p. 469. A rare reference to the origins of Eleanor's fatal illness. Placed here in the summer of 1917, it actually occurred in the winter of 1919.

p. 162 **Clover killed herself:** Daniels, *Washington Quadrille*, p. 18.

p. 163 **the Catholic Church:** Alsop, *A Centenary Remembrance*, pp. 70–71.

p. 163 **in matters of faith:** Eleanor stressed that FDR believed "religion was an anchor, and a source of strength and guidance" (ER, *This I Remember*, pp. 346–347). Frances Perkins, secretary of labor in all of President Franklin Roosevelt's cabinets, devoted a whole chapter of her book *The Roosevelt I Knew* (New York: Viking, 1946) to FDR's "religious experience" (pp. 142–144).

p. 164 **Rita Halle Kleeman**, *Gracious Lady: The Life of Sara Delano Roosevelt* (New York: D. Appleton-Century, 1935). A telephone interview with the biographer's grandson Peter Halle on November 1, 2003, revealed that Rita Halle Kleeman's ashes were scattered on the grounds of the Roosevelt mansion in Hyde Park at her request. FDR greeted Peter's father Roger Halle like family when the latter attended a casual meal on the lawn in Hyde Park in 1936.

p. 165 **Cardinal Spellman:** Joseph P. Lash, *Eleanor: The Years Alone* (New York: W. W. Norton, 1972), p. 190.

p. 167 **overheard at a tea party:** Ward, *A First-Class Temperament,* p. 479; Alsop, *A Centenary Remembrance*, p. 72.

p. 169 **"Will you get James":** ER to SDR, September 2, 1920.

p. 169 **"it was my grandmother":** James Roosevelt, *My Parents*, p. 61.

p. 176 **"one perfect rose":** Daniels, *Washington Quadrille*, p. 227; Alsop, *A Centenary Remembrance*, p. 71.

p. 178 **"a vibrant personality":** Elizabeth H. Cotten to Jonathan Daniels, January 29, 1967.

p. 179 **"his photographs of the moon":** "Rutherfurd," in *Historic Families of America*, edited by Walter W. Spooner (New York: Historic Families Publishing Association, no date given), p. 18.

p. 181 **Winty Rutherfurd had powerful appeal:** Mrs. Lucy Mercer Blundon to the author, with an enthusiasm that caused her husband some discomfort.

p. 182 **In a delightful coincidence:** Mrs. Lucy Mercer Blundon to the author.

p. 182 **"*not* for money":** Elizabeth H. Cotten to Jonathan Daniels, January 29, 1967.

p. 182 **"'Mrs. Carroll announces the marriage of her daughter'":** Quoted in Daniels, *Washington Quadrille*, p. 189.

PART TWO: LUCY AS MRS. WINTHROP RUTHERFURD

CHAPTER 7. ELEANOR, FRANKLIN, AND LUCY IN NEW ORBITS

p. 203 **would not keep the mosquitoes away:** ER, *This Is My Story*, p. 345.

p. 208 **allowing her to go home:** Willis, *FDR and Lucy*, p. 152.

p. 209 **Harry Worcester Smith,** *Life and Sport in Aiken and Those Who Made It* (New York: Derrydale Press, 1935); **Emily L. Bull,** *Eulalie* (Aiken, SC: Kalmia Press, 1973); **Emily L. Bull Cooper,** *Eulalie* (2nd edition; Columbia, SC: University of South Carolina Educational Foundation, 2005).

p. 209 **Palmetto Golf Club:** Smith, *Life and Sport in Aiken*, p. 7.

p. 210 **"most sought for in Aiken":** Quoted in Smith, *Life and Sport in Aiken*, p. 30.

p. 215 **Frank Freidel at Harvard:** Jonathan Daniels to Frank Freidel, September 6, 1967, Jonathan Daniels Papers.

p. 215 **"they didn't see each other":** Joseph P. Lash interview with Anna Halsted, October 29, 1968.

CHAPTER 8. FRANKLIN REACHES OUT TO LUCY, 1926–1928

p. 218 **she wanted to become his partner**: Asbell, *Mother and Daughter*, p. 39.

p. 219 **"stay with her cousin Susie Parish"**: Quoted in Asbell, *Mother and Daughter*, p. 33.

p. 219 **"serious tension between her parents"**: Quoted in Asbell, *Mother and Daughter*, p. 40.

p. 219 **"a stream called Val-Kill"**: Quoted in Asbell, *Mother and Daughter*, p. 40.

p. 228 **had never heard of Yale**: Curtis B. Dall, *F.D.R. My Exploited Father-in Law: An Intimate Account of the Man, the Regime, and the Legacy* (Torrance, CA: Institute for Historical Review, 1970), pp. 12–13, 15.

p. 230 **"did claim Charles Carroll of Carrollton"**: Note of Francis Brianne, December 27, 1966, Jonathan Daniels Papers.

p. 234 **"take a great interest in it"**: FDR to SDR, March 7, 1926.

p. 234 **"I know you were really interested"**: FDR to SDR, October 13, 1926.

p. 235 **"suffering from nervous prosperity"**: FDR to Auntie Bye (Anna Roosevelt Cowles), June 29, 1927.

p. 241 **made Anna an ally of Lucy Rutherfurd**: Dall, *My Exploited Father-in Law,* pp. 30–31.

p. 242 **when he "may have more leisure"**: Quoted in Daniels, *Washington Quadrille*, pp. 229–230.

p. 243 **Sergeant Earl Miller**: Blanche Wiesen Cook, *Eleanor Roosevelt, Volume 1: The Early Years, 1884–1933* (New York: Viking, 1992), pp. 439–440. Letter of Earl Miller to Miriam Abelow, August 22, 1966.

CHAPTER 9. LUCY AND THE PRESIDENT

p. 246 **"I shall call you Saint":** Quoted in Bull, *Eulalie*, pp. 120–123.

p. 246 **the sentiments Lucy evoked:** Interview of Eulalie Salley in the *National Observer*, August 22, 1966.

p. 247 **he "vaguely resembled FDR":** Elizabeth Shoumatoff, *FDR's Unfinished Portrait: A Memoir* (Pittsburgh, PA: University of Pittsburgh Press, 1990), p. 75.

p. 247 **"a gentleman of the old school":** Bull, *Eulalie*, p. 123.

p. 248 **"the way he looks at you":** Bull, *Eulalie*, p. 121.

p. 250 **"Everything was out in the open":** Bull, *Eulalie*, p. 152.

p. 252 **a memento from her own childhood:** Now owned by Lucy Knowles.

p. 252 **Minna's recurrent visits with the Rutherfurds:** Interview with Mrs. Lucy Mercer Blundon.

p. 255 **"knows more about dress":** Quoted in Bull, *Eulalie*, p. 122.

p. 260 **"alive in the political world":** Geoffrey C. Ward (ed.), *Closest Companion: The Unknown Story of the Intimate Friendship Between Franklin Roosevelt and Margaret Suckley* (Boston: Houghton Mifflin, 1995), pp. xv–xvi.

 p. 261 **"adamantly opposed to sex":** Quoted in Ward, *Closest Companion*, p. xiii.

p. 270 **"I know you'll bring us through":** John Rutherfurd to FDR, June 23, 1941.

p. 274 **the kind of political blackmail:** Joseph Persico, *Roosevelt's Secret War: FDR and World War II Espionage* (New York: Random House, 2001), p. 208.

CHAPTER 10. SUNDOWN SOLACE

p. 277 **an important lengthy document:** Anna Roosevelt Halsted Papers, FDR Library, Box 70, Rutherfurd File.

p. 281 **"he can not [sic] relax and really rest":** Quoted in Ward, *Closest Companion*, p. 148.

p. 281 **her cousin Franklin's perennial favorite:** Ward, *Closest Companion*, p. 209.

p. 283 **Lucy met FDR on his home ground:** Ward, *Closest Companion*, p. 288.

p. 286 **She called her "a lovely person":** Quoted in Ward, *Closest Companion*, p. 323.

p. 286 **dated November 15 and 19, 1944:** ER to Esther Lape, quoted in Joseph P. Lash, *A World of Love: Eleanor Roosevelt and Her Friends, 1943–1962* (Garden City, NY: Doubleday, 1984) p. 150. In another letter to Esther, of January 3, 1944, Eleanor juxtaposed her obligations as a grandmother and her career interests. When her daughter Anna appeared to be able to join her husband in London, Eleanor mused, "Can I take care of the children satisfactorily? Not without giving up many other things, perhaps I should. . . . Oh, well, if I keep from thinking selfishly they'll probably come out all right" (quoted in Lash, *A World of Love*, p. 117).

p. 287 **"all the time, to watch over him":** Quoted in Ward, *Closest Companion*, p. 290.

p. 287 **"wondering how he can 'escape' afterwards":** Quoted in Ward, *Closest Companion*, p. 315.

p. 288 **"to help her fellow man":** Quoted in Ward, *Closest Companion*, p. 346.

p. 288 **"Franklin was left entirely alone":** Quoted in Ward, *Closest Companion*, p. 353.

p. 289 **until she was fifty years old:** Ward, *Closest Companion*, p. 352.

p. 291 **"That's where they had their plantation":** Joseph P. Lash, interviews with Anna Roosevelt Halsted.

p. 292 **Arthur, the president's valet, left for the night:** Ward, *Closest Companion*, p. 403.

p. 293 **Nicholas Robbins:** Bernard Asbell, interview with Mr. Robbins, assistant to Madame Elizabeth Shoumatoff.

p. 294 **"a mother more beloved":** Shoumatoff, *Unfinished Portrait*, p. 77.

p. 294 **"particularly in her smile":** Shoumatoff, *Unfinished Portrait*, p. 75.

p. 295 **"it should not be postponed":** Shoumatoff, *Unfinished Portrait*, p. 98.

p. 296 **"Nobody loves us, nobody cares for us":** Quoted in Shoumatoff, *Unfinished Portrait*, p. 101.

p. 297 **FDR was in high spirits:** Shoumatoff, *Unfinished Portrait*, p. 102.

p. 298 **he had come to admire:** Bernard Asbell, interview with Nicholas Robbins.

p. 299 **"a most idealistic, almost naive mind":** Shoumatoff, *Unfinished Portrait*, p. 79.

p. 301 **"What about Japan?"** Quoted in Shoumatoff, *Unfinished Portrait*, p. 107.

p. 302 **"she [Eleanor] would not consider a divorce":** Quoted in Shoumatoff, *Unfinished Portrait*, p. 109.

p. 303 **"though Sec. Morgenthau comes for dinner":** Quoted in Ward, *Closest Companion*, p. 414.

p. 303 **"the whole western front":** Quoted in Ward, *Closest Companion*, pp. 413–414.

p. 305 **"making others happy":** Quoted in Ward, *Closest Companion*, pp. 415–416.

p. 307 **"in the most inspiring way":** Quoted in Shoumatoff, *Unfinished Portrait*, p. 110.

p. 307 **Lucy would return to Q Street:** Mrs. Lucy Mercer Blundon to the author.

p. 308 **"My darling Clementine"**: Quoted in Jon Meacham, *Franklin and Winston: An Intimate Portrait of an Epic Friendship* (New York: Random House, 2003), p. 219.

p. 309 **"to address himself to her"**: Shoumatoff, *Unfinished Portrait*, p. 111.

p. 309 **"to put weight on me!"** Quoted in Ward, *Closest Companion*, p. 375.

p. 312 **that fateful night after FDR's death:** Pam LeBoutillier to the author.

EPILOGUE. TWO WIDOWS

p. 317 **William Turner Levy,** *The Extraordinary Mrs. R: A Friend Remembers Eleanor Roosevelt* (New York: John Wiley & Sons, 1999), pp. 178–179.

p. 319 **"Mother resented LM":** Joseph P. Lash, interview with Anna Roosevelt Halsted, November 27, 1967.

p. 321 **"[M]en and women who live together."** ER, *This I Remember*, p. 349.

p. 323 **"I sometimes acted as a spur":** ER, *This I Remember*, p. 349.

p. 323 **"not always on the militant march":** Daniels, *Washington Quadrille*, p. 310.

p. 323 **If anybody was to blame:** Members of the Delano clan believed that Eleanor had not been Franklin's choice as a prospective wife. Roland Redmond attested that it was his mother Sara who singled out Eleanor as the ideal mate for her son. Redmond was the husband of the young Sara Delano, FDR's first cousin, and a partner in FDR's first law firm of Carter, Ledyard, and Milburn. In an interview with Emily Williams on October 27, 1978, for the Eleanor Roosevelt Oral History Project, he attested that Eleanor's "meeting and marrying Franklin was largely the conclusion and decision of her mother-in-law." Eleanor "was a strong, healthy girl" and Aunt Sally was "keen to have her boy marry somebody with good background." In a letter of January 25, 1979, Redmond further explained to his interviewer at the FDR Library that "Sara Roosevelt may well have thought that Franklin and Eleanor could have waited [with the announcement of their engagement] until he was established in business."

p. 325 **"over one hundred requests for public appearances":** Levy, *The Extraordinary Mrs. R*, p. 5.

p. 326 **"he approached with such cheerful grandeur":** As indicated above, Lucy's writings have been preserved in the collection of the Rutherfurd Foundation.

p. 328 **a reproduction of a Shoumatoff portrait of FDR:** Levy, *The Extraordinary Mrs. R*, p. 12.

p. 335 **"My mother had many friends in Washington."** Mrs. Lucy Mercer Blundon to the author.

p. 337 **an apocryphal story:** Ted Morgan, *FDR: A Biography* (New York: Simon & Schuster, 1985), pp. 206–207.

p. 337 **"Betsey is about 100%!"** Unpublished correspondence between FDR and Dr. Harvey Cushing, President's Personal File 1523, FDR Library.

p. 340 **Monsignor Smith attended her funeral:** Bull, *Eulalie*, p. 122.

p. 340 **the banning of flowers:** Levy, *The Extraordinary Mrs. R.,* p. 245.

BIBLIOGRAPHY

Alsop, Joseph. *FDR, 1882–1945: A Centenary Remembrance*. New York: Viking, 1982.

Andrews, Marietta Minnigerode. *My Studio-Window: Sketches of the Pageant of Washington Life*. New York: E. P. Dutton, 1928.

Angelo, Bonnie. *First Mothers: The Women Who Shaped the Presidents*. New York: William Morrow, 2000.

Asbell, Bernard. *When F.D.R. Died*. New York: Holt, Rinehart & Winston, 1961.

Asbell, Bernard (editor). *Mother and Daughter: The Letters of Eleanor and Anna Roosevelt*. New York: Coward, McCann & Geoghegan, 1982.

Baker, Russell. Review of *Franklin and Eleanor: An Extraordinary Marriage* by Hazel Rowley, *New York Review of Books*, June 9, 2011, pp. 22–25.

Baker, Russell. Review of *Eleanor Roosevelt: Transformative First Lady* by Maurine H. Beasley. *New York Review of Books*, June 9, 2011, pp. 22–25.

Beasley, Maurine H. *Eleanor Roosevelt: Transformative First Lady*. Lawrence: University Press of Kansas, 2010.

Black, Allida M. "For FDR an Enduring Relationship." *Washington Post Outlook*, March 1, 1998, p. C03.

Black, Allida M. (editor). *Courage in a Dangerous World: The Political Writings of Eleanor Roosevelt*. New York: Columbia University Press, 1999.

Boettiger, John R. *A Love in Shadow: The Story of Anna Roosevelt and John Boettiger*. New York: W. W. Norton, 1978.

Brough, James. *Princess Alice: A Biography of Alice Roosevelt Longworth*. Boston: Little, Brown, 1975.

Bull, Emily L. *Eulalie*. Aiken, SC: Kalmia Press, 1973.

Caroli, Betty Boyd. *First Ladies*. New York: Oxford University Press, 1987.

Caroli, Betty Boyd. *The Roosevelt Women: A Portrait in Five Generations*. New York: Basic Books, 1998.

Clapper, Olive Ewing. *Washington Tapestry*. New York: McGraw-Hill, 1946.

Cook, Blanche Wiesen. *Eleanor Roosevelt, Vol. 1: The Early Years, 1884–1933*. New York: Viking, 1992.

Cook, Blanche Wiesen. *Eleanor Roosevelt, Vol. 2: The Defining Years, 1933–1938*. New York: Viking, 2000.

Cook, Blanche Wiesen. *Eleanor Roosevelt, Vol. 3: The War Years and After, 1939–1962*. New York: Viking, 2016.

Collier, Peter, with David Horowitz. *The Roosevelts: An American Saga*. New York: Simon & Schuster, 1994.

Congregation of the Daughters of the Divine Savior. *Ruf der Zeit* [Call of the times]. Vienna: Archbishop's Office for Education, 1983.

Congregation of the Daughters of the Divine Savior. *Volksschule Waldkloster Quellenstrasse, Festschrift anlaesslich der Eroeffnung des Neubaus* [Academic discourse on the School in the Forest, in celebration of opening ceremonies for the new building]. Vienna: Archbishop's Office for Education, 2004.

Cooper, Emily L. Bull *Eulalie*. Second edition. Columbia: University of South Carolina Educational Foundation, 2005.

Cox, Joseph W. *Champion of Southern Federalism: Robert Goodloe Harper of South Carolina*. Port Washington, NY: Kennikat Press, National University Publications, 1972.

Dall, Curtis B. *F.D.R. My Exploited Father-in Law: An Intimate Account of the Man, the Regime and the Legacy*. Torrance, CA: Institute for Historical Review, 1970. (Originally published by Christian Crusade Publications in 1967)

Daniels, Jonathan. *The End of Innocence*. Philadelphia: J. B. Lippincott, 1954.

Daniels, Jonathan. *The Time Between the Wars: Armistice to Pearl Harbor*. Garden City, NY: Doubleday, 1966.

Daniels, Jonathan. *Washington Quadrille: The Dance Beside the Documents*. Garden City, NY: Doubleday, 1968.

Davis, Kenneth S. *FDR: The Beckoning of Destiny*. New York: G. P. Putnam's Sons, 1972.

Davis, Kenneth S. *Invincible Summer: An Intimate Portrait of the Roosevelts*. New York: Atheneum, 1974.

Davis, Kenneth S. *FDR: The New York Years, 1928–1933*. New York: Random House, 1985.

Faber, Doris. *The Life of Lorena Hickok: E.R.'s Friend*. New York: William Morrow, 1980.

Faber, Doris. "Biography of Lorena Hickok." Undated manuscript. Papers of Doris Faber for *The Life of Lorena Hickok: E.R.'s Friend*. FDR Library.

Feldman, Ellen. *Lucy: A Novel*. New York: W. W. Norton, 2003.

Festschrift zum 100 ten Jahr. Privat-Hauptschule Melk der Kongregation der Schwestern vom Goettlichen Erloeser [Book commemorating 100 years since the founding of the private school of the Congregation of the Sisters of the Divine Savior]. Melk 2002. [This festschrift comes in the form of a small book celebrating a hundred years of service to the town of Melk, given by a parochial school under the direction of the Order of Sisters of the Divine Savior.]

Felsenthal, Carol: *Alice Roosevelt Longworth*. New York: G. P. Putnam's Sons, 1988.

Freidel, Frank. *Franklin D. Roosevelt: The Apprenticeship*. Boston: Little, Brown, 1952.

Freidel, Frank. *Franklin D. Roosevelt: The Ordeal*. Boston: Little, Brown, 1954.

Freidel, Frank. *Franklin D. Roosevelt: Launching the New Deal*. Boston: Little, Brown, 1973.

Freidel, Frank. *Franklin D. Roosevelt: A Rendezvous with Destiny*. Boston: Little, Brown, 1990.

Gallagher, Hugh Gregory. *FDR's Splendid Deception: The Moving Story of Roosevelt's Massive Disability – and the Intense Efforts to Conceal It from the Public*. Arlington, VA: Vandamere, 1994. (Originally published by Dodd, Mead in 1985)

Goodwin, Doris Kearns. *No Ordinary Time: Franklin and Eleanor Roosevelt – The Home Front in World War II*. New York: Simon & Schuster, 1994.

Gunther, John. *Roosevelt in Retrospect: A Profile in History*. New York: Harper & Brothers, 1950.

Gurewitsch, Edna P. *Kindred Souls: The Friendship of Eleanor Roosevelt and David Gurewitsch*. New York: St. Martin's, 2002.

Hagedorn, Hermann. *The Roosevelt Family of Sagamore Hill*. New York: Macmillan, 1954.

Halsted, Anna R. Interviews by Joseph Lash. FDR Library, 1966–1971.

Hassett, William D. *Off the Record with F.D.R., 1942–1945*. New Brunswick, NJ: Rutgers University Press, 1958.

Hickok, Lorena A. *Reluctant First Lady*. New York: Dodd, Mead, 1962.

Hoffman, Ronald, with Sally D. Mason. *Princes of Ireland, Planters of Maryland: A Carroll Saga, 1500–1782*. Chapel Hill: University of North Carolina Press, 2000.

Kleeman, Rita Halle. *Gracious Lady: The Life of Sara Delano Roosevelt*. New York: D. Appleton-Century, 1935.

Kleeman, Rita Halle. "Biography of Sara Delano Roosevelt." Undated manuscript. Correspondence and notes for *Gracious Lady: The Life of Sara Delano Roosevelt*. FDR Library.

Lash, Joseph P. *Eleanor and Franklin: The Story of Their Relationship Based on Eleanor Roosevelt's Private Papers*. New York: W. W. Norton, 1971.

Lash, Joseph P. *Eleanor: The Years Alone*. New York: W. W. Norton, 1972.

Lash, Joseph P. *Love, Eleanor: Eleanor Roosevelt and Her Friends – The Early Years*. Garden City, NY: Doubleday, 1982.

Lash, Joseph P. *"Life Was Meant To Be Lived": A Centenary Portrait of Eleanor Roosevelt*. New York: W. W. Norton, 1984.

Lash, Joseph P. *A World of Love: Eleanor Roosevelt and Her Friends, 1943–1962*. Garden City, NY: Doubleday, 1984.

Leuchtenburg, William E. *Franklin D. Roosevelt and the New Deal,*

1932–1940. Ithaca, NY: Cornell University Press, 1983. (Originally published by Harper & Row in 1963)

Leuchtenburg, William E. *In the Shadow of FDR: From FDR to Bill Clinton*. Ithaca, NY: Cornell University Press, 1992.

Levy, William Turner. *The Extraordinary Mrs. R: A Friend Remembers Eleanor Roosevelt*. New York: John Wiley & Sons, 1999.

Longworth, Alice Roosevelt. *Crowded Hours: Reminiscences of Alice Roosevelt Longworth*. New York: Charles Scribner's Sons, 1933.

McCullough, David G. *Mornings on Horseback: The Story of an Extraordinary Family, a Vanished Way of Life, and the Unique Child Who Became Theodore Roosevelt*. New York: Simon & Schuster, 1981.

Meacham, Jonathan. *Franklin and Winston: An Intimate Portrait of an Epic Friendship*. New York: Random House, 2003.

Meyer, Sr. Helena. Correspondence with the author, Society of the Holy Child Jesus, 2007–2008.

Miller, Nathan. *The Roosevelt Chronicles*. Garden City, NY: Doubleday, 1979.

Morgan, Ted. *FDR: A Biography*. New York: Simon & Schuster, 1985.

Page, Richard Channing Moore. *Genealogy of the Page Family in Virginia*. Bridgewater, VA: Carrier Company, 1883.

Page, Rosewell. *Thomas Nelson Page: A Memoir of a Virginia Gentleman*. Port Washington, NY: Kennikat Press,1923.

Parks, Lillian Rogers, with Frances Spatz Leighton. *The Roosevelts: A Family in Turmoil*. Englewood Cliffs, NJ: Prentice-Hall, 1981.

Perkins, Frances. *The Roosevelt I Knew*. New York: Viking, 1946.

Persico, Joseph E. *Roosevelt's Secret War: FDR and World War II Espionage*. New York: Random House, 2001.

Persico, Joseph E. *Franklin and Lucy: President Roosevelt, Mrs. Rutherfurd, and the Other Remarkable Women in His Life*. New York: Random House, 2008.

Richardson, Hester Dorsey. *Side-Lights on Maryland History: With Sketches of Early Maryland Families,* 2 vols. Cambridge, MD:

Tidewater Publishers, 1967. (Originally published by Williams & Wilkins in 1913)

Ridings, William J., Jr., and Stuart B. McIver. *Rating the Presidents: A Ranking of U.S. Leaders, from the Great and Honorable to the Dishonest and Incompetent*. Secaucus, NJ: Carol Publishing, 1997.

Rogers, William Warren, Jr. "The Death of a President, April 12, 1945: An Account from Warm Springs." *Georgia Historical Quarterly*, vol. 75, no. 1 (Summer 1991), pp. 106–120.

Roosevelt, Eleanor. "I Remember Hyde Park." *McCall's*, February 1963, p. 71. [A fraud exposed by the author in 2002–2003. The essay, reprinted in *Reader's Digest* in June 1963, was commissioned by the editor of *McCall's* and ghostwritten by the socialite Eleanor Harris, rather than by Eleanor Roosevelt herself. The fraudulent article's distortion of the relations between Eleanor and FDR's mother Sara has done much harm to historical truth.]

Roosevelt, Eleanor. "Ten Rules for Success in Marriage." *Pictorial Review*, December 1931, p. 4.

Roosevelt, Eleanor. *This Is My Story*. New York: Harper & Brothers, 1937.

Roosevelt, Eleanor. *This I Remember*. New York: Harper & Brothers, 1949.

Roosevelt, Eleanor. *It Seems to Me: Selected Letters of Eleanor Roosevelt*. New York: W. W. Norton, 1954.

Roosevelt, Eleanor. *The Autobiography of Eleanor Roosevelt*. New York: Harper & Brothers, 1961.

Roosevelt, Eleanor. *You Learn by Living: Eleven Keys for a More Fulfilling Life*. New York: Harper & Brothers, 1960.

Roosevelt, Eleanor, with Helen Ferris. *Learning to Live: Your Teens and Mine*. Garden City, NY: Doubleday, 1961.

Roosevelt, Elliott, and James Brough. *An Untold Story: The Roosevelts of Hyde Park*. New York: G. P. Putnam's Sons, 1973.

Roosevelt, Elliott (editor). *F.D.R.: His Personal Letters – Vol. 1, Early Years*. New York: Duell, Sloan & Pearce, 1947.

Roosevelt, Elliott, with James N. Rosenau (editors). *F.D.R.: His Personal Letters – Vol. 2, 1905–1928*. New York: Duell, Sloan & Pearce, 1948.

Roosevelt, Elliott, with Joseph P. Lash (editors). *F.D.R.: His Personal Letters – Vols. 3 and 4, 1928–1945*. New York: Duell, Sloan & Pearce, 1950.

Roosevelt, Franklin D., Jr., with Donald Day. *Franklin D. Roosevelt's Own Story*. Boston: Little, Brown, 1951.

Roosevelt, James, with Bill Libby. *My Parents: A Differing View*. Chicago: Playboy Press, 1976.

Roosevelt, James, and Sidney Shalett. *Affectionately, F.D.R.: A Son's Story of a Lonely Man*. New York: Harcourt, Brace, 1959.

Rowland, Kate Mason. *The Life of Charles Carroll of Carrollton, 1737–1832*. 2 vols. New York: G. P. Putnam's Sons, 1898.

Rowland, Kate Mason. *The Life of George Mason, 1725–1792*. 2 vols. New York: Russell & Russell, 1964. (Originally published by G. P. Putnam's Sons in 1892)

Rowley, Hazel, *Franklin and Eleanor: An Extraordinary Marriage*. New York: Farrar, Strauss & Giroux, 2010.

Schlesinger, Arthur, Jr. "FDR's Secret Romance." *Ladies' Home Journal*, November 1966, p. 66.

Shoumatoff, Elizabeth. *FDR's Unfinished Portrait: A Memoir*. Pittsburgh, PA: University of Pittsburgh Press, 1990.

Smith, Harry Worcester. *Life and Sport in Aiken: And Those Who Made It*. New York: Derrydale Press, 1935.

Streitmatter, Rodger (editor). *Empty Without You: The Intimate Letters of Eleanor Roosevelt and Lorena Hickok*. New York: Free Press, 1998.

Teague, Michael. *Mrs. L.: Conversations with Alice Roosevelt Longworth*. Garden City, NY: Doubleday, 1961.

Thomas, Lately. *The Astor Orphans: A Pride of Lions*. Albany, NY: Washington Park Press, 1999.

Totten, Christine M. "Remembering Sara Delano Roosevelt on Her 150th Anniversary." *Rendezvous: News and Notes from the Franklin D. Roosevelt Library and Institute*, Winter 2005.

Tully, Grace. *F.D.R., My Boss*. New York: Charles Scribner's Sons, 1949.

Van Rensselaer, Mrs. Schuyler. *History of the City of New York in the Seventeenth Century*. 2 vols. New York: Macmillan, 1909.

Ward, Geoffrey C. *Before the Trumpet: Young Franklin Roosevelt, 1882–1905*. New York: Harper & Row, 1985.

Ward, Geoffrey C. *A First-Class Temperament: The Emergence of Franklin Roosevelt*. New York: Harper & Row, 1989.

Ward, Geoffrey C. (editor). *Closest Companion: The Unknown Story of the Intimate Friendship Between Franklin Roosevelt and Margaret Suckley*. Boston: Houghton Mifflin, 1995.

Ward, Geoffrey C., and Ken Burns. *The Roosevelts: An Intimate History*. New York: Knopf, 2014.

Wharton, Edith. *The Age of Innocence*. New York: Collier, 1987. (Originally published in 1920)

Willis, Resa. *FDR and Lucy: Lovers and Friends*. New York: Routledge, 2004.

Zweig, Stefan. *The World of Yesterday: An Autobiography*. New York: Viking, 1943.

ACKNOWLEDGMENTS

I am indebted to the following persons.

Cynthia Koch was my earliest mentor. She inspired me to explore the influence of Sara Delano Roosevelt on her son Franklin, and in more recent years to focus on the three decades of joy and sorrow brought FDR by his beloved friend, Lucy Mercer Rutherfurd.

Mrs. Lucy Knowles and Mrs. Alice Knowles, Lucy Mercer Rutherfurd's granddaughters, as well as her niece the late Mrs. Lucy Mercer Blundon, contributed photos and other family documents and opened new views of Lucy Mercer Rutherfurd's importance.

In the last stage of the project, Ellen Foster's assistance in proofreading and resolving queries was invaluable.

And above all I thank my husband Don Edward Totten for his moral and practical support throughout the project.

INDEX

Page numbers in iltalics indicate
photographs.